Western Spirituality:
Historical Roots,
Ecumenical Routes

Western Spirituality: Historical Roots, Ecumenical Routes

Edited by

MATTHEW FOX, OP

Notre Dame, Indiana 46556

© 1979, Fides/Claretian
Notre Dame, Indiana 46556

Library of Congress Cataloging in Publication Data

Main entry under title:

Western spirituality.

  Includes bibliographical references.
  1. Spirituality—Addresses, essays, lectures.
I. Fox, Matthew.
BV4501.2.W435   230   79-18312
ISBN 0-8190-0635-1

To

Thomas Merton, a catholic monk
and
Abraham Heschel, a rabbinic prophet
two persons with the courage to explore
their roots and worldwide routes.
May we never forget them
or their courage.

Contents

PART II
ECUMENICAL ROUTES

Introduction: Roots and Routes in Western Spiritual Consciousness

Matthew Fox, OP

About Roots

All spirituality is about roots. For all spirituality is about living a nonsuperficial and therefore a deep, rooted, or radical (from *radix*, root) life. Roots are collective and not merely personal—much less are they private or individualized. To get in touch with spiritual roots is truly to leave the private quest for *my* roots to get in touch with *our* roots. Where roots grow and nourish in the bowels of the earth, there things come together and there a collectivity of energies is shared. No root that was ruggedly individualistic would long survive. In the earth's bowels roots feed on the same organisms as they twist and turn interdependently. among one another. The name we give this collectivity of roots is tradition.

Tradition is the common nourishing and searching and growing of our roots. We need tradition as much as we need one another. It has been said of the late Rabbi Heschel that he believed in the transmigration of souls because this doctrine "contains a profound religious truth. For one to know oneself, one must seek to understand one's past, one's heritage, the religious tradition from which one emerges. . . . The human soul is born with a past."[1] Westerners have been born with a past—indeed with many pasts—and the purpose of this book is to get us in touch with these roots once again. For the question arises: How

1

much in touch with our roots are we of the West? Roots, being underground energies, can easily be covered over and covered up. They can become forgotten and even be violently repressed. They can be put on a shelf or exalted on a pedestal where they never truly intersect our own lives and where they dry up and then die. They can become lost and unknown for centuries and only explorers into the bowels of the earth who journey from the light of day and the ego-separations of daytime to the dark caves of our collectively hidden unconscious can reclaim them.

It is especially the dominant Western tradition, that of Christianity, that is in the gravest danger of becoming rootless, that is, forgetful of its roots in our time. Much of this is due to the overly weighty influence of nonbiblical philosophies in the history of Christian spirituality—ways of thought like Stoicism, gnosticism, Platonism and Neoplatonism. Much also is due to the political, sexual, and economic dominance of Christianity and Empire, so that much that was authentic in biblical spirituality was twisted or repressed in order to put Christianity at the service of Empire building and Empire maintaining. Thus the passage from Christianity as a way of life (spirituality), which is how the early Christians saw themselves in the *Book of Acts*, to Christianity as a religion. Thus too the passage from creation spirituality, which sees life as a blessing, to the dominance of redemption motifs, motifs that instead of reminding all that they are of divine stock ("images of God") instruct even the young—especially the young!—in how corrupt they are or ought to consider themselves. Thus the unhealthy and unbalanced sexual dominance of the male and male images (for example, that of climbing Jacob's ladder) in Western mystical history.

Western spirituality has two basic traditions—that which starts with the experience of sin and develops a fall/redemption spiritual motif; and that which starts with the experience of life as a blessing and develops a creation-centered spirituality. This book's purpose is to put Westerners in touch once again with the more neglected of these traditions, namely that of blessing/

creation. This tradition will emphasize humanity's divinization rather than humanity's fallenness.

A Christian professor who is a fine and distinguished scholar of the Hebrew Bible said in a lecture recently that creation spirituality must never ignore the redemption tradition. As an abstract statement this declaration is true enough, but as a critical comment on the history of Christian spirituality it utterly misses the point and in fact continues the ongoing repression of the creation tradition. For the evidence is overwhelming that in Christian history the fall/redemption motif, so often championed by dualists like Augustine and Bossuet, has held overpowering sway—it condemned Pelagius and Scotus Eriugena, Thomas Aquinas, and Meister Eckhart, and it platonized and thus neutralized Francis of Assisi. It practically wrote women off the face of the spiritual map, locking them up whenever possible, virtually ignoring their experience and their writings, with only a few breakthroughs visible such as a Catherine of Siena or a Teresa of Avila. In the over-emphasis on salvation history and the silence vis-à-vis the history of nature, society, and creativity it has ignored rich and badly needed roots in scriptural and historical spiritual development—to say nothing of ecumenical spirituality. It has put the body down and called this repression holy; it has encouraged private conversions and sentimental pieties that have nothing to say to what Berdyaev in his essay in this volume wisely calls *theosis* or a "cosmic and social religion"—thus it renders sacraments and ritual trivial. It has substituted a private "righteousness" for biblical justice; it has taught sin-consciousness rather than peoples' capacity for the divine; it has more often fostered curses than blessings. It isolates: it isolates individuals from themselves, for example as regards their own passions, and it isolates individuals from one another. It thus very readily becomes a tool for dividing and conquering that sacralizes and legitimizes those who would lord it over others, whether in state or church. It has remained silent about that ultimate way of life that Jesus taught and died for—namely,

compassion, and when it has consented to include compassion as
a part of spirituality at all, it has sentimentalized this biblical
name for the divine which in fact is about setting captives free.[2]
It has failed to resist docetism and the dehumanizing of Jesus
and the incarnation event. In its dualistic view of the world it
pits salvation history against history, supernature against nature,
soul against body, redemption against creation, artist against
intellectual, heaven (and hell) against earth, the sensual against
the spiritual, man against woman, individual against society and
condemns all those with a cosmic vision (creation after all *is*
cosmic) as pantheists. Its one-sided spiritual theology does not
even have the term pan*en*theist in its vocabulary.

In short, I suggest that it is not creation spirituality that needs
to bend over backwards to include the redemption tradition,
since the latter is just about the only tradition most Christians
have been exposed to; rather, it is the redemption spirituality
that should quit its hegemony for a while, practice something of
the detachment it preaches to others, and listen and learn from
those who represent the creation-centered tradition and are trying to live it. Creation spirituality, far from ignoring redemption
themes, actually involves itself in reunderstanding the meaning
of redemption in different cultural and historical periods. This
is clearly the case in Latin American theology today, which is so
often called Liberation Theology but which is clearly a species of
creation spirituality. Creation spirituality is dedicated to what
Helen Kenik in her essay demonstrates to be justice as the act of
preserving creation and passing it on as a blessing to others. The
nature/grace dualism that haunts the Western psyche is rein-
forced by the hegemony of redemption spirituality *over* creation
spirituality, of grace *over* nature, as if nature itself is not graced.
Moreover, the fall/redemption tradition has become distorted
itself to the extent that it ignores the gracefulness of creativity
and creation. Just as creation-centered thinkers do not ignore
redemption motifs, so too must the redemption-thinkers begin
to include creation in their consciousness in a deep way and this

inclusion may begin to provide the correct setting for redefining what is meant by redemption in the West.

Nor are cries for "reconciliation" between the two traditions to be heeded at this time in Christian history. For, as Krister Stendahl has pointed out,[3] a reconciliation that comes too soon is nothing but a surrender by the powerless to the powers that be. When unequals reconcile what obtains is capitulation, not reconciliation. Reconciliation is for equals, not for those still bound in a powerful/powerless situation. The fact is that creation spirituality remains an unwanted step-child in Western Christianity whose mainstream has invested so heavily and so long in Augustinian original sin and redemption motifs. Instead of reconciliation at this date, what is needed is more and more scholarship that uncovers the wonders and beauties of creation spirituality on the one hand and more and more persons willing to throw themselves into living it on the other. For only out of this living will a lost tradition be refound and reborn. The purpose of this volume is to contribute to this ongoing scholarly rediscovery and thus, in its own way, to support and encourage those living or desiring to live creation-centered spirituality. While at first glance a book on *Western Spirituality* might appear to be a churchy affair, what is at stake in fact in the struggle to regain creation consciousness is at least as important to society as to spirituality. In his important book, *The Unsettling of America: Culture and Agriculture*, Wendell Berry makes explicit the issues at stake for society if religious faith ignores creation:

> Invariably the failure of organized religions, by which they cut themselves off from mystery and therefore from the sacred, lies in the attempt to impose an absolute division between faith and doubt, to make belief perform as knowledge; when they forbid their prophets to go into the wilderness, they lose the possibility of renewal. And the most dangerous tendency in modern society, now rapidly emerging as a scientific-industrial ambition, is the tendency toward encapsulation of

human order—*the severance, once and for all, of the umbilical cord fastening us to the wilderness or the Creation.*[4]

There can be no in-depth self-understanding or group understanding without root understanding. This is the purpose of Part I of this book: To get us in touch again with neglected, forgotten, repressed spiritual ways of our roots. All revelation is meant to be an unveiling of our hidden roots. The nature of a word, says Meister Eckhart, is "to reveal what is hidden." Christians who call Christ the Word welcome him as a revealor of what is hidden, as one who came to make the unconscious conscious, the forgotten remembered, the unknown known, dreams reality, the hidden less hidden, and perhaps the familiar and readily known a little bit less known. Truth does become hidden and covered over with cultural changes and laziness and superficialities and guilt. If the purpose of the word is to reveal, then its purpose is equally to lay open the cover-up. In our time and culture the term "cover-up" is a familiar experience indeed. It is the way so much in our society operates that it might even qualify as the reigning spirituality of our times, our unholy times. When people hear time and time again, for example, in television advertising for one of the country's largest corporations, that McDonald's "does it all for you" then an awareness sets in that our language is becoming corrupt. We begin to learn how words are now being used to cover up instead of to reveal.

The purpose of this volume is to contribute to an uncovering that will help to make the collective spiritual unconscious of the West less unconscious and more conscious. Less forgotten and more a part of our everyday living and loving of life and one another. Is the West out of touch with its own spiritual roots? E.F. Schumacher suggests that we are and that the experiment of the past few centuries to live without religion in the West (by which he means without spirituality) has been a failure.[5] We need to start again with a spiritual vision.

But one does not manufacture a spirituality. Spiritualities—like roots—are born and not made. One begins with tradition and develops it. Thomas Merton was equally harsh on what the West has made of its spiritual heritage. Speaking of how Christians should get back to an appreciation of history and become "as obsessed with history as" Marxists are, he comments:

> The Marxian idea that the key to everything is found in history is, curiously enough, the basic idea of the Bible. We, the Christians, have forgotten this. We have reduced our religious thought to the consideration of static essences and abstract moral values. We have lost the dynamic sense of God's revelation of himself in history.[6]

Merton's lament at our substituting static abstractions for the dynamic experience of God in history parallels the concern of Rabbi Heschel with the difference between biblical and Greek spirituality. Jewish biblical spirituality "is radically different from Greco-German philosophical thought" which is, in the Aristotelian God, "thought thinking itself." He contrasts the biblical God to the Greek God.

> The God of the prophets of Israel is a being characterized by his transitive concern about the human condition. The God of the philosophers expresses a self-reflexive concern; he is involved only with himself. The God of the prophets is emphatically involved in human affairs. The ideal personality for the philosophers, Heschel claims, is to be like God—sterile, static thought. The ideal personality for the Bible is to be like God—active, dynamic concern for the human condition.[7]

Thomas Merton and Rabbi Heschel—these two powerful voices of the West nourished by deep traditions of Christian and of Jewish spirituality respectively agree: The spirituality of our age will be biblical and Jewish instead of neoplatonic and hellenistic. It will involve the Spirit in history and above all will be characterized by an "active, dynamic concern for the human condition." It is to these two biblical believers, who lived as well as reflected on their spiritualities, that this volume is dedicated.

Persons interested in their spiritual roots will wonder how their ancestors demonstrated this kind of "active, dynamic concern for the human condition"—if at all. Such questions have too seldom been asked in Christian hagiography of late where miracles, dogmatic conformity or titillating supernaturalisms seemed so often of greater importance than relief of the pain of fellow human beings. Each of the essays in Part I dealing with our roots takes up such human involvement as a theme. Thus the period of the Hebrew Bible is examined as a source for creation spirituality in the lead article of this volume—I am convinced that the "Biblical Basis for Creation Spirituality" by Helen Kenick is more than an opening essay to this volume. It is, in my opinion, a lead and an opening to a long-awaited perspective on biblical and historical studies. There is a sense in which the salvation history approach to scriptures and the fall/redemption approach to spirituality has been too exclusive, too uncritical, too narrow, too unjoyful, and too dualistic. In short, too Augustinian and too introspective. Kenick opens the door to another perspective, another tradition, a way of blessing. Sobrino's contribution on prayer in the early church and its implications at the social and political levels of our lives carries through with Kenick's theme that justice is the preservation of creation, the passing on of its blessings. Nicolas Berdyaev, writing out of the spiritual riches of the Eastern Christian tradition—a tradition that never succumbed to the overly introvert journeying of Western psychologists like Augustine—acts as a prophet to us Westerners by the force of his argument: that creation is at least as important a tradition in spirituality as fall/redemption and that there is no way to recover our divinity and likeness to God without it. He outlines what a cosmic, creation-centered spirituality offers in contrast to redemption spirituality. Mary Schmiel's groundbreaking study on Celtic spirituality opens the door to understanding and appreciating Western efforts at creation spirituality. This tradition, influenced more by Byzantine than by Roman theology, was planted in the Rhineland area and in great parts of France and northern Italy. Thus Meister Eckhart and Francis of

Assisi, to cite only two Western mystics, owe much to this tradi-tion.[8] Rosemary Ruether puts a refreshing question to the period of church patriarchs: What were the women of the period developing as a spiritual alternative? Chenu considers Thomas Aquinas' much-neglected theory on the importance of human passions and society to spirituality, and Meister Eckhart, ignored for six hundred years by spiritual writers in the West, is allowed to speak once again on the subject of the spiritual jour-ney of a creation-centered person and people (Fox). We are presented with a new look at Catherine of Siena (Parks) through letters that have never before been available to English-reading persons, and we see therein a mystic who is just as much a social-political mover. We take a critical look at the remarkable psychological struggle and development of Teresa of Avila (Romano), thus taking her off a pedestal of pious otherness down to the level where we, like she, have to work out our liberation in fear and trembling. We see delineated in her jour-ney a map of how grace builds on nature: her creativity, her womanhood (including menopause), her struggle for identity in a very male society, her end to masochism and her courage all come to the fore with the help of insights from psychological sciences. And the seventeenth century in France which includes the milieu of Jansenism, of Pascal, of Cardinal Richelieu and which has proven to be so influential in modern Christian spirituality is reexamined (Didomizio).

Part I of this book on Historical Roots might just as well have been entitled "Readings in Creation Spirituality: Forgotten Ele-ments of Western Spirituality" since the Jewish biblical tradition of blessing found in the Hebrew Bible and in the New Testament church, creativity as a spirituality, women in Celtic society and in the Patristic world, Aquinas' passion and concern for society, Eckhart's realized eschatology and deified humanity themes, Catherine of Siena's social consciousness, the psychological struggle of Teresa of Avila, the Jansenists' political involvement have all been so neglected and forgotten in the churchy religions and the load of spiritualistic spiritualities that have so often

aristotelian

passed for spirituality in the West of late. The reading of hagiography and spirituality through neoplatonic instead of biblical glasses has to cease if the West is to regain touch with its deepest and richest spiritual roots. The authors of these articles contribute substantially to this return to biblical spiritual roots.

How much out of touch has the West become with its own spiritual traditions? It is telling, I believe, that the American school of consciousness psychologists such as Robert Ornstein, Charles Tart, Claudio Naranjo, et al., have next to nothing to say about Western spirituality. For all practical purposes their studies on mysticism and psychology turn exclusively to the East[9]—as if the West had nothing to offer whatsoever! What a harsh implicit judgment this is on the mainstream of religious concerns in the West. It is very likely that the flight from mysticism that has characterized so much of rationalistic and scientific and capitalistic piety of the past three centuries was more involved in a flight from prophecy than we were aware. How often I have listened to persons tell me that they never imagined any connection between spirituality and politics, spirituality and economics—a fact that makes one wonder just how the Sermon on the Mount has penetrated Western consciousness, if at all. The rekindling of mystical expansion that also includes political awareness may be underway, however, in Protestant no less than in Catholic circles. A fine example of this would be Bengt Hoffman,[10] a Lutheran theologian who finally demonstrates how indebted Luther was, as prophet no less than as mystic, to the Rhineland tradition of mysticism as represented in this volume, for example, by Celtic studies, by Meister Eckhart and Thomas Aquinas. (The direct influence on Luther was, of course, neither of these but rather Eckhart's disciple, John Tauler. The latter, however, being also a Dominican, was imbued with both Aquinas' and Eckhart's this-world spirituality. Still, however, Luther was also deeply affected by Augustine especially as regards his pessimistic view of the world and the human race.)

dialogue

As Westerners begin to explore spiritual roots other than those so heavily encrusted with Augustine's redemption-oriented Neoplatonism they will find themselves more and more in direct contact with the creation tradition of the Hebrew Bible. To explore a spirituality in the world is to take human history and the history of nature seriously. To speak of a New Creation presupposes a creation spirituality—one that takes human creativity as the meaning of the "image of God" tradition as a starting point for social development and that does not get caught up in the overly introspective quest of Augustine.[11] What Rabbi Heschel calls "the affairs of suffering humanity" are the proper subjects for spiritual development. A modest purpose behind this volume, then, is to help undo the guilt that platonic dualisms via Augustine have heaped upon Christian spirituality. And thus to reveal that Christians do have options beyond Augustine. Biblical ones and historical ones. The Western spiritual tradition is far richer, far more diverse, far fuller of celebration and of socially involved compassion than we Westerners give it credit for being. There are traditions of our past where history and body are integral to and not separate from Christian spirituality. For, in Fr. Chenu's words, "to admit that God creates is implicitly to confess that matter is divinely willed and therefore good."

It is especially creation-centered spirituality that contains untapped treasures and rich sources of spiritual nourishment for Westerners. Claude Tresmontant summarizes that tradition in the following manner: "God's method, the only method his love would allow, is to create a being that might create himself in order truly to become a god, a being in the image and after the likeness of the Creator."[12] A creation spirituality will encourage the creator and artist in every person. It will be actively involved, as every artist is, in making the unconscious conscious—not for an elite but for the people. The American historian Carroll Quigley has also commented on the difference between the redemption spirituality left us by Augustine and the creation spirituality of the biblical tradition. He distinguishes between "Left wing" spirituality which bases its appeal on "the Christian insistence on the need of the world and the body" and the "Right wing" which bases its appeal "on the Christian emphasis on the soul, God's grace, and the perfect rationality of God."

> Ultimately, in the history of ideas, the former extreme goes back to the Hebrews and to the Ionian atomists, while the latter extreme, goes back to Persian Zoroastrianism and to the Pythagorean rationalists, above all, to Plato.... The threat to the synthesized moderate middle ground from the Right has come from dualistic rationalism and especially from the influence of Plato. This influence has worked historically through Augustine of Hippo, who was a Platonist in philosophy although a Christian in religion.[13]

Christian spirituality, then, is a rootedness of being in the world. In history, time, body, matter, and society. Spirit is found there (or better, here) and not outside of these essential ingredients to human living. This means that economics and art, language and politics, education and sexuality are equally an integral part of creation spirituality. And, not least of all, joy. The joy of ecstasy and shared ecstasy in celebration. This is a nonelitest spirituality. A "folk" spirituality one might call it. Of the folks, by the folks and for the folks. It is a spirituality as if people mattered.

In this regard, it might have been appropriate to have subtitled this book: "The Death of Gnosticism and the Death of Neoplatonism in the West." For a biblical spirituality eliminates dualisms which are the essence of gnostic spiritualist sects.[14] Dualisms of male-female, mysticism-prophecy, art-life, this life-next life, spirit-matter, body-soul, have no future in a biblical spiritual vision. They are dead or deserve to be. A biblical spirituality eliminates Neoplatonism on the following grounds: First, creation is not, as a matter of fact, the way neoplatonist cosmology would have it. Creation is an ongoing process which includes the curved much more than the linear and flat. Profound consequences arise for spirituality depending on one's view of the universe, both micro and macro. Today's scientific discoveries about the evolution of matter and the curvature of earth and of space do havoc with the Ptolemaic universe that Neoplatonism presumes.[15] Secondly, redemption in the creation tradition does not mean redemption of the soul so much as redemption of the world. There is no need to redeem matter, much less to control it. There is a need to harmonize with it and to see that the human race celebrates in just fashion together. In many ways Part I of this volume undertakes a dialog with contemporary thinking in light of traditional spiritualities. That is why redemptive spiritualities are found so lacking and creation-centered ones are so richly represented. Critical biblical studies (Kenik, Sobrino), critical history (Schmiel, Ruether, Chenu, Fox, Didomizio), critical psychology (Romano, Berdyaev) all open up new areas for spirituality and spirituality research.

Neoplatonism *is* the issue in the history of Christian spirituality—Neoplatonism vs. the Bible. Thus nothing is more deliberate than the inclusion of three essays on Jewish spirituality. (Kenik, Hellwig, Miller) and our beginning this volume with Jewish spirituality. There will be no re*newal* of Christian spirituality (only mild reform at best) without a divorce from Neoplatonism and a rebetrothal to the creation spirituality tradition of Jewish, biblical thought.

About Routes

To investigate roots is to investigate routes. For roots are ever groping, ever stretching themselves, and ever interacting with other roots and nourishing and nurturing in the depths of the earth. Roots are not static, complacent, or satisfied. They grow. They move. They explore new (and old) territory.

So it is with the ecumenical routes. It is when a people's and a person's spirituality become truly rooted and detached from superficialities, that ecumenical routes take on a deeper importance: How do people from other cultures, other traditions,

other roots make this journey? What insights do they lend for
our underground nourishment? What contrasts? What criticism
can they lend that will in fact make our journeying that much
more rooted and richer? With all these questions in mind
scholars in Part II share with us insights from diverse spiritual
traditions.

We learn, for example, of the blessings that creation brings to
the Native American peoples and their response of reverence
for the land, for the dead, for eating, for nature and its beauty
(Hobday). We learn of how a nonelitest celebration lies at the
core of Hasidism and how redemption does not have to mean
redeeming of souls but means redeeming the world (Hellwig).
We receive insight into the Russian spirituality of emptying and
filling and the important role of the peasant in the development
of Russian spiritual consciousness (Kenney). We learn from the
Yoga tradition of the positive role that body can, and indeed
ought to play in spirituality (O'Brien), and we appreciate William
Hocking's struggle with the "Protestant principle" of cultural
criticism within mystical history (Woods). We learn of the only
partially successful effort by American Transcendentalists to
democratize religious experience in a country indebted to the
myth of democracy (Alexander). We learn of the struggle that
the Jewish philosopher Franz Rozenweig underwent in trying to
relate his Jewish roots to Christian routes (Miller).

One intriguing lesson I have learned in putting together this
volume is the relativity of all roots. What distinguishes roots
(Part I) from routes (Part II)? It all depends on where one
stands. As a Roman Catholic, I have determined that Hasidism
and Transcendentalists belong in Routes. Were I Jewish, however, clearly the former would belong in Historical Roots and
were I Protestant the latter would belong there. Here lies a lesson in itself: That the line between roots and routes, between
our tradition and others, is a fine one indeed. One might even
say it is a transparent one. It should not be taken too seriously
and yet at the same time it cannot be ignored. One needs to
know one's own tradition before another's is revealed for all the

richness it contains. This surely is one of the significant blessings of the ecumenical movement today: It is urging upon all of us a deeper appreciation and awareness of our own roots.

Another dimension to ecumenism today is the global nature of it and with that the urgency of it. One can speculate whether there is not invariably a resurgence of interest in mysticism every time that there is a population explosion—the scholar Phillipe Dollinger has demonstrated that this demographic influence was a key one, for example, in the mystical explosion in the Rhineland in the fourteenth century.[16] It would seem to make some sense as a basic cultural/spiritual law: That when people sense their physical frontiers closing in on them they are driven to exploring the frontiers of consciousness or spirituality. If that is the case, then the pressures that an awakened global village is subjected to, whether of population, food, energy resources, employment, etc., may be ushering in the greatest and most worldwide spiritual awakening the village has ever entertained. And that would truly be an ecumenical awakening, for humankind is simply too interdependent today and too well informed to deny that the Spirit travels more routes than one's own particular one. (This is not to imply, however, that as persons we do not need to travel particularized routes. For we, unlike the Spirit, cannot travel everyplace.)

When it comes to ecumenism of all world religions, the Second Vatican Council, putting an end to centuries of religious confrontation, could declare that:

> From ancient times down to the present, there has existed among diverse peoples a certain perception of that hidden power which hovers over the course of things and over the events of human life. . . . Other religions to be found everywhere strive variously to answer the restless searchings of the human heart. . . . The Catholic church rejects nothing which is true and holy in these religions. She looks with sincere respect upon those ways of conduct and of life which often reflect a ray of that Truth which enlightens all people.[17]

It is significant that the reference to creation (the spirit hovering over the waters; the striving of religions to respond to restless searchings of human hearts) and to creation spirituality in particular (religions are called "ways of conduct and of life") is what binds Christian theology to other spiritual theologies in this document. Creation spirituality is a condition sine qua non for ecumenism on a worldwide scale for it is precisely creation, the gifts of existence itself and the sustainers of that common existence, that all peoples and all faiths share in common. There will be no worldwide ecumenism without creation-centered spirituality. For ecumenism is not a pious duty or one more commandment, it is an overflow of the relationship we experience with all that is.

I think it is of more than passing interest that almost every author in this volume is from a Roman Catholic background including those doing work on Hocking, Rozenweig, Russian Spirituality, Hasidism, Native American, Yoga, Transcendentalists. Why is this of interest? Because it demonstrates how far ecumenism has already come in our lifetimes that Catholics could establish themselves as scholars in traditions and routes that they were not born into. It is an invitation to others, Jews and Protestants, to involve themselves too in routes other than their own. I would welcome, for example, a Jewish study on Meister Eckhart or a Protestant appreciation of Teresa of Avila. That would have to wait on other volumes.

Rabbi Heschel called for a "depth theology" as being the common ground wherein all religious traditions might plant their roots. It is a theology less of doctrine than of event; a theology bent on uniting instead of dividing peoples. It is a theology that respects mystery wherever it be found and does not put dogma before mystery. It respects the limits of our own roots and for that reason it opens us to routes.

> Depth theology seeks to meet the person in moments in which the whole person is involved, in moments which are affected by all a person thinks, feels and acts. It draws upon that which

happens to man in moments of confrontation with ultimate reality.... Depth theology warns us against intellectual self-righteousness, against self-certainty and smugness. It insists upon the inadequacy of our faith, upon the incongruity of dogma and mystery.[18]

I heartily endorse Heschel's concept of depth theology—it is only when theology has roots that are deeper than dogma alone (though dogma has a role to play in lending structure to these very roots) that it will have any worthwhile message to offer *or* receive from other traditions. That is why religious practice or spirituality as a way of living is what is at stake in the future of ecumenism and, one might imagine, in the future of the global village. Integral today to having "an active, dynamic concern for the human condition" is our orienting roots to routes and learning to be globally conscious in our spiritualities. There can be no spirituality worthy of the name today without ecumenism on a worldwide scale. There will be no deep roots without routes.

And yet, there can be no routes without roots. I am reminded of the Buddhist priest at the University of Hawaii who was frequently approached by Westerners asking to be taught Buddhism. His reply was: "Okay. But there is nothing in Buddhism that is not in Christianity." But do Christians even know what is in Christianity? Has religion in the West actually helped persons to explore these depths or has it, consciously or unconsciously, been a part of the cultural process called secularization that has in fact covered up and covered over and thereby repressed such roots?

On the Contributors

It is no accident that half of the contributors in this volume are women and half of the topics treated in this volume are about women and spirituality. No more disastrous distortion is so regularly repeated in spirituality circles than the overdominance of the male—as if our foremothers were not at least as rich in their roots and routes as our forefathers. Those who are embarrassed by Catherine Romano's psychic history of Teresa should ask this question before they object too vociferously: Have my previous impressions of this saint come to me exclusively through all-male sources? It is time that critically conscious women were heard from in the field of spirituality and in this volume every effort is made to see that happen.

The authors of this volume represent a new generation of spiritual theologians. Most all have been at one time or another world citizens, i.e., they have lived outside their own culture for extended periods of time. All have been tempered by racial, economic, sexual, and political injustices. They are critical and qualified thinkers who are young in heart though they vary in age and familiarity to the reading public. All of them you will be hearing from again. Their spiritual visions are people-oriented, politically conscious, and earthy. I think, therefore, it is correct to say they are biblical people. Each and every one is living an alternative life style and has resisted hiding behind pillars of security whether they derive from the comfort of piety or the comfortable benefits that big academia can bestow. I think you will enjoy meeting them and the not-to-be-forgotten spirits that they bring to life on these pages.

LIST OF AUTHORS

HELEN A. KENIK received her Ph.D. in biblical languages and literature from St. Louis University and is assistant professor of biblical theology at the Jesuit School of Theology in Chicago. Her articles appear in the *Journal of Biblical Literature* and *The Bible Today,* and she is working on a *Commentary on 1 and 2 Kings* for the International Theology Commentary Series.

JON SOBRINO, a Jesuit priest, is professor of philosophy and theology at the Universidad Jose Simeon Cañas of El Salvador. Born in Barcelona, he received an MA in mechanical engineering from St. Louis University and a doctorate in theology from the Jesuit Theologate of St. George in Frankfurt, West Germany. He is author of *Christology at the Crossroads* (Orbis Books).

NICOLAS BERDYAEV (1874–1948) was a Russian religious philosopher in the tradition of searching intellectuals of the nineteenth century such as Khomyakov, Solovyon, and Dostoevsky. He was deported from Russia in 1922 and settled in Paris where he continued lively dialogue with Protestant and Catholic thinkers. He edited the journal *Put'* (The Way) from 1925–1940 which served as a forum for many of the creative religious minds of the twentieth century and published over twenty books on cultural and religious issues.

ROSEMARY RUETHER is Georgia Harkness professor of Theology at Garrett Theological Seminary, Evanston, Illinois. She has published over a dozen books, including *New Woman, New Earth*; *Religion and Sexism*; *Radical Kingdom*, and hundreds of articles in religious and cultural journals. She holds her Ph.D. in patristic studies from Claremont Graduate School and is well known nationally and internationally as an articulate spokesperson of feminist consciousness and Christian culture. She is a visiting professor at the Institute of Creation-Centered Spirituality at Mundelein College, Chicago.

MARY AILEEN SCHMIEL is a lifelong student of mythology and history, particularly Celtic history. She has studied in France and Ireland, and has traveled extensively in those countries as well as Britain, Greece, Italy, Israel, and North Africa. She holds an MA in religious studies from Mundelein College and hopes to utilize her background in mythology in helping to develop feminist and ecological consciousness in Christianity and society.

M.D. CHENU, a French Dominican, has been actively engaged in theological writing, research, and teaching for five decades. His historical consciousness was one of the significant influences on the Second Vatican Council. His books translated into English include: *Toward Understanding St. Thomas*; *Nature, Man and Society in the Twelfth Century*; *Faith and Theology*; and *Theology of Work*.

MATTHEW FOX is director of the Institute of Creation-Centered Spirituality, Mundelein College, Chicago. He holds a doctorate in the history and theology of spiritualities from the Institut catholique de Paris. His books include *Religion USA*; *On Becoming a Musical, Mystical Bear—Spirituality American Style*; *Whee! We, wee All the Way Home: A Guide to the New Sensual Spirituality*; *A Spirituality Named Compassion and the Healing of the Global Village, Humpty Dumpty and Us*.

CAROLA PARKS, a Dominican Sister of Adrian, Michigan, is a French instructor at Aquinas Dominican High School, Chicago. Formerly a member of the faculty at the Catholic University of Puerto Rico, she did research at the Centro Nazionale di Studi Cateriniani in Rome and has studied languages at the University of Fribourg in Switzerland, the Catholic University of America, and Florida State University.

CATHERINE CRESS ROMANO is a graduate with honors from Barat College, Lake Forest, Illinois, and a Ph.D. candidate in the Clinical Psychology program at the University of Health Sciences, the Chicago Medical School. She is the mother of three daughters and is preparing a manuscript on Teresa of Avila from an Adlerian point of view.

DANIEL G. DIDOMIZIO is assistant professor and chairperson of the humanities studies division at Marian College of Fond du Lac, Wisconsin. He holds a doctorate in spirituality and historical theology from the Institut catholique de Paris and is a member of the National Young Adult Ministry Board of the United States. He and his wife, Jackie, are preparing a book on sexuality and spirituality for Paulist Press.

MARY JOSÉ HOBDAY is a Sister of St. Francis of Assisi and of Native American heritage—Seneca from her mother, Seminole from her father. She grew up in the Southwest, close to the Navajo and Ute Mountain Indians. Sister Jose did her graduate work in theology, Native American literature, and architecture and engineering. She has taught from secondary through university level, including the Native American Culture Center at UCLA. She has worked nationally and internationally in areas of prayer and spiritual renewal, and for the past eight years has lived and worked with the Sioux and Assiniboine tribes of Montana, and the Papago tribe of Arizona. She is currently working in the Diocese of Tucson, with emphasis on spirituality in relation to the three cultural streams of that area—Indian, Hispanic, and Anglo.

MONIKA K. HELLWIG is professor of theology at Georgetown University, Washington, D.C., mother of two adopted children, and author of several books including *The Christian Creeds*; *Tradition*; *The Eucharist and the Hunger of the World*; and *Death and Christian Hope*. Though raised in the Roman Catholic tradition, she comes from a family that was Lutheran in one branch and Jewish in another, and she has devoted considerable effort to the study of the Jewish heritage.

JAMES KENNEY is a Ph.D. candidate in the department of the history and literature of religions at Northwestern University, Evanston, Illinois. His dissertation topic is: "Mahayana Buddhism and Modern Theoretical Physics: The Philosophical Parallels and their Implications for Buddhist-Christian Encounter." He studied at the University of Leningrad and is the chairperson of religious studies at Barat College, Lake Forest, Illinois and a lecturer at the Institute of Creation-Centered Spirituality, Mundelein College, Chicago.

JUSTIN O'BRIEN is professor and director of graduate studies at the Himalayan International Institute in Honesdale, Pennsylvania. He has been a university teacher for thirteen years and has studied in America, Holland, and India where he trained with Swami Rama. His professional research concentrates on the field of human consciousness, religious experience, and a holistic philosophy of the human person. He is co-author of *Medita-tion in Christianity* and *The Art and Science of Meditation,* and his recent book is *Yoga and Christianity.*

JON ALEXANDER is a Dominican and faculty member at Aquinas Institute of Theology, Dubuque, Iowa. He holds a doctorate in history from Temple University and has done postdoctoral work at Harvard Divinity School. He has published articles in the *Journal of Church and State* and in *Listening Magazine.*

RONALD MILLER is founder and Director of Common Ground, an organization for interfaith study and dialogue. He holds a doctorate in history and literature of religions from Northwestern University and is assistant professor of religion at Lake Forest College and serves on the faculty of Loyola University's Institute of Pastoral Studies.

RICHARD WOODS holds his doctorate in philosophy of religions from Loyola University, Chicago, and is a visiting professor at the Institute of Pastoral Studies, Loyola University. His books include *The Occult*; *The Devil*; *Another Kind of Love.* An anthology on mystical writings which he is editing, *Understanding Mysticism,* will be published in 1980 by Doubleday Image.

To all these contributors I express my heart-felt thanks. And to Sister Mary Ann Shea, op, for her diligent work on the index to this book and to the students of the first class of the Institute of Creation-Centered Spirituality whose questions and probing contributed to the reason for this volume.

NOTES

1. Byron L. Sherwin, "Journey of a Soul: Abraham Joshua Heschel's Quest for Self-Understanding," *Religion in Life* (Autumn, 1976), p. 270.
2. See Matthew Fox, *A Spirituality Named Compassion and the Healing of the Global Village, Humpty Dumpty and Us* (Winston,

1979) for an in-depth treatment of this much-neglected theme in Christian spirituality.

3. Krister Stendahl, *Paul Among Jews and Gentiles* (Fortress Press, 1978), pp. 97–108.

4. Wendell Berry, *The Unsettling of America: Culture & Agriculture* (Avon, 1978), p. 130. Italics mine.

5. See E.F. Schumacher, *A Guide for the Perplexed* (Harper & Row, 1977). I consider Schumacher's religious vision to be far too male and hierarchical to announce a new future for us, however.

6. Thomas Merton, *Conjectures of a Guilty Bystander* (Doubleday Image, 1968), p. 102.

7. Sherwin, "Journey of a Soul," p. 274. See Abraham Heschel, *The Prophets* (Harper & Row, 1962), cc. 12–16, 18.

8. See Edward A. Armstrong, *St. Francis: Nature Mystic* (University of California Press, 1976), pp. 34, 41: Francis was "reviving and reproducing much that was of the essence of Celtic Christianity with its simplicity, evangelical fervor, community spirit, comparatively loose organization, love of neighbor, and devotion to adventurous missionary enterprises." (182f.). In many respects Francis, who was creation-centered, has more in common with the spiritual theology of the Dominican Meister Eckhart than with the Neoplatonism of the Franciscans Celano and Bonaventure.

9. For example, Robert Ornstein, *The Psychology of Consciousness* (Freeman, 1972); Claudio Naranjo and Robert Ornstein, *On the Psychology of Consciousness* (Viking, 1971); Charles T. Tart, ed., *Altered States of Consciousness* (Doubleday, 1972); Charles T. Tart, *States of Consciousness* (Dutton, 1975); Charles T. Tart, ed., *Transpersonal Psychologies* (Harper & Row, 1975). This last volume does allow for a forty-page treatment of Christian spiritual experience out of 479 pages on the subject.

10. Bengt R. Hoffman, *Luther and the Mystics* (Augsburg, 1976). Another fine study that Protestant scholarship brings to creation spirituality—in addition to the work of Krister Stendahl already referred to is Claus Westermann, *Blessing in the Bible and the Life of the Church* (Fortress Press, 1978).

11. Krister Stendahl demonstrates how Augustine's introspection has distorted the West's understanding of Paul in

Krister Stendahl, "Paul and the Introspective Conscience of the West," in Wayne A. Meeks, ed., *The Writings of St. Paul* (Norton, 1972), pp. 78–96.

12. Claude Tresmontant, *A Study of Hebrew Thought* (Desclee, 1960), p. 151. For more on Jewish as distinct from hellenistic thinking, see Thorleif Bowman, *Hebrew Thought Compared with Greek* (Norton, 1960).

13. Carroll Quigley, *The Evolution of Civilizations* (Macmillan, 1961), pp. 218f.

14. Cf. Hans Jonas, *The Gnostic Religion* (Beacon Press, 1963).

15. See Fritjof Capra, *The Tao of Physics* (Berkeley: Shambhala, 1975).

16. Philippe Dollinger, "Strasbourg et Colmar, Foyers de la Mystique Rhenane (XIIIe–XIVe siecles)," in *La Mystique Rhenane* (Paris: PUF, 1963), pp. 3–13.

17. "Declaration on the Relationship of the Church to Non-Christian Religions," in Walter M. Abbott, ed., *The Documents of Vatican II*, (Guild Press, 1966), pp. 661f.

18. Abraham Heschel, *The Insecurity of Freedom* (Farrar, Straus & Giroux, 1966), p. 119.

PART I:
HISTORICAL ROOTS

Toward a Biblical Basis for Creation Theology

Helen A. Kenik

Whatever our religious tradition, each of us comes under the influence of the dominant dualistic view of humanity. Following the Augustinian definition of the human being, we have been indoctrinated in the perspective that human nature is best distinguished into the natural and supernatural elements, the natural serving primarily as a hindrance to the experience of the full life of the spirit. The correlative of such thought is emphasis upon the evil potential of human nature and its need for salvation. In such thinking, the dominant rubric will understandably be salvation.

Prior to Augustine, hellenistic thought dominated the Western world. The hellenistic static perception of reality led to the presentation of ideas by distinction and contrast. One exemplar of such thinking is the great apostle Paul whose theology is structured upon the dichotomy between the flesh and the spirit:

> Those who live according to the flesh
>   are intent on the things of the flesh,
> those who live according to the spirit,
>   on those of the spirit.
>
> The tendency of the flesh is toward death
>   but that of the spirit toward life and peace.
>
> If you live according to the flesh,
>   you will die;

> but if by the spirit
>> you will put to death the evil deeds of the body,
>> you will live (Rom 8:5-6, 13).[1]

While Paul made the point of his message through the use of antithetic language that is typical of hellenistic thought, Paul cannot be accused of a dualistic view of humanity. The dualistic interpretation imposed on Paul's writings derives from those who have used the dialectic in Paul to serve the purpose of their own thought. Of these, Augustine most significantly influenced the church's use of Paul to support the view of humanity as a composite of flesh and spirit.

Even the Hebrew scriptures do not remain immune from the influence of dualistic thought. It must be emphasized that there is no distinction between nature and spirit in Hebrew thought, nor is there a dialectic in the presentation of ideas.[2] Hebrew thought and therefore the Hebrew scriptures are characterized by a holistic view of the human person and by a dynamic, as opposed to a static, perception of reality. Yet scholars, all of whom come under the influence of the dualistic concentration upon the human need for salvation, continue to be so dominated by this tradition that even the Hebrew scriptures are treated as if they, too, fit into the dualistic mode. The Hebrew scriptures are generally approached in their totality as a salvation history.[3]

The purpose of this study is to demonstrate that alongside salvation theology in the Hebrew scriptures, there is another dimension which is equally viable but generally ignored as insignificant. Yahweh, savior of Israel, is also creator of the world. The view of saving God fits into the broader context of God's will for life in all dimensions. God the creator gives life, sustains life and entrusts life to creatures. God does not only act for life in particular situations; God maintains created life and this is accomplished through human beings to whom the life in the world is entrusted. Along with an understanding of Yahweh as the God of a special and chosen people is the realization that Yahweh is Lord not only of Israel but of all peoples and all nations. The creator God reigns and rules over all. Both perspectives—Yahweh as an exclusive saving God and Yahweh as a universal creative God—are presented by the writers of the Hebrew scriptures.

It will be impossible in the short space of this study to fully develop every argument that serves the intended point. I intend to suggest the themes that when linked together supply a biblical basis for creation theology. In this presentation, I will outline and elaborate upon some traditions to demonstrate a possible line of development. In this essay when I speak of creation theology I mean the understanding of Yahweh, presented in the Hebrew scriptures, as God who gives life and takes life, who sustains and preserves life, and who entrusts human beings in the world as the agents of God for the continuation of life. The proposed line of development for creation theology will follow this schema of traditions:

1) Yahweh as creator/king and judge
2) Kingship as the role through which the created order in the world is preserved
3) Royal personhood demonstrated in
   a) the creation story in Gen 2:4b-3:24
   b) the ancestral history
   c) the Joseph story.

CREATION AND SALVATION

When Israel began to attribute the work of creation to Yahweh will be forever beyond our determination. The Hebrew scriptures do give witness that, very early, Israel praised Yahweh as the creator,[4] just as Israel acclaimed Yahweh as its savior.[5]

The world of which Israel was but a small piece honored many gods to whom were assigned different tasks. The Creator God and a variety of nature gods dominated the pantheon. The creator god was perceived to be involved in the coming into existence of the cosmos;[6] whereas fertility gods guaranteed the continuation and perpetuation of life.[7] Human beings who wished to ensure the continuing work of nature did service to the gods who, they believed, could give fertility to humans, animals, and plants. They appeased those gods who would guarantee the sequence of the sun and moon, of seasons and tides, of rains and harvest. The functions of the creator god as well as the fertility gods were attributed in Israel, of course, to the one God Yahweh. This was not without struggle, nor was it an automatic assumption. Witness the charge expressed by Hosea:

> She has not known that it was I
>   who gave her the grain, the wine, and the oil (Hos 2:10).

With undaunted conviction, on the other hand, Israel knew that Yahweh was the God who had saved her from the slavery of Egypt. The principal identity of Yahweh was recited as "your God who brought you out of the land of Egypt, that place of slavery" (Ex 20:2).[8] The experience of the Exodus proved to be the central event for Israel's self-understanding as a special people of Yahweh as well as the crucial event by which Yahweh acted in history to save the chosen people.

On account of the uniqueness of Yahweh as a God who intervenes in history as opposed to being a nature God, the Exodus event and the divine intervention are highlighted as if these are the totality of the divine revelation. The Hebrew scriptures are read almost exclusively out of this framework so that the acclamation of Yahweh as Savior seems to be the sum of faith. Yahweh is known and presented therefore primarily as an intervening, saving, helping God. It seems that interpretation of the Hebrew scriptures is controlled by the need to uphold the exclusivity of Yahweh as a god who acts in history to save. It may be true that the scriptures really do present a one-sided view of things; but it may also be the case that one-sided interpretation is the result of a biased view of theology.

The truth of the matter is that Yahweh was and is not a nature god. Being distinct from nature, however, does not imply denial of Yahweh as both the Creator God who preserves and sustains life and a Savior God. The attribution to Yahweh of creation and the life in nature seems more problematic to interpreters than it did to the believers in Yahweh and the writers of the Hebrew scriptures. It is time to pose the question bluntly: Is the God who was known by the Israelites and who is presented in the Hebrew scriptures only a saving God; or do the Hebrew scriptures equally present Yahweh as the God who gives life as well as sustains life by continual presence and care? This is to say: Did not the Israelites attribute *life* as well as *action* to Yahweh? I believe that the answer to this last question is "yes." The one-sided view of God has come down through the centuries under the aegis of interpreters motivated by the view of humanity in need of salvation. Only a Savior God makes sense when the primary need is perceived to be salvation from bondage, be this slavery or sin. Only an intervening God seems necessary when people perceive themselves as helpless and sinful and uninvolved in the creative process of life.

The Hebrew scriptures themselves present a more balanced image of Yahweh. Yahweh is indeed the God who saves; but Yahweh also gives and preserves life. Yahweh is creator as well as savior; Yahweh is preserver of life as well as intervener in history. No one would deny the fact of Yahweh's role in the totality of life—and yet we do so when we place too much emphasis on the limited scope of salvation. Nor would anyone deny that Yahweh is Lord of the entire world and all peoples. But when the issue becomes the chosen of Yahweh, the elect, the special people, then the lordship of Yahweh takes on a tone of exclusiveness.

We need to examine the broader context and insight about God presented in the Hebrew scriptures. That literature reveals that Yahweh was praised, known, and experienced as the creator/preserver as well as savior. Interpreters, having primary need for the latter role to address a sinful people, have exposed the salvific dimension to the almost total neglect of the alternative creative dimension. We will, therefore, deal solely in this

study with the image and function of Yahweh as Creator, a role
that implies the continual care and sustenance of life as well.

It is important to note that the focus in a creation theology
differs from the focus in salvation theology. In the latter, *God is
the actor*. The emphasis leans toward the God who saves by entering history as an intervenor on behalf of a needy and sinful
people. In the creation perspective, the arena of activity is the
world created by God. There the preservation of life and the
sustenance of nature are delegated to the highest of God's creatures, to human beings. The focus leans away from God toward
human beings who are created by God and charged with the
responsibility for the continuation of life. *Human beings are the
actors*. They are charged with a task for life which is a divinely
delegated task. This is to say that God's work is entrusted to
human beings.

In order that this last point become clear, it is necessary first of
all to hear the biblical presentation of Yahweh as Creator. Once
the divine task has been outlined, the correlation with the function entrusted to human beings becomes apparent.

YAHWEH AS CREATOR/KING

From earliest times, Israel acclaimed Yahweh its only king.
According to Martin Buber, "The unconditioned claim of the
divine kingship is recognized at the point when the people proc-
laim JHWH himself as king, him alone and directly (Exodus
15:18), and JHWH himself enters upon the kingly reign
(19:6)."[9] The understanding of Yahweh as king was as much the
consequence of the experience of God's leadership of the people
in the Exodus event and into the land, as it was the affirmation
that all life has its origin in God. The concept of kingship, in line
with these two separate notions, implies two distinct functions in
regard to the people—1) a leadership role and 2) an ordering
role.

As leader-king, Yahweh accompanied his people as they moved from place to place. Yahweh led them from Egypt (Ex 14-15), through the wilderness (Ex 16-17; Num 10:11ff), and into the land (Joshua). Yahweh remains present with the people and thus is the one who travels along with them (Ex 33:16), and who also goes on ahead of them (Ex 13:21). Imagery often used to designate the king-leader is that of the shepherd (Gen 19:24). Yahweh is the true shepherd of Israel who gathers his people, leads them, guards them, and cares for them.[10] The shepherd motif is significant because the national king, as the leader of Yahweh's people, was often titled shepherd at those times when he failed to meet his responsibilities of leadership. We will return to the shepherd motif when we speak of the responsibilities of the kings as leaders.

Yahweh as orderer-king is directly involved in the act of creation. To appreciate the significance of ordering for creation, we must recognize that Israel was influenced in her understanding of Yahweh by the experiences of reality as these were variously expressed in the ancient near eastern world. A basic notion in the ancient world very simply put was that when the earth was made, the king reigned; or when the king was established upon his throne, the world was set in order. Kingship and creation were inextricably linked ideas.

We find an example of the creation of the world or the ordering of the cosmos and the reign of the king in the Babylonian epic of creation, the Enuma elish.[11] This epic describes how the god Marduk, when the chaos goddess Tiamat had been killed, split her in two so that the earth as perceived by humans stood in the gash in her middle. The waters above the skies and below the earth were her remains. The whole functioned in such a way to serve as ordered cosmos under Marduk's dominion.

In Ugarit, the story of Baal and Mot/Death describes the victory of Aliyan Baal over "Death" who has power over life and fertility.[12] When Mot/Death is vanquished, life in the cosmos is able to go on in a dependable and orderly fashion. By his victory

Aliyan Baal rises in supremacy in the cosmos. His house is built and he reigns.

Both Marduk and Aliyan Baal assure life and order in the cosmos by their victory over chaotic forces. Their victory also establishes each as the reigning god. These myths, in particular, are often reflected in biblical accounts. The most obviously related text is the creation account in Genesis 1. There the creation of the cosmos is described as the ordering of the luminaries in their proper positions and the governing of the world under the dominion of mankind. The completion of creation is marked by the reign of Yahweh. Notice that the seventh day is the sabbath, the day on which the Lord reigns. His people worship him because life and order are assured when people assume their responsibilities in the world and acknowledge that Yahweh is their God and king.[13]

Like the peoples in the ancient orient, Israel identified Yahweh as both king and creator. In Ps 149, the association is explicit in the parallelism between the two roles:

> Let Israel be glad in their *maker,*
> let children of Zion rejoice in their *king* (Ps 149:2).

The parallelism between "maker" and "king" indicate that the two terms are considered coterminous. Yahweh is both "maker" and "king." In a milieu where the chief god was the creator god, the assimilation of that function to Yahweh would have been made early and asserted boldly as is attested in the psalm: "For the gods of the nations are things of nought, but the Lord made the heavens" (Ps 96:5). Not the other gods, but Yahweh and Yahweh alone is the creator of the universe.

The group of psalms called the enthronement psalms also celebrate the kingship of Yahweh.[14] These psalms express the affirmation that when the king reigns the world is in order.

> The *Lord is kind,* in splendor robed . . .
> and *he has made the world firm,* not to be moved (Ps 93:1; cf. 96:10).

Over and over the psalms assert that the existence of creation presupposes the rulership of God:

> For the Lord is a great God,
>   and a *great king* above all gods;
> In his hands are the depths of the earth,
>   and the tops of the mountains are his.
> His is the sea, for *he has made it,*
>   and the dry land, which *his hands have formed*
> (Ps 95:3–5).

Kingship implies creation. The divine reign and the life of the world go hand in hand.

It should be noted that kingship and the correlative act of creation extend to all the earth. The Lord is king/creator not only of Israel but of all peoples and all nations. All peoples everywhere come under the sovereignty of Yahweh, the creator. The divine rulership thus has universal application in contrast to the particularity of Yahweh's acts of deliverance on behalf of Israel. The universality of Yahweh's reign is expressly celebrated in Psalm 47:

> For the Lord, the Most High, the awesome,
> is the great *king over all the earth* (Ps 47:3).

> For the *king of all the earth* is God (47:8a);

> God *reigns over the nations,*
> God sits upon his holy throne (47:9).

In this psalm the "king of all the earth" is identified as Lord, i.e., the particular name Yahweh. Yahweh, in turn, is titled with another name, the *Most High.* In Hebrew, this title reads *Elyon.* In tradition the title *El Elyon,* God Most High, reflects the Canaanite tradition of the god who, as creator, is the high god above all gods.[15]

In the biblical narrative, the priest Melchizedek calls upon the God Most High (El Elyon) as "maker of heaven and earth" (Gen

14:19). In response, Abraham addresses Yahweh with the precise titles used by Melchizedek:

> I have sworn to the *Lord, God Most High* (Yahweh El Elyon),
> *creator of heaven and earth* (Gen 14:22).

Yahweh is here not only given the title which implicitly designates the creator god, but Yahweh is also explicitly identified as the creator of heaven and earth. The title *Most High* thus designates "creator." Looking again at Ps. 47, we read that "the Lord, the Most High . . . is the great king" (vs. 3). Again, kingship is related to creation. The creator god is also the king. The title *Most High* was used repeatedly to acclaim Yahweh's Lordship over the world and his supremacy over all gods:

> . . . you, O Lord, are the Most High over all the earth, exalted
> far above all gods (Ps 97:9; cf. 83:19).

Thus Yahweh's role as creator was presumed; his rulership was acclaimed. All peoples belong to Yahweh who is their maker; all nations come under the dominion of Yahweh because he is their king.

Yahweh The Creator/King as Judge

As creator/king, Yahweh fashions the world and determines its workings. God designs the movements of the sun and moon, places human beings over all creatures to care for them, just as God intends that human beings share the world and their role in it in mutuality and harmony.[16] There is an order in creation which is the plan of the creator/king.

As king/creator, Yahweh assures that the order intended in creation is preserved. God guarantees fertility and regularity in nature;[17] and God desires that human beings live harmoniously in community and society. To accomplish this latter, the king/

creator functions in the capacity of *judge*. Judgment is generally understood to be necessary when Israel has broken covenant. When one party to covenant is unfaithful, the guilty are brought to trial for disloyalty. Examples of such court scenes are reflected in the judgment speeches of the prophets.[18] In these trials, Yahweh accuses his people of infidelity and pronounces judgment. The role of the judge in these cases is that of the court magistrate as well as the prosecutor. Yahweh, in both roles, makes the indictment as well as issues the sentence.

There is another rubric by which to understand the role of the judge. This is the function of the one who gives life and who works to preserve the life that is ordered by creation. We are speaking of a nonethical judgment in the sense that the Torah per se does not supply the content for the indictment. The judgment is addressed to kings, in particular, and to all people; for Yahweh wills that order in society be preserved through the efforts of human beings. The content of the judgment is expressed precisely in that language by which kings and people are invited to participate in God's will for life.

God judges precisely because all the world belongs to him and therefore God continually oversees that the order intended in creation continues in the world:

> Rise, O God, *judge* the earth,[19]
> for yours are all the nations (Ps 82:8).

Out of the basic relationship that exists between the creator and creatures, God functions as the judge. This is the task by which God continually recalls all people to life. God's will is for *shalom* in society; God intends that life flourish and that all obstacles to life be removed. Hence the primary motivation for judgment can be expressed as *justice:* God's concern is for the poor, the captives, the blind, the stranger—all those who become the objects of abuse. The psalmist praises Yahweh the creator and judge:

> . . . . . the Lord
> Who *made heaven and earth,*
>   the sea and all that is in them;
> Who keeps faith forever,
>   *secures justice* for the oppressed,[20]
>   gives food to the hungry.
> The Lord sets captives free;
>   the Lord gives sight to the blind.
> The Lord raises up those that were bowed down;
>   the Lord loves the just.
> The Lord protects the strangers;
>   the fatherless and the widow he sustains,
>   but the way of the wicked he thwarts.
> The Lord *shall reign* forever . . . (Ps 146:5–10a).

Judgment finds its object in the concrete needs within society. Its purpose is to assure that society experience the peace and wholeness intended with creation. The Lord reigns, the world is made, and the people are judged, i.e., recalled to life in the order made by God—these are interdependent ideas about rule of God.

> . . . The Lord *is king.*
> He has *made the world* firm, not to be moved;
> he *governs* the peoples with equity (Ps 96:10).
>
> . . . (exult) before the Lord, for *he comes;*
> for he comes *to rule* the earth.
> He shall *rule* the world *with justice*
> and the peoples *with equity* (Ps 98:9; cf. 96:13).

God's rule is directed for peace in society. In mythical terms, we could say that the world exists upon the foundation of God's throne and that society flourishes under the rule of God. God's design for the world is peace and harmony for and among peoples. The psalmist expresses these ideas so much more clearly in the words:

... justice and judgment are the foundation of his throne (Ps 97:2b).

(history) of pronouncements
cases

The King in Israel

God as the creator/king/judge governs the world and has dominion over it. God alone is the source of life and the possibility for its continuance. The task for life belongs to God; the origin of life remains in God. But God has delegated the carrying out of the task of life to human beings who themselves are the product of creation. God has handed dominion in the world into the hands of human beings and has so endowed them that they participate with God in the preservation of life.

The peoples in the ancient oriental world perceived that the king, who reigned as a stand-in for the gods, carried out the task of life in place of the gods. To guarantee the continuous working in nature, the king participated in the yearly fertility rites. To assure peace and harmony in the family and society, the king functioned as chief judge among human beings. The ancients recognized the integrity between justice in society and life in all its dimensions. The king's right relationship with the gods was indicated by the fact that this king provided that all peoples in his realm were treated justly, and this in turn issued in the fertility and productivity of nature. Thus life in nature and society depended upon the king's right relationship with god. And conversely, the king's relationships within society and toward other human beings revealed the king's stance before God.

First among human beings in the Israelite nation was the king who mediates between God and the people. The king was the leader at one period in history through whom God worked to sustain order in the world.

There is a tendency in biblical scholarship to think of the king as the foil for apostasy and hence to interpret the period of the monarchy negatively in contrast to the era and leaders prior to the monarchy which are looked upon as the epitome of loyalty.

because
assembly of wealth,
is past not king

To speak of kingship is to conjure forth a negative image of one who usurps the divine authority, power, and presence.[21]

As a form of leadership, kingship ought not to be interpreted in such a biased fashion. In fact to do so is to remain blind to the impact of the royal ideal upon the biblical books. It is true that some kings were unfaithful. But there is an ideal of kingship which is vital for understanding how Israel understood God's working in the world. In regard to the ideal of kingship, Israel drew from various royal ideologies to express its own understanding of kingship. Israel's king was not like the king of any other single nation in the ancient world; but Israel's king was defined so that he was clearly recognizable as the servant of Yahweh, obliged to submission to Yahweh, and responsible for accomplishing the divine will on behalf of God's special people.

Moreover it is important to recognize that the period of the monarchy gave rise to the abundance of literature by which we have come to know and to appreciate the ancestors of Israel as well as all believers in Yahweh. Through that literature, composed under the influence of royal thought, later writers and especially some of the prophets, articulated the hope for a future ideal king who would indeed be the life-bearer for God's people. Thus the ideal of kingship profoundly influenced the biblical understandings. Even more, the insights regarding humanness and the relationships that constitute order derive from the ideology of kingship, as we shall see later in this essay.

The king's was a delegated task. His role was specifically that of judging or governing, the specific task by which Yahweh maintains the order of creation of the world. In Hebrew, the term for the king's charge is *shapat*. It could mean either "governing" in the sense of administering to people, or "judging," making decisions in a way that assures individuals their rights. In this one function is summarized the role of ruling by which life and order in society is maintained. When the king rules honestly and justly, peace, the sign of life, flourishes. On the other hand, a king who functions out of self-interest, who treats people according to status or with partiality, who accepts bribes, creates a climate of disorder and mistrust. The consequence is disunity, conflict, and a lack of communal vitality in the society. The indicators we have posed here carry a very contemporary ring. In general, the responsibility given to leaders is of a classic nature. But our concern is specifically the understanding of the king's role as it is presented in the biblical texts.

The psalm at 2 Sam 23:1–7 states that the king speaks by the Spirit of God. This is an acknowledgement of dependence on God. The psalm continues:

> He that *rules* over men *in justice,*
>   that *rules in the fear of God.*
> Is like the morning light at sunrise
>   on a cloudless morning,
>   making the greensward sparkle after rain . . .
> (vss. 3b–4).

Living faithfully before God means that the king, in his role as ruler, deals justly, which is another way of showing fear of God. The consequence of loyalty before God and justice in practice is described here in metaphors of nature—like sun that gives light to darkness and sparkle upon vegetation. This means that the just leadership of the king results in a community and society where life flourishes out of peace and trust and love. The king's loyalty before God is demonstrated in his actions toward people. The result is the flourishing of life which the biblical poet describes as natural phenomena.

That the king's function was delegated by God, and could be understood to be an extension of the work of God is expressed in the prayer for God's blessing on the king in Ps 72:

(part) earth

> O God, with *your judgment* endow the king,
> and with *your justice,* the king's son (Ps 72:1).

desire for care of creation

It is God's justice and judgment which are requested so that the king may truly act as God himself would act. It is the will of God and the people that the king deal with each individual as God himself would deal, for the people under the rulership of the king are God's own people:

> He shall govern *your people* with justice
> and *your afflicted ones* with judgment (Ps 72:2).

Kings need to be reminded that the people they serve are God's own. And it is especially those who are most in need who constitute God's very own. The function by which the king acts in God's stead is "governing." This is the one duty, *shapat.* Precisely what is meant by this role is explicitated in this particular psalm:

> He shall defend the afflicted among the people,
> save the children of the poor
> and crush the oppressor (Ps 72:4).

The king defends and saves God's people; he crushes the enemy of God's people.[22] As a result of the king's activity on behalf of God's people and his loyalty to God, "justice shall flower in his days, and profound peace . . ." (Ps 72:7). There is but one reason for the king's sovereignty—that the life of God's people may be preserved. The dominion of the king is meant to guarantee that each and every person receives justice, that the integrity of society is guarded because individuals gain an equal hearing.

There was no confusion in Israel about the task of the king and his responsibility before God. The people prayed for him that he "may rule from sea to sea" and that "all nations serve him" (Ps 72:8a, 11b). There is less a desire for universal rule in this petition in the sense of race for power than a profound desire to extend the rule of a just and faithful king:

> For he shall rescue the poor man when he cries out,
> and the afflicted when he has no one to help him.
> He shall have pity for the lowly and the poor;
> the lives of the poor he shall save.

From fraud and violence he shall redeem them,
and precious shall their blood be in his sight (vss. 12-14).

The sentiment about kingship expressed in Psalm 72 is echoed in various ways in the collection of sayings found in the Book of Proverbs.[23] These sayings were part of the instruction for the young men who would be leaders among God's people. The future leaders are charged with the practice of justice in particular, and because all people are God's own.

Injure not the poor because they are poor,
  nor crush the needy at the gate;
For the Lord will defend their cause,
  and will plunder the lives of those who plunder them (Prov 22:22-23).

By justice a king gives stability to the land;
  but he who imposes heavy taxes ruins it (Prov 29:4).

If a king is zealous for the rights of the poor,
  his throne stands firm forever (Prov 29:14; cf. 16:12).

Rich and poor have a common bond:
  the Lord is the maker of them all (Prov 22:2; cf. 29:13).

He who oppresses the poor blasphemes his Maker,
  but he who is kind to the needy glorifies him (Prov 14:31).

Open your mouth in behalf of the dumb,
  and for the rights of the destitute;
Open your mouth, decree what is just,
  defend the needy and the poor! (Prov 31:8-9).

The task given to the king, as his special responsibility for preserving the intended order of creation within the society, is clearly stated. No one can claim that the duty is ambiguous or that the focus is uncertain. The desired end is life; and the king, whose realm is the society of his world, works to preserve life through his task as ruler.

assembly of elders

This responsibility is so grave that when the king fails to work for life for the people, he comes under the divine judgment; for ultimately, it is God who is judge. Ps 82 presents the scene of the Divine Judge standing up in the midst of the divine assembly to make the indictment against the unjust rulers. The Divine Judge asks:

> How long will you judge unjustly
>   and favor the cause of the wicked? (Ps 82:2).

then continues with the exhortation, reminding kings of their obligations as rulers:

> Defend the lowly and the fatherless,
>   render justice to the afflicted and the destitute.
> Rescue the lowly and the poor;
>   from the hand of the wicked deliver them (Ps 82:3-4).

The kings of the earth are brought under judgment because they fail to do justice. Rather than ruling in a way that preserves the order that is God's will among peoples, the kings are bearers of death when they succumb to the enticement of bribery and the rewards of partiality. The consequence of their unjust actions is a situation of chaos; creation is undone: "All the foundations of the earth are shaken." (Ps 82:5b).

The Prophet and the King

Because the king carries out God's work in the world, the actions of the king need to be continually critiqued. The prophetic role is mainly that of "reminding" the king about his responsibilities.[24] The prophets undersood God's intent for his creatures and witnessed to the divine will for creation. They perceived God's will to be for life, a situation in which peoples are at peace. The prophets, therefore, dared to confront those who disrupted the peace. They were the messengers of the

creator/king/judge who spoke God's own words of judgment recalling peoples to right order.

Most vehemently, the prophets confronted the kings whose
primary task was ruling for the sole purpose of preserving the
integrity of the nation. The prophetic word was harsh and to the
point: "Hear, you leaders of Jacob, rulers of the house of Israel!
Is it not your duty to know what is right, you who hate what is
good, and love evil? . . . You who abhor what is just, and pervert
all that is right . . . her leaders render judgment for a bribe" (Mic
3:1, 9, 11). The prophetic indictment echoes the responsibilities
of kings:

> Every one of them loves a bribe
> and looks for gifts.
> The fatherless they defend not,
> and the widow's plea does not reach them (Isa 1:23).

The voice of the prophet is God's word of judgment against the
leaders who contribute to the inequities, discord, oppression,
partiality and all means of disruption within the created world.
The very ones who are God's agents in the world for order are
the creators of disorder, and therefore the object of divine
judgment. The voice of the prophet is God's word of judgment
on behalf of the plundered poor, the dispossessed, the widow
and orphan, the oppressed weak; "O my people, your leaders
mislead, they destroy the paths you should follow. The Lord
rises to accuse, standing to try his people. The Lord enters into
judgment with his people's elders and princes: It is you who
have devoured the vineyard; the loot wrested from the poor is in
your house. What do you mean by crushing my people, and
grinding down the poor when they look to you?" (Isa 3:12, 14–
15). The prophets stand on the side of the poor and in opposition to those who abuse the poor by the misuse of power and
authority.

While condemning the unfaithful kings in the name of
Yahweh, the prophet offers hope that one day there will be a

king who is indeed a royal person—who "shall judge the poor with justice, and decide aright for the land's afflicted, who shall strike the ruthless with the rod of his mouth, and with the breath of his lips shall slay the wicked (Isa 11:4). In the new age there would be shepherds after God's own heart "who will shepherd you wisely and prudently" (Jer 3:15; cf. 23:4). The prophet speaks for Yahweh, saying: "I will save my sheep . . . and I will judge between one sheep and another. I will appoint one shepherd over them to pasture them, my servant David . . ." (Ezek 34:22–24). The prophet reminds the people that a new king will come, one who will be prince under God, and who will rule the people in the new age, the time when the order intended for creation will be restored.

From Royal Power to Royal Person: The Messianic Tradition

Unfortunately, the ideal of kingship was seldom realized. It is therefore understandable that kingship carries such negative connotation and is interpreted so pessimistically. Yet it is the ideal of kingship, the model for involvement in the divine creative activity, that nourished hope that one day such a king would reign. Isaiah most eloquently gives expression to that hope:

A shoot shall sprout from the stump of Jesse (Isa 11:1a)

The spirit of the Lord shall rest upon him: . . .
    and his delight shall be the fear of the Lord. (Isa 11:2a, 3a)

Not by appearance shall he *judge,*
    not by hearsay shall he decide.
But he shall *judge* the poor *with justice,*
    and decide aright for the land's afflicted.
He shall strike the ruthless with the rod of his mouth,
    and with the breath of his lips he shall slay the wicked.
Justice shall be the band around his waist,
    and *faithfulness* a belt upon his hips (Isa 11:3b–5).

It is this ideal of kingship that is manifested most perfectly in the life and mission of Jesus of Nazareth. As is quoted in the gospel of Luke, Jesus came:

> To bring glad tidings to the poor;
> to proclaim liberty to captives,
> recovery of sight to the blind
>   and release to prisoners (Lk 4:18).

The ideal of kingship furnished the content for the messianic tradition, the tradition which was fulfilled in the life of Jesus Christ and which is the challenge to every Christian. This is to say that there is continuity between the ideal of kingship and the life of every human being, especially those who follow Christ. In a very real sense every Christian is called to be a *royal person*. Like the kings, every person is created to have dominion in the world, i.e., to be stewards of the world and builders of community within society. Like kings, each individual is created to be a mediator through whom God's life is generated in the world.

Since kingship can carry such negative connotations, it is preferable to speak of the *royal person* as the one who fulfills the responsibilities to be in the world for the life of others. The king could be simply a royal power; whereas the *royal person* is fully involved in relationships—totally dependent on God and actively involved in serving others an expression of love and dependence on God. The *royal person* is one through whom God's life flows and vitalizes all he/she touches. The *royal person* is a generator of life.

The association between the ideal of kingship, the royal person, and every individual human being is not mere transference or application of a theological expression for contemporary purposes. The Hebrew scriptures make the association clearly and boldly. Human beings are described as God's creatures with a royal status and kingly responsibilities. In Psalm 8, which expresses praise for the Creator and wonder at the nobility of humanity, the psalmist acclaims:

You have made them little less than God,
  and *crowned* them with glory and honor.
You have *given* them *dominion over* the works of your hands,
  putting *all things under* their *feet* (Ps 8:6–7).

According to this description, which corresponds to that of the
royal person, human beings share the divine life (made little less
than God); are elevated to a royal status (crowned with glory and
honor); and are given responsibility for the preservation of life
(given dominion), a concept conveyed also in the symbol of the
footstool (all things under their feet). Human beings are indeed
created to be royal persons. They are charged, by reason of their
status in creation, to be communicators of divine life within the
world. The blessings of life flow through royal persons to the
community. The sacred trust of responsibility for life derives
from God who ultimately is Lord of Life. Therefore, *royal persons* are absolutely and completely reliant upon God whom they
know to be the cause and the purpose of life.

THE ROYAL PERSONHOOD AND A THEOLOGY OF HUMANNESS

The Yahwist narrative was composed under the influence of
the monarchy.[25] The understanding of humanness as it is introduced in Gen 2–3, not surprisingly, reflects the understanding
of life and responsibility for kingship.[26] In a real sense. the
Yahwist presents human beings as kings. This writer understands that human beings are from among creatures and yet
somewhat above other creatures as the being that communicates
the presence of God to the world. Essentially, the king's function, as we have seen, is to be from and among people and raised
to the position through which he may ensure the preservation of
God's order in the world.

This is a very different focus from that in which the interest in
humanity's apostasy and need for reconciliation—a perspective

that dominates salvation history. The neglected side of the coin of salvation theology is a look at God as creator, the giver and preserver of life. From this perspective, the focus is not God; the focus is upon human beings as God's creatures through whom the divine work is accomplished in the world.

To demonstrate the divine presence in, with, and through human beings as they accomplish the work of God, God is featured in anthropological terms; God is immanent in creation. God "is with" individuals; communication is direct and to ordinary human beings, not cultic leaders. In this context, human beings are recognized in their reality of potential for good and evil. They are, however, challenged to respond from their basic goodness to responsible service in the world. Human beings are presented as gifted or "blessed" and as bearers of those gifts/blessings to others. In other words, human beings are recognized as graced individuals who are created and gifted to be the communicators of God's life in the world. The Yahwist narrator wrote out of the understanding that life is a gift to be lived and enjoyed and celebrated. Life has meaning simply as it *is* and the benefit to others comes because one accepts one's gifts and therefore lives vitally. These notions underlie the Yahwist presentation as well as the other writings of the tenth century, B.C. The emphasis in this literature rests on the power of life communicated from God through human beings to the world.

Humanness in the Yahwist Creation Account

The creation account in Gen 2:4b–3:24 records realities about humanness. This report was not written to describe historical beginnings. It is rather a reflection upon the mystery of humanness, setting the mystery of life forth in all its dimensions. The truths about humanity presented in this text pertain to all peoples; they do not refer only to the people chosen by God to be the special people. Essentially, the text affirms the reality that Yahweh is creator of all and that all human beings are dependent on God who is their maker.

The creation story is expressed poetically and with dramatic imagery so that what we have is a series of scenes which elaborate the facets of human life. The language is fresh and inviting. Significantly, however, the story is told theologically; for the point of the poetic dramatic presentation is the function of human life within the plan of creation.

Let us consider, first of all, the image of God that dominated the tenth century world when the Yahwist composed this narrative. We notice that God sees (2:19); she breathes (2:7); she plants (2:8); she forms in the manner of a potter (2:7); she builds like a builder (2:21); God walks in the garden (3:8); she calls to the couple (3:9), and dialogues with them (3:10-13); she clothes the couple (3:21). God is presented in every respect anthropomorphically. The reader gets the impression that God is very close, having very human characteristics. God is immanent. God is "with," "walking among" his people.[27]

The narrative, however, focuses upon human beings. Humanity is to be understood in the term 'adam. 'Adam indicates all humanity, both male and female.[28] The distinction between male and female is quite precisely in the use of distinct terms: 'ish for male or husband, and 'ishshah for female or wife. These terms are found in Gen 2:23-24 and 3:6, places where mutuality and companionship in society are intended. All that is said about 'adam is intended for both the male and female partners in the human family.

The narrative is artistically constructed with imagery to boldly state realities about human life. The composite of this imagery is the Yahwist understanding of humanness. It is, therefore, necessary to carefully consider the various motifs, metaphors, and themes.

The narrator tells us that human beings are made of *dust* "from the ground" (2:7) and that human beings return to the *dust* (3:19). The dust motif is not intended only to highlight the finiteness of human existence. To illustrate the transitoriness of life, the motif is indeed dramatic. In this narrative, the motif of dust contrasts with the exaltation of human life by the breath of God. In 2:7 the text reads, "the Lord God formed 'adam out of the dust of the ground and blew into his nostrils the breath of life, and so 'adam became a living being." From simple dust, 'adam is given life from God's breath. This is to say that human life *is* out of the divine life and therefore somewhat divine. The breath of God, according to the Yahwist insight, is the essence of the living human being. When the breath of God is taken away, the person ceases to live (Ps 104:29). Human beings are thus uniquely related to the Creator by sharing the divine life. In 2:9 we read that plants also are made to grow "out of the ground"; and in 2:19 all creatures are formed "out of the ground," the common element in creation. The distinctiveness of 'adam is the fact that human life is lifted by God from a state of nothingness (dust) to divine life (the breath of God). The motif of dust makes the contrast more pronounced.

The motif of dust is used in royal literature to state quite precisely the status of the king in royal society. The person who ascends the throne is understood to have been lifted from nothingness to a status of dominion: "I lifted you up from the dust and made you ruler of my people Israel" (1 Kgs 16:2a). In this context, the dust implies the preroyal status, a status like human existence which is transitory. The warning to the king threatens a return to dust, i.e., to the preroyal status: "I will utterly sweep you away . . ." (1 Kings 16:3). The obvious implication is that dust can be swept away. The motif of dust was borrowed by the Yahwist from the royal sphere where it expressed the limitations of the royal power, and where it depicted the radical transition from a status of nothingness to that of ruler among God's people.[29] The dust motif carries dramatic meaning in the royal context. The depth of meaning in the creation narrative is heightened in light of its meaning in regard to kings.

The connection made between the use of dust in the creation story and in royal literature has important implications. As such common elements are isolated, it becomes increasingly clear that there exists an interdependence between the two literatures, or rather that they share a common context and reflect similar concerns. In the instance of the dust motif, light is shed upon Israel's understanding that its king reigned from a very fragile position. The king comes from a status of nothingness, i.e., from among the people; and the king is raised to the throne to carry on God's work. Since the king is lifted to service, it is possible for the king to be reduced again. The imagery asserts that the king is limited in authority to the power and authority of Yahweh as no other statement could do.[30]

In the creation account, the dust motif together with the elevation of life through the divine breath establishes the first dimension of royal humanness, the relationship between human beings and God. Humanness in its essence is a participation in the divine life. The sharing of the divine life lifts human beings from nothingness to a status of rulership within creation. This rulership does not imply autonomous power but rather necessary dependence upon the Lord of all. The first dimension of royal humanness is realized when human beings acknowledge both their responsible position within creation and their utter and essential dependence upon the Creator. In this first dimension of relationship with God there is implied an acceptance of human life as blessed with potential to cooperate with God in making possible the continuation of life within the world.

The actualization of the human position within creation is explicitated in the second relationship outlined by the Yahwist. This relationship is one of stewardship toward nature and creatures, based on the premise that human beings are derived from the common element of "the ground,"[31] yet distinguished by being raised from dust to rulership. The narrative specifies the relationships very deliberately. Regarding humanity's relationship to nature, the narrative states: "Then the Lord God planted a garden in Eden, in the east, and he placed there the 'adam whom he had formed" (2:9). "The Lord God took the 'adam and settled him in the garden of Eden, to cultivate and care for it" (2:15). The reader gets the impression that God labored in the creation of the garden to assure its beauty and productivity. The garden of the world is given to 'adam for pleasure and for food

(2:9); it is given also to be nurtured and preserved (2:15). The words with which the Yahwist expresses the human charge are carefully chosen and carry a pregnant imperative. The word for "cultivate" is *'ebed*, literally meaning "to serve" the garden or to care for it that it may continue to have life. The term translated "care for" is *shamar*, which means "to keep," "to preserve," or "to maintain" its life. *'Adam* is charged "to serve" and "to preserve." In this task, *'adam* is named as the divine representative in the world and as the world's steward. Humanity is charged to serve and care for the world, that is to say, to love nature as God the Creator loves the object of her creation.

The responsibility of human beings extends also to the creatures of the world. This awareness is told in a simple and direct imagery by the Yahwist. When the creation of the creatures (also made "out of the ground" as are plants and humans alike) is complete, God "brought them to the *'adam* to see what he would call them; whatever *'adam* called each of them would be its name. The *'adam* gave names to all the cattle, all the birds of the air, and all the wild animals" (2:19–20a). This naming of the creatures implies the dominion of human beings over all the creatures. Though humans share a common origin with all creatures, they are charged with the task of seeing that creatures are cared for within the world. In this sense, human beings represent God in providing for the preservation and life of nonrational creatures. Better said, God acts through human beings in continuing her creative activity.

The second dimension of humanity's relationship is to the world and to all creatures in it. It is impossible for human beings to really live and be unrelated to the world and its creatures. The plants and animals are given for the pleasure, yes, the ecstasy of human beings, but also into the care and protection of human beings. Humanity is charged with an extraordinary responsibility: to be involved in the life of the world as a participant for its continuing existence. Living out one's responsibility as steward within the world is the second characteristic of the royal person. The royal person acknowledges one's dependence on God and the responsibility charged to him/her by tending, preserving, being involved in the divine creative activity as caretakers and co-creators with God for the perpetuation of life in the world.

Lastly, humanity symbolized by the generic 'adam becomes part of another kind of relationship. This is a relationship with "the suitable partner" (2:18, 20), for "it is not good for the 'adam to be alone" (2:18). The suitable companion is introduced through a second creation which is simply a device for making the transition from humanity in a general sense to the reality of the distinction between maleness and femaleness[32](2:21–22). The relationship between male and female is thus exemplified as a relationship lived out in the community: "the two of them become one body" (2:24). Human beings are created as male and female and intended to relate in society, the basis of which is sexual relationship.

With the bonding of the male and female into community, the third fundamental relationship is established. Human beings are meant to live in society as in a community and are called into mutuality and sharing of life. The royal person engages in life with others. Out of this sharing, life comes forth concretely in procreation and symbolically in the evidence of fullness of life that is the consequence of mutuality with other human beings.

The definition of royal humanness is complete with this intro-duction of partnership among human beings. By royal human-ness we mean the daily living out of the three dimensional reality of existence: relationship with God in the shape of dependence; relationship with nature in the shape of caring for the world with all its creatures; and relationship with other human beings in the shape of community be and mutuality in society. In effect, we are saying that to be human is to be related.

While the Yahwist distinguishes three separate lines of rela-tionship, the essential relationship with God is contingent upon the relationships within society and toward nature. This is spelled out in the example of human interaction, one individual against another, as in the report of Cain and Abel (Gen 4:2–16). The Yahwist demonstrates the interconnectedness between the relationships by positioning the account of alienation from God (Gen 3) and alienation between individual human beings (Gen 4), side by side.[33]

Humanness is indeed relationship. But there is the reality of human freedom that is equally a quality of humanness. The Yahwist does not ignore this human capacity to refuse to live in the relationships which are the basis of creation. Because human beings are free to choose participation and cooperation in the order of creation or to refuse, the Yahwist constructed another dramatic event to illustrate the power of choice. In the drama presented in Gen 3, the woman and serpent enact the freedom of choice which is an essential of humanness. Through this choice, the Yahwist addresses the problem of the human potential for good as well as for evil. In this drama, the writer makes the assertion that human beings are equally capable of good and evil. This is not the same as saying that human beings were created evil.

In the story, the power of choice is expressed through the imagery of eating or not eating from one tree. The use of "eat" as the action of human participation gives insight to the dramatic expression of the writer. Eating implies total involvement and participation. The force of this imagery is apparent in the no less than fifteen uses of the term "eat" or "food."[34] In the drama of choice, the Yahwist is saying that the man and woman are totally and completely involved in the choice; participation is from the gut level.

We notice that in 3:9 two trees are mentioned: the "tree of life" and "the tree of knowledge of good and evil." The first of these—the "tree of life"—is not mentioned again until the very end of the narrative at 3:22. The "tree of life" is symbolic of the human desire to live forever. It represents the desire for immortality. Of course, immortality is incompatible with humanness: human beings are formed from dust and return to dust. Since there is no human choice about immortality, the narrative states, using dramatic imagery, that the Lord God "stationed the cherubim and the fiery revolving sword to guard the way to the tree of life" (3:24). Immortality is forever out of the reach of human beings. The Yahwist asserts that immortality distinguishes God from her creatures and therefore will never be a property of humanness.

The second tree—the "tree of knowledge of good and evil"—symbolizes another human desire, the will to know all things. It is from this tree that the man and woman may not eat. Human beings may not desire a knowledge and therefore a control that exceeds the limits of human nature.

Knowledge is an essential of being human; knowledge provides humanity with the capability of being steward and preserver and companion. Tremendous power is placed into the hands of human beings with knowledge. It enables people to carry on God's work in the world. But knowledge is also the cause of great evil, the evil demonstrated in the narrative, the evil of exceeding the limits of human nature. Human beings, as we have said, are free to enter into relationships; and they are free to determine the quality of those relationships. Human beings have been created with power and authority which enables them to assume the position of responsibility for the preservation of the order in nature and the world which God intends. But given such authority, human beings may choose to assume a god-like authority, executing power in a way that conflicts with God's desire for creation. The evil demonstrated in the narrative is the choice to be self-sufficient, the desire to "be like gods who know what is good and what is bad" (3:5). Every human being has used the given freedom to act as if he or she were autonomous; we all at one time or another assume a god-like stance, taking to ourselves power and dominion that is inconsistent with the creative order which makes for life. The human action, in opposition to God's will for life, results in death. The Yahwist expressed this last reality of the human potential for evil with the statement: "See! The 'adam has become like one of us, knowing what is good and what is evil!" (3:22). Human beings *do* have tremendous power and authority. The continual challenge, the challenge to the royal person, is the use of that power in accord with God for life.

Both desires—for immortality and for knowledge—are illustrated in the narrative development in Gen 4–11. Two concrete events are told, each of which illustrates the attempt to exceed the limits of human nature. Gen 6:1–4, the intermarriage between gods and humans, demonstrates the attempt to transgress the limits of finiteness. The other, Gen 11:1–9, the account of humanity "making a name for (itself)" by building "a city and a tower with its top in the sky" (vs 4), demonstrates the attempt to transgress the limits of technology. Here human beings use their knowledge to effect what only God can give.

We have suggested that the trees—the tree of life and the tree of knowledge of good and evil—symbolize the basic desires of humanity: the desire for immortal life and the desire for knowledge. The meaning we have suggested is verified in the two narratives we have cited. Each of these explicitates the misuse of one of these desires. The desires themselves are, in fact, good; they are the capacities by which human beings live humanly. But they are also the capacities that allow human beings to ignore the sovereignty of God and to assume an autonomous reign. They are the capacities for both good and evil.

How are we to understand the consequences of the choice to eat of the tree of knowledge of good and evil, the consequences presented in the language of curse? We must, first of all, understand that curses and blessings together name the realities that are part of human life. Those dimensions of life that are called the curses specify a series of limitations within the scope of the totality of life. The mystery that is life is comprised of some aspects which are pleasant and some which are painful. That is the way life *is*! The world with its plants and trees and creatures and human beings are created for human delight. But these are also created to be served: the ground must be worked, the soil tilled and plants harvested; creatures are not all tame or pleasant to behold—some crawl on their belly in the dust; and there are children to be brought forth and human conflicts to be reconciled. Life in all its aspects is good and beautiful. But human beings may not merely passively exist; they are delegated with the task of serving life. The Yahwist understood well this human responsibility for creation and expressed the reality within a matrix that stands clearly in contrast to the blessedness of the gifts that grace life.

In order to view the contrast, we need to look at the overall structure of the narrative. The blessings which are given to *'adam* balance with the curses which challenge *'adam*. So also is there contrast between the other elements of the narrative which surround the central drama, the choice to eat of the one tree.

Human life is given (2:7)	- - - Human life is protected from immortality (3:24)
'adam is placed in the garden to serve it (2:8, 15)	- - - *adam* is alienated from the garden (3:23)
two trees: tree of life and tree of knowledge of good and evil (2:9)	- - - two trees: tree of knowledge of good and evil and tree of life (3:22)
the commandment and the threat, "you shall *die*" (2:17)	- - - Eve is called "the mother of all the *living*" (3:20)

blessings
    'adam in relationship with the ground, plants, and creatures
    male and female relationship (2:15–25)
	curses
	    woman and a creature male and female
	    'adam with the ground and plants (3:14–19)

drama of choice
(3:1–13)

The narrative is structured upon an inclusio, that is, the writer makes a complete circle with the elements of the narrative.

There is direct contrast and continuity between the first element of the narrative and the last: human life is given, and in the end, life remains human. This element about humanness is undoubtedly the single most important tenet of the narrative. All else depends on it. Though human beings become alienated from the world given to them, still they are blessed with life. Though they are threatened with death when they exceed the limits of humanness, still Eve, the actress in the drama, is called "mother of the living." Though the ground, plants, creatures and human beings impose hardship upon humanity, these very gifts constitute the blessings of human life. In the center of the narrative stands the drama of choice. In this section is dramatized the choice before every human being *to receive* human life and its gifts with the incumbent responsibilities, or *to take* power and authority that are not given.

In this discussion, we have suggested that Gen 2–3 situates persons in basic relationships which demand of persons particular responsibilities. These relationships and responsibilities are:

1) to God the Creator who shares her very life with human beings and charges them to be the divine representative in the world;

2) to nature and creatures with which persons are entrusted for sustenance and preservation; and

3) to other human beings with whom individuals are co-creators and cosharers in the nurturing of life.

We have suggested also that Gen 2–3 names the realities of human life as these were understood by the Yahwist theologian. In articulating his theology of humanness, the Yahwist worked from certain presuppositions which we have attempted to uncover in our analysis of the creation narrative. It is apparent that the Yahwist presumes both the human potential for good and for evil. Clearly, the Yahwist affirms the basic goodness of humanity who shares the spirit of God as the essence of life. The Yahwist also affirms the fact that humanity often misuses the gifts or abuses the relationships that are constitutive of humanness. As such, human beings betray their basic goodness. It is significant that the Yahwist explains the human potential for

good and evil as an expression of human freedom which is presumed to be given. The freedom, enacted in the dramatic choice of obedience to God's commandment, can be played out in each of the basic relationships. Human beings are free
— to acknowledge dependence on God or to claim self-sufficiency,
— to accept responsibility for the world and its creatures or to pollute and waste the world's resources;
— to recognize the mutuality among persons or to claim superiority.

The Yahwist, furthermore, makes the positive assertion through narrative technique that there are limits imposed upon humanity. One limitation is mortality; human beings by nature must die. The other limitation, traditionally seen as an imposed punishment for sin, is really the Yahwist's way of stating the fact that life is not all bliss. It is consonant with humanness to work, to experience pain, to fear some creatures, to know human conflict, etc. These are the problems that each individual confronts in the journey of life. Far from being impediments, these challenges motivate humanity in the use of freedom toward accepting responsibilities.

It is noteworthy that though man and woman took from the tree of knowledge, they did not die. Life was not ended though they disobeyed God's word and misused their freedom. The human response, it is true, diminishes the relationship with God but it does not destroy it, and clearly, life is not ended. This insight of the Yahwist is remarkable. He made every attempt to make a clear statement about the limits of life and also about God's will for life. Generations of Christians have done quite another thing in the interpretation that has been imposed on the text. The text makes a series of statements that indicate that, in spite of human unpredictableness, life continues precisely through these same human beings. The woman, though she had seized the fruit and had shared it with her husband, is called Eve, "because," as the text says, "she became the mother of all the living" (3:20).[35] And the couple, though they had overstepped the bounds of their humanness, were clothed by God with garments of skin made for them (3:21).[36] Each symbol indicates that God remains with the people of her creation. Each is a symbol for life.

God's Will for Life in the Narratives of Genesis

This theme of God's will for life continues in the Yahwist narrative development. In spite of the human penchant to abuse the divinely intended relationships, in each instance, life perdures. In the case of Cain and Abel in Gen 4, there is a dramatic illustration of the struggle between brothers. Cain murders Abel. Though life had been denied another, though Cain had exceeded human authority which does not encompass the taking and giving of life, Cain does not die. He becomes a wanderer on earth; and he lives in fear for his life (4:14). But God protects his life by marking him so that no one will kill him (4:15). Not only is Cain's life protected, but the narrative makes the point that Cain reared children and built a city (4:17ff.). Life and progeny and prosperity flow from him.

A second illustration of God's will for life is found in the flood narrative (Gen 6–9). When all the earth was inundated, plants ceased to grow and creatures failed to survive, there was one family and one pair of each of God's creatures which came forth from the ark. Through this family and the creatures with them, life continued upon the earth. God had willed that life should continue and had provided that creatures would be protected so that there would be the capability of a new beginning. God did not destroy and re-create. God provided that life would continue through human beings who loved God and who cared for the creatures of God's world.

With creation, God *entrusted* the world to human beings. God does not interfere, but rather *trusts* that human beings will engage in the task of life. God wills that human beings live in, care for, and serve the world doing God's work. This task is not done by single individuals; it is a matter of mutuality, i.e., sharing the

task in a harmonious endeavor and in a common purpose to
make/keep creation in the order designed by its Maker.

Humanness and Blessing in the Ancestral History

Underlying the ancestral history are the presuppositions about
humanness which the Yahwist introduced in the creation narrative. In Gen 12–26, each of the ancestors is presented as a royal
person. These are not cultic officials nor officers whose primary
service is worship or the shrines. Rather, the people involved are
the mothers and fathers, the grandparents, the aunts and uncles
who live loyally before God in the world and who therefore
mediate God's life to others.

The ancestral history is structured upon a number of important themes, such as the promise of land and of numerous progeny. The theme with which we will concern ourselves is that of
"blessing," for it is through this idea that God's power for life is
expressed in and through the central characters.

The Yahwist writer introduced a programmatic statement into
the call of Abraham. Upon this statement, the whole of the narrative presentation is constructed. The various sagas, legends,
and etiologies drawn from tradition were selected and woven
into the masterful narrative upon the crux of the program set
forth in the carefully articulated statement:

> Go forth from the land of your kinsfolk and from your
>   father's house to a land that I will show you.
>   I will make of you a great nation,
>   and *I will bless you;*
>   I will make your name great,
>   so that *you will be a blessing.*
>   I will bless those who bless you
>   and curse those who curse you.
>   *All the communities of the earth shall find blessing in you.*
> Abram went as the Lord directed him (Gen 12:1–4a).[37]

The promise of God to Abram is addressed to the people living
in the newly formed monarchy. It reminds them that the land

they possess so proudly is the fulfillment of God's promise and that their greatness and fame is the sign of God's fidelity. Moreover, the statement makes the assertion that this people is not only abundantly blessed and that they are a blessing to others, but that all communities of the earth receive blessing through them. These are bold declarations that can be understood only in concrete reality.

We ask, just as God's people must have asked long ago: What is the meaning of this blessing? And, In what ways can Israel be a blessing for others? The narrative does answer both these questions and in so doing gives insight to the profound theological understanding of the narrator. The Yahwist worked out of the realization that God remains present in and with all of her creatures, caring for them and sustaining their life. The sign of that ever-present life is, according to the Yahwist, God's blessing. For this theologian, life is blessing and blessing is life. Even more, wherever there is life, God is present; God's presence is evident whenever there is the sign of blessing. Blessing is thus the indicator of God's faithful and sustaining care for her creatures.

In Hebrew thought, the notion of an abstract divine presence would be incomprehensible. To be real signs, God's blessing must be concretely seen and experienced. Thus Abraham is described as one who "was very rich in livestock, silver, and gold" (Gen 13:2; cf. 24:35). These possessions meant, in Hebrew thought, that Abram was very gifted with blessing. These possessions were the signs by which everyone could know that God "was with" Abram and also that Abram was, in fact, a loyal servant who walked faithfully before God (Gen 24:40; 48:15). This is to say that the blessings witnessed concretely to the relationship between God and Abram.

To Isaac, Yahweh reiterated the promise, "I am with you. I will bless you . . . " (Gen 26:24). As a sign that Isaac was a royal person, one living in relationship, "the Lord blessed him, he became richer and richer all the time, until he was very wealthy indeed. He acquired such flocks and herds, and so many work animals that the Philistines became envious of him" (Gen 26:12b–14). This elaborate description of Isaac's richness serves to make the listerner aware of Isaac's power among the peoples. Because of this blessing, Isaac is identifiable as one who lives faithfully before God, one whom God has blessed, and who therefore must be a blessing, a giver of life, for others. The Philistine king recognized the power for life in Isaac and the potential for participating in that life. Abimelech said: "We are convinced that the Lord is with you, so we propose that there be a sworn agreement between our two sides.... Henceforth 'The Lord's blessing be upon you!' " (Gen 26:28-29). The pact between the two parties signaled peace (vs 31), which is the consequence or sign of living in accord with the order in God's creation. The narrative describes one way in which individuals or the nation can be a blessing for others. Here that way is by concluding an agreement of peace and thereby establishing *shalom.*

Jacob, the ancestor of Israel, is described in contrast to Laban, the ancestor of the Arameans, as one who "grew increasingly prosperous, and came to own, not only large flocks, but also male and female servants and camels and asses" (Gen 30:43). This abundant prosperity says more clearly than any abstract description that God is with Jacob. Jacob is God's loyal servant and God blesses him with abundance. The blessing given to Jacob cannot be contained or possessed but is meant to flow from the blessed individual to others. This is the point of the programmatic statement: "I will bless you ... so that you will be a blessing" (Gen 12:2). In narrating the history, the Yahwist made sure that the point is emphasized: God intends that life come to others through human beings. Having experienced God's blessing through Jacob, Laban is prompted to say: "I have learned through divination that it is because of you that God has blessed me" (Gen 30:27). Jacob agrees and acknowledges that the increase which came to Laban as the result of Jacob's ingenuity was actually God's blessing: "You know what work I did for you and how well your livestock fared under my care; the little you had before I came has grown into very much, since *the Lord's blessing came upon you* in my company" (Gen 30:30).

The point cannot be stressed too much that, for the biblical theologian, blessing was the way for expressing God's loving, provident care, and presence with his people. Furthermore, God's people were gifted, not for their own glory and advantage, but that others might be gifted through them. In every instance, others touch the source of life through people whom God has touched. It is to be expected, therefore, that the royal person Joseph would make a difference in Egypt. The story states that "from the moment that (Pharaoh) put (Joseph) in charge of his household and all his possessions, *the Lord blessed the Egyptian's house* for Joseph's sake; in fact, *the Lord's blessing was on everything* he owned, both inside the house and out" (Gen 39:5).

In presenting each of the ancestors, the Yahwist narrator was controlled by the awareness that each of these individuals was a royal person. This is to say that their lives are firmly rooted in God, the source of life, and that out of that rootedness life is given to others. The point of these stories is to show that God's life flows through human beings to the world.

Let us look more carefully at the elaboration of the statement about blessing: "All the communities of the earth shall find blessing in you" (Gen 12:3b). The ancestral narrative is told in a way that shows all the people of the then known world receiving benefit through the blessed individuals. Each of the leaders who interact with Abram, Isaac, and Jacob are representatives of a neighboring people. For example, Lot, with whom Abram shares the land, is the ancestor of the Ammonites and Moabites (Gen 19:37-38). Laban, who benefits from Jacob's work, is the ancestor of Arameans (Gen 28:5; 31:20-24). Of course, Jacob is the ancestor of the Israelites (Gen 32:29). A full treatment of the way the narrative shows God's people to be a blessing for the communities who interact with the monarchy is impossible here.[38] As an illustration, let us consider only summarily the one narrative in which Abraham intercedes for Sodom and Gomorrah in Gen 18:16-33.

Abraham's dialogue with Yahweh is positioned between two dramatic events, each of which contributes to the literary context for this scene. In Genesis 13, we are told that, when given a choice of land, Lot selected the Jordan plain and settled there near Sodom; while Abraham remained in the land of Canaan

(Gen 13:8–13). In Genesis 19, the cities Sodom and Gomorrah are destroyed because those in the city are evil. The destruction does not occur, however, before Lot and his family are sent away from the city: "(God) was mindful of Abram by sending Lot away from the upheaval by which God overthrew the cities where Lot had been living" (Gen 19:29). Subsequently from Lot are issued two sons, Moab and Ammon, the ancestors of the Moabites and Ammonites (Gen 19:37–38). The life spared to Lot results in life for the two nations who are neighbors to Israel in the time of the monarchy.

The scene of Abraham's intercession on behalf of Sodom and Gomorrah is set against the backdrop of the story of Lot. It is positioned here by the Yahwist as a concrete example of one way the communities of the earth receive blessing through Israel. While Abraham's pleading for the people of the cities appears to be of no avail on account of their evil, still life continues. Lot is spared and two nations are given life.

In the intercessory scene itself, almost every statement is laden with significant meaning. There is, first of all, the rumination of God about revealing his mind to Abraham: "Shall I hide from Abraham what I am about to do, now that he is to become a great and populous nation, and *all the nations of the earth are to find blessing in him?*" (Gen 18:17–18). From this statement we know that the concern of the narrative is Abraham's power for life in regard to this neighboring people. Its point is to present one way, the way of intercession, by which Abraham can be a blessing for the cities and also Israel can be a blessing for its contemporaries.[39]

It seems that the crux of the problem underlying the narrative is God's justice. As judge, God maintains life by preserving the order intended in creation. In order to do this, God may punish or even destroy those who are disrupters of life. It is God as judge whom Abraham addresses: "Will you sweep away the innocent with the guilty? . . . Far be it from you to do such a thing, to make the innocent die with the guilty, so that the innocent and the guilty would be treated alike! Should not *the judge of all the world* act *with justice?* (Gen 18:23, 25).[40] Abraham, who is "but dust and ashes!" (vs 27) that is to say, a human being, implores the "judge of all the world," who can only be God. This fact alone dramatizes the power of human beings for life. The Yahwist intends to demonstrate that power in Abraham's challenge to God, the point of which is the vindication of God's justice. Is God just in resolving to destroy Sodom? Is God right in taking the lives of the people in this city? The dramatic diminishment of the numbers brings the reader to the awareness that there were not even ten innocent. Since the city was destroyed, all must have been guilty for God would not "make the innocent die with the guilty" (vs 25). No one from the city was spared save Lot, through whom life continued and flourished in the two nations of Moab and Ammon. In a very concrete way, Abraham is shown to be a significant human being through whom the ruler of the world, who is creator and judge, acts for the life of others.

The Joseph Story

Joseph stands apart from all others because he is a royal person par excellence. In every respect, Joseph is a generator of life. He is presented as a model human being in whom are idealized the qualities of humanness. In Hebrew thought, humanness means relationship between God and the individual. In the case of Joseph the statement about God's presence with Joseph and the sign of that presence is repeated like a refrain:

But since *the Lord was with him,* Joseph got on very well and was assigned to the household of his Egyptian master. When his master saw that *the Lord was with him and brought him success* in whatever he did, he took a liking to Joseph and made him his personal attendant; he put him in charge of his household and entrusted to him all his possessions. From the moment that he put him in charge of his household and all his possessions, *the Lord blessed the Egyptian's house* for Joseph's sake; in fact, *the*

Lord's blessing was on everything he owned, both inside the house and out (Gen 39:2-5; cf. vss 21, 23).

There are two literary levels to the Joseph story. In both, Joseph is presented as the one whose life makes a difference for others. In the original story about Joseph in Egypt, the Egyptians are blessed through Joseph. The household of the pharaoh prospers (Gen 39:5); the people are provided with food during the famine (41:56); and, in fact, "all the world came to Joseph to obtain rations of grain, for famine had gripped the whole world" (41:57).[41]

The story about the young Joseph in Egypt was used by redactor to account for the presence of the tribes of Israel in Egypt. In order that Israel might be brought out of Egypt, all of the tribes would first have had to move to that land. The story accounts for the transition from Canaan to Egypt.[42] In this telling, the image of Joseph is consistent. Through Joseph, the life of his father and brothers is preserved during the famine. They go to Egypt "that they may stay alive rather than die of hunger" (42:2). To preserve the life of the Israelites, God had prepared that Joseph would be in a position in Egypt that through him the life of the brothers would be spared:

> It was really *for the sake of saving lives* that God sent me here ahead of you (45:5b).

> God, therefore, sent me on ahead of you to ensure for you a remnant on earth and *to save your lives* in an extraordinary deliverance. So it was not really you but God who had me come here; and he has made of me a father to Pharaoh, lord of all his household, and ruler over the whole land of Egypt (45:7-8).

The purpose of Joseph's life is summarized in the statement spoken by Joseph to his brothers:

> Though you meant harm to me, God meant it for good, to achieve his present end, *the survival of many people* (Gen 50:20).

CONCLUSION

The outline of traditions—the creator as king and judge; the king as representative of Yahweh; the royal personhood—demonstrates the continuity between the function of the creator and the purpose of human life in biblical thought. I have lifted out of the biblical literature a line of development which focuses upon the responsibilities charged to human beings. The literature reveals that a serious task is delegated to human beings by God for the purpose of preserving life as intended in creation. This line of thinking is introduced as a possible basis for formulating a creation theology.

In suggesting that the Hebrew scriptures contain the fundamental elements for creation theology, I do not negate the classical focus upon God as savior. Rather, I am suggesting that there is an alternative to the one-sidedness of salvation theology. This latter has been accepted as if it is the totality of faith. Creation theology offers the fresh perspective of the divine activity *through human beings.* This viewpoint together with the perspective of divine intervention *on behalf of human beings* makes the message of the scriptures complete.

This study indicates that, in formulating a creation theology, the central tenet will be: *God wills that life be for others.* God created human beings and blesses them for the single purpose that, through individuals, life will continually flow into the world.

The New Testament scriptures reveal that the ideal human life was lived by Jesus Christ. This man embraced the world as God created it; he "came that (the world) might have life and have it to the full" (Jn 10:10b).

NOTES

1. Biblical quotations are taken from *The New American Bible:* the new Catholic translation prepared by the members of the Catholic Biblical Association of America.

2. On the differences between Hebrew and Greek thought, see: Thorleif Boman, *Hebrew Thought Compared with Greek* (W. W. Norton & Company, 1960); and Claude Tresmontant, *A Study of Hebrew Thought* (New York: Desclee Company, 1960).

3. To illustrate this, we refer to the most recent publication in biblical theology by a renowned scholar: Walther Zimmerli, *Old Testament Theology in Outline* (John Knox Press, 1978). The orientation of this theology is the divine activity and human response with salvation being the controlling action. Minimal space is allotted to the work of God as creator (pp. 32–43), and there primarily as this mode serves salvation. No mention is made of God's continuing work and presence in the world in and through created life.

4. Pslams which give praise exclusively to the creator of the universe are: Pss 8, 19:1–6; 104, 148.

5. Some psalms in which the events of salvation are recounted are: Pss 78; 105; 106; 135; 136.

6. E.g., at Ugarit and in Canaan the supreme god El was called "creator of creatures." El was honored as the high god in the pantheon and all other gods were sons and daughters of El. See. F. M. Cross, "Yahweh and the God of the Patriarchs," *Harvard Theological Review* 55 (1962), pp. 242–244.

7. E.g., the Canaanite Baal was responsible for maintaining the regularities of the earth in the face of change and contingency. Baal was the male principle of fertility. After battle with Mot/death, Baal has intercourse with the goddess Anath, is enthroned in his palace, and life continues.

8. This formulary occurs throughout the narratives with particular frequency in Deuteronomy. It is one of the statements of faith that is recited in the basic creeds. Cf. Deut 6:21–22; 26:8; Josh 24:17.

9. *Kingship of God* (Harper & Row, 1967), p. 119. Cf. Isa 6:1–5 for a dramatic description of Yahweh as king.

10. Cf. Pss 80:2; 77:21; 78:52; 23:1–4; Jer 23:3; 31:10. Shepherd is a common Ancient Near Eastern title for both kings and gods. The kings Lipit-Ishtar of Isin and Hammurabi are shepherds of the people, and the god Shamash is addressed as shepherd. See, James Pritchard, ed., *Ancient Near Eastern Texts Relating to the Old Testament.* 3rd Edition with Supplement

(Princeton University Press, 1969), pp. 159, 164-5; 387. (Hereafter this work will be indicated ANET.)

11. Enuma elish is found in *ANET,* pp. 60-72.

12. The Baal myth is found in *ANET,* pp. 129-142.

13. For a full treatment of the use of these myths in the bible, see Bernhard W. Anderson, *Creation Versus Chaos* (Association Press, 1967).

14. The enthronement of Yahweh was thought to have been celebrated each year in Israel at the beginning of the New Year. When the rains had ended and there was promise of a fruitful agricultural year, the New Year festival commemorated the enthronement of Yahweh as king over the universe. The psalms that reflect that festival are thought to have been patterned after the Babylonian creation epic which was recited in Babylon at the beginning of each year. For the development of this hypothesis, see Sigmund Mowinckel, *The Psalms in Israel's Worship,* Vol. I (Abingdon, 1962), pp. 106-189.

15. On the attribution of the title "El Elyon, procreator of heaven and earth" to Yahweh, see Norman C. Habel, "Yahweh, Maker of Heaven and Earth: A Study in Tradition Criticism," *Journal of Biblical Literature* 91 (1972), pp. 321-337.

16. Humanness as relationship will be discussed below in our presentation of the Yahwist creation narrative.

17. The continual care and preservation of life is biblically expressed as "blessing." See the recent study, Claus Westermann, *Blessing in the Bible and the Life of the Church,* Overtures to Biblical Theology (Fortress Press, 1978). In this study, Westermann proposes that God's activity in blessing is the alternative of God's activity in salvation. Describing the different concepts of God perceived in these differing modes, Westermann says, "The God who saves is the one who comes; the one who blesses is the one who is present (or dwelling or enthroned)" (p. 8).

18. Some judgment speeches are: Am 4:1-2; Hos 4:1-3; Jer 2:4-13.

19. The Hebrew word *shapat* could be translated either "judge" or "govern" or "rule." In the examples quoted here, each of these different translations is used for the same term.

20. The Hebrew *mishpat* (justice or judgment) derives from the verbal root *shapat* (judge or govern). I prefer to translate

mishpat as "what is right," implying that each person is given what is one's right according to the divine intention for impartiality. See Ps 103:6: "The Lord secures justice and the rights of all the oppressed."

21. Contemporary biblical scholarship does not present a clear view of Israel's understanding of kingship. Many prefer to interpret the position through the eyes of other oriental models of kingship, and therefore, carry over ideas which may not at all have dominated Israel's understanding of its kings. As an example, see Frank Moore Cross, "The Ideologies of Kingship in the Era of the Empire: Conditional Covenant and Eternal Decree," in *Canaanite Myth and Hebrew Epic* (Harvard University Press, 1973), pp. 219–273. It is my opinion that Israel drew upon the various ideologies of kingship in the known world to articulate its own understanding. The borrowed ideas were notably those which highlight the subordination of the king to Yahweh. At some future date, this opinion will be prepared for publication. For the present, I cite, H. A. Kenik, "The Design for Kingship in 1 Kings 3:4–15: A Study in the Deuteronomistic Narrative Technique and Theology of Kingship," (Dissertation, St. Louis University, 1978).

22. With this psalm, compare Ps 101. Cf. H. A. Kenik, "Code of Conduct for a King: Psalm 101," *Journal of Biblical Literature* 95 (1976) 391–403. In this study the author isolates the duties of kingship and demonstrates that these are intended for the purpose of preserving life in the community.

23. On the sayings in Proverbs as collections used in education, see William McKane, *Proverbs: A New Approach* (Westminster Press, 1970), pp. 262–412; and R. N. Whybray, *Wisdom in Proverbs: The Concept of Wisdom in Proverbs 1–9:45* (London: SCM Press, Ltd., 1965).

24. The prophets address not only the kings but all leaders and all peoples. The prophets call people to accountability for failure to assume responsibility as royal persons. Cf. W. A. Brueggemann, *The Prophetic Imagination* (Fortress Press, 1978), for a fresh and exciting articulation of the prophetic task as that of criticizing and energizing. Professor Brueggemann focuses upon the role of the king and the prophetic critique of the king's execution of that role. In so doing, he over-emphasizes the nega-

tive dimensions of the royal position and thereby fails to recognize that there is the ideal of the royal person which, in fact, kings are challenged to be. This negative view of the royal position does not, however, diminsh the powerful statement about the prophetic task.

25. The close association between the royal court and the Yahwist narrative is widely accepted after the significant contribution in this regard by Gerhard von Rad in *Old Testament Theology, Vol. I, The Theology of Israel's Historical Traditions* (Harper & Row, 1962), especially pp. 36–57. See also: P. F. Ellis, *The Yahwist: The Bible's First Theologian* (Fides Publishers, 1968); Hans W. Wolff, "The Kerygma of the Yahwist," in *The Vitality of Old Testament Traditions,* edited by W. A. Brueggemann and H. W. Wolff (John Knox Press, 1975), pp. 41–66; and W. A. Brueggemann, "Yahwist," in *The Interpreter's Dictionary of the Bible, Supplementary Volume* (Abingdon, 1976), pp. 971–975.

26. Current studies have successfully demonstrated parallels between events in the court and the illustrative scenes in the creation account. See W. A. Brueggemann, "David and his Theologian," *Catholic Biblical Quarterly* 30 (1968), pp. 156–181; and *In Man We Trust: The Neglected Side of Biblical Faith* (John Knox, 1972), pp. 29–63.

27. "Being with" is a leitmotif markedly present in the Yahwist narrative. When the narrator tells us that God "is with" one of the Israelite ancestors, for example, we immediately know that this person is a royal person, one through whom God accomplishes her purpose in the world. This person is described as "blessed" and as being the communicator of blessing for other people or even for nature (e.g., the increase of flocks). The indicator, "God is with," tells the reader that the life of this individual serves God's purpose for the life of the world.

28. Two terms are used in the narrative: *'adam* and *'ish.* These are not synonymous. Only *'ish* connotes male or husband. See, Alison M. Grant, "*'adam* and *'ish:* Man in the O. T.," *Australian Biblical Review* 25 (1977), pp. 2–11.

29. Cf. 1 Sam 2:8; Ps 111:7–8; and the study: W. A. Brueggemann, "From Dust to Kingship," *Zeitschrift für die alttestamentliche Wissenschaft* 84 (1972), pp. 1–18.

30. Dependency upon Yahweh is a necessary stance for any

leader. The biblical theme of "littleness' conveys this idea very powerfully. See, H. A. Kenik, "The Little Child Shall Lead," *The Bible Today*, No. 101 (March, 1979), pp. 1947-1953.

31. Cf. Gen 2:7, 9, 19.

32. The implication of the introduction of the male and female counterparts of humanity is precisely for the purpose of demonstrating the unique relationship among human beings. See, Walter Vogels, " 'It Is Not Good That the "Mensch" Should Be Alone; I Will Make Him/Her a Helper Fit for Him/Her' (Gen 2:18," *Eglise et Théologie* 9 (1978), pp. 9-35.

33. For the fuller development of this point, see, Claus Westermann, *Creation* (Fortress, 1974), pp. 17-31.

34. Gen 2:16, 17; 3:1, 2, 3, 5, 6^2, 11, 12, 13, 17, 18, 19, 22.

35. The name Eve reflects two concepts, that of creatress and the created. As the creatress, Eve cooperates in creation; she creates with the help of God. As the created, Eve is made by God. The two-edged meaning is significant for what has been said about the task of humanity in this study. Eve/humanity is herself creature; she is made by God. But Eve/humanity shares with God in the act of giving life; she is co-creatress. See, I. M. Kikawada, "Two Notes on Eve," *Journal of Biblical Literature* 91 (1972), pp. 33-37.

36. This verse must be read together with Gen 2:15; 3:7, 10. The Hebrew terms for "naked" and "skin" derive from a common root and therefore are related by sound, an important feature for a narrative that was undoubtedly recited. The relationship between the terms is significant theologically as well. The narrative demonstrates a progression from the couple being fully open before God, to a sensitivity about that openness, to, finally, God covering or accepting the couple as they are.

37. This statement was shown to be programmatic for the construction of the Yahwist narrative by Hans W. Wolff in *The Vitality of Old Testament Traditions,* pp. 41-66.

38. For a fuller presentation of the way the Yahwist shows Israel to be a blessing for the various nations, see ibid., pp. 55-63.

39. Abraham in an intercessory role is really a reflection of one role of the king. An example of a king interceding before God is found in 1 Kings 8:27-61.

40. Compare this address with the description of God as judge, presented above.

41. It is thought that the basic story was used as a text for the education of young men for the court. See, Gerhard von Rad, "The Joseph Narrative and Ancient Wisdom," in *The Problem of the Hexateuch and Other Essays* (McGraw-Hill, 1966), pp. 292–300.

42. This is the theory introduced by George W. Coats, *From Canaan to Egypt: Structural and Theological Context for the Joseph Story* (CBQMS/4; The Catholic Biblical Association of America, 1976).

2

Christian Prayer and New Testament Theology: A Basis for Social Justice and Spirituality

Jon Sobrino, SJ

In this work we are attempting to develop an outline of ideas around the important theme of prayer. We are interested particularly in what might be the focal point of Christian prayer, the basic structure of what we can call its Christian elements, and its relationship with the whole of the Christian faith. We limit ourselves particularly to the prayer of those Christians who can be considered "followers" of Jesus. We would like to help that group of Christians—priests and religious men and women—who have traditionally dedicated themselves to prayer within a life of apostolic action. We also want to help those numerous groups of lay persons who, while committed to Christian praxis, search for meaningful Christian prayer. In all of this we are mindful of today's difficulties over prayer, especially its integration into the whole of the Christian life and specifically into a liberating Christian praxis.

Translation by Kathryn Mc Clung
*By "praxis" is meant conscious action on the world. It implies more than the word "practice" in that praxis stems from theory which people (usually in intentional groups) have personally studied and elaborated for themselves. Their actions are used to critique their theory and newly critiqued theory reforms praxis in dialectical fashion. [Editor's note.]

The Issue of Prayer Today

Prayer in general can be described as one of the ways of communicating with the Deity.[1] It therefore has to do with how we experience meaning and totality and how we interpret what we consider to be the ultimate. Prayer is thus distinguished from other ways of trying to master the problem of meaning, such as rational-analytical discourse on the Deity and praxical-ethical experience and activity.

Within the whole of faith, the role of prayer is to be a means of access to the Deity. Traditionally no one disputed that prayer was something "good" and "religious" which did not need to be justified. However, from the very beginning it must be made clear what it is about prayer that is "Christian."[2] In order to determine what is specifically "Christian" we could compare the traditional content of Christian prayer with the prayer content of other religions, including the Hebrew Bible.[3] Such a comparison would be a first attempt to decide what is "Christian" about the prayer of Christians.

But more important than that comparison is the systematic study of the relationship between prayer and the other aspects of Christianity, such as analytical discourse on God and praxical-ethical activity. In the special nature of that relationship we will also find the special nature of Christian prayer.

Still on a descriptive level, we can show that Christian prayer has undergone a generalized crisis both in its practice, which is no longer traditional, as well as in the theoretical understanding of its meaning. It is no longer so evident that we should pray. It is not that the issue of meaning has disappeared, but rather that non-Christians have questioned the very search for meaning. Meanwhile, there is a new historic understanding of Christian faith.

In the so-called "first world" that controversy was generally associated with the secularization of religion, Christianity in particular. The aim of religion was assumed to be, at first glance at least, the aim of prayer as well. The secular conception of the world no longer leaves it obvious that prayer is a means of "mak-

ing contact with God."[4] In the third world the process of secularization has not had such a direct influence on most people,
although some groups have felt its effects. For these groups the
issue of secularization has turned into the issue of politicalization. Consequently, the crisis of prayer does not have its beginnings primarily in the difficulty of getting in touch with the
divinity, but rather in the effectiveness or ineffectiveness of
prayer to influence public life and, furthermore, in its potentially alienating nature.

At present, even for those Christians who have questions
about their prayer, describing the crisis of prayer has become
rather more complex. In the "first world," it is evident that there
is a decrease in prayer and those activities—such as Mass
attendance—which we can call forms of prayer. On the other
hand, there is at least an outward revival of some forms of
prayer. This revival may take the form of new religious expressions such as we see in the resurgence of transcendental
meditation, the popularity of oriental spiritualities, and the various kinds of "Pentecostal" prayer which, in their origin and aim
at least, are Christian. There is also postreligious prayer, meaning that which is not based on the "religious" structures of Christianity far removed from us. An example in point is Dietrich
Bonhoeffer who on the one hand announced the end of religion, the end of the "religious" understanding of Christianity,
and on the other, told himself that "he was one of the few men to
whom his God was something real and close."[5] People have attempted to overcome the crisis of prayer by resacralizing our
understanding either of Christianity or of the world in general.
This latter effort is carried on by persons who do not consider
themselves Christian but nevertheless are searching for the
meaning of their existence. Still others try to maintain a secular
understanding of Christianity.

With respect to the third world and Christians committed to
the process of liberation, the new orientation of their faith based
on Christian praxis has led them on occasion to abandon prayer
altogether. However, Arturo Paoli, Ernesto Cardenal, Raul
Vidales, Leonardo Boff, and Gustavo Gutiérrez have raised their

voices to affirm that prayer is necessary from within and in the
midst of Christian praxis if we are ever to find the meaning of
that praxis.[6] The experience of transcendence and meaning occurs within that praxis, but the "beyond" which springs up from
that praxis must be considered by itself in order for the experience of gratuitousness to appear. In this way Christians find
themselves as Christian by living out that praxis. Grasping the
necessity of prayer is something done dialectically. It cannot be
simply programmed a priori independently of praxis. It is
dialectical to the extent that the "beyond", the excess of meaning, appears in praxis and to the extent that this "beyond" is
grasped as such. Then it unchains a new Christian praxis.

For many, all that might be necessary would be to quote the
following paragraph by Gutiérrez on the prayer of the committed Christian.

> Prayer is an experience of gratuity. This 'pointless' act, this
> 'squandered' time, reminds us that the Lord is beyond being
> categorized as useful or useless. God is not of this world. The
> gracious nature of his gift creates deeper needs, frees us from
> all religious alienation and, in the final analysis, from all kinds
> of alienation. The committed Christian in the Latin American
> revolutionary process has to find the paths to an authentic—
> and not an evasive prayer. The person cannot deny that there
> is a crisis here and that we easily slip into blind alleys.... But
> there is no going back; new experiences, new demands have
> made some familiar tranquilizing paths impassable.... If it
> really is true... that it is necessary to go through people to
> arrive at God, it is equally true that "going through" this gra-
> cious God strips me, lays me bare, makes me expand my
> understanding and leads toward a synthesis.[7]

In describing the situation of prayer today, we cannot overlook the relatively new phenomenon of "communal" prayer.
The issues raised by this phenomenon go far beyond, although
they include, the various techniques and group dynamics developed by psychology and sociology. It points to a communality
of faith which, though obvious, has been forgotten: Christians

live out their faith as members of ecclesial communities: Religious within a religious community, conscienticizied lay persons within a base community.* Today's communitarian expression of faith, and so of prayer, is a historical current that can be justified theologically. This new situation, however, calls for reflection on the relationship between "individual" prayer and "collective" prayer. I introduce the phenomenon of communitarian prayer here to complete the picture of prayer today. I will deal with it in depth later on.

As we enter into the real issue of prayer, we maintain that it is impossible to deduce the essence of Christian prayer by a historical, anthropological, or phenomenological examination of what was understood to be prayer in the history of religion, even though some or many of its elements had to necessarily be incorporated as Christian prayer took historical form. The ultimate reason why we say this is that Christian prayer does not simply presuppose "contact with the divinity" or with the absolute, but rather with the Father of Jesus, the God to whom Christian faith and prayer are directed. Beginning with this fundamental affirmation, we wish to state the background, purpose, method, and presupposition of this essay.

The background is that for prayer to be Christian it must have the originality of the Christian faith itself. From this perspective it is possible to formulate questions which put into relief some aspects of that originality which need to be present in prayer, although bringing them up may lead us to ask whether prayer is really possible. If the "reign of God" is the ultimate horizon of all

---

*Base Christian Communities (*comunidades eclesiales de base* in Spanish) are intentional groups of 8–40 persons who, though usually not living together, share their life of faith in the world together. They share an on-going commitment to deepen their faith by mutually critiquing their often joint praxis. For a description of the phenomenon in the United States and its theological grounding, cf. Tomas G. Bissonnette, "Comunidades Eclesiales de Base: Contemporary Grass Roots Attempts to Build Ecclesial *Koinonia*," *The Jurist:* 35 (Winter-Spring, 1976), pp. 24–58. [Editor's note.]

Christian reality, what does it mean to "pray for the reign of God?" (The same question can be asked analogously of celibacy or other Christian conditions.) If the ultimate experience of meaning, the gratuitous nature of the Christian life, ultimately becomes real only in the act of doing, what can "contact with God" in prayer mean? If the Christian is always on the path to the Father, if God is yet to be all in all, what can search for the will of God in prayer mean when counterposed to possessing God which "contact with God" seems to imply? If a person becomes Christian only through realizing the reign of God, wherein lies the truth between the contradictory generalizations that all life is prayer and nothing is prayer?

The purpose of this essay is theological, that is, to lay out and resolve the aforementioned problems theologically. Obviously, in the reality of life the problem of prayer is much more complex. All prayer is formulated within a very specific psychological, sociological, and political context. We want to clarify Christian prayer using the ultimate Christian presuppositions, namely, God, the reign of God, Jesus, the following of Jesus, the demand to do justice, the experience of God's gratuitousness, etc. Evidently even these presuppositions are conditioned and limited by particular historical situations. Inasmuch as these presuppositions are drawn from Jesus' own history, they cannot be considered as abstract or independent of time. They are historically situated. So in our theological analysis we will treat prayer within its historical context.

I have dealt with the prayer of Jesus elsewhere for English-speaking readers.[8] The method there was simple: if Jesus is the Son, the first-born, the first of the believers, he is also the first of those who pray. Throughout the history of the church many schools and forms of prayer have arisen. These were necessary so that Christianity could take historical form. We will restrict ourselves to what seems to be fundamental: we will look to uncover the nucleus and fundamental structure of Christian prayer beginning with Jesus' own prayer. That nucleus and structure continues to take diverse historical forms.

The presupposition of this essay is that prayer, especially Christian prayer, is an area of life that enjoys relative autonomy. It therefore deserves and demands detailed study. To concentrate on prayer does not mean giving it absolute autonomy or ignoring its relationship to the whole of the Christian faith. On the other hand, we must recognize—on the basis of Jesus' example as well as systematic reflection—that prayer responds to a typically human contexturing and that it is not fully identical to other areas of life, such as the rational-analytical or the ethical-praxical, although it is related to them.

THE PRAYER OF THE CHRISTIAN: THEOLOGICAL BASIS AND STRUCTURE

In the history of the church, there has been rich and diversified thought concerning Christian prayer. Moreover, there is a diverse history of the practice of prayer; there are various schools of spirituality and various forms and techniques for individual and group prayer.

What we are now attempting to do is to show the basis and structure of those Christian elements that must be in any prayer which claims to be Christian, whatever its form. In the following sections we will touch on two important points for present-day prayer: its relationship to achieving justice and the communal aspect of prayer.

The first and fundamental answer to the question concerning the prayer of the Christian is that it must be like that of Jesus, since it is he who first lived in the fullness of faith (cf. Hebrews 12:2) and who in his mortal life also offered up supplications and pleas (cf. Hebrews 5:7). This is also the implicit teaching, at least of the synoptic writers who while presenting the doctrine and praxis of Jesus' prayer also present it as a model for prayer for the first Christian communities.

Even though this seems obvious, it ceases to be so when we ask whether or not the situation changed substantially after Jesus' resurrection. Must the prayer of the Christian therefore be different from that of the historical Jesus? In short, it can be asked whether or not the prayer of the Christian who lives after the resurrection of Jesus will be as radically historical as that of Jesus or if with the resurrection that fullness has already been given which would make "communication with the Deity" possible, no longer by way of search but of possession. If, with Jesus' resurrection, the full and total revelation of the Father has already been given, then it seems that the prayer of the Christian could not be like that of Jesus.[9]

This presentation of the question seems very theoretical. Nevertheless, we believe it is and has been operative to a great extent in the history of Christian spirituality and prayer. It has made possible a notion of prayer as pure "contemplation" of a God who has been known since Jesus' resurrection; and in like manner it has paid less attention than it should to the historical character of prayer, the homo viator nature of the one praying, and the analysis of a specific praxis as the locus of prayer. For this reason it is not superfluous to recall the early Christian experience after the resurrection to see if, in this new situation, the prayer of the Christian was like that of the historical Jesus or if anything had substantially changed.

From an understanding of the fundamental Christian experience of the first communities we can state the following: the Christian faith asserts that something new has occurred. This innovation is described in two different but correlative ways: that is, God has appeared in a new form, and Christians experience themselves as new persons. The latter is clear when throughout the New Testament it is repeated in various ways that the Christian is "the new person," that Christians are the "community of the saints," "the new Israel," "the eschatological community," etc.

Christians relate the new reality they experience to the new expression of God. When they put this newness of God into words, they do so against the background of the surrounding religions and the Old Testament. Instead of simply saying

"Yahweh" to express who their God is, they are forced to find new terminology with which to express their experience of objective reality.

For this reason the New Testament speaks of the Father, who continues to be the ultimate mystery of existence—a sacred mystery which cannot be manipulated and who in his substance continues to be the transcendent creator, origin of everything and absolute future (cf. 1 Cor 15:28). In the words of John, the Father is "love" who expresses himself in various ways, such as redeemer and reconcilor. Moreover, the Father is placed in relationship with history beginning with the mystery of evil and sin: his wisdom is shown on the cross which is madness and scandal.

The New Testament also calls Jesus the only-begotten Son of the Father. This means on the one hand that since the time of Jesus, the Father as transcendent mystery has clearly expressed his will, has broken the abstract symmetry of a God who—as power—could in essence be both salvation and condemnation. Since Jesus, what is known about the Father is that he leads people to salvation, not condemnation. On the other hand, when speaking of the Son they say that the correct way of relating to and thus gaining access to the mystery of the Father has appeared in history; in this Son the road of access to the Father has appeared.

The New Testament also speaks of the Spirit to affirm that the mystery of God has not only appeared in the history of Jesus but that it has entered into people and the human community. It means that newness of life is not only something exemplarily proposed in Jesus as the Son, nor is it only a possibility we have invented or a new way of understanding nature, history, and humankind; instead it is a true change in one's life. It means that people become godlike by becoming children of God in the Son. On a wider plane it means that God has entered into history and that history has been assumed in God.

This novel concept of the mystery of God who is at the same time transcendent, close-by in Jesus, and internalized in the Spirit is certainly circular. However, this circularity is typical of the Christian reality, and it is this which will explain the structure of Christian prayer. In this structure the Father is known through the Son and the history which the Spirit releases. In turn whether the Son acts in a certain way or whether the Spirit releases a specific history depends on the ultimate reality of the Father. The same can be said of the interaction of Jesus and the Spirit. This is not simply any spirit, rather the Spirit of Jesus, the one which makes us like Jesus, the one which releases a history according to Jesus. Jesus is not known unless it is from the history released by the Spirit.

The circularity is essential to Christianity. The most radical expression of this circularity lies not only in the fact that a mutual relationship is formed between our question and God's answer, as if we were a mere receiver of the revelation of God; revelation understood simply as communication would remain external to ourselves. The radical circularity lies in the fact that God-in-himself who wants to be God-for-us is not so without the we-in-God.[10]

Christian Prayer According to Paul

This trinitarian reality is what explains the prayer of the Christian in the New Testament.[11] Obviously, the New Testament describes many types of prayers; but in theologizing on prayer it calls upon the deepest experience of the new faith. This is what Paul does in chapter 8 of his letter to the Romans.

In describing the situation of the Christian who prays, Paul lists the essential elements of that prayer. First of all, he affirms that the mystery of God the Father continues to be a mystery which is sacred and unable to be manipulated even in prayer. He affirms this noting the basic inability of people to pray. This inability does not refer to the psychological difficulties of people in prayer nor even our intellectual inability to think of God as a mystery; instead the inability rests first of all in the God to whom we pray. The Christian prayer must begin by maintaining the fundamental mystery of God, and because of this the "not knowing how we ought to pray" (Rom 8:26) is paradoxically the condition which makes all true prayer possible.

Paul also points out the place of Christian prayer. This is none other than history and the insertion of the Christian into it. Paul selects those characteristics of history which most of all seem to make prayer impossible; they are the very conditions which make it possible for prayer to be Christian: sufferings (Rom 8:18), vanity of the creation (v. 20), and our infirmities (v. 26). Also, Paul asks for our solidarity with history and not evasion of it, overcoming it intentionally or ideologically through the body. This solidarity is expressed through the "groanings" of prayer (v. 22) and the groanings of Christians (v. 23).

From within history Christian prayer is done in the Spirit. So it is the life in the Spirit makes true prayer possible. It is important to note that when Paul introduces the Spirit he makes two statements which are apparently contradictory, but in his specific dialectic they encompass the prayer of the Christian. On the one hand it is in the Spirit that God can be called "Abba" (v. 15); on the other hand the Spirit enables us to continue groaning (v. 26). This means that life in the Spirit makes it possible to pray like Jesus, who calls God "Abba," while continuing to search for his will, expressed in "unutterable groanings."[12]

What Paul is saying then is that the prayer of the Christian is first prayed from real life, in the misery of history and in solidarity with it, without trying to overcome our specific history in searching for some other place for prayer which is seemingly more peaceful, but actually less favorable and even impossible for Christian prayer. The first thing the Spirit does is to make our life Christian. Within Christian life prayer is done "in trinitarian fashion." We pray to the Father as the ultimate mystery of reality which continues to be transcendent; still he can be called "Father." We pray as Jesus, using his own expression, "Abba," and like him inserted in history, in solidarity with it, addressing ourselves to the Father with the same trust and with the same groanings. To pray in the Spirit must be done from within a true Christian life.

The prayer of Christians is then, even after the resurrection, like that of Jesus. The resurrection facilitates the concretization of God into a trinitarian form, and Jesus now belongs to this concretization of God. However, the basic structure of the Christian's prayer continues to be like the prayer of Jesus. The last thing the Spirit can do is to make Christians sons and daughters in the Son, and the prayer which can be released in Christians can be nothing other than the prayer of Jesus. The resurrection of Jesus adds a grounded hope to the history of Christians but does not deprive this hope of its historic nature, does not cease to make it "against hope," and therefore even after the resurrection prayer subsists from the dialectic of calling God "Abba" and not knowing what to request. It is the dialectical way of declaring that the prayer of the Christian is addressed to a Father who is "love" but who continues to be "forever greater."

Beginning with Paul's theology we have sought to find the basis of Christian prayer: it is nothing more than life in the Spirit of Jesus.[13] No matter how trivial it may seem, it must be repeated. Prayer is not an activity of humankind or the Christian who has full autonomy; it must not be assumed that because of the desire to pray one is actually prepared to do so right away. The problematic nature of prayer cannot be resolved on the basis of intention, as if the desire to "communicate with God" is at once effective in itself. The basis of prayer is not found in prayer itself, but in the reality of the Christian life.

A Structure for Christian Prayer

According to this we can systematically and briefly analyze the structure of prayer. This is the fundamental theological structure which will show up in various forms depending on the actual methods of prayer, none of which must be lacking; otherwise "Christian" prayer will not exist, although it may be prayer in the religious sense. This structure can be summarized in three basic steps.

The first step of prayer is hearing the word of God. By this hearing it is implied that the mystery of God is personal and wills to save and liberate us. The specific forms of conveying this understanding will be the life of Jesus itself, that which has been set apart in the scriptures as the word of God, and that which Christian tradition has been accumulating by listening to the word; and in another vein it is hearing the word of God through the concrete historical situation in all its personal, social, political, and ecclesiastical dimensions. This hearing is the experience of meaning in the form of a demand and of initial grace.

The second step of prayer is doing what one has heard. Obviously in prayer one already can and must respond to the word which is heard, but this response does not reach its fullness until it turns into a response to the real nature of God, whose word is heard. And this response can no longer be intentional but must be real; it is what we call doing. At this time we are not trying to introduce the nominalist problematic issue of whether "doing" is or is not prayer. What we are trying to assert is that it fits into the overall structure of Christian prayer.

The third step of prayer is a word of thanksgiving or request for forgiveness, depending on the deed. This is the place to utter "Abba," either as Jesus did in giving thanks, or as the prodigal son did in asking for forgiveness.

These three steps are logical and we believe they have to be present in a Christian prayer. Their chronology may be more complex: hearing may occur in what may be described as action: action may be that which makes us able to hear, etc. However, the important thing is that the three steps of Christian prayer are executed.

These three steps have not been chosen arbitrarily but proceed from observing Jesus and the true nature of the God of Jesus. The necessity of hearing is the anthropological interpretation of God's being greater; it is the expression of the theological deficiency of all people before God. And it is therefore the necessity of discerning the will of God, who because he is a God who overcomes absolutely everything, cannot be adequately grasped through nature, the inertia of history, the traditions of men, nor even church dictates. All of these may be elements of discernment but not its solution. For this theological reason God's word must be heard.[14]

The doing, in addition to its necessity from the aspect of Christian ethics, is also essential to prayer since it is in the doing and not merely in the internal part of prayer that the attitudes of the Christian are being solidified. These attitudes allow the internal element expressed in prayer to correspond to the objectivity of the Christian requirement and not merely to the willingness of the individual. In short, doing is the condition which makes possible and confirms that the attitude of the one praying is Christian. As has been repeated elsewhere, Christian faith, hope, and love are not universal postures which can be generated on the basis of intent, but are a faith against disbelief, a hope against hope, and a love against alienation. However, it is only in Christian doing, in the practice of love and justice that the "substance" of the abovementioned virtues comes into view, as well as their historical verification. The "inner attitude" necessary for praying to the God of Jesus is being developed, is recovering its concrete nature through doing; and that is what will be expressed in the moments which are defined as prayer, differentiating them here from the moments of action.

The word of response is the doxological expression of belonging to, of being akin to the reality which we call God. The word of "giving thanks" or "asking forgiveness" is the expression of the affinity experienced with God as ultimate mystery, or the expression of his absence. In that word there is a very personal or communal surrender of the "I" which no longer controls what it says itself, but which feels the need to say it. Only when this surrender of the "I" at the level of the word of prayer lives from the real surrender of the "I" in doing, without being based on intentionality, can one request in prayer the real surrender of the "I" to the mystery of God.[15]

According to all that has been said the prayer of the Christian is the history of his prayer. Obviously, the three steps outlined continually occur in life, and they form the history of prayer, placing it on a different plane every time depending on the quality of the hearing, doing, and speaking. This assumes first of all the possibility and necessity of changing external forms of prayer, the possibility of different types of prayer according to the various ages, psychologies, historic eras.

On a deeper level, however, it means that the prayer of the Christian must have a history if the correlate of that prayer is truly the God of Jesus. Prayer is not nor can it be on a timetable, something which at least momentarily assumes definitiveness; and it can be even less a routine repetition of plans already acquired and worked out. Scheduled prayer is necessary, and given human psychology a minimum of "routine" or at least rhythm, even institutionalized, will also be necessary; but the truth of prayer will depend on the whole of its history. The goal is what gives meaning and truth to the whole process of prayer.

What the process implies is passing from the first general Christian prayer—in which the great Christian truths such as trust in God, hope, the decision to make love a way of life, can already be operative—to specific prayer which with the same formal subject matter manages to have a different, more profound, significance and a greater and more effective concentration on the attitude of the Son regarding trust and surrender to the mission.

That Christian prayer has a history is also confirmation of its truth since it is confirmation that prayer is not offered up to simply any deity but to the Father of Jesus, who is forever greater. The change which is effected within prayer signifies that God is not owned even in prayer, but that the Christian possession of God is always in the form of a search.

All this means that the Christian experience of God, in order to be historical, needs time to take form. We are not talking about a particular length of time but a kind of time in which sufficient historic events take place so that Christians can experience them as destiny and praxis. It must be these events, not mere inner feelings or mere natural or aesthetic experience, that move people to prayer.

The important thing about Christian prayer is that it has a history which came into existence in a novel way, which has the fortitude to repeat the hearing, doing, and speaking to the end, and that it is aware of its own deficiency and does not take delight in itself. In the final analysis what counts is the last "Abba" which is uttered at the end of life; and with what real weight history has been hearing this word of trust.

To recapitulate, the prayer of the Christian must be like that of Jesus. It is prayer made possible by the reality of being a "son" or "daughter" and in the measure that one is a son or daughter; but this refers prayer to the Christian reality; the surrender of the "I" in the practice of love, from which the surrender of the "I" in prayer subsists. Thus, one can say, as Jesus did, "Abba," and also like Jesus maintain the not knowing how to pray, that is, asking that the will of the Father be done or allowing the Spirit to continue groaning when the Christian no longer knows what to say, since he finds himself before a God who is on the one hand love, wherefore be calls him "Abba," and on the other hand forever greater, wherefore he continues groaning.

PRAYER AND ACTION FOR JUSTICE

We have already seen the relationship of action to prayer when considering the structure of the latter. Now it is helpful to see this relationship in greater detail because of the real problem it involves on our continent, and because of the specific history which this relationship has had, especially for priestly spirituality and the religious life.[16]

At the descriptive level we can see how the world of prayer has in fact diverted attention from action, has justified lack of action, and many times has objectively alienated the people who have devoted themselves to prayer, even though subjectively they might have the best of intentions. From this point of view the urgency of relating prayer and action in a Christian way is evident. On the other hand the absolutization of action is not infrequent today either, in such a way that its relationship to prayer, when it continues to be sought, sometimes gets no further than the nominalism of affirming that prayer is life. As it has been pointed out, however, if "all is prayer," it is not impossible that "nothing is prayer." For those who want their action to be Christian, it is also urgent that they find the correct relationship between action and prayer.

This difficulty can be systematically expressed by saying that an attempt is made to transfer the common conception of the "ex opere operato" of sacramental theology either to prayer or to action, as if any mechanism of prayer or action were at once in itself saving. The "ex opere operato" functions effectively when the dialectic between prayer and action is broken.

The difficulty is clearly seen when in fact the inner moment of prayer is made absolute so that it attempts to substitute on the basis of intent what can only be manifested in Christian action. However, it is also seen when it is taken for granted that a specific action is already saving through itself. What action has in its favor is that it has found the proper place for the manifestation of the Christian faith, but it is not automatically determined that this action is already Christian.

The solution to the problem lies not in making one of the two poles of prayer/action effectively absolute, but in connecting them. In order to analyze this relationship, we are going to present two theoretical models which have grown up throughout the history of Christian spirituality and which in their nucleus continue to influence theory and practice, as can be seen, for example, when analyzing the specific spirituality which affects groups of priests and nuns. The two models are as follows: (1) "contemplata aliis tradere" (to surrender to others the things one has contemplated); (2) "contemplativus in actione" (to be contemplative in action).

These two theoretical models have been developed within the religious life and are presented as a solution to the problem which concerns us. This means that the problem of contemplation and action has been seen by those—especially priests and nuns—who are dedicated to a life which includes prayer and the apostolate as basic dimensions. For this reason it is very informative to analyze more precisely these two proposed models.

Contemplata aliis tradere

The model "contemplata aliis tradere" seems to us inadequate for expressing the proper relationship between prayer and Christian action. We are not concerned here with making a historical exegesis of the principle, and even less with judging those who allow themselves to be guided, at least theoretically, by this model. If it is given as an example, it is because we believe that it is still operative in the formation of young seminarians, priests, and nuns; and it is presented as the theoretical justification of a type of spirituality which we do not believe is in agreement with the core of the gospel and certainly does not seem adequate for the present moment.

The model "contemplata aliis tradere" assumes that prayer and action are sufficiently separate and separable dimensions; the "tradere" implies the surrender of a reality already established, or at least of that which has already been contemplated in prayer as something established, to a receiver who does not influence the establishment of what is contemplated. In addition to presenting both dimensions as separate realities, supremacy is given to the moment of contemplation over the moment of action in this model. This supremacy is certainly chronological here since one must contemplate beforehand in order to be able to surrender; but it also suggests actual supremacy of contemplation over action.

The criticism of this model can be made based on what philosophy and the social sciences have made clear today: theory, in this case contemplation, cannot take form as such without a time of praxis and on the other hand human knowledge seems to be conditioned by biology, psychology, sociology, and economics. It is therefore philosophically naive to claim that the thing contemplated can be established by itself solely on the basis of con-

templation, without taking into account that practice also constitutes the substance of the thing contemplated; and the structure
within which one contemplates conditions this substance.

More profoundly still, however, and for whomever the philosophical argument might not be compelling, it must be added
that we do not learn to contemplate by doing theology but by the
praxis of love. In this model attention is also called to the role of
the receiver of the action and to the action on the receiver. The
receiver is seen merely as passive. He does not influence the
establishment of the thing contemplated; but this is not correct
from a Christian viewpoint. It is basic to the Christian faith that
that which has to do with "communication with God," or "access
to God" is mediated by history in general and people in particular, and much more specifically by the poorest and most oppressed people, whom the gospel declares are the privileged
place of access to God. The "aliis" therefore cannot be considered purely as receivers but also as the ones in the contact with
whom the content of the thing contemplated—or at least a basic
part of it—is established.

With respect to action itself, summed up in "tradere," we must
ask what it means in concrete terms, whether it is a "surrender"
which merely announces what has been contemplated, or
whether in announcing it tries to do what has been contemplated. This issue goes beyond the issue of prayer; it is the
whole question of Christian ethics, but it also has to do with
prayer. It involves seeing in depth what kind of action is going to
be an indispensable element in order for contemplation to be
Christian, whether it is the mere announcement to others that
salvation exists or it is announcing it through a historical action
which at once makes it somehow present.

The criticism made of this model does not ignore or disdain
the positive aspect of it, which is affirming the necessity of contemplation for Christian action. What is criticized is the type of
relationship between prayer and action. Basically, it is criticized
because it is a way of looking at it which separates both dimensions at the beginning, though it tries to unite them afterwards.
This way of approaching things has always been dangerous in

the history of Christianity. It is instead a matter of searching for an approach which takes account of the unity of both dimensions at the outset, within which what is proper to both can be analyzed.

Contemplativus in actione

This is what the second approach attempts, with the reservation we will discuss hereafter. The "contemplativus in actione" first of all assumes philosophically that the individual is being formed in his individual inner being into a "doing" outside this inner being. Contemplation is then a dimension within a more overall process of doing and becoming an individual, the need for which appears so that the doing and the becoming are really from the individual and not a merely mechanical doing and becoming.

From the biblical and Christian point of view, this model presents a greater closeness to the structure of the revelation and the personal adaptation of it. It implies that the revelation of God, that is, the God who is going to be contemplated, occurs in history and occurs in the making of history. In the scriptures there are many parallels to this fundamental affirmation: to know God is to do justice, truth is carried out in charity, he knows God who loves his brother. These are very general statements which require a meticulous exegesis, but in all of them it is affirmed that there can be no "contemplation" without some type of "action," and this action should be "in favor of humankind," not simply any action whatsoever.

Lastly, this model does not greatly emphasize the chronology of the prayer/action relationship. It does not properly analyze whether the first moment is defined as an initiation to prayer or an initiation to contemplation. Its attraction rests more in the same process of the relation between both of them and their dialectic.

Upon a more detailed analysis of what is meant by "contemplativus in actione" in the Christian sense, we must be aware that the formal unity of this model can be destroyed easily by a definite conception of what action is or what contemplation is. It involves going beyond the formal unity of the model in order to formulate that unity which historically joins action and contemplation today. This formal unity must be made concrete today as "contemplative in acts of justice."

When criticizing "action" from a Christian standpoint the first thing which must be stated is that not simply any action allows for "Christian" contemplation. Obviously, they are not acts which are made possible by sin; neither are they just any action supposedly neutral or abstractly good. It is customary to assume too frequently that any action which is at least generally good is at once the appropriate place for contemplation, where the difficulty would lie in the "contemplating" but not so much in the "doing." However, this supposition is not very critical. There are actions which would allow a contemplation of the aesthetic sort or actions which, on the basis of the aesthetic vigor they demand, would make possible a contemplation based on the overcoming of the "I." This is, however, not enough so that contemplation based on such kinds of action can be the doxological prayer of Jesus explained previously.

In principle the action which facilitates contemplation of the God of Jesus and the contemplation of history from the time of this God is precisely following Jesus in that which is central. And if this nucleus were not present it could not be made up for on the basis of purifying the intent of other actions which are neither good nor evil in themselves.

Fundamentally it must be said that the nucleus of Christian action is love according to the tradition of the scriptures and the history of the church; but this is still very general. If this love is not made real and historicized it runs the serious risk of not being love or even being effectively converted into anti-love, that is, into something which is of absolutely no benefit to what must be done.

The concrete historical form of a praxis of love cannot be deduced a priori, precisely because it is a concrete form. In the current situation of the third world there is no doubt that this primordial form of love is the service to and the struggle for justice for the large oppressed masses. This does not mean that love does not have other expressions also necessary in order for action to be Christian, such as personal love, charity, friendship, mercy, etc., since there continue to be areas in our lives in which love must be made concrete in these ways. However, in our situation all these manifestations of love must include justice as the most obvious and urgent expression of love, since it is from the relationship with this superior-in-number and oppressed "other" that the theological category of "other" comes from, which category will also be found later in the "other" of family, marriage, religious life, profession, etc. At the psychological level it is evident that the "other" functions in various ways according to the relationship which links it to the subject (marriage, family, friendship, religious life, etc.), and that this fact must also be taken into account. Theologically, however, it seems to us that by autonomasia the "other" which mediates the experience of God and thus of contemplation is the "other" of the oppressed majorities (cf. Matt 25:31–46).[17]

In a closer analysis of "action for justice" as the place of Christian contemplation, it must first be noted that it is the contact with and action on behalf of the oppressed masses is the privileged place in which the unconditional, radical "no" which God pronounces on the world of sin is found. The experience of this "no" is neither the last nor the most basic word of God concerning the world, but it is necessary and indispensable in order to contemplate the God of Jesus and to contemplate history as God sees it.

In the second place, in action for justice there is a type of surrender of the person and the group which is different from the surrender which occurs in other spheres. It is ordinarily in the struggle for justice that more is required of people: their virtues, their time, their security, and even their lives. Obviously, there is also a real, authentic surrender in other expressions of love, such as friendship, charity, wedded love, etc.; but the surrender to others rarely reaches as great a fullness as in the struggle for justice in which the element of gratification may be more lacking than in the other expressions of love.

In the third place, it is in the struggle for justice that the Christian tension and the necessity of taking sides against living our faith, hope, and love normally appear. Maintaining this tension in real life is one of the indispensable conditions for an experience with the God of Jesus, and therefore for prayer. This is therefore the privileged place for the conversion of the individual and the group. It is a great evangelical, though perhaps not philosophical, truth that the poor person is the one who is capable of converting others. Any other conversion which is not in terms of the poor and which does not lead to a life of doing justice is illusory. It will remain at the level of change in the self-understanding of the individual, but with difficulty will the person's life effectively change so that life is lived in order to surrender it.

Action for justice, therefore, seems to us to be the type of action which is required not only for those who already have come to Christian faith but it is also an indispensable element for coming to Christian faith as such. "The roads to faith and justice are inseparable."[18] For this reason action for justice seems to us to be the favored place for contemplation, since it specifies the place in which contemplation can be contemplation of the Christian God, and thus the place for also contemplating the reality of the world and history in the light of God.

In the "contemplativus in actione" model it must also be assured that within this action there is contemplation of the God of Jesus and hence of history as God sees it. It goes without saying that if there is Christian action for justice, the contemplation which stems from it will automatically be Christian. However, in order to be concrete, we must clarify the presuppositions of the viewpoint of the contemplative individual or group. These are moreover the conditions which make action for justice Christian. These presuppositions are deduced from Jesus' prayer, from the overall experience of the New Testament, and also from accumulated historical experience.

First, we must recall that in the primary experience of Jesus and the first Christians God takes the initiative. In the words of John: "God first loved us." This basic experience of gift and gratuitousness is necessary so that our entry into history by a praxis of justice might be truly Christian. In the New Testament the relationship of love of God and love of neighbor is not presented as if there were double recipients when we love people, as if God and neighbor were a duality which ought to be joined afterwards. Instead, the plan of the New Testament is that love of neighbor arises out of our being loved by God. The gratuitous experience encompasses two moments: knowing we are loved by God and finding ourselves in a praxis of love, in this case, justice. This whole gratuitous experience is a condition so that the action for justice makes contemplation possible.

Secondly, we need to look at the individual or group that prays. The basic way for the person or group to become Christian is through action for justice. However, the verification that the individual and the group are becoming Christian lies in their permanent disposition to conversion. They cannot take for granted that the choice of the correct path of Christian life, the struggle for justice, in itself resolves all the problems involved in conversion. In short, the inclination to overcome "our own" sin, the constant necessity of denying our own will for power, the acquiring of the inclinations and virtues listed in the Sermon on the Mount, must be kept in mind. Basically, it is a question of the Christian's becoming a person of pure disinterested gaze which is also a condition for contemplation.

In the third place, and as an a posteriori criterion, there will be contemplation in action for justice if this contemplation does in fact bring new action for justice, that is, contemplation should not only be the channel for action, but also release new action in favor of justice. If we contemplate God who is greater than we, then no particular praxis of justice, inasmuch as it is particular, can exhaust the demand of the God whom we contemplate.

Finally, we must insist that contemplation does exist, that it is verifiable and that it can be described. This implies concrete places, times, and forms of prayer. We will not stop to analyze these specific points at this time but will explain their general necessity. We have already listed the basic content of prayer within action for justice: hearing the word of God and responding with thanksgiving or a request for forgiveness. However, this content, the doxological nucleus of which we have stated, must be accompanied by certain reflections and conditioning factors which, though external, allow such a nucleus to take form.

The designation of times, places, and forms of prayer, in addition to being the self-disciplining normally required by human psychology, is already a statement that one really wishes to hear the word and that one really wants to direct that which is done in the action for justice to the Father of Jesus, to the source of that first love. The difficulty of theologically demonstrating a priori the necessity of these external disciplines is well known. Nevertheless, a posteriori it can be stated that where there really is desire to hear and an awareness of gratitude or guilt, silence is impossible, and that which is not voiced ends by not motivating.

If it is difficult to point out the necessity of the formalities of prayer as positive, what occurs when these formalities are totally abandoned can be observed as negative. The doxological nucleus of prayer also requires "substance" in order to take shape; and the abandonment of this substance may also signify the disappearance of the central nucleus of prayer.

We are not entering into the issue of the forms of prayer here. We believe what we have said holds for personal and community prayer, for liturgical and sacramental prayer, for prayer based on Bible reading or for prayer which comes from reflection on historic events. The important thing is to emphasize that although reflection is basic to action, the moment defined as contemplation has its relative autonomy. Also, in the same way that action for justice cannot live solely from the ethical intentionality of wanting to execute justice, but must find ways and tools so that justice is truly served, contemplation cannot live solely from intentionally wanting to contemplate in action but must become concrete in some way, choosing some tools which make it possible and also serve as verification of what really is being contemplated in action for justice. Otherwise, it can fall into pure intentionalism either of action or contemplation or both.

In summary of what was said in this section, we can state that the fundamental problem for committed Christians today lies in relating prayer and action. The difficulties for prayer come neither exclusively nor primarily from the environmental difficulty caused by secularism, although these difficulties obviously do exist. The fundamental difficulty is theological: what it means to communicate with the God of Jesus.

The primary solution is found in considering prayer not as something absolutely autonomous within Christianity, but as something related to it. The meaning of prayer will lie in finding its proper relationship with that which is absolutely central to faith; and this is nothing other than the practice of love, as it is unmistakably asserted in the synoptics and by Paul, James, and John.

On the other hand, love too, like any Christian reality must be historicized. In our situation this love is made concrete in the first but not only place in the advancement of justice in the sense described. The primary problem of prayer is resolved in relation to this execution of justice, since that is the place of access to God; and for this reason, from this place and not from any other one, one can have what we call experience with God, without which speaking of prayer has absolutely no meaning.

Hence, an appropriate model for describing Christian prayer seems to be that of being "contemplative in action." Thus, the matter of the Christian faith could be expressed as: gaining access to a God who is love, becoming like God. The form of Christian faith: gaining access to a God greater than us because the "beyond" rises out of history when we do justice. It is also because only in history as we take sides "against" can we grasp the transcendence of the God of Jesus, some thing not possible with other deities.

In speaking of "action for justice" therefore, no claim is made to horizontal reductionism, but rather to finding the place of true

Christian verticalism; and this place cannot be determined only by intention but also according to an objective basis which is in contact with the true nature of the God of Jesus. Otherwise, though attempting to be profoundly religious and Christian, it is being presupposed that it is the intention which judges what God should be and which judges his true nature, which is the most subtle form of atheism for a Christian. As Porfirio Miranda says, "the question does not lie in whether or not someone looks for God, but in whether he looks for him where he himself said he was."[19]

Finally, we have spoken about those criteria which can confirm a posteriori whether true contemplation exists or only mechanical action for justice: the experience of grace, permanent conversion, new action for justice, and the clarification of contemplation in the material conditions of existence, that is, in times and places.

PERSONAL AND COMMUNITY PRAYER

The prayer that has been current in the history of the church until recent times has generally been individual prayer. It has also been personal, and this type of prayer is still necessary. Certainly Jesus gives us an example of the "personal" prayer alone with God; and throughout the whole of scriptures it is evident that there are occasions in the history of the human race which demand this solitude, even though in this being alone with God the social realities which condition and make possible the very solitude of the person are also present. In the classic figures of the Old Testament, such as Abraham, in the calling of the prophets, in the lamentations of Jeremiah, in many prayers from the psalms, in the prayer of Mary, it appears that before God and in the moments of profound decisions, neither hearing his word nor responding to it can be fully relegated to the group. Even though individualism and existentialism have stressed this dimension of human life and made it unilateral, listening to

God's word as a group has not ceased to exist. Today it is plain that even the most personal decisions are influenced by social conditionings, but this does not exclude the fact that within them the individual person must discern, choose, and pray.

Also, in the recent history of the church there has been another type of prayer which, to differentiate from the personal one, can first of all be called collective. This kind of prayer implies the gathering, at least physical, of various people. Liturgy has always viewed the convocation of the people of God to celebrate the eucharist and other liturgical procedures as ideal, even though it has also permitted private mass, for example. We do not yet call this type of prayer communal. The fact of physical meeting or of intention to join forces can be a path to communal prayer, though it does not necessarily have to be so. So-called collective prayer may be communal prayer or the prayer of a community of individuals.

Lastly, a type of prayer which we fittingly call communal has been developing. In it an attempt is made to produce the aforementioned three steps of prayer no longer strictly as an individual person, but also in a group or community. What we are now endeavoring to show are the theological presuppositions which make this type of prayer a Christian necessity, although it neither excludes nor frees from the responsibility of times of personal prayer.

It is a historic fact that the Christian faith has existed in church form from the beginning. This means that even before any theologizing on the new, true nature of the believer, Christians did not conceive of their faith in Jesus as individual—which would have been theoretically possible—but communal. It is plain that proceeding from Judaism which is religiously organized as a people, they would take this step with the greatest of ease.

The new faith lived in communal fashion from the start. This is shown at the level of church organization and administration, at the level of edification of the community from within, at the eucharistic and liturgical level and at the level of the practice of penitence, in the form of excommunication as well as readmission.

The communal comprehension of the faith is also evident in the theologizing which Christians apply to themselves. Church, people, body, temple, etc., are named. In the theological treatments of subjects it can be said that the Trinity is the Father, the Son, and "us." The work of the Spirit does not appear so much in the individual, renewed person as in the renewal of the plural nature of "us."

This confirmed ecclesiology of the new life still does not solve the problem of communal prayer, if it is true that prayer signifies a means of access to the God of Jesus such as we have described it. What it involves is the communal character of the experience of God in action for justice. It therefore involves explaining what a communal experience with God and a communal action for justice signify. In order to try to explain how the communal character can reach the deepest roots of the faith, we will make some brief biblical observations and some other systematic ones.

Beyond the communal character of the organization, the liturgy, and the theologizing itself concerning the church, in the New Testament some clear indications appear that at the very level of faith this communal dimension exists. That means that for faith to spring up and develop, mutual interaction of Christians is needed.

The most extreme example is seen in chapters 11 and 12 of the letter to the Hebrews in which, after giving a definition of faith (cf. 11:1), not only objects of faith are proposed as chiefly important, but also individuals of faith. In chapter 11 models of faith in the Old Testament are held up, from which it is not only said abstractly that they had faith, but also what this faith was made up of in their actual life, what trials they had to undergo for it, and what consequences resulted from it. Also, in chapter 12 Christ is presented, here not so much as an object of faith but as the favored individual of faith, as one who has lived the faith in newness and fullness. Eyes must be fixed upon this Jesus. The fundamental presupposition is that those models of faith presented, especially that of Jesus, are witnesses of faith, and are those which release faith in others. From the eyes of faith we take it for granted that faith does not occur because someone presents objects for belief. Rather, people who already believe cause the growth of faith in others. The Christian faith has a clearly specific content: God, the kingdom, Jesus, etc., but this content matter does not become a part of the individual beginning with a direct communication of the content and acceptance of it. Christian faith of the individual is mediated by witnesses of the faith.

What is given as an affirmation concerning the witnesses of the past and the great witness of Jesus in the letter to the Hebrews appears in other places in the New Testament as an affirmation in the present. In Colossians it is said that being a church is "forbearing one another" (Col 3:13). This basic affirmation is in a definite admonitory context, but we believe this context must be universalized to also include faith in this mutual forbearance. In other passages this is presented more explicitly. When Jesus prays for Peter so that his faith should not fail, he adds that Peter in turn should strengthen his brothers (Luke 22:32). There is no reason to reduce what is said here to the level of hierarchic management of the church, rather to simply accept that in the church some have to be prepared to strengthen others in the faith. There are those in the faith who are strong and those who are weak, and there must be a mutual interaction among them. Christians must be ready to strengthen the faith of others and to allow themselves to be strengthened by others. The presupposition is that the aim of the Christian life is not the Christian life of the individual as such, but that there is a church, meaning a community of faith.[20]

The mutual interaction of the faith of Christians is seen impressively described in Romans 1:11ff. Paul writes that "I am longing to see you either to strengthen you by sharing a spiritual gift with you, or what is better, to find encouragement among you from our common faith." These verses have greater significance if one considers that Paul does not speak here of a visit to the Romans as one who has authority. Paul has this authority (cf. 1:5), but he does not speak of an official visit. What he really hopes for is a mutual consolation at the Christian level; he, though he is an apostle, needs faith from others as they need it from him, which is even stressed linguistically in the repetition of the "you and I," "sharing," "our common faith."[21]

In the New Testament it therefore appears that the church form reaches deepest into the life of Christians into that which constitutes its very faith; and that an interaction among the faith of Christians exists. This seems to us to be the first and foremost supposition of that which is communal in prayer.

These brief biblical observations may be accompanied by other systematic ones. In short, we believe that in order to understand communal prayer two things must be kept in mind: (1) God's greatness, (2) the theological conception of communion of the saints and intercession. The first indicates that God is not only greater than nature but also greater than the individual himself, and thus individual subjectivity cannot exhaust the experience with God. One therefore has to be open to the manifestation of God through others. The second signifies that Christians are not saved as individuals but that there is a communion in salvation. The traditional statements on the communion of the saints and intercession enclose a profound truth, even though they have been understood very often in the mechanistic manner of the "ex opere operato." The basic intuition is nevertheless profoundly biblical: we come to God as a people. Communion and intercession are automatically given when the individual joins a community and lets himself be influenced by it. What we are trying to do is to treat this communion and intercession objectively and not pretend they are intentional or a supposed heavenly interchange of spiritual gifts. Theologically it is very important to remember that in baptism the renewal of the individual life is brought about within and by joining a community, to church. And historically it is an everyday observation that when there is a profound individual conversion, people seek either a religious order or a base Christian community in which to cultivate their new life. In theology as well as in history, the faith of the individual Christian is accompanied by his introduction into a community of faith. Communion in faith and intercession for each other is, therefore, first of all a very historical and visible reality.

This final communal aspect of faith is that which theologically explains the meaning and necessity for communal prayer. If we consider the aforementioned three steps of prayer, their communal dimension can be appreciated. The first step is hearing the word of God. What is involved here is actually hearing what the objective will of God is. Doing this in a community is, in addition to being the expression of the inclination of the individual to really hear and to avoid self-deceit as much as possible, also the effective historical way of better coming upon this will. With respect to the will of a God also greater than one's own individuality, as well as with respect to the complexity of the historical world concerning which one wishes to discern the will of God, it is undeniable that hearing the word as a community is a requirement that the community can fulfill better than the isolated individual. This is nothing more than tackling the problem of discernment, which must be taken in complete seriousness in order to respond to the historical will of God. That the individual also has to discern by himself and that he has to make his decisions himself is evident. However, the discernment of the individual does not reach its fullness if the individual does not include at least the inclination and openness to a group with whom to discern.

With regard to the second step of prayer which is the doing, the practice of love, the community has importance at a dual level: as mediation of the experience of grace and as a release for action for justice. Christian action, the practice of love, is the response to knowing one is loved by God; but again this reality needs mediation. Obviously, and according to the New Testament, the first and favored mediation of this love of God to us is Jesus. Through him we know that God loves us. However, to us this person of Jesus also comes to us mediated by the behavior of actual contemporary people. The communal group is the place, though not the only place, to repeat the experience of knowing oneself to be loved by God.

The community is also the place where one finds sufficient imagination and courage so that the practice of love is a fight for justice in a world of conflict. That which confirms the daily experience is already shown in the New Testament. Action for justice carries risks with it; it is a test for faith. It is therefore necessary to find the means of overcoming the temptation of inertia, of not taking the necessary step forward. Also, Christians of today, especially when they decide to make a clear commitment of their faith, need "so many witnesses in a great cloud" (Hebrews 12:1) which gives them strength in this task. By one "the world was convicted" (11:7), another "set out without knowing where he was going" (11:8), others "defied the royal edict" (11:23), and another preferred "to be ill-treated in company with God's people" (11:25). If the total process of prayer needs witnesses of the faith, it also needs witnesses of justice.

With regard to the third step of prayer, that is, the doxological word of thanksgiving or request for forgiveness, that which is communal also pertains to it precisely because it is a word of doxological meaning. "Meaning" and "exclusive individuality" seem to be mutually exclusive. "Meaning" which is not shared lacks meaning. This appears theologized in the scriptures every time the Christian Utopia is presented in its communal dimension: kingdom, brotherhood, etc. However, this meaning manifested is the one which is also expressed in prayer. It is simply to be remembered that when they asked Jesus to teach them to pray he began with the invocation, no less important because it is well-known, of "our Father." No matter how well-known it is, the ultimate meaning of the Christian faith is properly expressed in this way and not merely as "my" Father.

Hence, Christian prayer must have a communal dimension not only because psychology thus approves it, or because it will in this way overcome the fear of modern man and woman in being alone, but also because of the God to whom it is addressed. If prayer is the means of communicating with God, going to God, it cannot be forgotten that this God is the God of the kingdom: a word is heard concerning the kingdom, the kingdom is built, and thanks is given or forgiveness requested for the manifestation or absence of the kingdom. For this reason, Christian prayer is impossible in total solitude.

Obviously, moments of personal prayer must exist in the life of the Christian, but this prayer will also derive from the prayer which is prayed together, first with Jesus, then with the "witnesses" of faith and of Christian justice throughout history and with present-day witnesses. Personal prayer, although necessary, cannot be an absolute end in itself. It will also be the contribution to community prayer, and the consequence of this communal prayer.

Christian prayer also takes part then in the basic church law of "bearing and being borne" which rejects the pride of whomever pretends he does not need to be borne as well as the timidity of the one who thinks he cannot bear others. The traditional "prayer for others" draws its sharpest reality from the "pray with others" in the three steps described.

CONCLUSIONS

Prayer is a phenomenon typical of all religions. It can be defined as "communicating with the Deity." Prayer has gone through a crisis due to the fact that the phenomenon of secularization takes away the obviousness of this point of contact with the divinity, and because the process of politicalization may make prayer look ineffective and even alienating.

Nevertheless, from a Christian point of view the radical crisis of prayer proceeds from whether it is contact with the God of Jesus or attempted contact with divinity in general. In order to discern Christian prayer, one must basically keep in mind the prayer of Jesus since the favored model of access to the Christian

God is given in it. In other words, one must ask in Christian terms what "prayer for the kingdom of God" means.

Jesus is familiar with and practices the prayer of his people; but he is not naive with respect to it. He knows the temptations and manipulations latent in prayer. Notwithstanding, his life is marked by prayer. The typical characteristics of it lie in searching for the will of the Father, carrying it out, and responding doxologically by way of thanksgiving. There is a mutual interaction between his prayer to the Father and his ministry of announcing and establishing the kingdom and denouncing and removing sin against the kingdom.

The prayer of Jesus depends on the true nature of the person whom he called "Father." This personal reality makes its appearance to Jesus in the formality of transcendence, that is, of being forever greater, and in the substance of love as the ultimate reality which gives meaning and releases history.

The prayer of the Christian, even after the resurrection of Jesus, must be like that of Jesus. The Christian prays to the Father as the ultimate mystery; he prays like the son; and he prays in the Spirit, meaning while following Jesus. This is the Trinitarian basis for prayer.

The basic structure of Christian prayer consists of hearing the word of God, doing the word listened to, and responding with thanksgiving or a request for forgiveness. This threefold process is not taken one time and never again; rather it is the very process of life. The prayer of the Christian is the history of his prayer.

In order to understand what is by definition called "moment of prayer" and its relationship to "moment of action," the "contemplata aliis tradere" does not seem adequate, but instead that of "contemplativus in actione." This action within which there is contemplation can be nothing more than that of love. In the present situation of our history love is shown to be favored, although not exclusively, in action for justice. The theoretical model of relating prayer and action would then be that of "contemplative in action for justice."

In addition to traditional personal prayer, communal prayer is developing at present. This is not merely the prayer which is prayed collectively, but is also that in which the three steps of prayer are shared with the community. The necessity of communal prayer is deduced from theology: at the level of faith and of being loved and loving others, the Christian is not merely an individual but a member of a body. Also, the basic law of the establishment of the church ad intra is valid for prayer: to bear and be borne; and ad extra: to accomplish the mission, which leads into the kingdom of God.

NOTES

1. For a general introduction to the phenomenon of prayer, *cf.* J. Sudbrack, "Prayer" in *Sacramentum Mundi* (Herder & Herder) vol. V, 1970, pp. 74-81. See also *Concilium* 79 (1972) which is dedicated entirely to prayer.

2. We have elaborated on the issue implied in the distinction between "religious" and "Christian" in *Christology at the Crossroads* (Orbis Books, 1978), pp. 179-235.

3. In this article it has not been possible to treat prayer in the Hebrew Bible. Persons interested may consult: W. Eichrodt, *Theology of the O.T.*, vol. II (Westminster, 1967), pp. 172-176; Haag-Ausejo, *Diccionario de la Biblia* (Barcelona, Herder, 1967), col. 1363-1368; A. Hamman, *Prayer: The New Testament* (Franciscan Herald Press, 1971), pp. 5-59; P. van Imschoot, *Teología del A.T.* (1969), pp. 532-541.

4. The following quotations from John A. T. Robinson, *Honest to God,* serve to illustrate this: "(According to the prophets) a right relationship to God depended on nothing religious: in fact religion could be the greatest barrier to it." (p. 61) Further on Robinson makes the following confession: "I believe the experts have induced in us a deep inferiority complex. They tell us that this is the way we ought to pray, and yet we find that we cannot maintain ourselves for any length of time even on the lowest rungs of the ladder, let alone climb it. If this is the *scala santa,* then it seems it is not for us. We are evidently not 'the praying type'" (Westminster Press, 1963, p. 93).

5. E. Bethge in the Introduction to D. Bonhoeffer, *Letters and Papers from Prison,* (Macmillan, 1953), p. 11.

6. In *Estudios ENCUENTRO* 3-4, Bogotá, which is dedicated to prayer from a liberating praxis, there is a series of prayers typical of committed Christians in Latin America. Along with the psalms of E. Cardenal appear other prayers, creeds, Lord's Prayers and eucharistic canons. See also G. Bessiere, "Do Revolutionaries Pray? Testimonies from South America" in *Concilium* 79, pp. 109-114.

7. G. Guitiérrez, *A Theology of Liberation* (Orbis Books, 1973), p. 206.

8. See Jon Sobrino, S.J., "The Prayer of Jesus and the God of Jesus in the Synoptic Gospels," *Listening* (Fall: 1978), pp. 189-213.

9. Although it might appear to be a purely theoretical consideration, it is important to note that Jesus, even after the resurrection, never makes himself the object of our prayer. The ultimate object continues to be the Father. This means that even after the resurrection Jesus continues being the Son, the First-Begotten, and consequently the person who is the firstborn in the fullness of prayer. With regard to the perspective of Jesus regarding the Father after the resurrection, *cf.* W. Thuessing, "La imagen de Dios en el N.T." in *Dios como problema,* edited by by J. Ratzinger, (1973), pp. 80-120.

10. To speak of the trinitarian structure of the Christian experience even today sounds like a nominalistic exercise or a mere doctrinal task, with which it would seem easy to assign a real and less operative meaning to the life and prayer of a Christian. Perhaps the fundamental reason for this is that we have pretended to have found a doctrinal teaching about the Trinity in the New Testament and have overlooked the fact that the doctrine of the Trinity is really rooted in the experience, praxis and life of Christians. To throw more light on this from a biblical perspective, *cf.* I. Schierse, "La revelación de la Trinidad en el N.T." in *Mysterium Salutis* II/I, 1969, pp. 117-135. From the point of view of systemics we believe that the great advance in our conceptualization of the Trinity and its working in the Christian life came about in two steps: (1) from considering the Trinity-in-itself to considering the Trinity-for-us. Cf. K. Rahner,

"El Dios trino como principio y fundamento trascendente de la historia de la salvación" in *Mysterium Salutis* II/I, p. 360–449 and (2)from considering the Trinity-in-itself to considering ourselves-in-the-Trinity, cf. J. Moltmann, *The Crucified God* (Harper & Row, 1974), pp. 200–290.

11. From the very beginning it should be made clear that the trinitarian structure of prayer does not mean simply "praying to the three Persons." Rather the trinitarian reality of God is going to be present in prayer. Perhaps it would be worthwhile to remember that when we speak of "believing in the three Persons," we are not proposing three objects of faith, all at the same level. Rather we are keeping present the trinitarian structure of faith. To believe "in the Father" supposes placing ultimate confidence in him; to believe "in the Son" supposes the definitive exemplarity of faith realized in Jesus; to believe "in the Spirit" supposes a realization of faith in the Father in the same way as Jesus did.

12. Cf. M. de Goedt, "The Intercession of the Spirit in Christian Prayer," *Concilium*, 79, pp. 26–38.

13. For a descriptive study of prayer in the diverse communities of the New Testament, cf. Hamann, *Prayer*, pp. 185–238.

14. For a theological treatment of discerning the will of God, cf. K. Rahner, *The Dynamic Element in the Church* (Herder & Herder, 1969).

15. It may seem that calling Christian deeds an essential presupposition for prayer, not merely an ethical exigency of an already constituted faith, appears to be evident; but it is not. In a recent article, a specialist in prayer, L. Boros enumerates the following as presuppositions of Christian prayer: surprise, astonishment, obligation, loneliness, doubt, temptation, hope and calm silence. All these presuppositions can be necessary to place oneself before the mystery of God. Nevertheless, Christian deeds do not appear on the list. We believe that without those deeds the other presuppositions can only be presuppositions for "religious" prayer, but not necessarily for Christian prayer (*Concilium*, 79, pp. 52–62).

16. For this section, cf. E. Ellacuría, *Fe y Justicia*, 1976 (material compiled as a publication of the Centro de Reflexión Teológica, San Salvador); Jose Porfirio Miranda, *Marx and the Bible*

(Orbis Books, 1974); Jose Miranda, *Being and the Messiah* (Orbis Books, 1977); J. Miguez Bonino, *Christians and Marxists: The Mutual Challenge to Revolution* (Orbis Books, 1976); J. Alonso Días, "Términos bíblicos de justicia social y traducción de equivalencia dinámica" in *Estudios Eclesiásticos* (enero-marzo, 1976), pp. 95-128.

17. Cf. E. Dussel, "Domination-Liberation: A New Approach" in *Concilium* 96 (1974), pp. 34-56; also *Para una ética de la liberación latinoamericana*, I (Buenos Aires: Siglo XXI, 1973), pp. 97-156; II, pp. 52-64.

18. Congregación General XXXII de la Compañía de Jesús *Jesuitas Hoy*, n. 8.

19. P. Miranda, *Marx and the Bible*, p. 57.

20. This historical communitarianism in the faith appears frequently in the New Testament. We will limit ourselves to citing some examples from the pauline letters. In I Thes. Paul sends Timothy to them to fortify their faith (3,2); Paul consoles himself with the Thessalonians' perseverance in the faith in the midst of trials (3,7); he desires to pay them another visit in order to complete what is still lacking in their faith (3,10). He announces his up-coming visit to the Philippians for their progress and to add joy to their faith (Phil 1,25). He exhorts the Romans to readily accept the person who is weak in the faith (Rom 14,1). He writes the Corinthians to console them in their tribulations in the same way as God has consoled him (II Cor 1,4). What these and other examples show is that faith, perseverance in faith in the face of trials and growth in faith does not occur merely by virtue of the objective announcement of the Kerygma which proposes the content of the faith, but only by virtue of the concrete actions of the Christian community.

21. Paul "does not speak of the paraclesis which can bring them consolation and counsel, since preaching, if it is evangelical, always offers power and creates demands on the hearers. Paul even painfully avoids any pretension which sounds authoritative. . . . The only thing which appears as an exception is the *mutua fratrum consolatio* in which he himself hopes to share." E. Kaesemann, *An die Roemer*, (Tübingen: Mohr, 1973), p. 16.

3

Salvation and Creativity: Two Understandings of Christianity

Nicolas Berdyaev

"As each has received a gift, serve one another as good stewards of God's varied grace" (Peter 4:10).

The most central, the most tormenting, and the most acute problem of our epoch is the interrelation between the ways of human salvation and the ways of human creativity. The human being is perishing and has a thirst for salvation. But the human being is also by nature a maker, a creator, a builder of life, and the thirst for creation cannot be extinguished in him. Can the human being save himself and at the same time create? Can he create and at the same time save himself? And how is one to understand Christianity? Is Christianity exclusively a religion of the salvation of the soul for eternal life or can Christian consciousness[1] also advocate the creation of a higher life? All these questions torment the contemporary soul, although one does not always realize their full depth. The Christian wishes to justify his vital vocation, his vital creative work, but he is not always aware that this justification involves the very understanding of Christianity and concerns the assimilation of its fullness.

Creativity and the Church

The anxiety over the problems of salvation and creativity reflects the schisms between the church and the world, the

Translation and notes by Carolyn Gifford.

115

spiritual and the mundane, the sacred and the secular. The church is concerned with salvation; the secular world is concerned with creativity. The church does not justify and sanctify[2] the creative works with which the secular world is concerned. The church world deeply disdains and holds in contempt that creative work in cultural life, in the life of society, creative work which fills the movement occurring in the world. At best the church allows creativity; but the church merely tolerates it and creativity does not receive real acceptance. Salvation is the primary task, the first necessity; creativity is a secondary or tertiary task, a supplement to life, but not its very essence.

We live under the sign of the most profound religious dualism. Hierocracy, that is, clericalism as the way in which the church is understood, expresses and justifies this dualism. In such an understanding of the church, the hierarchy in its essence is angelic and not human.[3] This heavenly angelic hierarchy is only symbolized in the human world. The system of hierocracy—the exclusive rule of the clergy in the life of the church—and by way of the church also in the life of the world— is a suppression of the human nature,[4] a subjection of the human nature to the angelic nature as the one destined to rule life. This system always means the domination of conventional symbolism.[5] But the suppression of the human nature, the barring of its original creative expression destroys Christianity as the religion of God-humanity. Christ was the God-human and not the God-angel; he perfectly united divine nature and human nature in one person, and by this, human nature ascended to divine life. Christ the God-human founded a new spiritual race of humanity and the life of God-humanity, not God-angelhood. The church[6] of Christ is God-humanity. The angelic nature stands between God and the human being acting as a passive, intermediary source[7] transmitting God's energy, bearing God's grace. The angelic nature differs from the active, creative nature assigned by God to humanity. But humanity, in its sinful, limited condition,[8] does not contain the fullness of Christian truth. And the repressive rule of the angelic, hierocratic nature is the mark of the inability of sinful humanity to express its creative nature, to understand Christianity in its fullness and completeness. The way of salvation for sinful humanity needs above all the angelic, hierocratic nature. The way of creativity has remained an arbitrary human way, unsanctified and unjustified, and in it the human being is left to his own resources.

Religion's failure to express the revelation of the human nature as an organic part of the life of God-humanity, religion's lack of openness about the free vocation of the human being creates a dualism of church and world, church and culture, a sharp dualism of sacred and secular. Such dualism creates two orientations toward life within the faithful Christian, a division of sacred and secular within him. And this duality within the life of the Christian reaches particular acuteness in the Christianity of modern times. The Christianity of the Middle Ages had a theocratic, hierocratic culture in which all the creativity of life was subordinated to the religious nature, a subordination which meant the supremacy of the angelic hierarchy over the human. Medieval culture and society were sacred, but religious justification was conventionally symbolic. Culture as it was understood in the Middle Ages was angelic not human. The supremacy of the angelic nature always leads toward symbolism, toward the conventional, symbolic representation of heavenly life in the human world without real achievement of it, without real transformation of human life. Modern times dispensed with symbolism and accomplished a break. Humanity rose up in the name of its own freedom and went its own arbitrary way. A small corner of the soul remained for religion. Christians began to understand the church as a compartment of life.[9]

The Christian of modern times lives in two conflicting rhythms—in the church and in the world, in the ways of salvation and the ways of creativity. Theocratic societies and theocratic cultures suppressed human nature; human freedom did not yet give its consent to the realization of the kingdom of God. In the humanistic societies and cultures of modern times, human nature broke away from God and from the operation of divine grace. The union of the Divine and the human was not reached. The ways of creativity of the humanistic world were without God and against God. The drama of modern humanistic history is a drama of the deep separation of the ways of the life of creativity from the ways of salvation, from God and God's grace.

Now the dualism between the church and the world reaches forms of expression which former epochs did not know, since in those epochs the sacred was understood as organic. In the world, enormous creative movements have taken place in science, philosophy, art, civil and social life, in technical achievements, in peoples' moral attitudes, in religious thought and mystical attitudes. All of us, not only unbelievers but faithful Christians as well, participate in this movement of the world, this movement of culture; we give to it a considerable portion of our time and effort. On Sundays we go to church. Six days of the week we give to our creative, constructive work. And our creative attitude toward life remains unjustified, unsanctified, unconnected with the religious nature of life. The old, medieval, theocratic, hierocratic justification and sanctification of the entire process of life no longer has power over us, it has become lifeless. The most faithful, most Orthodox people participate in the unjustified and unsanctified life of the world. They subject themselves to secular, not sacred, science; secular, not sacred, economics; secular, not sacred, law, to life that has long since lost its sacred character. Faithful Orthodox people live a religious life in church: they go on Sunday and feast days to the church, fast during Great Lent,[10] pray to God morning and night, but do not live a religious life in the world, in culture, in society. Their creativity in civil and economic life, in the sciences and in the arts, in inventions and discoveries, in everyday morality remains outside the church, outside of religion, secular, worldly. Creativity is an entirely different rhythm of life from the rhythm of salvation.

Turbulent creative movement has occurred in the world and in culture. Yet for a long time relative immobility, a kind of petrification and ossification, has come over the church. The church began to live exclusively by preservation, through a bond to the past, that is, it conveyed only one side of church life. The church hierarchy became hostile to creativity and suspicious of spiritual culture; it belittled humanity and was frightened of its freedom. It opposed the ways of salvation to the ways of creativity: it said: we are saved in one plane of existence and we create life on an entirely different plane. And the fear always remains that on that plane in which we create, we perish and do not achieve salvation. There is no hope at all that we can overcome further unbearable dualism through the submission of our entire life and all of our creative bursts to a hierocratic nature, through a return to theocracy in the old sense of the word. We cannot return to the conventional symbolism of hierocratic society and culture. Such a return could only be a temporary reaction, rejecting creativity. The religious problem concerning humanity, its freedom and creative vocation, has been posed in all its acuteness. And this is not only the problem of the world, the worn-out and belabored problem in contemporary culture; this is also the problem of the church, the problem of Christianity as the religion of God-humanity.

All the thought of modern times was subjected to the corrupting influence of nominalism.[11] In the consciousness of humanity, ontological reality was corrupted and dispersed. This process affected even church consciousness. The most reactionary current of church thought adopted a nominalist understanding of the church. It ceased to understand the church integrally as a universal spiritual organism, an ontological reality, a Christ-filled cosmos. A compartmentalized understanding of the church prevailed, that is, an understanding of the church as an institution, a society of believers, hierarchies, and church buildings. The church was turned into a therapeutic institution into which individual souls come for healing. A Christian individualism indifferent to the fate of human society and the world is maintained in this way. The church exists for the salvation of individual souls but is not interested in creative life, in the transfiguration of social and cosmic life . . . Yet Christianity cannot be reduced to the individual salvation of separate souls. The church inevitably addresses itself to the life of society and the world; it must inevitably participate in the building of life.

The understanding of Christianity exclusively as a religion of personal salvation—narrowing the scope of the church to something existing alongside all the rest, while in reality the church is the positive fullness of existence—has been the source of the greatest disorders and catastrophes in the Christian world. The humiliation of the human being, his freedom and his creative vocation has resulted from such an understanding of Christianity; it has caused humanity to revolt and rise up in the name of its freedom and creativity. In the empty place which was left in the world by Christianity,[12] Antichrist began to build his tower of Babel and went a long way in his construction. The freedom of the human spirit and the freedom of human creativity definitely perishes when it has been enticed down this path. The church sought to protect itself from the evil elements in the world and from evil movements in it by discouraging creativity. But true protection of the sacred will be possible only when Christian creativity is allowed.

Creativity and Humility

On what spiritual foundation is Orthodox individuality based? How can Orthodoxy justify an understanding of Christianity as a religion of personal salvation, indifferent to the fate of society and the world? In the past, Christianity was exceptionally rich, varied, and many-sided. One can find the basis for various understandings of Christianity in the gospels, the apostolic letters, patristic literature and church tradition. The understanding of Christianity as a religion of personal salvation, suspicious of any creativity, rests exclusively on ascetic patristic literature, that is, on writings which do not reflect the whole of Christian literature, nor even all of patristic thought. Asceticism expresses an eternal truth which enters into an inner spiritual path as an inevitable feature. But it is not the fullness of Christian truth.

The heroic battle with the nature of the old Adam, with sinful passions, emphasized a particular side of Christian truth and exaggerated it out of all proportion. The truths revealed in the gospels and in the apostolic letters were put into second place, suppressed. Humility was laid down as the way of salvation for eternal life; humility was at the foundation of all Christianity and at the base of every spiritual way. According to this type of thought, the human being must humble himself and all the rest will come of itself. Humility is the only method of inner spiritual work. But humility hides and stifles the love which is revealed in the gospels and which appears as the foundation of God's New Covenant with humanity.

The ontological meaning of humility lies in the real victory over the human being's sinful inclination to place the center of gravity of life and the source of life within himself. Thus humility lies in overcoming pride. Humility means a real change and transfiguration of human nature, the supremacy of spiritual humanity over psychic and carnal humanity. But humility must not stifle and extinguish the spirit. Humility is not outward obedience, submissiveness, and subordination. Christianity cannot deny humility as a stage of the inner spiritual way. But humility is not the goal of spiritual life; it is, rather, a subordinate means. And humility is not the only means nor the only way of spiritual life. Inner spiritual life is infinitely more complex and multifaceted. One cannot answer all the demands of the spirit by preaching humility. Furthermore, one can understand humility falsely and much too superficially. Absolute primacy belongs to the inner spiritual life and the inner way; it is more primary, deep, and fundamental than all our relations to the life of society and the world. Our entire relation toward life takes shape in the spiritual world, from the depths of the spiritual world. This is an axiom of religion, an axiom of mysticism. But one can understand humility in a way which distorts all one's spiritual life, a way which does not contain the divine truth of Christianity or its divine fullness. And in this misunderstanding lies the full complexity of the question. While the ontological meaning of humility lies in the liberation of spiritual humanity, decadent humility keeps humanity in a condition of repression and oppression, chaining its creative power.

Decadents of humility begin to oppose humility to love. They consider the way of love to be a daring, not a humble way. A decadent of humility would ask: How can I, sinful and unworthy, claim to have love for my neighbor, to have brotherhood? My love will be infected by sin. First I must humble myself; love will appear as a fruit of humility. But I must humble myself all my life and I will never achieve a sinless condition. Therefore, love too will never appear. How can I, a sinful person, dare to strive toward spiritual perfection, toward courage and the elevation of the spirit, toward the attainment of a higher spiritual life? First I must conquer sin by humility. But this will expend all life and will not leave time and strength for a creative spiritual life. This spiritual life is possible only in that other world, and even there it is scarcely possible. In this world only humility is possible. Thus decadent humility creates a system of life in which ordinary, average, bourgeois, everyday life is considered more humble, more Christian, and more moral than the attainment of a higher spiritual life, of love, of contemplation, of understanding, and of creativity. Decadents of humility always suspect such a life of a lack of humility, and of pride. To sell in a shop, to live the most egoistic family life, to serve as a police official, or in the excise department—such activity is humble and not arrogant or daring. But to aim toward a Christian brotherhood of people and toward realizing the truth of Christ in life, to be a philosopher or a poet—a Christian philosopher or a Christian poet—such activity is not humble but proud, arrogant, and daring. Even if a shopkeeper is not only self-interested but dishonest as well, he runs less risk of the danger of eternal damnation than the one who through his entire life pursues absolute truth and justice, who thirsts after the life of beauty. A religious philosopher, a poet of life, a seeker after the truth of life and the brotherhood of people runs the risk of the danger of eternal damnation because he is not sufficiently humble, but instead is proud. The result is a hopeless, vicious circle. Decadents of humility declare that striving toward the realization of God's truth, the kingdom of God, spiritual elevation, and spiritual perfection is actually spiritual imperfection since it shows lack of humility.

What is the basic flaw of decadent humility and its system of life? The basic flaw is latent in a false understanding of the relationship between sin and the ways of liberation from it and the attainment of a higher spiritual life. I cannot argue thus: the world lies in evil; I am a sinful person and therefore my striving toward the realization of Christ's truth and toward brotherly love between people is a proud claim, a lack of humility. For any authentic movement in the direction of the realization of love and truth is a victory over evil and a liberation from sin. I cannot speak thus: striving for spiritual perfection and spiritual elevation means pride and a lack of humility, an insufficient realization of human sinfulness. For any step toward spiritual perfection and spiritual elevation is the way of victory over sin. I cannot speak thus: I am a sinful person and my daring to know the secrets of existence and to create beauty are pride and show a lack of humility. For authentic knowledge and authentic creation of beauty are already victories over sin and transfiguration of life. One cannot say: sin distorts and perverts love, spiritual perfection, knowledge and all else and that is why no victory over sin can be gained by these ways. For, in the same way, it is perfectly possible to say: the way of humility is distorted and perverted by human sin and self-interest, and thus is a distorted, decadent, corrupted, humility, humility turned into slavery, egoism, and cowardice. Humility is no more guaranteed against distortion and degeneration than are love and knowledge.

The central idea of the Eastern Fathers was that of *theosis,* the divinization of all creatures, the transfiguration of the world, the idea of the cosmos, and not the idea of personal salvation. It was not by chance that the greatest Eastern teachers of the church inclined toward the idea of *apocatastasis,*[13] not only Clement of Alexandria[14] and Origen,[15] but also St. Gregory of Nyssa,[16] Gregory of Nazianzus,[17] and Maximus the Confessor.[18] Mainly

Western Fathers—Augustine[19] and, later, Western scholastics—
express the juridical understanding of the world process, that
is, the juridical understanding of atonement, the creation of
hell, the salvation of the elect, and the eternal damnation of
all remaining humanity. For the classical Greek Fathers, Christianity was not just a religion of personal salvation. It was oriented toward a cosmic understanding of Christianity; it advanced the idea of the enlightenment and transfiguration of
the world and the *theosis* of all creatures. Only later Christian
consciousness began to value the idea of hell more than the idea
of the transfiguration and divinization of the world. Christianity
understood as a religion of personal salvation from eternal
damnation through humility led to panic and terror. Human
beings lived under dreadful pressure of the terror of eternal
damnation and agreed to anything if only to avoid it. An au-
thoritarian system of obedience and submission was created
through a fit of passion caused by fear of damnation, a panic
fear of eternal torment in hell. A creative attitude toward life is
very difficult with such a spiritual orientation and such a condition of consciousness. One cannot create when one is threatened
with damnation. All life is placed under the sign of terror and
fear. When the plague rages and death threatens constantly, one
cannot create; one is interested exclusively in the means of salvation from the plague. And sometimes Christianity is indeed understood as salvation from a raging plague.

Human beings found creativity and the building of life possible only because of a dualistic system which allowed them to
forget about salvation from damnation for a time. They turned
to sciences and arts or the building of society, having forgotten
for a moment about menacing damnation and discovering for
themselves another sphere of existence separate from that in
which salvation and damnation occur. In no way did they connect these two spheres. The understanding of Christianity as a
religion of personal salvation from damnation is a system of
transcendental egoism, or transcendental utilitarianism and
eudemonism. Transcendental egoism and eudemonism naturally deny the way of love and cannot be true to the gospel com-

mandment which orders us to lose our own soul in order to
gain it, to give it up for our neighbor, and which teaches, above
all, love—selfless love for God and our neighbor. One slanders
Christianity when one claims that it is a religion of transcendental egoism which does not know selfless love for Divine
perfection. Such a claim would mean either a barbaric Christianity, a Christianity suppressing the wildness of passions and
itself distorted by these passions, or a decadent Christianity,
damaged and impoverished.

Christianity always was, is, and will be not only a religion of
personal salvation and terror of damnation but also a religion of
the transfiguration of the world, the *theosis* of all creatures, a
cosmic and social religion, a religion of selfless love, love for God
and humanity, promising the kingdom of God. In the individualistic, ascetic understanding of Christianity as a religion of
personal salvation in which one cares only about one's soul, the
revelation of the resurrection of all creatures is incomprehensible and unnecessary. The religion of personal salvation has no
universal eschatological perspective, no personal connection of
the individual human soul with the world, with the cosmos, with
all creation. The religion of personal salvation denies the hierarchical[20] order of existence in which all is united with all and in
which no individual fate can be isolated. The individual understanding of salvation is more typical of Protestant pietism than
Catholic Christianity.[21] I cannot save myself alone, I can save
myself only together with my brothers and sisters, together with
all of God's creation. I cannot think only of my own salvation, I
must think also of the salvation of others, of the salvation of the
whole world. And even the idea of salvation is only an exoteric
expression for the achievement of spiritual heights, of perfection, of becoming like God—which is the supreme goal of the life
of the world.

Creativity and Transfiguration

The greatest Christian mystics of all creeds placed love for
God and union with God above personal salvation. Exoteric

Christianity[22] often criticized mystics because for them the center of gravity of spiritual life does not lie in the ways of personal salvation; they proceed by the perilous ways of mystical love. Mysticism is, after all, an entirely different stage of spiritual life than asceticism. One may learn the originality of mysticism by reading the hymns of St. Symeon the New Theologian.[23] Christian mysticism understands salvation as enlightenment and transfiguration, as the *theosis* of all creatures, as the overcoming of "closed creation," that is, overcoming isolation from God. The idea of *theosis* prevails over the idea of salvation. St. Symeon the New Theologian has expressed this very well:

> I am filled with his love and beauty and I am being filled with divine joy and sweetness. I become a communicant of light and glory: my face shines like that of my beloved and all my members become radiant. Then I become more beautiful than the beautiful, richer than the rich; I become stronger than all the strong, greater than emperors and much more honorable than anything ever seen, not only of the earth and what is on earth, but also heaven and everything that is in heaven.

I quote from the greatest mystic of the Orthodox East. One could cite an innumerable number of passages from Western mystics, both Roman Catholic and German Protestants, which confirm the idea that for the mystic the center of gravity never lies in striving toward salvation. Catholic mysticism overcame the legalism of Catholic theology, the juridical understanding of the relationship between God and humanity. Bossuet's debate with Fénelon[24] was precisely one between a theologian and a mystic. The mystical way always included a lack of self-interest, renunciation, forgetfulness of self, a revelation of boundless love for God. But love for God is a creative condition of the spirit; it means liberation which overcomes any repression; it is a positive disclosure of spiritual humanity. Humility is only a means; it is still negative. Love for God is the aim; it is already positive.

Love for God is already a creative transformation of human

nature and love for spiritual elevation, for the divine in life. *Eros,* love of the divine, is spiritual ascent, spiritual growth, a victory of the creative condition of the soul over the condition of depression; *eros* is the soul's sprouting wings of which Plato speaks in *Phaedrus.* The positive content of existence is love, creative transfiguring love. Love is not some sort of special, isolated aspect of life but, rather, all of life, the fullness of life. Knowledge is also a revelation of love, of cognitive love through a cognitive merging of the one who loves with the object of his love, with existence and with God. Creation of beauty is also a discovery of the harmony of love in existence. Love is an affirmation of the image of the object of love in eternity and in God, that is, an affirmation of existence. Love is the ontological source. But love for God is inseparable from love for one's neighbor and for God's creation. Christianity is precisely the revelation of divine-human love. What saves me, that is, transfigures my nature, is not only love for God but also love for humanity. Love for my neighbor, for my brothers and sisters, matters of love enter into the way of my salvation, my transfiguration. Into the way of my salvation enters love for animals and plants, for each blade of grass, for stones, for rivers and seas, for mountains and fields. I am saved by this love and the whole world is saved as well; illumination is achieved.

Lifeless indifference toward humanity and nature, toward all life in the name of the way of personal salvation is a disgusting manifestation of religious egoism; it is a drying up of human nature, a preparation for becoming one of the "cold-hearted *skoptsi*."[25] Christian love must not be "glass love,"[26] that is, abstract spiritual love. Only spiritual, psychic love in which the soul changes into spirit is living love, divine-human love. Sometimes one encounters monastic, ascetic malevolence toward people and the world, a cooling of the heart, a numbness toward all life and creation. Such an attitude toward creation represents the degeneration and decay of Christianity. The replacement of the commandment of love for God and love for the neighbor given by Christ himself with the commandment of external

humility and obedience which cools all love evidences a degeneration of Christianity, an inability to contain the divine truth of
Christianity.

One should note that it is the Orthodox East which is closest to
the idea of cosmic transfiguration and enlightenment. Western
Christianity is nearer to the juridical idea of justification; thus
for Catholic and Protestant consciousness the central idea is justification. Hence arguments concerning freedom and grace,
faith and good works acquire particular significance in the West.
Western Christianity also searches for authority and an external
criterion of religious truth.* Only the mystics rose above the
repressive idea of God's judgment and demand of justification
from humanity; they understood that God does not need the
justification of human beings but the love of human beings and
the transfiguration of their nature. This is the central problem
of Christian consciousness. Is the essence of Christianity in justification, in judgment, in God's implacable justice? Or is this
essence in real transfiguration and illumination, in God's unend-
ing love?

Christianity reared people full of sanguine instincts which
were cruel and barbarous in the juridical understanding of
Christianity, a severe method creating a genuine spiritual terror.
But one may contrast to the juridical understanding a deeper
understanding of Christianity as the revelation of love and freedom. The human being is called to be creator and a participator
in the work of God's creation. It is God's call addressed to
human beings toward which they must respond freely. God does
not need submissive and obedient slaves, always trembling and
egoistically preoccupied with themselves. God needs sons and
daughters, free and creative, loving and daring. Humanity
frightfully distorted the image of God and ascribed to him its

---

*In a certain sense the dogma of papal infallibility and the gnoseology
of Kant rest on one and the same principle of an external, juridical,
justifying criterion of truth [Berdyaev's note].

own distorted and sinful psychology. The Christian revelation is above all the good news of the coming of the kingdom of God, which we must seek before all else. The search for the kingdom of God is not only the search for personal salvation. The kingdom of God is the transfiguration of the world, universal resurrection, a new heaven and a new earth.

The Christian understanding of the world does not obligate us and moreover does not permit us to think that only the separate souls of people are real, that only they make up God's creation. God created society and nature and they are also realities. Society is not a human fabrication. It has always existed and has ontological roots just as the human person does. One cannot uproot the human person from society just as one cannot detach society from human persons. The person and society belong to one concrete whole and exist in vital interaction. The life of society reflects the spiritual life of persons. Society is a specific spiritual organism which is nourished by the life of persons and also nourishes them. The denial of the reality of society is nominalism, and such nominalism has fatal consequences for the consciousness of the church, that is, for the church's understanding of its nature. The church is a spiritual society and this society possesses ontological reality. It cannot be reduced to the interaction of separate souls each saving itself. In the society which is the church not only isolated souls are being saved; the kingdom of God is also being realized. It is possible that the understanding of Christianity as a religion of personal salvation alone reflects the decline and ossification of Christianity. Christianity has become uninspired, dull, uncreative and has ceased to inspire and direct the life of human societies and cultures. It has been driven into a small corner of the human soul, and conventional and external dogmatism and ritualism have replaced the actual realization of Christianity in life. Had it not been for such a decline there would not have been such godlessness and depreciation of the spirit. The future of human societies and cultures depends on whether Christianity will receive a creative meaning which transfigures life; it depends on whether spiritual energy capable of engendering enthusiasm, capable of leading us from decline to ascent will once more be revealed in Christianity.

The official people of the church, the professionals of religion tell us that we need only personal salvation, and creativity is not necessary for this goal—it is even harmful. Why knowledge? Why science and art? Why invention and discovery? Why social truth? Why the creation of a new, better life when eternal damnation threatens me and I need only salvation? Such a depressed and panicky religious consciousness and feeling cannot justify creativity. Nothing is necessary for the work of the personal salvation of the soul: knowledge is not necessary, nor are art, economics, the state, the very existence of nature, of God's world. Human creativity—knowledge, art, invention, the perfecting of society—are necessary, not for personal salvation, but for the realization of God's plan for the world and humanity, for the transfiguration of the cosmos, for the kingdom of God into which all the fullness of existence enters.

The Nature of Creativity

The human being has been called not only to save himself but to be a creator, a participator in God's work of the creation and building of the world. And a person can sometimes forget about himself and his soul in the name of the creativity to which God has called him, in the name of the realization of God's work in the world. God has given people diverse gifts and no one has the right to bury them in the earth; all must creatively make use of these gifts which indicate the true vocation of persons. The apostles Paul and Peter speak about this with great power (1 Cor. 12:28; 1 Peter 4:10). God's plan concerning humanity includes the creative nature of human personality. Personality is saved, but in order that it be saved it must be affirmed in its authentic nature, that is, as the center of creative energy. Outside of creativity there is no personality. The creative personality is saved for eternity. The assertion of salvation in opposition to creativity means the assertion of the salvation of emptiness, of nonexistence. Psychology of creativity is inherent to humanity in its positive existence; it may be suppressed and hidden, it may be revealed, but it is ontologically inherent in humanity.

The creative instinct in a person is not a mercenary one, in it a person forgets himself, he goes outside of himself. Scientific discovery, technical invention, artistic and social creativity can be necessary for others and can be used for utilitarian goals, but the one who is creating is not self-interested and is detached from himself. Such is the essence of the psychology of creativity which is quite distinct from the psychology of humility and cannot be built on it. Humility is an inner spiritual action in which a person is occupied with his soul, with overcoming his self, with perfecting himself, with saving himself. Creativity is a spiritual action in which a person forgets about himself, moves outside of himself in the creative act, absorbed by his task. In creativity the human being experiences a state of the extraordinary ascent of his whole being. Creativity is always a shock in which the ordinary egoism of human life is overcome. And a person consents to forget about the salvation of his soul in the name of creative action. It is impossible to make scientific discoveries, to contemplate philosophically the mystery of existence, to create artistic works, to originate a social reform in a state of humility alone. Creativity is a different quality of spiritual life than humility and asceticism; it is the revelation of the god-like nature of humanity. Sometimes people reason thus: "first one should save oneself, conquer sin, and then afterwards create." But such an understanding of a chronological relation between salvation and creativity contradicts the laws of life. It never happened in this way and it never will. "I must save myself during my entire life, and I will not manage to conquer sin finally until the end of my life. Therefore the time will never come when I am strong enough to begin to create life." But just as one must save oneself all one's life, one must create all one's life, participating in the creative process in conformity with one's gifts and calling. The correlation between salvation and creativity is an ideal and inner correlation and not the correlation of an actual chronological sequence. Rather than interfering with salvation, creativity helps toward salvation because creativity is the fulfillment of the will of God, obedience to God's call, participation in God's work in the world. Whether I am a carpenter or a philosopher, God calls me for creative building. My creativity may be distorted by sin, but a complete lack of creativity expresses the final repression of humanity by original sin. Ascetics and saints were not only saving themselves; they also created and were artists of the human soul. The apostle Paul was in his spiritual type more a creative genius than a saint.

Creativity: Enchurching the World

In modern times all spiritually significant people have been spiritually alone. The genius, the creative pioneer, was terribly and tragically alone. There was no religious consciousness of the fact that the genius was a heavenly messenger. And only rarely did one hear voices such as those of isolated Catholics who demanded the canonization of Christopher Columbus. This isolation of the creative genius was caused by the kind of dualism mentioned above. Only a creative Christian renascence can overcome this dualism. But one cannot conceive of a renascence in hierocratic categories. One cannot squeeze such a renascence into the framework of church professionalism. One cannot view it as an exclusively "sacred" process in contrast to "profane" processes. A creative church renascence will come from a movement in the world, in culture, from the accumulation of creative religious energies in the world. We must believe more firmly that Christ acts in his spiritual human race; he does not abandon it, even if this activity is invisible to us.

The Christian stands before the problem of the "enchurching" of all life. But enchurching does not necessarily mean submission of all aspects of life to the church as understood compartmentally, that is, it does not mean theocratic and hierocratic repossession. Enchurching inevitably includes the recognition that spiritual creativity is churchly; a compartmentalized and hierocratic church consciousness has considered this same creativity to be unchurchly. The church in the most profound sense of the word has also lived in the world, unconscious churchly processes have occurred in the world. The fulfillment of the church as the life of God-humanity, the revelation of an integral church consciousness, signifies enrichment through a new spiritual experience of humanity. This spiritual experience cannot remain unjustified and unsanctified. The human being endlessly longs for and craves the sanctification of his creative search. The church is life; life is movement, creativity. The Christian should no longer tolerate the condition in which creative movement remains outside the church and in opposition to the church, while the church is without movement and devoid of creative life. Certain forms of church consciousness willingly recognized a theophany in frozen forms of existence, in immovable historical bodies. But times are coming when church consciousness will have to recognize a theophany in creativity.

Outside the church, secular, humanistic creativity is exhausted; everywhere it turns down a blind alley. Culture is banal and a thirst for eternity torments the best people. And this means that an epoch of churchly, Christian, God-human creativity must come. The church cannot remain a small corner of life, a small corner of the soul. We hope that every creative, transfiguring attitude toward life will pass from the world into the church. Only in the church can the image of the human being and his freedom be preserved and revealed; both his image and his freedom are being annihilated by processes taking place in the world. In a godless civilization the image of the human being and the freedom of the spirit will perish and creativity will dry up; already a barbarization is beginning. The church must once again save the spiritual culture and spiritual freedom of humanity. This I call the coming of the new middle ages. The will is being awakened for a real transfiguration of life, not only a transfiguration of the person but also one of society and the world. And this good will must not be brought to a stop by the consciousness that the kingdom of God on earth is not possible. The kingdom of God is realized in eternity and in each moment of life, and its realization does not depend on the extent to which the power of evil outwardly prevails. Our task is to devote our entire will and our entire life to the victory of the power of good, to the truth of Christ in everything and everywhere.

Two tragedies split and crush human life: the tragedy of the church and the tragedy of culture. These tragedies are caused by the dualistic damage, the impoverishment of the church through its compartmentalized, hierocratic self-understanding in which it always opposes itself to the world. Certainly we Christians must not love the "world" and that which is of the "world"; we must conquer the "world." But this "world," by definition of the Holy Fathers, is passions, sin, and evil; the "world" does not mean God's creation, the cosmos. The church is opposed to the "world" but not to the cosmos, to God's creation, to the positive fullness of existence. The solution to the two tragedies lies in the vital, and not merely theoretical, understanding of Christianity as the religion not only of salvation but also of creativity, as the religion of the transfiguration of the world, universal resurrection, love toward God and human beings, that is, in the entire content of the Christian truth about God-humanity, about the kingdom of God.

NOTES

1. The term *xristianskii soznanie* = Christian consciousness indicates Christianity's self-consciousness about its nature and its function, that is, its understanding of itself.

2. The verbs *opravdavat'* (to justify) and *osvjaščat'* (to sanctify) indicate in this context that the church does not support creative work in all areas of life either through providing a theological basis for creativity or through encouraging those who attempt to create.

3. Berdyaev means by this that the hierarchy of the institutional church as such performs an angelic function: it is the

medium through which the sacraments are dispensed (and
therefore the one medium through which grace is always available), and by which the church as an historical institution is
administered.

4. The word *načalo* which has been translated here as "nature" could also be translated as "principle." It has been translated "human nature" to emphasize the way in which Berdyaev
has invested a familiar phrase with renewed and deepened
meaning, as he defines human nature in relation to activity and
creativity and in opposition to the passive, intermediary angelic
nature which functions simply as a channel for grace.

5. The term *uslovango simvolizma* (conventional symbolism)
refers to the condition in which one assumes outward historical
manifestations of the church such as the ecclesiastical hierarchy
to be filled with spiritual qualities, when they may actually be
devoid of truth, love, beauty, freedom, mercy—true spiritual
qualities. The faithful living under the domination of conventional symbolism may give their allegiance to an outward form
which no longer incarnates spiritual qualities. Berdyaev speaks
of the tsardom as such a historical form which no longer displays
spiritual qualities. When the angelic nature rules life through
the ecclesiastical hierarchy, conventional symbolism flourishes
because the creativity which is the essence of human nature is
not encouraged. Thus true spiritual life can only be symbolized
and not incarnated, since true spirituality requires human
creativity.

6. The word "church" here and some other places in the essay
refers to the church in its fullest, deepest meaning, the church
as *sobornost,* as an ontological reality which is the realization of
the kingdom of God. It must be distinguished from the church
in those historical manifestations which have not fully incarnated
spiritual qualities.

7. The angelic nature, as a passive, intermediary source which
transmits the grace of God, stands lower in the hierarchy of
created being than the human nature as the active, creative nature.

8. The sinful, limited condition of humanity is the result of
the fall as an existential event in the life of humanity and the
lives of individual human beings. The event of the fall leaves

human beings inwardly divided, separated from God and able to perceive only objectively. Thus, human beings are unable to understand the fullness of Christian truth, since that truth presupposes an intuitive mode of knowing (*gnosis*) in which division and separation from God are overcome.

9. The word *differencial'no* (differentially) has been translated here as "compartmentally" and specifically in this sentence as "a compartment of life" in order to indicate more clearly the process Berdyaev believes to be taking place in the understanding of the church. As he explains in the article, Christians are losing their awareness of the Church as cosmos, as the Body of Christ which is the center of human life and gives meaning to that life. Christians begin to view the church as one of several institutions to which they are related.

10. *Velikij post'* (Great Lent, or simply Lent) is the period of fasting for the seven weeks preceding Easter.

11. Berdyaev understands by "the corrupting influence of nominalism" the tendency to deny the existence of the universal church as an ontological reality and to regard the church as real only in its individual instances, as isolated entities. Berdyaev does not believe in the existence of Platonic universals, ideal essences of which individual instances only more or less conform to the essence. Rather than either Platonic realism or nominalism, Berdyaev believes in what he calls ideal-realism in which he apprehends the universal in the particular.

12. The "empty place" refers to the so-called secular sphere in which creativity takes place (according to prevailing church thought) and from which the church withdrew, refusing to have anything to do with either creativity or the secular.

13. The Greek word *apocatastasis* means for Eastern theology in general "the final consummation of the end . . . the restoration, when Christ will return in glory to judge both the living and the dead." (Timothy Ware, *The Orthodox Church*, p. 265) However, for Berdyaev, the meaning of the word carried with it the idea of Origen and other Greek Fathers that in the final restoration all created being will be restored to spiritual life everlasting, and that the pains of hell will not be eternal. Berdyaev sets this idea over against the idea of hell as a place of eternal damnation to which the wicked are consigned at the last judgment. He

cannot accept the idea of the existence of an ontological hell as part of God's plan for creation.

14. St. Clement of Alexandria (c. 150-c. 215) was head of the famous catechetical school of Alexandria which was the center for much advanced Christian thought. He taught that there was a true Christian *gnosis* through which a believer could fully comprehend Christian truth.

15. Origen (c. 185-c. 254) succeeded St. Clement as head of the catechetical school of Alexandria. Although he was an outstanding thinker of the early church, his work provoked controversy within the church as to his orthodoxy so he was never canonized.

16. St. Gregory of Nyssa (c. 335-c. 395) was one of the three Cappadocian Fathers, an outstanding Post-Nicene thinker who dealt particularly with the subject of the image of God in the human being, the effect of the fall on this image and the nature of Christ's redemptive activity.

17. St. Gregory of Nazianzus (329–389), another of the great Cappadocian Fathers (the third being St. Basil the Great), is called Theologian by the Eastern Church in honor of his outstanding work. The Cappadocian Fathers developed Christian thought about the nature of the Trinity as a mystery of unity in diversity.

18. St. Maximus the Confessor (c. 580–662) wrote mystical and ascetic works, among them the *Four Centuries of Charity*.

19. Augustine (354–430), Bishop of Hippo in North Africa, is credited by Berdyaev with introducing the juridical interpretation of Christianity to which Berdyaev refers later in the sentence. Eastern Orthodox Christianity in general tends to reject Augustine's interpretation of grace and free will as two forces opposed to one another. Orthodox believe instead in a cooperation of God's grace and the free will of human beings acting synergistically. Grace for Orthodoxy is resistible.

20. Berdyaev here uses "hierarchical" not in the sense that those higher on the hierarchical scale (for example, human beings, the highest in the hierarchy of created being) have rights and privileges that others lower down on the scale do not possess, but rather to indicate special responsibilities of those higher on the scale for those lower than themselves. In this understanding of

"hierarchy," human beings have a responsibility to transfigure the rest of the animal creation, as well as plants, the mineral world, etc., making them part of the cosmos—the transfigured creation.

21. Here Berdyaev opposes Catholic Christianity [literally, "church Christianity"] to sectarian tendencies and what he calls "spiritual Christianity"—an individualistic religious attitude. Neither of these latter types is concerned with universal salvation, as Berdyaev is. The sentences following describe the attitude of Catholic Christianity.

22. "Exoteric Christianity" is objectified Christianity, the faith of vast numbers of believers. It is a faith characterized by a concern for saving souls from eternal damnation and preaching a religion which advocates the sort of humility which precludes creative striving toward God and the achievement of the kingdom of God.

23. St. Symeon the New Theologian (949–1022) was a mystic and the abbot of the monastery of St. Mamas. The title "New Theologian" indicates that the Eastern Church has placed his writings on the spiritual level of St. John the Evangelist. Some of his writing is found in the *Philokalia* (English translation by Kadloubovsky and Palmer, *Writings from the Philokalia on the Prayer of the Heart.* London: Faber and Faber, 1973.) and also in *Hymns of Divine Love,* translated by George A. Maloney, S.J. (Dimension Books, n.d.).

24. Francois Fénelon (1651–1715) and Jacques Bossuet (1627–1704), two leading figures of French Catholicism, became involved in a controversy over a spiritual movement which spread through France, Italy and Spain during the seventeenth century. This movement evidenced a reaction of mystical spirituality (represented by Fénelon) against bureaucratic ecclesiasticism (represented to some degree by Bossuet). Fénelon was convicted of Quietism.

25. The *skoptsi* (meaning "self-castrators" from *skopec* = eunuch) were a sect which appeared in Russia in the 1770s as an offshoot of the *xlysti* (flagellants). The act of self-castration apparently was a protest against the immorality of Russian society, and intended as a sacrificial act to redeem fallen society. Berdyaev's objection to the activities of the *skoptsi* would most likely stem

from their repudiation of sexuality as sinful in itself, and their attempt to destroy their sexual nature rather than to transfigure sexual energy in creative activity.

26. Berdyaev defines the term "glass love" more explicitly in *The Destiny of Man* as "spiritual love, abstracted from the emotions and from all concreteness and individuality" (p. 187), and in *Solitude and Society* he writes that glass love is "impersonal love which is not concentrated on any individual image" (p. 119).

4

Patristic Spirituality and the Experience of Women in the Early Church

Rosemary Radford Ruether

The patristic church inherited from the New Testament period an ambivalent view of women and spirituality. On the one hand, the church of the first century made some significant changes in the traditional status of women which had been inherited from Judaism. The Judaism of the temple cult had strictly excluded women, not only from priesthood, but even from proximity to the sanctuary. Purity laws distanced women even more from the cult during much of their lives. Childbirth and menstruation were regarded as rendering them ritually unclean. The synagogue took over this body of purity laws and applied them to the daily lives of men and women. In rabbinic Judaism women were not "called to the Torah." The highest occupation of a Jew is to study the Torah in the circle of disciples around the rabbi. Women were not called to participate in this pursuit. Theirs was to manage the cult of "pots and pans," sending their husbands and sons off to the higher pursuits of religious scholarship. The secondary status of women is evident in all the rites and festivals. Judaism is basically a male religious assembly in which women play secondary supportive roles.[1]

Women in the Apostolic Community

The early church, by contrast, seems to have brought women much more into the center of its life. The synoptic gospels do not model the church after the patriarchal family or kinship group, but rather see it as a voluntary community of those who have accepted a call to discipleship, in tension with the family and social hierarchies. Those who follow Jesus must be willing to break with family loyalties and even stand in tension with them: Matt 10:37–39; Luke 14:26–27. This originally was not a call to celibacy, but rather the stance of a movement community that was shaped by a sense of the urgency and crisis of the times. Jesus also rejects relations of hierarchy and domination as models for the leadership of the church. Those who would be leaders must emulate the roles of the lowest of the society, servants or slaves. The disciples are to call no man father, master, or teacher: Matt 23:1–10. Relation to God and to Jesus brings people into a new community where all are brothers and sisters and are to serve one another, rather than to have power over each other. The iconoclastic view of the Messiah: "The Son of Man comes not to be served, but to serve," sums up this new vision of leadership as service, rather than dominion.[2]

These breaks with traditional role models, based on the patriarchal family and the leadership classes, must have had a liberating effect on the early church's understanding of new relations between men and women. Traditional hierarchies of class, race, and sex were leveled in the new messianic community. This is summed up theologically in Paul's dictum: "In Christ there is neither male nor female, slave nor free, Jew nor Greek": Gal 3:28. This formula was not created by Paul, but reflects an early Christian theology of baptism. It is a formula constructed in conscious repudiation of the dominant traditions of the Jewish and Greek worlds, where the master group was accustomed to thank God that they were born "male and not female, free and not slave, Jew and not gentile" or, in the case of the Greeks, "Hellene and not barbarian."[3]

The church expressed this new equality in Christ for women in certain levelings of role and function. Women in the Christian assembly were equally called to be students of the scriptures and teachings. The story of Mary and Martha is an early Christian affirmation of the right of women, equally with men, to sit at the

feet of the Christian teacher: Luke 10:38–42. The parallelism of
male and female examples in the parables; i.e., the kingdom of
heaven is like seed which a farmer sowed in a field; the kingdom
of heaven is like leaven which a woman sowed in a measure of
wheat: Matt 13:31–33; Luke 13:18–21; Mk 4:30–32, showed the
awareness of the Christian catechists that they were dealing with
an audience of men and women, unlike the synagogue.[4] Those
who were catechumens were also in training, in turn, to be
Christian teachers. Paul shows us that women functioned in his
churches as local church leaders, and traveling evangelists: Phil
4:2–3; Rom 16:3. The book of Acts declares that the pentecostal
Spirit is poured on God's maidservants and men servants alike:
Acts 2:17. Prophecy, an essential element in early Christian
leadership, was exercised by women as well: Acts 21:9.

But we find also in Paul the ambivalence of the church toward
this new parity for women. Paul understands women's new
equality in Christ "eschatologically." He sees it as a part of a new
transcendent order that has begun in the redeemed community,
the church. His view of slavery is very similar. Women and slaves
have a foretaste of this eschatological liberation of all creation
within the Christian community. This is expressed, for Paul, not
merely "spiritually," but in the ability of women and slaves to
exercise leadership roles, to teach, prophesy, and spread the
good news. But Paul regards society outside the church, including Christian family life, as still governed by the hierarchical
order of the "world." Paul's theology equates social hierarchy
with the "order of creation": 1 Cor 11:2–16. This is the sphere
which is still governed by the Law. The state too is a part of this
"natural order," to which Christians should continue to adhere
until Christ comes and the redemption of the body and the
physical cosmos should be complete: Rom 13:1–10.

Paul, in other words, sanctions an unfortunate dualism in
Christian theology, a dualism of "two spheres." Equality in
Christ belongs to an eschatological order which has its foretaste
in the church. But in the social order the hierarchy of men over
women, masters over slaves, still obtains. Christians should not

seek to change this social order, but regard it as continuing to be authoritative and divinely created. It is abolished only with the transcendence of the natural order itself. For the woman, virginity or widowhood may be regarded as a foretaste of this eschatological emancipation from male domination, similar to emancipation of the slave. But there is no mandate from the gospel to change or reform the social order of marriage and slave relations as such: 1 Cor 7:17–40.

In the pastoral epistles and other deutero-Pauline works this social conservatism becomes more pronounced. The deutero-Pauline community that produced the pastorals also edited the original corpus of Paul: i.e., 1 Cor 14:34. In this community much of the leadership of women found in the Pauline church was suppressed. Creation and the fall were regarded as normative patterns for the secondary and punished status of women in both society and the social structure of the church.

> Let a woman learn silence in all submissiveness. I permit no woman to teach or to have authority over men. She is to keep silent. For Adam was formed first; then Eve. And Adam was not deceived, but the woman was deceived and became a transgressor. Yet the woman will be saved through bearing children. . . .
>
> 1 Tim 2:11–15

In the pastorals the patriarchal family emerges as normative for the church, unlike the synoptics and Paul where the church as a messianic movement stands in some tension with the family. Bishops, elders, and deacons are to be selected from male heads of families who have proven their worth by their ability to manage their marriages and households. The ministry of women survives in the pastorals in a female deaconate: 1 Tim 3:11. But it has become a separate, marginal office, unlike Paul's reference to Phoebe the deacon: Rom 16:1, which makes no distinction between her office and that of a male deacon. The church of the pastoral epistles was also engaged in a struggle with radical gnostic Christians who regarded the marital order as superseded by Christ: 1 Tim 4:1-7.

These contradictory tendencies—on the one hand, a belief in the beginnings of a new eschatological order in the church that overcomes the hierarchy of male over female, and, on the other hand, the idea that the hierarchy of male over female is the order of "nature" and is to be affirmed as the normative social order of the world—shape the response of the early church to the question of women. There is evidence that this was a "question" in the early centuries of the church. Belief that a messianic order has already begun set off utopian thinking about the levelings of class, race, and sex distinctions. Pagans were aware that even slave girls were given an "unseemly" authority in the Christian community.[5] Gnostic radicals wished to push the idea of eschatological transcendence to a doctrine of total rejection of marriage as normative for the baptized.[6]

Women in Patristic Anthropology

The pattern of thinking toward women and sexuality was shaped by the balancing of these contradictory tendencies, as understood within the dualistic religious culture of that time. The church rejected the idea of celibacy as normative for all Christians, affirming the goodness of marriage and procreation as a part of the created order. But it gradually came to sanction the idea of a celibate elite who were regarded as anticipating the eschatological order of heaven "in which there will be neither marrying nor giving in marriage."[7] Within the married world the patriarchal headship of men over women was firmly maintained. But the concept of a celibate elite relativized the normativeness of marriage. It now came to be regarded as a secondary vocation of those who did not have the virtue or self-discipline to aspire to the higher holiness.

Moreover, the patriarchal pattern of headship of males was regarded as normative for the institutional order of the church, as well as that of society. This divided the celibate elite of males from the celibate vocation for women. Although equal in holiness, they were not equal in authority. For the male celibacy and priesthood were united. Those who wished to be priests and bishops should aspire to the holiness of celibacy and set aside marital relations.[8] Women, on the other hand, were not called to the priesthood or even to the ministry of public teaching. Therefore celibacy did not open for them opportunities of public authority in the church. It remained a vocation of private holiness.

As we come to the church of the fourth century, the period of the establishment of the church under the Emperor Constantine and his heirs, and the age of the great Church Fathers and doctrinal councils, we see the pattern I have outlined above achieve its fixed and normative form. Jerome and Augustine in the West, the Cappadocian Fathers in the East, reflect a concept of Christian life molded by ascetic and monastic spirituality. We also can recognize a certain pejorative influence of the ascetic dualism on the image of both sexuality and femaleness. Although women were no more bodily and sexual than men, the male perspective tended to equate the dualism of soul or mind over body with the dualism of male over female. Women come to be regarded as closer to the flesh than men. The negative view of sex and the body is assimilated into a negative view of women as spiritually inferior to men and more identified with the carnal instincts. This creates a fearful view of sex and a fanatical misogyny toward women that becomes characteristic of the Christian monastic tradition. This is different from Judaism, which, although it regarded women as socially subordinate, had a much more positive view of sexuality.

The analogy of male and female to soul and body is characteristic of the anthropology of the Church Fathers. The analogy is found in Greek philosophy, especially Aristotle, who equates the male with the principle of headship and women with the carnal or material principle.[9] This idea is developed in ascetic spirituality in the hellenistic Jewish philosopher, Philo. The Greek Church Fathers, especially Origen, were directly dependent on the exegetical tradition which Philo had established in

Alexandria in the first century A.D. Philo interpreted the original image of God in humanity of Genesis 1:27 as asexual. The image of God refers to the asexual, spiritual or intellectual principle of the soul. Sexuality, or the dualism of male and female, for Philo, does not refer to the same principle as the image of God, but is a distinct and lower element added to human nature with a view to its fallenness and mortality (and, therefore, need to reproduce itself). Both men and women are dualistisms of spirit and body. Spiritually they partake of the principle of the image of God. In their bodily beings, they partake of the lower principle of sexual dualism.

But Philo also read the intellectual principle of the image of God as analogous to maleness; the bodily principle as analogous to femaleness. This allows him to regard women as images and paradigms of the lower material principle that drags down the spiritual principle and mires it in sinful flesh. The creation of Eve is regarded as an image of the fall of the original androgenous Adam in which the lower female or material principle separates out and is no longer under the control of the male mind. Instead it becomes an antagonist and tempter. Salvation, for Philo, consists in a struggle against the flesh and an aspiration toward the single, contemplative life in which the spiritual principle of the intellect would be freed from the flesh to commune with the mind of God.[10]

The Greek Church Fathers, such as Origen in the third century and Gregory of Nyssa in the late fourth century, followed Philo in these views. Nyssa believed that the image of God in humanity is monistic. Bisexuality refers to the bodily nature, which is not made in God's image, but with a view to the fall of the soul into carnality, sin, and death. Humanity is a compound of the divine, incorporeal nature, to which the soul corresponds, and the irrational, material nature of brutes, toward which the body tends. Only the spiritual part partakes of the divine image, while bisexuality has no correspondence to the divine archetype. The original, unfallen Adam in paradise would not have married or procreated sexually, but would have been immortal like the angels. Sexuality appears through the fall. Monastic celibacy is a return to the original monistic Adam of paradise, an anticipation of the angelic state of heaven.[11]

Augustine tells the story of human creation and fall with a somewhat different emphasis. For him bisexuality would have been a part of the original humanity of paradise. The unfallen Adam would have been a compound of male spirit and female corporeality. When Eve was taken from Adam's side, she was taken from him in order to be his helpmeet. But she is a helpmeet only in procreation. For any intellectual task another male would be more suitable.[12] In paradise the female and bodily "side" of "man" would have been strictly subordinate and obedient to its male head. The unfallen Adam would have experienced a complete harmony of spirit and body, the one commanding, the other obeying. In paradise, moreover, there would have been no experience of lust or libido in sexual procreation. In paradise the male would have "used" the woman without sensual feeling, just as he moves his hand or foot, dispassionately, and totally under the control of the rational will. There would have been no uncontrolled rush of disordered affection and spontaneous tumescence of the male sexual organ. But the male would have sowed his seed in the woman with the same objectivity as a farmer sows seed in field.[13]

For Augustine, the essence of the fall is the disordering of rational control over the body and its feelings. The male mind loses control over the body. His sexuality becomes disordered, so that he now experiences uncontrolled erections. Augustine looks at the male erection and sexual libido as the seat of that fallen or disordered state of humanity after the fall; the "law of the members that wars against the law of the mind." Here in the fallen state, therefore, it is impossible to engage in the sexual act, even within marriage, without sin. Every sexual act is sinful because of the lust that accompanies it. This taints every child with original sin, which Augustine believes to be transmitted through the sexual act. In marriage this sin is forgiven (venial), if the intent of the sexual act is solely to produce a child. Sex in marriage may also be seen as a "remedy of concupiscence," thus preventing disordered lust from breaking its legal bounds. But if a married couple engages in sex for pleasure and prevents conception, the sexual act is seriously sinful (mortal), and tantamount to fornication.[14] Thus Augustine's view of sexuality is the foundation of unfortunate views which have continued to shape Western Catholicism down to recent times.

In Augustine the image of God becomes more specifically a male principle. The domination of male over female is seen as analogous to the domination of mind over body. This leads Augustine even to deny that women possess the image of God autonomously, in their own right. The woman possesses the image of God only when taken together with the male who is her head. In herself alone, however, she symbolizes the bodily principle that must be subordinate to its head, the male. Thus in his treatise on the Trinity, Augustine says:

> How then did the apostle tell us that the man is the image of God and therefore he is forbidden to cover his head, but that the woman is not so, and therefore she is commanded to cover hers? Unless forsooth according to that which I have said already, when I was treating of the nature of the human mind, that the woman, together with her own husband, is the image of God, so that the whole substance may be one image, but when she is referred to separately in her quality as a helpmeet, which regards the woman alone, then she is not the image of God, but, as regards the man alone, he is the image of God as fully and completely as when the woman too is joined with him in one.[15]

One could hardly state more clearly the theological underpinnings of the view of the male as normative and generic humanity, while the woman is nonnormative and auxiliary to the human species!

For Augustine the sexually "loose" or the willful woman is regarded as the essence of sin. She expresses the disorder of the carnal nature in revolt against its head. The only proper role for woman is complete submission to the male, even to his unjust commands. His own mother, submissive to the demands even of a crude husband, stands, for Augustine, for the highest aspirations of woman.[16] Here woman helps restore the lost harmony to the human species by restoring that domination of mind over body, male over female, of the ordinal hierarchy of creation. Yet even as totally submissive woman in her sexual nature symbolizes, for Augustine, the fall of the soul. As he puts it in his *Soliloquies:*

> I feel that nothing so casts down the manly mind from its heavenly heights as the fondling of woman and those bodily contacts which belong to the married state.[17]

Thus, for Augustine, as for Nyssa, the higher salvation for humanity, and indeed the normative salvation, now that Christ has come, is to eschew marriage for celibacy.

Augustine believes that the blessings upon marriage and procreation in the scriptures were given only in reference to the old dispensation of the Jews.[18] Here even polygamy was allowed for the purpose of hastening the completion of the race of Israel from which Christ was to be born. Polygamy was allowed only for males, of course, not for females, since, as he puts it, "Nature allows multiplicity in subjugations, but demands singularity in dominations."[19] Many members can serve one head and many slaves one master, but not vice versa. Here we see how fundamental for Augustine is the analogy of male and female to head and body, domination and subjugation.

Now that Christ has been born, the blessings upon procreation have been rescinded. The virginal order is the command of the New Testament which finds its completion in the eschatological realm of heaven. Marriage is still allowed, but it has become a secondary option; permissible, but no longer necessary. As more and more people become Christians and choose the celibate life, the end of the world will be hastened. The whole creation will approach its transcendence in the eschatological order of the resurrection. Here and now pagans produce enough children from the physical point of view. Christians can take over these children and raise them to the higher Christian vocation.[20] Here we see how closely Augustine's views approach a gnostic dualism, although he stops short of its ultimate logic. The bodily and the material world were created by God and are good, when dominated by the mind and used by them within their own place. Then they are to be transcended by the higher order of the spirit. When they assert demands of their own to which the mind must conform, they represent sin and the fall.

The analogy of femaleness and carnality in patristic thought creates contradictory views of woman when it comes to considering her salvation and the possibility that she too might aspire to the celibate life. The Fathers never deny that woman, as much as men, have been redeemed by Christ and are capable of aspiring to the eschatological life of the spirit. Indeed it was evident to enthusiasts of the monastic life, such as Jerome, that many of their best followers came from the female side. Here we get an unexamined contradiction in patristic anthropology between what women "are" and what they "symbolize." In themselves they have to be accepted as beings who have minds as well as bodies, who are as capable as men of disciplining the body and aspiring to the life of the spirit. Yet, from the male perspective, they symbolize the carnal nature. The Church Fathers seldom can eschew the tendency to speak about women as though they have a lesser capacity for virtue. The female "nature" is described as though it were peculiarly prone to the vices of pettiness, sensuality, materialism, and maliciousness. The virtues of the mind, such as chastity, patience, wisdom, temperance, fortitude, and justice are equated with masculinity.[21] Consequently when a woman rejects marriage and procreation and aspires to the contemplative life, she is spoken of as if she has transcended not only the bodily nature, but her female nature. This accounts for the peculiar habit in patristic and medieval spirituality of referring to the female ascetic as if she had ceased to be a female. By rejecting the flesh, the female has become "manly."[22]

At least on the level of holiness, celibacy is treated in patristic writing as if it released woman from male domination. Celibacy releases woman from the curse of Eve, which is to bear children in sorrow and to be under the domination of the male. The celibate woman no longer has the male as her head, but rather she rises to the manly estate and is directly under Christ. In the words of the African doctor of the church Cyprian, in his address to virgins:

> You do not fear the sorrows of woman or their groans. You have no fear of the birth of children. Nor is your husband your master, but your Master and Head is Christ, in the likeness and in the place of man.[23]

Thus as celibacy allows men to transcend human nature and anticipate the angelic nature, it allows women to transcend female nature and become equivalent to the male. Here we see how fundamental hierarchical thinking is to the Church Fathers. The ladder of being is a great hierarchy of superior and inferior, ranging from God to the angels, to male and then female, then the brutes and material world. The fall is a slippage down the hierarchy. Redemption is a return back up the hierarchy to its spiritual and divine pole. Dionysius the Areopagite, in the fifth century, would spell out even more elaborately this hierarchical "Great Chain of Being" in patristic neoplatonic thought.[24]

To sum up our discussion of patristic anthropology so far; ascetic spirituality gave a double message to women. On the one hand, it habitually equated soul and body with male and female, thus giving a pejorative image to female nature. On the other hand, it treated women as persons as equally capable of aspiring to ascetic salvation and suggested to them that by so doing they could transcend their female nature, as well as their bodily finitude. Asceticism redeemed woman from the female condition. It gave women a license to reject the traditional demands placed upon them by society; to marry, often older men chosen by their families for political reasons; to have children for the patriarchal family; to remain confined to the narrow lifestyle of domesticity; to be denied the adventures and higher education of their brothers.

Celibacy opened up to women new vistas. Those unhappily married or reluctant to marry, burdened with too early and frequent childbearing, could reject these roles. They could withdraw into female communities to engage in intense study and cultivation of their minds and spirits. They could even throw over the traces of their lives in the family and take off for high adventures in the mysterious East to found monastic communities in Palestine or the Egyptian desert. These female monastic communities were founded and run by women, often with very little ecclesiastical supervision in this early period of "do it yourself" monasticism when there were no organized religious orders. It should not surprise us, therefore, that ascetic spirituality was very attractive to many women in the fourth century. Many women heard this liberating side of the monastic message and ignored or overlooked the misogynist side.

We tend to be impressed by the antisexual aspects of asceticism, since this no longer corresponds to our own beliefs about human nature and how to go about making it "whole." So we tend to think of the ascetic call as very oppressive, especially for women. But I believe that it was not experienced this way in the fourth century. However hard it may be for us to understand, ascetic dualism was the normal *zeitgeist* of the fourth century, accepted by all higher culture, hellenistic as well as Christian. It corresponded to the "normal" presuppositions of the times. Women would not have been put off by this. Instead they would have been impressed by the freedom it gave them to shed the oppressive aspects of their female condition and role and aspire to a new life of inward development and constructive activity whose rewards were no less than heaven itself! It allowed women to move from being an object, governed and defined by others, to being a subject, in charge of and defining one's own life as a spiritual person. This is the essence of the liberating choice, and was experienced as such by women in this period.

Mothers of the Church in the Fourth Century

If we read between the lines of the patristic letters and treatises, it becomes evident that women flocked to asceticism in large numbers. The Egyptian deserts were filled, not only with male, but with female monastic aspirants. Not surprisingly, many of the powerful foundresses and leaders of this movement were women of the upper classes, who often became Christians earlier than their husbands, fathers, and sons. The males of the upper classes were more closely tied to paganism, as the religion of political power and civil life. Political life entailed obligations to the old religion as a part of the male public identity. Women had no such ties to the old religion. Christianity often entered the families of the upper classes through the distaff side. Those women of the upper classes of the Roman and provincial nobility played an important role in promoting enthusiasm for monastic spirituality. Often it was their money which bankrolled the foundations of their more famous associates, such as Jerome and Rufinus of Aquileia. The male bias of the public tradition of the church conceals the fact that often it was these women who were the originators and stronger partners in shaping their monastic communities.

I will mention several examples of such female leadership in monastic foundations in the fourth century. There was Macrina, the sister of the Cappadocians, Basil the Great, and Gregory of Nyssa. She was the originator of the ascetic life for this family circle, and perhaps should be credited with being the first source of that monastic plan that came to be called the Basilian Rule. She opted for the ascetic life in her teens, resisting family efforts to marry her. She is described as the "father, teacher, paedagogue, and counselor" for her brother Peter, born post-humously.[25] She brought her mother into the ascetic life and converted the family estates into a monastic community of prayer and charitable service some decades before either of her more famous brothers turned away from "the world." Nyssa describes her as the primary influence in converting Basil to monasticism after he returned from many years of study of rhetoric in the great seats of learning, "puffed up" with worldly ambition.

> But Macrina took him over and lured him so quickly to the goal of philosophy that he withdrew from worldly show and began to look down upon acclaim through oratory and went over to this life full of labors for his hand to perform, providing for himself through his complete poverty a mode of living that would without impediment lead to virtue.[26]

Gregory Nyssa acclaims Macrina as the chief source in his own spiritual development. Not inappropriately he makes her the voice of spiritual authority and inspiration in his treatise on the soul, which he writes as a dialogue with Macrina.[27]

Another powerful group of women in monastic leadership came from the circle of Roman aristocratic women whose family connections linked them to the most powerful senatorial class. The foundress of this circle was Marcella who adopted an ascetic regime of prayer, fasting, and study in her palace on the Aventine about 352 A.D. She was inspired by models of asceticism from Egypt, popularized in Rome during the exile of Athanasius in the early forties.[28] She gathered about her a band of like-minded women who met for scripture study in her home. The circle included her sister, Asella, her mother, Albina, and the patrician widow, Lea. Marcella was described by Jerome as the "head of a monastery who showed herself a true mother to the virgins in it."[29] The prominent widow Paula was drawn into this circle in the seventies, along with her children, especially her daughter, Eustochium. About a decade earlier, in the mid-sixties another well-born widow, Melania, also joined this circle of noble ascetic women who converted their palaces into refuges for the practice of monastic life.

About 372 A.D. Melania left Rome to tour the monastic settlements of Egypt. After several years of work and involvement in the life of these solitaries of the Egyptian desert, as well as the controversies of the Alexandrian church, she moved to

Jerusalem and there founded a monastery on the Mount of Olives (about 377 A.D.). Her friend, Rufinus, joined her there some years later (c. 379/80). Together they developed a monastery for men under his care, as well as her own community for some fifty virgins. It was primarily Melania's funds that constructed both communities. They followed the rule of Basil in developing their monastic order. There was also a *scriptorum,* and the monasteries partially supported themselves by copying manuscripts. Melania pursued her own studies in the writings of such Christian authorities as Origen, Gregory (of Nyssa?), and Basil.[30]

In 382 A.D. the learned monk Jerome arrived in Rome and was drawn into the learned circle of women on the Aventine as their mentor, especially in the controversial study of the scriptures in the original Hebrew, which he pioneered. His promotion of asceticism in Rome led to increasingly acrimonious conflict. Finally he was given his walking papers by the Roman synod of clergy, thus ending his hopes for leadership in the Roman church through his office as secretary to the bishop of Rome, Damasus.[31] He had grown particularly close to Paula and her daughter Eustochium. When he was forced out of Rome in 385 A.D., Paula and her daughter arranged to leave also and to meet him in the East, probably in Antioch.

Together Paula, Jerome, and Eustochium made the customary grand tour of the hermit communities of Egypt, an adventure that was de rigeur for those attracted to monastic life. They also drew on Jerome's biblical lore to make an extensive tour of the holy places of the scriptures throughout the Near East. During this tour they visited Jerusalem, and there stayed with Melania and Rufinus in their monastic community. It was this double monastery that provided the model for their own. After their travels, Jerome and Paula returned to Palestine. In Bethlehem they planted a monastic settlement that was to be their homes for the rest of their lives.[32] With Paula's funds they constructed on the site of the nativity three monastic complexes for women and one for men, as well as a basilica and a hospice.

The leadership of this "spiritual kingdom" was to be inherited by Eustochium when her mother died in 404 A.D. Paula's granddaughter, Paula the Younger, child of her son Toxotius (who had remained in Rome), was born in 400 A.D. Jerome wrote a famous treatise on the ascetic upbringing of this Christian babe. A few years after her birth the child was brought to Bethlehem to grow up in her grandmother's monastery.[33] Similarly Melania's granddaughter, Melania the Younger, was to journey to Jerusalem in 418 A.D. to found additional monastic communities in the neighborhood of those of her grandmother.[34] Thus monastic establishments not only were outlets for women's autonomous creative energies. For a while they became something of a matrilineal establishment, drawing in the daughters and granddaughters of their foundresses.

Yet, despite the great scope provided women's energies by celibacy and monasticism, the church put significant limits on their ability to function as public leaders of the church. Not only were even these most holy women forbidden any ordained leadership, but it was dogmatically decreed that women could not be regarded as public teachers of the church. Despite their great learning in theology and biblical exegesis (Jerome testifies that these women's Greek and Hebrew abilities rivaled his own),[35] they could be consulted as teachers only in private. Publicly it was forbidden that they should be regarded as sources of teaching authority. This view undoubtedly accounts for the fact that no writings are preserved under their name. Although study and exegesis was a central part of their monastic lives, they produced no treatises for public circulation.

They wrote extensive letters of theological and scriptural inquiry and advice. In the case of the Church Fathers, such as Jerome, Basil, Gregory Nazianzus, Augustine, and others, the classical custom of collecting and preserving a corpus of such letters brings this genre of writing down to us. But no such collection was made of the letters of the women. We have only the male side of the correspondence. Thus we are in the unfortunate position of having to read the lives of these women through the pens of their male admirers (or detractors!). The repression of these women as public teachers is evident in the following comments on the scholarly acumen of Marcella, which appears in a letter of Jerome:

> Whatever in me was the fruit of long study and, as such, made by constant meditation a part of my nature, this she tasted, this she learned and made her own. Consequently, after my departure from Rome, in case of a dispute arising as to the testimony of scripture on any subject, recourse was had to her to settle it. And so wise was she and so well did she understand what the philosophers call *to prepon;* that is, what is becoming, that when she answered questions she gave her own opinion, not as her own, but as from me or someone else, thus admitting that what she taught, she had learned from others. For she knew what the apostle said, "I suffer not a woman to teach" and she would not seem to inflict a wrong upon the male sex, many of whom (including some priests) questioned her concerning doubtful and obscure points.[36]

Whether Marcella really took such a retiring view of her authority, we shall never know. It is clear that she did not wait for male leadership to start her community. She certainly felt able to form exegetical judgments in her own right, however much she may have represented them as coming from Jerome or others. In any case Jerome makes clear what the male church regarded as "becoming" for women, indeed necessary for her to be regarded as "saintly." The loss of any writings from these women themselves is a direct result of the official view of women as banned from the public teaching tradition of the church by reason of their sex. Thus what the monastic tradition gave to women with one hand, the church took away with the other. Women were regarded as freed from the curse of Eve and elevated to equal holiness with men through asceticism. But perish the thought that this equality in holiness should give them a public status of authority equal to men in the church! This ambiguous attitude toward women continues to plague the Catholic tradition down to the present time.

Patristic Mariology

Another important development of ascetic spirituality in relation to women is found in the development of mariology. Mariology flowered in Western spirituality in the late fourth century and must be regarded as a direct expression of the ascetic movement. The idea of the virgin birth and the suggestion that Mary, Jesus' mother, is a paradigm of the believing Israel, make their appearance in the New Testament: Luke 1:26-56. But any sustained reflection on mariology is absent in New Testament theology. Justin Martyr and Irenaeus of Lyon develop the theme of Mary as the New Eve.[37] But mariological reflection does not play any important part in their thought. Mariological piety probably makes its first inroads in gnostic circles, with speculation on Sophia, the figure of cosmic wisdom. It is in the apocryphal gospels, rejected by mainstream Christianity, such as the second century *Evangelium of James,* that the themes of perpetual virginity *in partu* and *post partum* are first elaborated.[38]

However, by the fourth century, particularly among ascetic enthusiasts like Jerome, these themes are embraced and raised to the status of doctrines which must be accepted by all orthodox Christians. Mary as perpetual virgin becomes the model of monastic life and the vindication of the superiority of virginity over marriage in the new dispensation. Jerome considers it horrifying and blasphemous to imagine that the mother of Christ, having first experienced the higher state of virginity, would have lapsed after the birth of Christ into the lower state of ordinary marital relations! Those, such as the churchmen Helvidius and Jovinian, who suggest that both marriage and virginity are equally honored in the church, and that Mary is a model for the equality of the two vocations, are repulsed by Jerome and Ambrose with angry denunciations. Their views are defined as heretical and scandalous.[39] The earlier church's tradition that Jesus had siblings is repressed. These figures in the scriptural tradition are redefined as "cousins," although this interpretation is of doubtful historicity. Thus a new emphasis on the virginity of Mary, not merely as a condition of Jesus' sinless birth, but also as a theme of mariological piety in its own right, flows from ascetic spirituality. As women are scorned as physical objects of love, a new spiritual mother and mistress takes their place as an object of sublimated adoration of a sinless and virginal "femininity."

Patristic spirituality also focuses upon the feminine image of the church. Both the Old and New Testaments image the People of God in feminine terms, as a wife or bride of God. In the New Testament, this is particularly expressed in the theme of the church as bride of Christ: Eph 5:25-27. But this is understood as an eschatological union, a revelation of the redeemed church. It cannot easily stand as an image of actual physical marriage. Instead the bridal church comes to be understood as a union which expresses a rejection and transcendence of carnal marriage in the new Christian dispensation. Physical marriage lowers the partners into carnality and produces children tainted with sin. By contrast, the church is a virginal mother. Birth in her womb is rebirth from the carnality of sinful birth. The womb of the church is the waters of baptism. Those reborn through the virginal womb of the church have left behind the carnal state of their original birth. From the bridal union of Christ and the church are born, not sinners, but virgins! Many of the Church Fathers speculate upon this virginal union of Christ and the church which reverses the sinful effects of carnal union. Thus Cyprian, speaking of the virgins of the church, hymns them as the flower of the church's insemination by Christ:

> Through them Mother Church rejoices in her glorious fruitfulness, and in them it flowers in abundance; and the more an abounding virginity adds to its numbers, the greater is the mother's joy.[40]

These themes of the virginal motherhood of the church were readily assimilated into mariological piety, despite the historical difficulty of speaking of Jesus's mother as also his bride! In the doctrinal disputes of the early fifth century, the title Mother of God was defended, despite the earlier connections of this title with a monophysite Christology.[41] The first apocryphal accounts of Mary's Assumption also were written in this period. Although they were originally condemned as unhistorical by the Roman pope, they quickly came to occupy a firm place in popular piety.[42]

Thus the church, which despised and feared the physical sexuality of women, also promoted, as a sublimated compensation, a spiritual image of the feminine as object of elevation and adoration. The female virgins of the church could look to the virginal mother of Jesus as their model, as they themselves reflected her dignity in the church. On the plane of institutional authority, the virginal woman and her daughters were denied a voice. But on the plane of equality in holiness, she mounted up to heaven to take her place beside the Ancient of Days, and his Son, the Christ. Christians could direct their prayers to her, knowing that her mother's heart would assure that pleas that went to Christ through her would gain a particularly persuasive hearing.

Thus we see that the spirituality of the patristic period is fraught with particular ambiguities for women. On the one hand, the idea of equality in Christ might have suggested an understanding of salvation which overcame the traditional subordination of women. On the other hand, ascetic dualism, with its equation of femaleness and carnality, deepened the negativity toward women and injected a pathological misogyny foreign to biblical tradition. The theme of a new equality is maintained in asceticism, but at the price of a negation of female sexuality and an inferiorized image even of marital procreation. Men and women are equal only in an eschatological transcendence of the bodily and the female natures. But this equality does not become a prophetic power to transform the inequality of women in their actual institutional relations in society or the church. Instead it deepens the doctrine of their servitude.

If the pastorals taught that women are saved by bearing children, patristic spirituality taught that women are *better* saved by an exaltation of self-abnegation that entails the discarding of physical motherhood. Catholic spirituality today has only begun to come to terms with the contradictions of this legacy toward the sexual and the female. We have only begun to imagine a more biblical understanding of creation and salvation in which redemption in Christ affirms the equal dignity of persons, not against, but in and through history and the flesh. Only when redemption in Christ is understood as historical, as an affirmation of God's original intention for creation, rather than a rejection of creation, will it become possible to see the great New Testament theme of equality in Christ as a mandate, not merely of flight from the world, but of transformation of the world in the direction of justice.

NOTES

1. C.S. Vos, *Women in Old Testament Worship* (Delft: Judels and Brinkman, 1968). Raphael Loewe, *The Position of Women in Judaism* (London: S.P.C.K., 1966).

2. See R. Ruether, "You Shall Call No Man Father: Sexism, Hierarchy and Liberation" in *Women and the Word: Sermons,* ed. Helen G. Crotwell (Fortress, 1978), pp. 92-99.

3. Elisabeth Fiorenza, "Die Rolle der Frau in der Urchristlichen Bewegung," *Concilium* 7 (1978), pp. 3-9.

4. See Constance Parvey, "Women in the New Testament," in *Religion and Sexism: Images of Women in the Jewish and Christian Traditions,* ed. R. Ruether (Simon and Schuster, 1974), pp. 138-9.

5. See the letter of Pliny the Elder to the Emperor Trajan, X.8 where two Christian slavegirls are described as holding the office of deaconess.

6. Arthur Vööbus, *Celibacy as a Requirement for Baptism in the*

Early Syrian Church. (Stockholm: Papers of the Estonian Theological Society in Exile, 1951).

7. See William Phipps, *Was Jesus Married?* (Harper and Row, 1970), pp. 142–63.

8. For the union of the power of celibacy and that of priesthood, see Samuel Laeuchli, *Power and Sexuality: The Emergence of Canon Law at the Council of Elvira* (Temple University Press, 1972).

9. Aristotle, *Politics* Bk. 1, ch. 5.

10. Richard Baer, *Philo's Use of the Categories of Male and Female* (Leiden: Brill, 1970), *passim.*

11. Gregory Nyssa, *De Opif. Hom.* 6.

12. Augustine, *De Grat. Ch. et de Pecca Orig.* II, 40; *De Genesi ad Lit.* 9, 5.

13. Augustine, *De Civitate Dei* 14, 24–26.

14. Augustine, *De Grat. Ch. et de Pecca Orig.* II, 41; *De Nupt. et Concup.* I, 6–7, 21, 33.

15. Augustine, *De Trinitate* 7.7.10.

16. Augustine, *Confess.* 9.

17. I.10.

18. Augustine, *De Nupt. et Concup.* I, 14–15; see also Jerome's *Adv. Jov.* I, 36.

19. Augustine, *De Bono Conj.* 17–20.

20. Augustine, ibid., 10; also *De Bono Viduit.* 9–11, 23–28.

21. Ambrose, *De Cain et Abel* I, 4.

22. For example, Leander of Seville, *De Instit. Virg.* preface.

23. Cyprian, *De Habitu Virg.* 22.

24. Pseudo-Dionysus the Areopagite, *De Caelesti Hierarchia* and *De Ecclesiastica Hierarchia.*

25. Gregory of Nyssa, *The Life of Macrina* in *Ascetical Works,* Fathers of the Church, vol. 58.

26. Ibid., p. 167.

27. Gregory of Nyssa, *On the Soul and the Resurrection.*

28. Jerome, *Ep.* 127.5.

29. Jerome, *Ep.* 23.2. See also J.N.D. Kelly, *Jerome* (Harper and Row, 1975), pp. 91–103.

30. Palladius, *The Lausiac History,* 46: see also F. X. Murphy, "Melania the Elder: A Biographical Note," *Traditio* 5 (1947), pp. 62–5.

31. Kelly, *Jerome*, p. 113.

32. Jerome, *Ep.* 108 (Life of Paula).

33. Jerome, *Ep.* 107.

34. Gerontius, *Vie de St. Mélanie.* Texte, Trad., et Notes, Deny Gorce, *Sources Chrétiennes* 90 (Paris: Ed. du Cerf, 1962).

35. Jerome, *Ep.* 108, 26–7.

36. Jerome, *Ep.* 107.7.

37. Justin Martyr, *Dialogue with Trypho* 100, 3; Irenaeus, *Adv. Haer.* 5, 19.

38. See H. Campenhausen, *The Virgin Birth in the Theology of the Ancient Church* (Allenson, 1964).

39. Jerome, *Adv. Helvid.;* Ambrose, *Ep. 48.* See Giovanni Miegge, *The Virgin Mary* (London: Lutterworth Pr., 1955), pp. 36–52.

40. Cyprian, *De Habitu Virg.* 3; See Joseph Plumpe, *Mater Ecclesia: An Inquiry into the Concept of the Church as Mother in Early Christianity* (Catholic University Press, 1964).

41. Miegge, *Virgin Mary*, pp. 58–67.

42. Pseudo-John the Evangelist, *The Book of the Falling Asleep of Mary* and Pseudo-Melito, *The Passing of Mary,* Ante-Nicene Fathers, vol. 8, pp. 587–600. See also R.L.P. Milburn, "The Assumption of Mary" in *Early Christian Interpretations of History* (Harper and Row, 1954), appendix.

5

The Finest Music
in the World: Exploring
Celtic Spiritual Legacies

Mary Aileen Schmiel

> I, proclaiming that there is
> Among birds or beasts or men
> One that is perfect or at peace,
> Danced on Cruachan's windy plain,
> Upon Cro-Patrick sang aloud;
> All that could run or leap or swim
> Whether in wood, water, or cloud,
> Acclaiming, proclaiming, declaiming Him.[1]

Early in the fifth century, one of the most decisive struggles in the history of Christianity was enacted. The principle contenders were a North African bishop and a British or Irish lay theologian. Their contest was centered in individual perceptions of human will and experience. But more importantly, a clash of whole cultures may be seen reflected there. St. Augustine was a son of the Roman Empire, which was then in the last phase of its decadence. His vision was profoundly colored, even molded, by the political chaos and philosophical negativism which pervaded the Mediterranean mindscape during that time of disintegration. Pelagius, on the other hand, came of that vast Northern civilization which the Romans called Gallic and the Greeks, *Keltoi*. If Augustine's thought is a manifestation of a marriage between disillusioned Neoplatonism and Christian hope, the worldview of Pelagius can be seen as a blend of healthy Celtic practicality and earthiness and Judaeo-Christian love-responsibility. We shall say more about their argument, but first let us look briefly at some of its results and examine the effects of Augustine's vistory on our own spiritual consciousness.

Judaism and Augustine

The Hebrew mind had no notion of the soul as separate from the body or of a life after death except through progeny until late in its history when it came under Persian influence. The early story of Adam's expulsion from paradise is a myth of origin, a way of explaining the human condition which was never intended as literal historical "truth" by its authors. Sin and evil entered the world through human disobedience, not through the act of creation as in Persian doctrine. The human being remains the image of a good God even after its "mistake," and the created earth is beautiful and good also. The idea of an objective state of metaphysical fallenness would be antithetical to the Hebrew perspective.[2]

The Hebrew consciousness from the very beginning was a political one. God and his Chosen People have a contractual relationship, with obligations on both sides. "Sin" is primarily a social phenomenon, related to the falling-away of kings, tribe, or individuals from their promise to live by "God's" laws. These laws, as in any tribal society, are largely concerned with justice within the community. Being faithful to Yahweh and behaving justly toward other people, especially the less fortunate, were really inseparable. The function of prophets and holy people was to call the people away from their chronic state of political "fallenness," i.e., worship of the material "false gods" of the neighboring peoples. The promised Messiah was always conceived of as a political champion more than an atonement offering, although that element is included also.[3]

Augustine, wrestling with these concepts, had no positive social experience upon which to draw, and being still somewhat under Manichean influence he had no real affinity for the natural world either. Like his spiritual mentor, Paul, he felt that he and the "true message" stood virtually alone against decadent tradition. Augustine conceived of sin, law, and nature as internal processes. Both the state of fallenness and that of "grace" or blessedness existed for him on an entirely metaphysical plane. He saw the story of Adam and Eve through both his philosophical background and his personal conversion experience. Having embraced Christianity he could no longer accept either the Manichean teaching that the material world is corrupt in essence, or the neoplatonic idea that corporeal existence is a punishment for sins committed on the ideal plane. But the experience of fallenness and of a redemption centered in Christ and his grace as an external agent were so immediate and indisputable to Augustine that he had to find some way of explaining them doctrinally. Unfortunately, it was not in his nature to admit of the possibility of different interpretations of the same experience.

In the course of his conflict with Pelagius, Augustine's theories of the fall and original sin, of grace and free will, evolved into full-grown doctrines which have formed the backbone of Western Christianity. Humankind was created pure but sinned through its own choice, and the resulting corruption is substantial and hereditary. All human beings since Adam and Eve have been born in a fallen state. Only the "elect" are redeemed (both election and salvation thus removed to a metaphysical level!), and then only through faith in Christ as atonement offering, through the arbitrary intervention of God, and through the sacraments of the institutional church.

The Exile of Human Creation Capacity

Reinhold Niebuhr has commented that Augustinian-based Christianity over-emphasizes the grace of *pardon* to the great detriment of the grace of *power* (the Creator's original gift).[4] This imbalance has so steadily dominated Western theology, particularly since the Reformation, that we are scarcely even aware of it. In concentrating exclusively on the fall-redemption process in a metaphysical context, we have systematically exiled all of the elements of positive creative power which are ours as creatures made in the Creator's image. In adopting a dualistic cosmology, by separating the City of God from the city of man/woman, we have divorced the law from the spirit, or political justice from religious consciousness. Even within religion, we have concentrated entirely upon "worship," which is directed toward transcendence of everyday life, and excluded celebration, which brings God-consciousness to earth. We are directed to consider the entire natural and sensual world a distraction, a stumbling-block to true spirituality.[5]

In focusing our spiritual questing upward and inward instead of outward, we ignore the gift of wonder which is the key to the kingdom of Heaven.[6] We forget what image-ination really means: the creating of images, which find their origin in the world of natural phenomena. In neglecting this capacity for sub-creation, we neglect the greatest of our potentialities.[7]

William Blake, in his revolt against the deadness of eighteenth century rationalism, made the statement that to be a Christian one must also be an artist. In his poetic cosmography, it was the exile of imagination, sensuality, passion, earth-consciousness that constituted the fall. It is our *perceptions* of our creative capacities which have "fallen," not their essence. "If the doors of perception were cleansed everything would appear to man as it is, infinite. For man has closed himself up, till he sees all things thro' narrow chinks in his cavern."[8] In constructing his mythical redemption saga, Blake called on prophetic models from the Judaic tradition, and also from the Celtic. The bard is for him a manifestation of the eternal redeemer of fallen consciousness, both individual and institutional.

Because of historical and theological bias, the Celtic mythological and philosophical legacy has been traditionally belittled or viewed with suspicion. The attitude that the classical Mediterranean is the only acceptable model for civilization has been the underlying assumption in Western thought since the Renaissance. However, now that "humanistic" trends seem to be over-reaching themselves and falling into decadence, the flaws inherent in our modern worldview are increasingly evident. The most obvious manifestations of this are the psychological and actual separation of technical knowledge from wisdom, power from love-responsibility, and most of humanity from its very source of being, the earth.

In seeking to repair the fragmentation of modern consciousness, many people turn to non-Western sources. The traditions of the Orient, of Africa, and of native America act as guidelines for many disillusioned Christians who find their own heritage corrupt beyond redeeming. But there is another route which presents itself. By going back and searching through some of the submerged parts of our own tradition, calling them to the foreground and restoring their importance, we may be able to resolve our dualistic spiritual consciousness into a more holistic one. The purpose of this essay is the exploration of Celtic spiritual models which may be helpful in our desire to restore creation-consciousness to religion and to secular life. I will begin with a brief discussion of early Celtic Christianity in general,[9] and will then present some of the main ideas of two medieval Celtic thinkers, Pelagius and John Scrotus Eriugena.

A Look at Pagan Ireland and the Coming of the Gospel

Although popular legend has Christianity coming to Ireland with St. Patrick in 432, the truth is that the faith had flourished there for more than a century before. In fact, the real reason for Patrick's mission was not to convert heathens but to try to bring the determinedly independent and antiauthoritarian Irish church under Rome's aegis. This was not to be accomplished for another four hundred years, however. Patrick and his helpers were if anything converted to the Celtic system rather than the other way around!

No one knows exactly when or how the Christian message first came to the island, but we do know that it assimilated itself peacefully into the existing political structure.[10] There seems to have been contact with the Greek and Judaic world even before the advent of Christianity, and these influences remained throughout the Middle Ages.

Early Irish society was tribal in nature. Its laws and general order bear a distinct resemblance to the Hebrew. The justice system was complex and all-pervasive, concerned with blood-ties, debts, injuries, and the rights of the disadvantaged. Judicial matters were formally presided over by the king or clan-chieftain, but the real mediator was the poet-priest, who sat at the king's right hand. These *filidh* (seers), also called druids (literally, "oak-sages"), were the guardians of all knowledge both legal and mystical. Beneath them were the house-poets, or *bardai,* whose job it was to compose verses of praise or satire, as the occasion warranted. It is easy to see how these poets also served an informal judicial function. In a clan society, the worst possible fate is ostracism, and this would inevitably result from a bard's reproach. There were also several orders known as "superfluous poets" in that their only court function was entertainment. In this category were harpers, pipers, jesters, and acrobats, and their persons were also respected and held sacred.

The Celtic peoples relied on oral transmission almost exclusively. In fact, the only place they used writing was on burial monuments, for which they used an alphabet based on the Druidic tree-calendar.[11] Laws, history, family trees, and religious knowledge were all memorized and passed on from generation to generation by the *filidh.* The reason for this custom is not that they lacked knowledge of "civilized" language; their command of the Greek alphabet has been attested to by Greek visitors in the centuries before Christ. But the Celts held the memory in the highest regard and feared to weaken it by cultivating a dependence on artificial tools. This was remarked upon by no less illustrious an observer than Julius Caesar.[12] They had several hundred forms of metre, all of which had to be mastered by the poet-priests. Rhymes and symbolic constructions helped as a mnemonic device in the case of the laws, and in mystical rites they were instrumental in evoking moods by incantation.

In addition to their social, legal, artistic, and religious functions, the *filidh* were also indispensable in warfare. Before a battle the chief poets of the opposing sides would hold a frenzied verbal contest. If one was clearly victorious, the battle might not have to be fought at all. If not, they would have succeeded in arousing their armies to the state of *furor* which so terrified their enemies.

The Celtic mind acknowledged no real dichotomy between reality and fantasy, between this world and the world "beyond." The doors of perception stood perpetually ajar, and all people were open to visionary states. The special function of the *filidh* was to live on the threshold of the two worlds. Physical death was considered merely "a pause in a long life."[13] Facing death courageously, fulfilling one's duty, and behaving with respect toward companions and enemies alike were the obligations of a warrior.

The concept of divine power diffused through all nature forms the basis of the ancient religion of the Celts. The scattered tales that survive are concerned with shamanism, sorcery (in the sense of simple earth-magic; the demonic connection was a late Christian invention) and animal shape-shifting by both gods and humans. Unlike the Hebrews, the Celts had no notion of a God who was "wholly other" nor of the human as something radically different from the rest of the natural world. Consequently there was no linear, discursive history per se, everything was conceptualized metaphorically.

> Till Greece and Rome created a new culture, a sense of the importance of man, ... nobody wrote history, nobody described anything as we understand description. One called up the image of something by comparing it with something else. ... One was less interested in man ... than in divine revelations, in changes among the heavens and the gods, which can hardly be expressed at all, and only by myth, by symbol, by enigma. One was always losing oneself in the unknown and rushing to the limits of the world. Imagination was all in all.[14]

It is because of this metaphorical mindset, so different from the literalism of the Levant at that time,[15] that the "letter" and "spirit" of the law never diverged in Celtic tradition. This is an important point to keep in mind in regard to the assimilation of Christianity into the pagan tradition.

The tales of the wandering carpenter who was the son of the Lord of the Universe had appeal for the Irish people on many levels. His method of teaching through symbolic parables resembled their own bardic tradition, and the virtues he extolled were in many ways similar to their own ideals. They took him to their hearts as a human guide and friend. But they also related him to the mystical side of their cultural consciousness. His death by tree-hanging parallels sacrificial fertility rites dating back to pre-Celtic times.[16] And in his glorious aspect he was compared with Lugh of the Long (or generous) Hand, the kind and beautiful sun god who also died and rose again. The two worlds, practical and mystical, are thus perfectly joined in Jesus.

The Old Testament, too, become very important to the early Celtic Christians. This was no doubt partly due to their love of a good story. But the idea that law is an integral part of faith is clearly evident also. In St. Paul's "Letter to the Galatians" he deplores the dedication of those Eastern Celts to the Judaic law and customs such as circumcision.[17]

Another typically Celtic trait is reflected in the same epistle where Paul finds it necessary to rebuke the congregation for their unwillingness to forego their attachment to "elemental spirits, seasons, solstices," etc.[18] The Western Celts were more fortunate and escaped such severe criticisms until many centuries later. The pagan deities, forces, and festivals found their way naturally into the Christian calendar, and the cult of Jesus brought a host of personalities who blended with native ones with whom they had something in common. Great Pan never died in Celtia.

Poetic Remnants of the Assimilation

The highest ideals of pagan Celtic society are found expressed in the triad "truth in the heart, strength in the arm, eloquence in the tongue." In the poetic sagas we find constant emphasis on these and on preservation of balance and harmony between human and natural forces, between head and heart, and between masculine and feminine wisdom. Heroes were taught the art of war by wise-women who laid as much stress on healing as on killing.[19] Of Conchobar, son of a Druid and a great queen and himself king of Ulster at the time of Christ, we read: "There was no wiser being in the world. He never gave a judgement until it was ripe, lest it be wrong and the crops worsen."[20] Such was the link between fertility and justice,[21] which is reminiscent of the Hebrew idea that natural disasters are caused by breaches in the justice contract with God.[22] Conchobar is a pivotal figure in mythology between the two eras. According to the story, he met his death on the day of the crucifixion when he saw a vision of the events at Calvary. He was so overcome by grief and anger at the injustice of what he saw that he, in effect, died of compassion. Some accounts add that he foresaw the coming of the risen Christ as a wiser king than he, and so allowed himself to slip through to the other world, the last of the old order.

Myth and history meet with St. Patrick. He plays a leading role in the tales of the hero Fionn McCool and his companions, who exemplify the pagan virtues and are the precursors of the Arthurian characters. Fionn's son Oisin returns from three hundred years in the enchanted Western Isles to find the Fenians long dead and Patrick's monastery where their fort had been.[23] The saint and the unrepentant pagan argue, but it is friendly squabbling. Again, the values are more similar than different:

> Just by the strength of their hands
> The Fenians battles were fought,
> With never a spoken lie,
> Never a lie in thought.
>
> Whatever your monks have called
> The law of the King of Grace,
> That was the Fenians law;
> His home is their dwelling-place.[24]

Generosity was for pagan as well as Christian the chief virtue, as this *rann* illustrates:

> If only the brown leaf were gold
> The wood sheds when the year is old
> Or if the waves had silver spray
> These too would Fionn have given away.[25]

Patrick, as mentioned earlier, was sent by Rome to reform the rebellious Irish church. But being a Briton himself, his orientation was very close to what he was sent to combat. Even after he succeeded in establishing some form of Roman-style hierarchy, his personal preference remained with the simple monastic structure so favored by all of Celtic Christendom. Patrick seems to have been very creation-oriented in his own thought, if his poetry is any indication. The *Creed*, written in answer to the following pagan querent perhaps, shows a marked contrast to the Redemption-focused Nicene one:

"The Questions of Ethne Alba":

> Who is God and where his dwelling?
> Is he ever-living, is he beautiful,
> Was his son fostered by many?
> Are his daughters dear and beautiful
> To the men of the world?
> Is he in heaven or on the earth?
> In the sea, in the rivers, in the mountains,
> In the valleys?
>
> Speak to us tidings of him:
> How will he be seen.
> How is he loved, how is he found?

Patrick's reply:

> Our God, God of all men,
> God of heaven and earth, seas and rivers,

God of sun and moon, of all the stars,
God of high mountains and lowly valleys,
God over heaven, and in heaven, and under heaven.
He has a dwelling in heaven and earth and sea
And in all things that are in them.

He inspires all things, he quickens all things,
He is over all things, he supports all things.

He makes the light of the sun to shine,
He surrounds the moon and the stars,
He has made wells in the arid earth,
Placed dry islands in the sea. . . .
He has a Son coeternal with himself . . .
And the Holy Spirit breathes in them;
Not separate are Father and Son and Holy Spirit.[26]

There are many half-historical legends surrounding the Irish saints who founded small monastic communities in Scotland and the far islands in those early centuries. Like the monasteries in Wales and Brittany, these settlements were nonhierarchical, upholding the ideals of true poverty, sharing, and living in accord with natural surroundings. The monks seem to have followed in some ways the same patterns as holy men of the old religion. They were skilled in martial arts, they had animal companions, and they kept up the study of poetry and music and herb-lore. Communities of women, carried over from the pagan worship of the goddess Brigid (Christianized as St. Bridget), flourished also.

Some men and women found even the monastic life distracting and sought total solitude in the green wilderness, taking the whole world for their oratory. They manifest a genuine Franciscan spirit; possessing nothing, they were free to "possess" and be a part of all creation. Still others chose a third mode of Christian life, to stay at court and continue the best of the old traditions within the structure of the new. It is not difficult to see the origins of the age of the chivalric legends in this.

Two brothers who exemplify the latter modes are the seventh century king Guaire and the hermit Marbán. Guarie was called "the Hospitable" and there are many beautiful legends surrounding his perfect charity. Marbán, on being asked by his visiting brother if he did not miss the court life, replied with this poem:

> I inhabit a wood unknown but to my God,
> My house of hazel and ash, as an old hut in a rath.
>
> My house small, not too small,
> Is always accessible:
> Women disguised as blackbirds
> Talk their words from its gables.
>
> The stags erupt from rivers,
> Brown mountains tell the distance:
> I am glad as poor as this
> Even in men's absence.
>
> Young of all things bring faith to me,
> Guard my door:
> The rough unloved wild dogs, tall deer,
> Quiet does,
>
> In small tame bands the badgers are,
> Grey outside:
> And foxes dance before my door
> All the night.
>
> Black-winged beetles boom
> And small bees:
> November through the lone geese
> A wild winter music stirs.
>
> Come, fine white gulls all sea-singing
> And less sad;
> Lost in heather, the grouse's song,
> Little sad.
>
> For music I have pines,
> My tall music-pines,
> So who can I envy here, my gentle Christ?[27]

Celtic Christianity Abroad: Pelagius and the Grace of Creation

No one knows for sure where Pelagius came from originally; some authorities claim him for Ireland, others for Britain, still others guess that he was born in Britain as the child of Irish missionary parents. His real name is frequently given as Morgan, "sea-born" (in Greek Pelagios), which is a Brythonic form. We do know that he was born in 354, the same year as Augustine, and that he came to Rome in the 390s. He was appalled by the moral laxness he found among Christians there, and quickly became known as a bitter opponent of the dualistic mindset of Levantine Christianity. He decried the pleading of the "corruption of the flesh" as an excuse for not behaving with a sense of responsibility. The Manichean influence was not only intolerable, but positively incomprehensible to one of his cultural background and personal temperament.

From Rome, Pelagius traveled to Sicily and Carthage and finally to Jerusalem where he met Jerome. It was inevitable that there would be a clash, and though the Celt is better known for his conflict with Augustine some years later, this struggle is also worth examining. The backbone of Pelagius' dispute with Jerome is the question of human capacity for "sinlessness," in other words the very nature of earthly existence. Pelagius, for whom the body-soul dichotomy as such did not exist, claimed that the possibility for leading a totally virtuous life was a part of God's original gift to man/woman, even though the possibility had never been realized. Jerome, however, argued that the flesh itself precluded this capacity. This dispute grew out of the Jovinianist controversy (Jovinian claimed that marriage was as holy a state as celibacy). In this contest, Jerome violently opposed the Jovinianists.

Pelagius came under Jerome's censure of what Jerome perceived as Jovinianist leanings, and also for his peripatetic teaching methods and association with "unclean types." "How can he claim any moral purity for himself, he who is in the midst of the crowd and a man of the people?" asks the desert scholar.[28] Jerome's ridicule also extends to Pelagius' many friendships with "mere women," and he writes scornfully of the "Amazons who attach themselves" to the Celtic master.[29] Pelagius' attitude to women is consistent with his culture, where women were counted equal with men in most areas, and even superior in some magical and religious dimensions. He is recorded as saying that "women also ought to have a knowledge of the law" and "should sing unto God," and Jerome's complaint that he "discusses the doctrines of divine law with young ladies whom he is in the habit of visiting" is no doubt well grounded in fact.[30]

In order to understand the heavy emphasis which Pelagius gave to the "law," it is essential to keep in mind what most religious historians never seem to realize: to a Celt of that time law meant a living body of metaphor, symbol, story, and eloquence which was a part of spiritual ecstasy. It is the farthest thing from the "Pharisaic" attitude to the law, which was justly deplored by Paul and Augustine. In the category of the Word, Pelagius included both the Old Testament and the gospel. He conceived of the law of Moses as pouring itself out into the further revelation of Christ's life and teachings, much in the same way Patrick looked at the Irish legal system. His attitude might be easily compared with the psalmists of the Davidic period who wrote with such exuberant love of the justice and beauty of the statutes of Yahweh. To call such a perspective "legalistic" is to entirely miss the point.

By the same misconception, Pelagius is also sometimes accused of "rationalism." But his "reason" cogitatio) is never empty or philosophically linear. It is a reason of the heart, the source of the free will which he considers the human being's greatest attribute. From this dynamic reasoning capacity comes creativity and imagination, and also justice and responsibility.

In a letter to the young nun Demetrias, Pelagius outlines his conception of the joys and struggles of the ascetic Christian life. He uses the Greek term *askein* in its original sense: "to work at something (as an art)." He encourages her to ceaselessly strive

toward the *perfectio morum,* distinguishing those actions which
are harmonious with being a child of God from those which are
not.[31] Life was for Pelagius as for his pagan forbears a balance of
mystery and action. He perceived the human journey as a
trinitarian structure, and used the terms *posse, velle,* and *esse.*
These three aspects of the life process form the touchstone of
Pelagius' theology.

Posse, Velle, Esse: An Exposition

Posse can be translated as the "ground of possibility," and is
inherent in being made in the image of a creative (good) God.
Velle, will, is the actualization force of this capacity, and *esse* is its
ongoing existence or meaning. *Posse* is the endless and boundless gift of God, the beginning and end of all human potential,
the "grace of power." *Velle* and *esse* proceed from that source as
the Son and Holy Spirit proceed from the Father.

Augustine's principal complaint against Pelagius was that he
denied the need for God's active intervention in the process of
salvation. According to the bishop, Pelagius "claims that man's
nature is sufficient" as is, that "man disputes as a bird flies or a
hare runs" with no need for the grace or wisdom of God to
"descend upon him."[32] With this, Pelagius would not argue, for
as we have seen, Celtic Christians were constantly taking note of
the natural grace behind running, flying, leaping, and in man/
woman's case, speech. The wisdom of God for the pre-Christian
Celts was made manifest from the ground up, and it was no
"darkness of heart" on their part which "changed the glory of
God into the likeness of (corrupt) man, birds, four-footed beasts,
and creeping things."[33] Their pantheism was rooted in a deep
desire to know God with the senses, to participate in the essential
oneness of all things both temporal and eternal.

Pelagius, far from denying grace, considered it such an obvious given that there was no need to speak of it as such. The grace
of creation is that *posse* which is our birthright, not to be as gods,
but to be fully human. "If you wish to measure the goodness of
human nature, look to its author," he wrote to Demetrius.[34]

This gift carries with it a heavy responsibility, however. Having free will means making the choice to move from *posse* to *esse* by means of *velle*. Pelagius' advice to Demetrias on the nature of the ascetic life has been compared with one of the Pythagorean *Sentences of Sextus*, with which he was probably familiar: "You possess something within yourself that is similar to God . . . you should manage yourself as if you were the temple of God."[35] Potentiality for virtue and creativity can only become actualized into being through a deliberate willed effort. Nor is this a one-time occurrence; Pelagius says that "the minute we stand still we begin to fall." The image of Dante's Purgatorio comes to mind, but also that of Blake's Los, the spirit of imagination working through eternity in his forge and sending his emanations into the world as rekindlers of the flame.

For Pelagius, sin is not a substance having any objective reality. It is only an act. Therefore Adam's sin is not transmissable by birth as it is for Augustine. Every human being is born as pure as Adam before the fall. Pelagius conceived of mortality as primordial and not related to any sin. But the possibility of sin and of *spiritual* death entered the world through Adam's example when he turned away from God. Like Blake, Pelagius saw human perceptions as the key to both fall and redemption. The *posse* which makes us human is infinite, but we close ourselves off from it and forget it entirely, and this prevents our taking hold of *velle* and moving toward self-actualization.

According to Pelagius, it is the *habit* of sin which holds us in a fallen state, and weighs heavier and heavier until finally it acquires the "force of nature" and "holds the sinner as if by necessity of sinning."[36] Pelagius' philosophy of "falling" bears some resemblance to that of Martin Heidegger, and his idea of the nature of the redemptive experience has much in common with modern philosophy as well.

Augustinian-based theology has always tried to belittle Pelagius' Christology, saying that he emphasized creation at the expense of redemption. But actually he evolved a complex and beautiful relationship with Jesus which was in some ways more complete than that of Augustine. Like the life process itself, the redemptive experience has three parts which correspond to *posse, velle,* and *esse.* For Pelagius, the redemption comes when something makes the creature, sunk in sinful habit, remember its *posse* and choose to turn back to God and its own true self. Like Blake, he envisions the person of Christ as a reminder, a rekindler of the sacred flame, who touches a chord deep in the heart and reaffirms that the potential for being "without sin," i.e., fully human, is there. Christ's three redemptive functions are these: he forgives past sins, he reveals through his teachings, and he provides an example through his life.

Of the first aspect, Pelagius writes: "Christ . . . submitted to the curse for us, because we were all guilty of death; as standing under a curse we were deserving of the tree ourselves, in that we did not abide by . . . the law."[37] The language and especially the tree image are reminiscent of the ancient Celtic and Middle Eastern propitiation sacrifice which corresponded to the Judaic scapegoat ritual. This is the point at which the past is wiped clean. Christ says to the repentant one: "Your sins are forgiven, your faith has made you well, now go and sin no more."

The importance of this "grace of pardon" is the clearing of the vision which enables us to reexperience the gift of *posse,* the "grace of power." The doors are then reopened for the use of free will to choose *esse,* authentic being. After participation in the cleansing experience has lifted the guilt of the past, it is to the teaching and example of Christ that one must look for guidance in striving toward a sinless life.[38] The stories of Jesus, with their rich earth-images and grounding in everyday experience, can provide the key to living in the present in a state of awareness rather than slipping back into the habit of "forgetting." And Jesus' active example of a life lived in truth, strength, eloquence, and generosity and a death faced with ultimate humility and courage was for Pelagius as for many others of the Celtic mindset a star to be followed.

For Pelagius, the secret of the state of creative being lies in achieving a balance between inner revelation and outward man-

ifestation. In fact, it can be said that the Celtic mind acknowledged no real inner/outer duality. As in the bardic tradition
poetry and politics were one, so for the Christian with *cogitatio*
and *iustitia*. The ideal should be to actualize the individual self as
fully as possible while learning how to live and die as a servant, at
one with the universe. The source of all sin is pride, just as it was
in the pre-Christian Celtic sagas.[39] But the remedy for too much
I-consciousness is not self-denial or mortification; that to
Pelagius was another form of pride. The Pelagian ideal could be
described as a state where the natural, healthy *I* pours out into
the I/Christ, which is the human community, the natural world,
the invisible Creator Spirit, and in turn takes its strength from
the whole. The self and the not-self should not co-exist in a state
of feud, but in a loving symbiosis, a free dance of joy. Gerard
Hopkins captured this whole image:

> As kingfishers catch fire, dragonflies draw flame;
> As tumbled over rim in roundy wells
> Stones ring; like each tucked string tells, each hung bell's
> Bow swung finds tongue to fling out broad its name;
> Each mortal thing does one thing and the same:
> Deals out that being indoors each one dwells;
> Selves—goes itself; *myself* it speaks and spells,
> Crying *What I do is me: for that I came.*

> I say more: the just man justices;
> Keeps grace: that keeps all his goings graces;
> Acts in God's eye what in God's eye he is—
> Christ—for Christ plays in ten thousand places,
> Lovely in limbs, and lovely in eyes not his
> To the Father through the features of men's faces.[40]

Although Pelagius himself was excommunicated and faded
into oblivion after his hopeless struggle with the Latin hierarchy,
his ideas survived in various ways in the next few centuries,

especially in the Celtic countries. Among the monastic communities of southern France there flourished the "error" which came to be known as semi-Pelagianism, and which sought to unite some of the doctrines of Augustine and Pelagius. This movement was condemned for heresy also, but the mindset of Pelagius was so basic to a large part of Celtic Christendom that it could never be successfully squelched.[41]

Wandering Artists and Sages: John Scotus Eriugena

In Ireland, although the Roman church had finally conquered the autonomous synod in the seventh century, the monastic temperament continued as vigorously independent as before. Irish scholars and ordinary monks continued to travel throughout Europe teaching and adventuring. Some of those who chose to stay in one place became expert at manuscript illumination, developing a distinctly Celtic style with animals both plain and fantastic and even symbols from the pagan tree-alphabet.[42]

The most reliable information we have as to what these anonymous artists and scholars were really like comes from poems written graffiti-style in the margins of their manuscripts. One of the more endearing of these is a testimonial by a scholar in praise of himself and his boon companion, who happens to be a white cat.

> Each of us pursues his trade,
> I and Pangur my comrade,
> His whole fancy on the hunt
> And mine for learning ardent.
>
> . . . .
>
> Master of the death of mice,
> He keeps in daily practice,
> I too making dark things clear
> Am of my trade a master.[43]

Here are two *ranns* with a typically practical Celtic outlook:

> King of Stars,
> Dark or bright my house may be,
> But I close my door on none
> Lest Christ close his door on me.
> ....
>
> To go to Rome
> Is little profit, endless pain;
> The Master that you seek in Rome
> You find at home or seek in vain.[44]

The court of Charlemagne became the center of European learning early in the ninth century, and continued so during the reign of his grandson, Charles the Bald. Among the illustrious scholars who lived and taught in France in the mid-century was one known as John Scotus Eriugena (literally, John the Irishman born in Ireland!). John, like several of his countrymen, devoted his career to the study of the Greek language, philosophers, and mystics at a time when the knowledge of Greek had virtually died out in the West. His thought is an attempt to reunite the divergent strains of Greek and Latin Christianity, but his own heritage is also a strong influence. The synthesis of his East-West dialectic has a distinctly Celtic feeling.

In his lifetime, John was principally known for his stand against the theory of predestination and for bringing the works of the Pseudo-Dionysius (then believed to be the real Areopagite), Maximus the Confessor, and Gregory of Nyssa into Latin. Although his own great work, *On the Divisions of Nature*, remained obscure while John was alive, in the succeeding centuries it became influential in certain heretical circles.[45] This eventually led to its being condemned for pantheism in the thirteenth century. But Eriugena's thought survived to have a profound effect upon several well-known mystics of the late Middle Ages and early Renaissance. Among these were Meister Eckhart, Ramon Lull, and Nicholas of Cusa.

John conceived of divinity in much the same way as his Greek "masters," especially the Pseudo-Dionysius. God is a "cloud of unknowing," unknowable to humans and even to itself. All attempts to define or classify it, to give it face, gender, and personality, are concessions to the human mind's inability to conceptualize infinity. But our greatest gift (or grant) from this ineffable source is the ability to try to image-ine God, to impose our own thought structure upon the ground of being. It is upon this premise that John attempts his description of the *Divisions of Nature.*

Whereas the Greek Christian Platonists envisioned the search for God as a climb upward out of natural being, John's cosmography is more circular. His "divine darkness" is like an underground river which flows through and nourishes the world of phenomena, rather than a cloud which is somehow above it. This inversion from upward to outward is consistent in Eriugena's adaptation of metaphysical ideas. He combines mystical speculation with love of the participation in the natural world, just as the pagan Celts had done for many centuries.

John describes the first division of nature as *non creata creans,* the uncreated creating. This is God the Alpha, the beginning motion toward theophany. The Greek image of *kenosis,* God emptying itself out into creation and remaining diffused there, appealed to John. But he is definitely not a pantheist, for he makes a clear distinction between creator and creation. His philosophy is properly called *panentheism;* God is at the same time immanent and transcendent. This conception of God probably has its origin in the sun, whom the early Irish called Lugh (Brythonic-Welsh Llew), the Light of the Long Hand.[46]

The second division, nature which is created and also creates (*creata creans*), is the ocean of "primordial causes." These are Plato's ideal forms, Jung's archetypes. They exist in the mind of God and in the human mind as the images or ideas underlying all creation; they are the source of creativity. Just as all numbers proceed from the monad and are reducible back to one, so the primordial causes are infinitely deversifiable yet unified in the Logos.[47] Primary among these causes is the human being itself, as unique blend of God and creature. The concept of the trinity also is found here; Eriugena says that consciousness itself has a threefold structure. The three stages are *ousia, dynamis,* and *energeia;* being, force, and operation. In terms of the human process these correspond closely to Pelagius' *posse, velle,* and *esse.* As relates to our God-image they are Father, Son, and Holy Spirit.

As in the depths of the psychic ocean, so in the forest of natural phenomena. All that is, in all its wonder-ful diversity, appears to John as a living theophany, a manifestation of the Word. He would agree with Blake that "everything that lives is holy." The grace of creation sings through the world in endless *phantasiae* (material images) which are re-created in the human soul as *phantasmae* (memory-images). "The Vegetative Universe opens like a flower from the Earth's center, in which is Eternity. It expands in Stars to the Mundane Shell, and there it meets Eternity again, both within and without...."[48] These words of Blake's could easily have been written by John the Scot!

Eriugena is fascinated by the particulars of external creation and by the ability of the human mind to play with these images. He devotes much space to discussion of the physical sciences; astronomy, the habits of birds, the nature of animals. He believes that animals have souls of a kind, and remarks upon the fact that Odysseus' dog recognized him after his twenty-year absence. John's style is lively at all times, in his literary dialogue between master and student, but never more than in his discussion of the dialectical relationship between God as unchanging source and as perpetual outpouring. One catches a glimpse of the Sufi idea that God needed to cause the creation to save him from loneliness, and perhaps also an echo of the Celtic stories about the Dagda, the Good God, and his bottomless cauldron of plenty.

Glory be to God for dappled things—
 For skies of couple-colour as a brinded cow;
  For rose-moles all in stipple upon trout that swim;
Fresh-firecoal chestnut-falls; finches' wings;
 Landscape plotted and pieced—fold, fallow, and plough;
  And all trades, their gear and tackle and trim.
All thing counter, original, spare, strange;
 Whatever is fickle, freckled (who knows how?)
  With swift, slow; sweet, sour; adazzle, dim;
He fathers-forth whose beauty is past change:
                                        Praise him.[49]

The last category, nature neither created nor creating, is the
Omega, the completion of the circle. It is not a terrifying emptiness, but the divine darkness, the mother night to which all
being returns. Eriugena did not believe in an anthropomorphic
heaven or hell, but he did have a notion of an afterlife, or rather
a continuation, which is in some ways reminiscent of the pagan
Celtic idea of the "other world." On some surreal plane outside
of time, the memory lives forever with its *phantasmae*. If during
its lifetime an entity had lived in accordance with the laws of its
nature, this would be a state of bliss. If it had gone against those
laws and lived by cruelty and disregard for natural balances, the
same *phantasmae* could become instruments of torture. But John
cannot really conceive of any soul having to suffer through eternity. He believes that there will come a time when the universe
will be utterly transformed. Then all the "numbers" will return
to the source of unity and "God alone will appear in everything
just as only light shines bright in the clearest air."[50]
  Evil is for Eriugena "the irrational motion of a misdirected
will." To employ an astronomical metaphor: when a body allows
its centrifugal force to overcome the gravity which pulls it toward the center, it goes flying off into space with such momen-
tum that it is difficult to stop. In the same way, when a soul
chooses to turn against God and its own true self, the very force
created by its action compels it to keep going in the wrong direc-

tion. This is something like Pelagius' "force of habit" and applies to the "fall" away from clear perceptions of *posse*.

How can one recover from this fallen state? Eriugena's idea of grace is a true blend of the Augustinian, the Greek, and the Celtic. The grace is present all along, in the Word through creation, but a catalyst is needed to remind us of it. For John as for Pelagius, Christ provides this catalyst, though with a slightly different emphasis. John agrees with the Greek fathers that the incarnation is the single most important event in history, the ultimate theophany. But here again he takes things a step beyond them, bringing speculation down to earth. Everything that the Greeks attribute to Christ, particularly his free will, John applies to every individual (potentially, not actually). Perceiving the primordial cause which is Christ-Logos in its conjunction with the man Jesus who lived as all people live, we re-cognize (re-know) ourselves. The conjunction of the "two worlds" which exists in him is in all of us. The simple remembrance of our potential Christ-hood and the free will option to strive toward it can make it possible to turn around and rediscover our rightful place at the center of the "cross" of the universe. "I am all at once what Christ was, since he was what I am, and this Jack, joke, poor potsherd, patch, matchwood, immortal diamond, *is immortal diamond*."[51]

Conclusion

The cross with the mystical rose at its center, which radiates into infinity both horizontally and vertically, represents the balance between the two dialectical "persons" of the human being. In one dimension, s/he is a part of the universe and made of the same stuff as plants, trees, birds, and rocks. In the other, s/he is *imago dei*, subcreator. As the image of God, the human is the only creature gifted with the ability to bring creatures of its own out of the abyss of ocean-images; to incarnate itself in art and in an artistic *life* in the sense of Pelagian *asketikos* and Blake's Christian art-prophecy. But this capacity is not limitless, and the creations and systems born of it are not automatically "good." It is in the primordial nature of man/woman to tend to fall away from the balance between capacities and natural limits in one direction or the other. To fall too much into the creature side leads to stagnation; to fall the other way leads to madness and destruction.[52]

In our society, it seems that collective institutions have fallen in the latter direction. This in turn produces a strong tendency in individuals toward the former. It is a deceptive stagnation because it is often camouflaged by frantic activity. We seem not only to have lost the center, but even the means of looking for it. We project irreconcilable dualities upon the universe and call them absolutes. We have constructed a desert of "civilization" and exiled the sea and the stars both objectively and in imagination. The ability to sit still, take notice of the world, and let our creative *phantasmae* surface is no longer even in our consciousness. We desperately need to learn to let life *happen* and celebrate it instead of rushing in to *direct* it constantly.

In recreating this rough sketch of some spiritual legacies of the distant past, I have deliberately given a very one-sided picture. Pagan Celtic society was no Golden Age, nor was the whole of Irish Christian life nearly as idyllic as I have portrayed it. I present it as an ideal form to be looked at metaphorically rather than literally. The Celtic cosmography contains some "ocean-images" which have been helpful to me in my personal quest. In traveling through the Celtic landscape in both imagination and physical reality, I have glimpsed what these poets and philosophers learned among their green hills and standing stones: that there is no real dichotomy between inner/outer, body/soul, poetry/practicality, imagination/reason. This contact (even on an imaginary plane!) with a cosmography where correspondences matter more than differences and revelation and action are as one can be very encouraging in the struggle to reinfuse society and church with a genuine Christian consciousness. The idea begins to emerge that it might actually be possible to turn around, both individually and collectively, and begin to live with imagination; to recover the true perception of our creative gift and turn it into theophany.

Epilogue

Once, as they rested on a chase, a debate arose among the Fianna-Finn as to what was the finest music in the world.

"Tell us that," said Fionn, turning to Oisin.

"The cuckoo calling from the tree that is highest in the hedge," cried his merry son.

"A good sound," said Fionn. "And you, Oscar," he asked, "What is to your mind the finest of music?"

"The top of music is the ring of a spear on a shield," cried the stout lad.

"It is a good sound," said Fionn.

And the other companions told their delight: the belling of a stag across water, the baying of a tuneful pack heard in the distance, the song of a lark, the laughter of a gleeful girl, or the whisper of a moved one.

"They are good sounds all," said Fionn.

"Tell us, chief," one ventured, "What do you think?"

"The music of what happens," said great Fionn, "that is the finest music in the world."[53]

NOTES

1. William Butler Yeats, "The Dancer at Cruachan and Cro-Patrick," in *Collected Poems of W. B. Yeats* (Toronto: Macmillan, 1950).

2. Claude Trésmontant, *The Origins of Christian Philosophy* (Hawthorn Books, 1963), ch. 1.

3. It seems that in most primitive cultures, the mystical human sacrifice/fertility element was bound up with political continuity or salvation. This is no doubt why Christianity was

adopted so readily in the Celtic world (which stretched from Spain to Turkey) and in the Levant of the Orphic mysteries. See Joseph Campbell, *The Masks of God: Occidental Mythology* (Penguin Books, 1976), and Frazer's *Golden Bough*.

4. Reinhold Niebuhr, *The Nature and Destiny of Man* (Scribner's Sons, 1964), p. 135.

5. Cf. Sam Keen, *Apology for Wonder* (Harper and Row, 1969).

6. Cf. Jesus: "Unless you become as little children you shall not enter the Kingdom of Heaven" (Luke 18:17).

7. Cf. J.R.R. Tolkien, in his essay "On Fairy-Stories," in *The Tolkien Reader* (Ballantine Books, 1966), pp. 22, 46-7.

8. William Blake, "The Marriage of Heaven and Hell", in *The Poetry and Prose of William Blake*, ed. David V. Erdman (Doubleday, 1970), p. 39.

9. For lack of space I will limit myself primarily to Ireland; I am aware that this is arbitrarily going to exclude much of equal value from Scotland, Wales, Brittany, etc. and I regret it.

10. See Gerhard Herm, *The Celts* (St. Martin's Press, 1975), ch. 15.

11. For a full explanation of this fascinating system see Robert Graves, *The White Goddess* (Farrar, Strauss, & Giroux, 1966).

12. Herm, *The Celts,* p. 146.

13. Lucan, quoted in ibid, p. 152.

14. W. B. Yeats, in Lady Gregory's *Cuchullain of Muivthemne* (Gerard's Cross: Colin Smyth, Ltd.), pp. 265-6.

15. Cf. Campbell, *Masks of God,* pp. 449-3.

16. Herm, *The Celts,* p. 157.

17. St. Paul, "Letter to the Galatians" 5:2-4, etc. For an account of Celtic migrations and settlements, see Herm, *The Celts.*

18. St. Paul, "Galatians," 4:8-10.

19. See accounts of Cuchullain's training with Scáthach in the Isle of Skye, which bears her name. For example, in Thomas Kinsella's translation of *The Táin* (London: Oxford University Press, 1970).

20. Ibid., p. 4.

21. For cross cultural insights into the link between the sun-king-vegetation see Mircea Eliade, *Patterns in Comparative Religion* (Sheed & Ward, 1958), pp. 127-8, *passim.*

22. Campbell, *Masks of God,* p. 207.

23. For one of many poetic accounts of this encounter see

Seumas MacManus, *The Story of the Irish Race* (Devin-Adair, 1977), ch. 13.

24. Frank O'Connor, *Kings, Lords, and Commons,* translations from the Irish (Dublin: Gill & McMillan Ltd., 1959). From "The Praise of Fionn," p. 29.

25. "Generosity," in ibid; p. 33.

26. James Carney, trans. *Medieval Irish Lyrics* (Dublin: Dolmen Press Ltd., 1967), from "The Questions of Ethne Alba" and St. Patrick's Creed," pp. 3–7.

27. John Montague, ed., *The Book of Irish Verse* (Macmillan, 1974), "Marbán, a Hermit Speaks," trans. Michael Hartnett, pp. 57–8.

28. Robert F. Evans, *Pelagius: Inquiries and Reappraisals* (Seabury Press, 1968), p. 32.

29. Idem.

30. Evans, *Pelagius,* p. 35.

31. Pelagius, "Letter to Demetrias," in Evans.

32. St. Augustine, "On Nature and Grace," in *Basic Writings of St. Augustine,* ed. Whitney J. Oates, (Random House, 1948), 1:xii.

33. Idem.

34. Pelagius, "Letter," in Evans.

35. The *Sentences of Sextus,* no. 35, cited in Evans, p. 50.

36. Pelagius, "Letter," in Evans, p. 101.

37. Pelagius, "Expositiones" (on the Pauline Epistles), cited in Evans, p. 106.

38. Evans, *Pelagius,* p. 108.

39. In Celtic myth, the hero or heroine's downfall always comes about through irresponsibility and growing insensitivity to the balance of self universe. It is usually the forces of nature which act as chastening agents. For example, Maeve's ambition and all the bloodshed of the Táin comes to nought when the two bulls who were its object kill each other; Cuchullain's luck and strength desert him after he kills his natural son in a moment of drunken boasting.

40. Gerard Manley Hopkins, "As Kingfishers Catch Fire," in *A Hopkins Reader,* ed. John Pick (Image Books, 1966), p. 67.

41. See Campbell, *Masks of God,* chapter on "Europe Resurgent."

42. Ibid., p. 467–70.

43. O'Connor, *Kings,* "The Scholar and the Cat," pp. 14–15.

44. Ibid., p. 16. "The Open Door," and "A Word of Warning."

45. Particularly the Almaricians. See Lambert, *Medieval Heresies* (Holmes & Meier, 1977), p. 102.

46. Primarily in Book III. To try to write an annotated exposition of the *Divisions of Nature* would require much more space than I have. The edition I have used is *Periphysean: On the Division of Nature,* by John the Scot, ed. & trans. by Myra Uhlfelder, summaries by Jean A. Potter (Bobbs-Merrill Company, 1976).

47. At a recent conference, the poet Robert Bly stressed the need for every individual to find his or her own personal term for these images, primordial causes, archetypes. Bly calls them "seed-images"; my own preference is "ocean-images," which is mainly derived from another early Irish poem. In it, the hero Bran is in the midst of a storm at sea and has a "double vision." At the same time that he is himself and seeing waves, fish, and sea-horses, he is also the trickster sea-god Mannanán, who perceives a scene as on dry land. The salmon become cattle and sheep, the currachs chariots, and the waves, forests. See Montague, pp. 45–7 "The Double Vision of Mannanán."

48. Blake, *Poetry,* "Jerusalem", ch. 1, 1ns. 34–36.

49. Hopkins, *Reader,* "Pied Beauty."

50. John Scotus Eriugena, in *Periphysean,* Book V, p. 358.

51. Hopkins, *Reader,* from "That Nature is a Heraclitian Fire and of the Comfort of the Resurrection."

52. These insights are gleaned from a combination of sources interacting with personal reflections; among them are Sam Keen, *Apology for Wonder,* J.R.R. Tolkien, "On Fairy-Stories", and Martin Heidegger, *Being and Time.*

53. James Stephens, from *Irish Fairy Stories,* reprinted in John Montague, *Irish Verse.*

6

Body and Body Politic in the Creation Spirituality of Thomas Aquinas

M. D. Chenu, OP

Creation spirituality is a way of life that takes body and body politic, nature and human history, as serious arenas where the Spirit of God is met on the one hand and put into motion on the other. Thomas Aquinas (1225–1274) was a champion of creation spirituality in a period of rising suspicion about it. He trusted the Creator and the creature to work dialectically with the spirit of creation. Indeed, no fuller epitaph for this creation spirituality can be rendered than that one which emanated from his pen on several occasions when he wrote: "To take something away from the perfection of the creation is to abstract from the perfection of the creative power itself." This statement, which contains both a metaphysical and a mystical principle for Aquinas, lays open the key to his entire spirituality. For him (as for Francis of Asissi), nature is not a mere shadow of the supernatural but contains spiritual energies in itself. To study nature and existence was for Aquinas a form of prayer and meditation, indeed a "liturgy" as he insisted in his running debates with cloistered monks of his day.[1]

In this essay I wish to explore two dimensions to creation spirituality which Aquinas dealt with and paid a severe price for investigating, and which contemporary thought continues to

Translation by Madeleine Doerfler.

wrestle with—that of the role of body and of body politic in spirituality. I approach the first question by way of the subject of human passions: Is the virtuous person necessarily a passionate person? Spiritualists and dualists of many stripes will respond automatically in the negative to this question, so crucial a one for feminist philosophers and others in our day. Aquinas, however, resisted any simplistic dualistic response to this issue of body, spirit, and bodily spirit as we shall see.

The second question, that of body politic, I will consider under the title of history, society, and spirituality. How integral are history and society (and the changing of both) to the spiritual existence of human persons? For Augustine, history was an embarrassment. People are not meant to be at home in the world, much less in changing the world. Not so for Aquinas. While St. Thomas has nothing of the historian about him and while he emphasizes history only when interpreting scriptures, still his conception of being-in-the-world furnishes a sociological basis for acknowledging time and history as a place for the holy no less than the profane.

I. THE ROLE OF PASSIONS IN SPIRITUALITY

St. Thomas maintains, in opposition to his Augustinian contemporaries, that the passions of aggression (*irascibilis*) and of desire (*concupiscibilis*) are properly speaking the subjects of virtues even in their physiological engagement. This conviction on his part follows from the principle of consubstantiality of body and soul that he defended when analyzing the morality of the passions as actions of the sensitive powers of people. This radical opinion on the nature of the human unity was not a popular one in his day, and Thomas found it necessary to treat the subject on at least three separate occasions. He took this position in his very first assignment in Paris when commenting on Peter Lombard's *Sentences* in the years 1254–1257 (thus before Averroes' works entered the Parisian academic world) and in doing so opposed previous commentators on the book of the *Sentences*.[2] He treated the subject again and in the same manner during the highly polemical debates on Aristotelian philosophy of man (1268–1277) and wrote of it in the disputed questions, *De virtutibus,* and again, in his *Summa theologica,* he raised the same question.[3] Significantly, his opinion never wavered on this subject throughout his lifetime.

How important is the question of the "seat" of the virtues? After all, in both moral philosophy and in psychology it is by their object rather than their "seat" or origin that the powers of the soul are defined.[4] But this regulating objectivism does not exteriorize or disincarnate either virtues or vices making of them a kind of spiritual ether. Rather, passions enter into play through and in the sense organs of the body complete with their physiological changes *("corporalis transmutatio"),*[5] and a keen observer of human nature will seek actively to render to the subject its role as "seat" of human values, moral options (*electio*) and, above and beyond that, the seat or subject of the Christian graces. Otherwise we have to put these patently absurd questions: Is the soul alone virtuous so that the body has only superfluities to perform? Is matter only incidental to our existence and moods and feelings and choices? If so, then my experienced sensations would remain exterior to my strictly intellectual life and even more exterior to my spiritual Christian life. Just how important is my body to being a Christian or believer or person of faith? These are the questions at stake depending on one's position about the seat of the virtues and passions.

The Dualistic Answer

St. Thomas has left us a near dossier of the arguments against the passions having a significant role to play in the virtuous person in his listing of sixteen arguments in *De virtutibus* referred to above. St. Bonaventure was one of Aquinas' opponents in this controversy as he followed Augustine's position quite rigorously. These persons all insisted that reason or the mind or spirit (what the Augustinians call *mens*) is the prime subject of the cardinal virtues of prudence, justice, courage, and temperance. For this is why virtues are proper to men and women and not to animals. The typical act of the virtues is to make a choice for better or for worse (*electio*). This choice arises from free will and is therefore incapable of having anything but reason as its operating subject.

In this treatment of human passion the sensitive powers of desire and of aggression are the subject of virtue only insofar as they participate in reason, being penetrated and finalized by the mind and the will. In this psychology, passions are considered passive—they can only obey what the soul dictates. Passions lack richness and energy that in fact sustains virtue. Passions are appendages to virtue much as a hand that gives a gift to someone is not itself virtuous but only the mind and intention of the giver is virtuous.

Aquinas' More Holistic Answer

Confronted with this spiritualism which recognizes no true virtue except that of the mind, Thomas Aquinas first of all divorced himself from a theoretical presupposition behind it: the dualistic distinction between a superior zone of the passions—which alone can be virtuous—and an inferior zone coming from sensual and animal nature. In the Augustinian world view this dualism was commonly invoked as the distinction between *ratio superior* and *ratio inferior*. Thomas consistently rejected this dualism which said that only the *ratio superior* (the nonanimal side to human nature) was capable of knowing "eternal truths," the wisdom of the sage, or of experiencing sanctifying grace.[6]

Thus, in Aquinas' view, the irascible and the concupiscent powers are themselves the true seat of virtues. Their perfection, even though emanating from reason (intelligence, will, and free choice) is proper to them: reason governs corporal emotions not by despotic commands as a lord dominates his serfs who cannot resist him, but rather by a "political" power as a sovereign governs his free subjects who have the right and the power to contest his authority. The human dignity of the passions is such that they enjoy in the active outflowing of the spirit (*derivatio*)[7] their natural energy and even their freedom of direction. In this way they are subjects of virtues and possess authentic moral value, for better or for worse.

Some might suggest that the difference between the two positions is subtle, resting only on a verbal distinction between virtue properly speaking, which has the mind for its subject, and virtue in the improper sense whose seat can be passion that is docile to the spirit. But it is precisely on this matter of docility that everything hinges. If it takes an exterior imposition (*"obtemperat rationi"* to use Bonaventure's phrase) to integrate our sensitive powers of confrontation (anger) or desire (love), then indeed we lack an ontological and psychological bond of senses and spirit. There is no consubstantiality of body and spirit.

Paradoxically, it is because the sensibilities are consubstantial in an ontological unity that, in Aquinas' opinion, they possess an autonomy which calls up a participation appropriate to the virtuous mastery of mind and liberty. They are not virtuous by a simple docile subordination or by simple habituation, as Bonaventure would concede if necessary,[8] but by an intimate penetration. It is thanks to this penetration—or better interpenetration—that the spirit finds a home in our sensibilities or passions.

Moreover, the test of the virtuous act for Aquinas is delight. If we become spiritual only by an imperative issuing from reason and will, virtue is in some way forced. It lacks a harmony with the nature of passion. It would proceed with repugnance and frustration that leads to sadness instead of blossoming into a state of delight.[9] The extreme intensity of the appetites is felt in proportion to their dynamism in and by the very impregnation of the spirit at the same time that the spirit perfects reason and will in the appetite of the senses. "The work of appetitive virtue is consummate in the sensitive appetite and on account of this the sensitive appetite is the subject of virtue."[10] It is from this that pleasure and spontaneity arise which, far from diminishing the virtuous value, increase its quality and merit. "The more delectably something is done out of a virtuous habit, the more delectable and meritorious is its action."[11] He who still has to struggle is weighed down by the struggle; the "continent" person does not fully possess the virtue of temperance. The "temperate" person, in the mastery of his passions in a healthy state where reason prevails, experiences greater joy than the one who remains under the influence of the brusque movements of his sensualities.[12]

Here lies the very meaning of the word "virtue" ("et hanc virtutem vocamus"[13])—magnanimity and gentleness in an even balance with fear and audacity; sobriety and chastity in an even balance with concupiscence. Harmony, not mastery; flow, not control; spontaneity, not will power; bigness of soul, not temerity— these are the virtuous consequences of Aquinas' passion-oriented spirituality. They resemble in a powerful way the biblical prophet as described by Rabbi Heschel:

> Asceticism was not the ideal of the biblical man. The source of evil is not in passion, in the throbbing heart, but rather in hardness of heart, in callousness and insensitivity. . . . We are stirred by their (the prophets') passion and enlivened imagination. . . . It is to the imagination and the passions that the prophets speak, rather than aiming at the cold approbation of the mind.[14]

This understanding of the unity of the human personality is in turn complemented by the biblical studies of Claude Tresmontant who indicates that "precisely because it is not dualist, Hebrew, more than any other language, has an understanding, a love of the elements and of the flesh."

> In our dualist system it is the custom to attribute passions and organic fuctions to the body, and all that is of a psychological order to the soul. In Hebrew, because there is no dualism, passions, organic functions, sensations, are just as easily re-

lated to the soul as they are to the organs and, conversely, thoughts and sentiments are ascribed to the organs and to parts of the body.[15]

Because for Aquinas there is only one substantial form which both causes a person to be a person and also to be body, animal, being—in short, a passionate spirit, we can cry with him "mirabilis Communio!"—Oh, wonderful Communion.[16]

History of Aquinas' Position

As a result of his rejections of the Augustinian dualistic spiritualism, Aquinas found himself embroiled in controversy after 1270 at the University of Paris over the subject of the unity of body and spirit and of the virtuous qualities of the passions in particular. His ethics of the passions did not prove to be any more successful with Christians than was his anthropology, for on March 7, 1277 (three years after his death) a most solemn doctrinal jurisdiction of the church, the Corporation of Masters of the University of Paris meeting under the authority of Bishop Etienne Tempier, condemned 219 propositions of which twenty were aimed at Aquinas' holistic philosophy of the human person. Ten years later the archbishop of Canterbury, Robert Kilwardby, censured a list of thirty propositions, the majority of which concerned Aquinas' position on the consubstantiality of soul and body, spirit and matter.

Thomas' aging professor, Albert the Great, hurried from Cologne to Paris to defend his former student but to no avail. It took the canonization of Aquinas (1323) to remove the cloud of suspicion. But intellectually Aquinas' holism never took hold. The central position in that controversy, as in many spirituality debates today, was precisely the issue of the oneness of human existence. This holism vigorously opposes the traditional position of a dualism of body and soul, a position originating with Saint Augustine (you do not find it in the Bible) and in fact favorable to a certain Christian spiritualism which has endured right down to our own day. Thomas Aquinas paid dearly for his holism and so too has Christian spirituality since his time.

Spiritualists believe that the human person has a value and meaning and personality to the very extent that he or she transcends matter with its limitations. But to admit that God creates is implicitly to confess that matter is divinely willed and therefore good. When it comes to discussing passion and spirituality, Christians should not forget the fact that Augustine was a victim of Manicheism for no small part of his life and that all life long he was haunted by an unusually negative experience of uncontrolled passion. Aquinas' spirituality does not operate out of so sad a personal experience. Aquinas is not guilt-ridden at being a human being and not an angel. As I have written elsewhere, "In the dynamic unity of the human reality the instincts, the sensuality, and the tensions which are at the root of the passions are all authentic elements of the virtuous life; they share in the dignity of reason and love, and therefore in the human—and divine—value of our lives."[17]

II. HISTORY, SOCIETY, AND SPIRITUALITY

We have seen how Aquinas' spirituality attempted a holisitic psychology and what a scandal this provoked for the dualistic masters of his era. Now we shall consider how his spirituality attempted a social holism as well. Thomas Aquinas attempts to establish in creation itself the historical reality of the universe and the theological origin of history. What a welcome contrast this provides to the general education of so many Christians for whom evolution is a stumbling block or for whom creation is expressed in pictures or language that imply miracle and disdain history; or to certain metaphysical expressions that suggest that creation, whether the act of creation by God or the spiritual dependency of the created being, is somehow oblivious to time. Even those thinkers who have succeeded in coordinating an evolving vision of the cosmos with the Absolute Creator fail to link creation as such, in its pure state as a relationship of creator and the created being, to time.

Aquinas taught tenaciously and to the great scandal of the "murmurantes" of his day that a beginning of the world is not included in the intelligibility of the creation. If the image of divine transcendence is presented exclusively in an "eternal" God in all his self-sufficiency, history then is only an accidental, though urgent, element to the conception of the act of creation. But here lies the distant and silent and motionless God of deists from Voltaire and Newton to Sartre. Aquinas thought very differently about the relationship of time and history to Providence.

The Anthropological Basis of History

The divine plan of the creation cannot be understood without the human race whose existence gives earthly and heavenly meaning to it. For humanity, created for itself but also as master of the world and its history, participates in the creation in this way. Humanity is a partner of God in the continuing building up of the world. A co-creator. The realization of that creative potential in humanity implies in turn the experience of becoming and of reality as history. For humanity, the co-creator, is unthinkable apart from history and it is through humanity that the universe receives a historic dimension.

Something more is involved in creation besides the history and the becoming of the universe: namely, multiplication and distinction.[18] The act of creating implies in its unfolding a multiplication of existences. God cannot emanate "something" without it being, in the original sense of the word, a *universe*. A oneness in multiplicity, a multiplicity in oneness. In Genesis it says that "God created man in his image, in the image of God he created him" (1:27). But whoever says "image of God" finds himself facing this inevitable multiplicity. Since God cannot be sufficiently well represented by one finite creature, the diverse multiplication of the creatures provides a compensation for their individual deficiences. Diversity is a blessing, not a curse! Diverse beings reflect the multiple beauty of God.

> God has produced things in the human being in order to communicate his goodness to the created beings and to represent his goodness in them. And because his goodness cannot be represented efficiently in one single creature, he created multiple and diverse things in such a way that whatever is lacking in one creature in representing the divine goodness may be made up for by another. Thus the goodness which in God is simple and unique is found in countless and differentiated creatures. Consequently it is the entire universe which shares perfectly the goodness of God and represents it more than any one creature by itself.[19]

This unity and interrelatedness by power of emanation, this union of the One with the Good is the reason for the sovereignty of the Creator.

Some mystical traditions within and without Christianity consider multiplicity and its metaphysical necessity to be a radical weakness. The Neoplatonists consider it the origin of a dispersion, a permanent failure that the incessant proliferation of beings cannot counteract.[20] The "dyade," that is, the first rupture with the Unity is the source of distress and the original curse upon the world. The fact that humankind is thus given over to the flux of history is the sign of an irreparable blow to this unity. This explains the repugnance of certain theologians for history, for prophetic challenges to history, and even to the history of salvation. For Neoplatonists, life on earth is an exile. We merely "put in our time" on earth much as a prisoner puts in his time. We are "doing time" one might say. Time becomes a wound through which our life pours out.

St. Thomas does not succumb to so pessimistic an interpretation of history and multiplicity. For him, the enterprise is just the opposite from being a curse: It is a work of "wisdom." To bring about the emanation of the Being into a coordination of those finite beings is itself to recreate the universe. Indeed, this activity of interrelatedness is the universe; it is an *ordo,* a sacred ordering of the sacred creation. It is God's work in the world, a constant creation and preservation fulfilling itself. It is humanity's sacred vocation.

At the summit of this creation of creation which is called universe or "hierarchy" in the sense of *ordo sacer* (Denys' expression), humanity recapitulates its steps in being and in value. Each stage becomes imprinted with its ontological dynamism in a progressive articulation of their levels. In humanity, all energies from matter to spirit lead to consciousness. Humanity thus humanizes nature. History becomes the human setting of the creation. This vision corresponds closely with the biblical one as pictured by Tresmontant.

> The Greeks seem to have been especially impressed by the movements of corruption and dispersal. Biblical becoming shows the fecundity and goodness of the Creator. The Hebrews showed a passionate attention to the process of fecundity, the maturing process. . . . Biblical time is the measure of this parturition, this universal maturing. It is essentially positive and good. . . . As regards man especially, something is still being accomplished, something is still growing. History is this *maturation.* . . . History is a constant invention in which innumerable free wills cooperate: the creative action of God and the co-creative action of man. History is not an unfolding in time of a preexisting model in which all is fore-ordained. For this reason it is impossible to forecast the precise "hour of fulfillment."[21]

History and Society

Through this progressive realization of the image of God in the world the human person, the microcosm of the universe, is constituted as the nerve center where the act of divinization is infused into humanity. The infusion of divine energy is not restricted to ephemeral individuals but finds its way in the continuity of the universe including all matter of the universe and of human history. It is cosmic in scope.

The multiplication that takes place at the fuller levels of consciousness certainly are part of the creative enterprise. Surely human individuals are "persons" and as such are worthy of love in the common sharing of the image of God. They are wanted for themselves and the multiplication of persons is an end in itself. However, each individual is radically insufficient in realizing his or her own nature fully. People are persons only in a community with all other persons. It is at this point that people are, by nature, "social." Being social means connection of the individual and of the species in order that perfection be concretely relizable. It is not by some vague provision that nature is fully satisfied by the aptitude of the species for permanent proliferation; the intention of nature coincides with the goal of creation which as we have seen is to give an enduring representation of the Creator in an extra-divine reality. The biological preservation of the species is not at all the material manifestation of an eternal renewal in individuals placed in juxtaposition. It is much more historical and sensual and interior than that. It is a web, a network, an interwoven fabric of a multiplication that gives its meaning to temporal evolution. Time is not only the exact succession of physical moments or the inherent number of a movement. It is far more relative than that. Time is the interior measure of a destiny. Time as destiny is itself part of the eternal design of a transcendent Providence that becomes real in the personal and collective consciousness.

In contrast to his contemporaries who condemned him for his "materialism," Saint Thomas believed that the genesis of history was accomplished through the development of the species and of the individual by and in matter. Matter is the principle of individuation. An individual does not become a person except in a body; one's own personal "incarnation" is at the same time the principle of individuality, sociability, and historicity. The angel who has neither sociability nor history is sterile and sufficient unto itself. Because a person is not a pure spirit but a spirit that takes on life when he or she is in matter, a person is not present to oneself except when he or she comes out of oneself. One does not see oneself in one's interior reality except by turning toward the world of objects and other people. We are nobody except when we are with another person. Self-awareness is awareness-of-oneself-in-the-world, an awareness of being with other people. Thus the metaphysical structure of humanity entails a radical access to history and a dependency upon history. It is therefore in the basic social fabric that the act of creation takes place historically, if it is true that a person is, by his or her body, not only a being-in-the-world, but also an individual who is fully realized only by openness to another individual.[22]

Certain forms of personalism which center exclusively on the interior state of the person do not give any account of social development in spite of their frequent exhortations to mutual love. In fact, such spiritualisms are cold and callous in their sentimentalism for they remain insensitive to the reality of history and to human interests. They have nothing to say to the impersonal harshness of the systems of justice on which society bases its rights. St. Thomas, in contrast, insists that the common good is more divine (*divinius est*) than personal liberties.[23] Freedom does not consist in an escape from social life in a protest of solitude and of pure interiority but in constructing a world of justice and peace that flows from justice. But to do this takes body (justice) and spirit (love) working in mutual harmony as body and soul do.

Aquinas goes far beyond Aristotle from whom he inherited the principle of hylomorphism in insisting on the historical fact of humanity. Lived time appears to increase its intensity geometrically for Aquinas for it is doubled by the richness of the generations which make up society. History is, by definition, social. And the history of the human race meshes with the history of nature. The moments of time and the liberties of individuals do not become history except by and in a society of people who live in this time. History is the human setting for the creation. It becomes richer when consciousness and the rights of liberties of all become more widespread.

There is a double-dimension to creation that is dialectical, and this dialectic is itself a kind of unity in *l'ordo*. Things that are created have not only a relationship with the Creating Being (*ordo ad deum*) but also a relationship with one another (*ordo ad invicem*). Undoubtedly that second articulation is reducible to the first one to the extent that its reason for existing is to lead the universe is to its final goal, an analogous representation of the perfection of the pure Being. But still it has a consistency of its own. The perfection of the universe is entirely immanent to the world. "After the divine goodness which is the end separate from things, the principle good existing in things themselves is the perfection of the universe" St. Thomas says.[24] This *ordo rebus inditus* has a meaning that can be deciphered without any detriment to the transcendental sense in the reality of God in the beyond, the *bonum separatum*. This dialectic of interrelatedness is precisely the "mystery" of the creation.

All this implies that, if the absolute and unique relationship with God forms the fundamental and co-conscious horizon of our multiple conscious relations with the world and with the interior of those relations, then absolute relationship enters into the awareness that humanity has of itself in and through relationships with other persons in society and with the world. Therefore we cannot separate that absolute relationship with God from our historically conditioned relationships with this world and with others who inhabit this world. Nor can we formalize that relationship with God and abstract it from the historical fabric of our existence.[25] Creation spirituality is truly a spirituality in and through creation and re-creation and not in spite of it.

Creation itself is bi-polar and to live deeply in it is to live dialectically. A double current animates the creation. On the one hand, each thing is magnetically attracted toward the Creator ("for this each and everything tends, namely that it might participate with the Creator and be assimilated to the Creator insofar as it is able"[26]) and on the other, things are ordered to achieve the perfection of the created whole of which they are parts. Creation fails when humanity fails. Infidelity to the social body, such as it is, in the construction and building up of the universe that goes beyond the agreements of individuals and of liberty of love is a failure for the creation of whom humanity is the demiurge. Bonhoeffer has said as much in his *Ethics* when he declares: "It is a matter today of taking part in the reality of God and of the world in such a way that I never experience the reality of God without that of the world and vice versa." Such is the law of the "return" toward God or of re-creation according to the very dynamics of emanation.

Theological Basis for History

St. Thomas is very nuanced in his theology of creation and borrows some aspects of his thought from Neoplatonism and some from Aristotle. But he is as careful in what he borrows as in what he rejects. A case in point is the Emanation-Return theme which is so dear to the Neoplatonists. Aquinas uses this theme of Exitus-Reditus to actually support his historical view of humankind. He accepts the dynamic of the Exitus-Reditus as the basic architectural plan for his *Summa Theologica* and the substance of neoplatonic metaphysics enters the very tissue of his thinking on creation. One need only consult his treatise on the creation to see how telling these influences are. Paradoxically, Thomas has recourse to Neoplatonism to establish the historical dynamism of the creation and to articulate temporality and eternity. Yet in doing so he rejects the idealistic and essentialistic logic of the neoplatonic system. The paradox is highlighted because the movement is led in opposition to Aristotelianism which does not recognize the theory of creationism in a divinity that is pure Act.

While Aquinas treats Denys with great reverence, he rejects his absolute transcendentalism and asserts the individualization of the relations of creatures with God. The Thomist notion of creation remains founded on the axis of being and not on an emanation beginning with the One. Such a One would remain inaccessible beyond the multiplicity of "ideas" that are creative and created at the same time and are manifestations of that One who, in his surexistentialism, can no more be involved in a creation of beings than he can be known by them. If it is by an internal necessity that the "many" proceed from the One, then individual beings are not known or desired for themselves.[27]

Pseudo-Denys' thought is still present, however, in an underlying way when Aquinas attacks the doctrine of the One as being too anthropomorphic. To represent the divine intelligence as the place of "ideas" that will produce determinations and multiplications through ideological activity is a projection in Aquinas' opinion. There are no "eternal truths" for if everything has already been made in the mind of God, then temporal realities such as the universe and humanity itself would only be projections and would lack their firmness and reality. Preexistence in the ideas of God is only a creative essence. The One is only a stock or reserve of essence. The One is the first, not the last word, in the creative process. There is no complexity in God because there is no real reference to his creatures; their knowledge and with it their capacity for participation is implied in the knowledge that God has of himself. Consequently, the relation of creatures to the divine has something disconcerting about it from the point of view of human logic about relationships: it is unilateral and from the side of the creature alone. God cannot be relative to another because if another exists, it exists in God.

Diversity and multiplication as laws of the creative emanance and of the perfection of the universe do not at all contradict the absoluteness of the Creator. Immanence is guaranteed by transcendence—transcendence is dialectically the guarantee of immanence. These two dimensions of the creative act make up the density of history at the same time that they compose the truth of nature. Because the creative mastery is total, *profundens totum esse,* it does not compete with creatures: rather, the relationship is one of interpenetration ("impermixtio causae primae ad res alias"). Transcendence guarantees, with the total purity of the creative act, the self-realization of the created being, which in humanity culminates in consciousness and history.

One will understand better the influences of Dionysian Neo-platonism and the necessary corrections that St. Thomas brings to that theory by comparing it to Augustinian Platonism, which was in Aquinas' time very well cultivated in the exemplarism of St. Bonaventure. As a Christian believer Augustine is necessarily imbued with the immanence of God in nature and history both personal and collective. However as a philosopher he is brief and to the point in developing an ontology of the unchangeable tran-scendence of the Essence in order to explain a development in which time is merely the unintelligible decomposition of eternity which alone is the place for being and for truth. The activities and the growth of beings are only a display of what the eternal forms precontained. The existence of each thing and the dura-tion which measures its existence are only the visible refraction of the invisible essences which, in their own truth, are neither born nor perish. History is no longer anything but a shadow. The world is not the dwelling place of humanity. We are not at home in history.[28]

While St. Thomas can hardly be labeled an historian in the contemporary sense of the word, nevertheless his spirituality of being-in-the-world—unlike that of Augustine and Denys and other Neoplatonists—respects the world and its development in time. His thought furnishes a basis for a sociology in which the efficacy and intelligibility and importance of secondary causes, far from competing with the eternal providence of God, actually bring God's plan to realization. And this completion of God's plan is accomplished in time and in the terrestrial truth of his-tory both sacred and profane. In Aquinas' world-view, "the crea-tive hold of God gives consistency to temporal duration."[29] God nourishes and supports all beings in existence including even the being of time itself.

Love and Creation

If God has no real relationship with the created being as with an object, one cannot seek in the created being the cause of the creative initiative; it is entirely in God. God cannot want anything but himself, even when by a super-abundancy he wants himself and loves himself in the perfect sharing of his own perfection. This he did of course in the creation of the human race in his image wherein the reason for the divine enterprise is found in the urgency of a love which feels the need—if we dare talk that way—of communicating with another being in whom to place its joy. This production is both autonomous and indwelling at the same time, since no being can be outside the Being or in any addition to it in any way. To the extent that there is a motive in the Creator it is coessential to him. His will, his goodness in expansion are his very being and his essence.[30]

But it is precisely this goodness that is by essence communicative; the Supreme Goodness is supremely communicative. "Good is diffusive of itself" *(bonum est diffusivum sui)*—Thomas makes admirable use of this Dionysian axiom that inclines toward a "natural" emanation. For it underlies the supreme gratuity of the creation undertaken in the sovereign freedom of the Creator. The initiative proceeding from love breaks down the apparent contradiction between transcendence and immanence and meaning to the monstrous logic of unilateral relationship of creature to its Creator. Such is in fact the great power of this communication of the Good, that the creatures are not at all the projection of an egoism but rather are beings that are wanted, made real, loved for themselves. In that aspect once again we see how the universe has consistency in its natures whose "uniqueness" is not dissolved, not instrumentalized, for that would be a mockery of love.

God wishes the universe with all its creatures *for their own sake,* although he also wishes it *for his own sake;* these two things are not repugnant. For God wishes that creatures exist on account of his goodness specifically in order that they might imitate and represent it in their own way; this they in fact do insofar as they have existence from his goodness and *subsist in their own nature....* For thus God has instituted each and every single nature, in order that it not lose *its own uniqueness (pro-prietatem)*.[31]

In this understanding of love, love itself is carried along according to its own law to its incandescence and conferred on "the other" who is totally emanated from it, a consistency that is so total that the other is truly another. It is as if God were entering into the dependency of the one whom he loves. What could be more contrary to the alienation of the creature? By the mystery of the creative act we are elevated to the mystery of gratuitous and free love. The identity of Being and of Love, there lies the meaning of the creative genesis. Our being is born of love. The ontological dependency is handed on by the certitude of love.

If everything that exists is seized by a love like this love that permeates each and every creature, then truly we can say that:

> The universal movement of nature is defined as a self-realization and a surpassing of self at the same time. Every being is possessed by a sense of transcendence. In St. Thomas' terminology this feeling of transcendency is called *love*. Thus every creature loves the all more than himself, and God more than the all.[32]

This "ecstatic" behavior belongs to the lived condition of the creature, that is to say, of complete being who is dependent and who finds in this very dependence the only possible and adequate achievement for his nature. Here is Aquinas' vision of the "return," by way of the very dynamism of each one's nature, according to their "emanation." Here lies the ecstatic re-creation of creation.

When we consider and situate humans who are the demiurge and conscience in this universe of beings and of natures, we cross over the threshold of the instinct of spirit (will as nature), of intelligence, of freedom, of responsibility. All things, every form, every value becomes recapitulated in humanity and takes on a new existence in the unity of the universe, macrocosm and microcosm, where nature and history interlock. "Man achieves at his level the process of interiorization and of reflection that the dialectic of movement was already marking out. He achieves it in a spiritual immanence whose affinities with the whole confer on things of the earth a new harmony and a new existence."[33] It is when the Christian at last invests his or her faith in the incarnation of God in "this creature waiting for its own liberation" (Rom 8:22) that Christians will have the right to call it the New Creation.

Having introduced the subject of Christian faith we are leaving in some manner the line of our meditation on Creation. We cannot do otherwise, however, if Creation truly implies history and if God himself is believed to have entered history. But this belief was preceded by the notion of Creation—an idea that flooded the pure philosophical analysis of causality and of pure act. This analysis opened itself up to "religion"—the relation of creature to Creator—let us say it without any ambiguity—to the "mystery." The word mystery is without doubt adequate if it is true that only love resolves the contradiction between a God who, if he is God, is incommunicable and inaccessible in his self-sufficiency and a God whose goodness is substantially communicable in itself. A God, therefore, who is *unum et bonum,* one and good all at once.

III. CONCLUSION

As we have seen, neither body nor body politic lie at the periphery of a creation spirituality as Aquinas understood it. Providence or divine history itself depends on the cooperation of creation with Creator and in particular of that passionate, social and historical and spiritual animal called man and woman acting in cooperation with the eternal and ever-creating God. Human history is truly history when individuals make interpersonal love externalized in objective acts of social justice. Then does the human race find itself home in the world. And the name for home is a verb and a divine name, called Love.

NOTES

1. Cf. Yves Congar, "St. Thomas, Servant of the Truth," in his *Faith and Spiritual Life* (London: Darton, Longman & Todd, 1969), pp. 83–85.

2. III, dist. 33.

3. See *De virtutibus*, art. 4 and *Sum. theol.* I, II, q. 56, a.4.

4. See *Quest. disp. De anima*, art. 13.

5. *Quest. de virtutibus*, art. 4, ad. 4.

6. *Sum. theol.*, I, q. 79, aa. 8–10. Aquinas agrees, however, that "the principal act of moral virtue is *electio*, which is the act of the rational appetite" (*Quest. de virtutibus cardinalibus*, art. 4, arg. 2.).

7. "These virtues are in the irascible as to their derivation." (*Quaest. de virtutibus cardinalibus*, art. 4, ad 13.

8. St. Bonaventure, *In III Sent.*, lib. III, dist. 33, art. I, q. 3, ad I. Here Bonaventure uses the phrase "obtemperat rationi."

9. St. Thomas, *Quaest. de virtutibus*, art. 4. Aquinas warns that sadness (or what we might term depression today) derives from the "violence" done to the sensible appetite.

10. Ia, IIae, q. 56, a.5, ad. 1.

11. *In III Sent.* dist. 23, q. 1, a. 1, ad. 4.

12. Ibid., dist. 33, q. 2, art. 4, sol. 2.

13. *Quest. de virtutibus*, art. 4.

14. Abraham J. Heschel, *The Prophets* (Harper & Row, 1962), p. 258.

15. Claude Tresmontant, *A Study of Hebrew Thought* (Desclee, 1960), pp. 47, 100.

16. *Cont. gent.*, II, 68.

17. M.D. Chenu, *Faith and Theology* (Macmillan, 1968), p. 110. The American historian Carroll Quigley points out, "in a figure like Augustine, we find a Christian religious outlook combined with a platonic philosophic outlook with which it is really not compatible. One consequence of this situation was a great prevalence of dualistic heresies. These were condemned as part of the religious settlement at Nicaea in 325, but they were not really overcome in philosophy until the twelfth century." (Carroll Quigley, *The Evolution of Civilizations* [Macmillan, 1961], p. 217.)

18. In treating the subject of creation Aquinas develops in particular the categories of "production" and "distinction." See *Sum. theol.*, I, q. 47 and *Cont. gent.*, II cc. 40–46.

19. *Sum. theol.,* I, q. 47, ad. 1. Cf. *Cont. gent.,* II, c. 45.

20. According to Aquinas, the perfection of each individual in unity is realizable only in a universe that is itself unified. See *De Potentia,* 3, 16; *Sum. theol.,* q. 47, a. 3.

21. Tresmontant, *Hebrew Thought,* pp. 26f., 29.

22. Cf. Karl Rahner, *Hearers of the Word,* trans. by Michael Richards (Herder & Herder, 1969), pp. 130ff.

23. *Sum. cont. gent.,* II, 45.

24. *Sum. theol.,* I, q. 22, a. 3.

25. Schillebeckx says: "In relation to myself, God, the Transcendent, has no other fundament than the contingency and gratuity of my historical existence" (in *Theologie d'aujourd'hui et de demain* [Paris, 1967] p. 125.).

26. *Sum. theol.,* I, q. 103, a. 2.

27. Pseudo-Denys, *De divinis nominibus,* c.5. By ignoring the dialectic of Creator and co-creator, ideas annul the autonomy of things. Secondary causes are eliminated so that God and not parents produce children; the artist creates nothing new and the farmer grows no new food.

28. Cf. Carroll Quigley, *Civilizations,* p. 219: In the West, "the threat to the synthesized moderate middle ground from the Right has come from dualistic rationalism and especially from the influence of Plato. This influence has worked historically through Augustine of Hippo, who was a platonist in philosophy although a Christian in religion. In the field of religion itself, this influence has given rise to dualistic heresies of which the chief, as might be expected, have appealed to Augustine. Augustine himself was not a heretic (however)."

29. A. Hayen, "La connaissance humaine selon saint Thomas," *Rev. phil. de Louvain,* 1956, p. 589.

30. See *Expositio super Librum de causis,* prop. 20.

31. Cf. *De potentia,* 5, 4.

32. St. Breton, *Saint Thomas d'Aquin* (Paris: 1965), pp. 51f.

33. Ibid., p. 59.

7

Meister Eckhart on the Fourfold Path of a Creation-Centered Spiritual Journey

Matthew Fox, OP

In this article I intend to explore the dynamics of creation spirituality as seen through the spiritual theology of the German Dominican Meister Eckhart (1260–1327). What route does the way of creation spirituality take? What paths does creation spirituality follow? In Eckhart's perspective, the way of creation spirituality is a fourfold one which can be identified as following: 1. Creation. 2. Letting Go and Letting Be. 3. The break-through and giving birth to God. 4. Re-creation by love-justice and compassion. This path can best be grasped not in linear fashion (Eckhart is profoundly nonlinear) but in one of two images: Either as interconnected spirals or as concentric circles.

I. BACKGROUND TO CREATION SPIRITUALITY IN ECKHART

One of the severe prices that the West has paid for the condemnation of Meister Eckhart a week after his death has been the near extinction of creation spirituality from the Christian consciousness. Beginning with the antiintellectual *devotio moderna* movement which took root shortly after Eckhart's death, a sentimentalized redemption spirituality took over Western spirituality for the most part. (An exception would of course

be the Renaissance humanists like Erasmus—but how many
Christian spirituality courses teach Erasmus in comparison to,
for example, Thomas a Kempis?). Thanks to significant discoveries by scholars of the past century and a half, there is a growing
consensus of opinion that Eckhart did not deserve to be condemned at all[1] but that he was a victim of ignorance (the Inquisitors never even read his Latin works), politics, and jealousy.

Another consequence of Eckhart's condemnation is that over
the years spiritual theologians have been reluctant to study him.
They have left the field exclusively to philosophers, philolo-
gers, and historians of philosophy who have naturally been putting their particular questions to Eckhart. Many of these scholars—when it came to Eckhart's spiritual theology—misrepre-
sented Eckhart's views on important subjects or indeed ignored
them altogether. For example, they have invariably concentrated on steps two and three (letting go and birthing God) of
Eckhart's journey and ignored steps one and four (creation and
re-creating society). Abstracting from Eckhart's love of creation
and ignoring altogether his political consciousness, they have
frequently performed a neoplatonic or monastic eisegesis on the
spirituality of the Dominican friar who, like his brother Thomas
Aquinas, broke so dramatically with Augustine about pivotal issues in spirituality such as body, holistic psychology, history,
women, politics, and institutional triumphalism. Some authors
have actually led students to believe that Eckhart's spiritual
journey stops with stages two or three whereas for Eckhart the
journey never stops, for, like God whose children *and* parents
we are, creation is continually unfolding and we and our society
with it. In Eckhart's understanding, stage four, or compassion
toward others, is at least as important as are experiences of letting go or breakthrough (stages two and three). Indeed, all of
the stages are interrelated and repeated often. From the point of
view of the practice of spirituality it would be a disaster to ignore
stages one and four as in fact so many commentators on Eckhart
do. While Eckhart often takes them for granted, twentieth century spiritual journeyers cannot afford to.

I have discussed elsewhere the elements implicit in a creation spirituality and all these elements are present in Meister Eckhart's spiritual theology.[2] But it might assist the reader to outline just a few instances of his deep commitment to a creation-centered spirituality.

Realized Eschatology

Eckhart is a champion of realized eschatology, which is the position found in Johannine theology and the late theology of Paul that eternal life begins in the present life. Says Eckhart: "Just think what an amazing and blessed life the person 'on earth' has in God himself—a life 'as it is in Heaven.' "[3] Commenting on the Our Father prayer, Eckhart says that Christ "teaches us to receive heavenly things, saying 'your kingdom come,' even before any of us get to heaven. He has ordered the earth itself to become heaven, saying: 'Your will be done on earth as it is in heaven.' And the kingdom too will come whether here by grace or in the future by glory."[4] Here we see not only Eckhart's commitment to realized eschatology but also his rejection of any triumphalist tendencies that would identify institutional church with the kingdom. He makes clear that the kingdom is still to come, though he is eager to hasten its arrival.

Commenting on 1 Jn 3:1, Eckhart declares that "It is in this life that a person is begotten as a Son of God and that he or she is born to eternal life" (DP, 318). So capital is realized eschatology in Eckhart's spirituality that Vladimir Lossky considers the failure to grasp this perspective the very reason why "puny-minded masters in theology" misunderstand Eckhart, for Eckhart "projects this eschatology onto his doctrine of humanity."[5]

Panentheism

Eckhart's theology is profoundly panentheistic. He rejects all subject-object images for God's and humankind's relationship and instead insists on how all is in God and God is in all things.

"God created all things in such a way that they are not outside himself, as ignorant people falsely imagine. Everything that God creates or does he does or creates in himself, sees or knows in himself, loves in himself" (M, 77). Eckhart cites time and again—and even at his trial—a favorite scriptural locus of panentheists, that of Acts 17: 28. "God in whom we live, move, and have our being." The label of pantheist was stuck on him by the Inquisition; however, to come to this conclusion his detractors actually had to change his words. He said "everything that is in God is God" (DW I, 56). This classical phrase is found not only in Alan of Insulies and Thomas Aquinas but also in a solemn declaration of the Synod of Rheims in 1148. The inquisitors altered Eckhart's words to "everything that is is God" and then condemned him.[6] In fact, Eckhart took pains to make clear how different his panentheism, or what Kelly calls the "all-inclusiveness of God," is from pantheism, as in the following instance. "God is in all things. The more he is in things, the more he is outside things; the more he is within, the more he is without" (SK, 58).

Eckhart thus rejects any dualistic suppositions that theism or popular religious sign-making might suggest as regards God and creation. Still respecting the transcendence of God, he grasps as a primary starting point the fact of all being in God and God in all. His is not heterodox pantheism (which only sees everything as God and thereby destroys God's transcendence) but an altogether orthodox panentheism.

Christ as Reminder, Not Redeemer

True to the theology of creation spirituality, Eckhart does not consider the entrance of Jesus Christ into human and creation's history to have been primarily to redeem sinful humankind. Rather, he sees Christ's historical presence to be first of all a Reminder—Christ came to remind us of our blessed and divine origins as images and likenesses of God in a grace-filled universe. The purpose of his coming is more our divinization than our redemption from sin and guilt. "God assumed our clothing so that he might truly, properly and substantially be man and that man might be God in Christ. But the nature assumed by God is common to all men without distinction of more or less. Therefore it is given to every man to become the son of God, substantially indeed in Christ but in himself by adoption through grace" (SK, 221). These words, "that a man might be God in Christ," summarize well the deification motif that Eckhart, indebted to Eastern spiritual theologians, preached.

He says: "Christ became a human child in order that we might become a God child" (DP 431). And again, "Why did God become a person? So that I might be reborn as God himself" (DW V, 415). Eckhart's preferring our divinization over our redemption as the reason for Christ's coming is one more instance of his significant break with Augustine.

Christ comes as Reminder more than as Redeemer. "For this reason therefore has the wisdom of God wanted to show our redemption by himself assuming flesh—in order that our instruction in divine, natural and moral matters *would be remembered*" (LW III, 156). Thus, for Eckhart, redemption *means* reminding: Christ came to call us back to our being made in the image and likeness of the Creator. "Christ is before all else the 'Reminder.' He reminds us of the truth that has been 'forgotten' and hidden from our conscious and subconscious minds. . . . "[7] After all, Christ is the Word and, according to Eckhart, "the nature of a word is to reveal what is hidden" (DP, 421f.). But if Christ is Reminder he is also prophet. For the prophets of Israel were sent by God to remind the people and to call them back to Torah, a way from which they had strayed. Christ then for Eckhart is primarily a prophet. He is a prophet indeed who "endured martyrdom" (DW V, 414). We find here none of the docetistic tendencies that so much neoplatonic spirituality falls victim to.

Having considered some basic themes fundamental to Eckhart's creation-centered spiritual theology, we can now turn our attention to the fourfold path of creation spiritual experience as Eckhart envisioned it.

II. PATH ONE: CREATION AS GRACE

For Eckhart, our first experience of God is in creation itself. He describes his own creation in the following way: "When I flowed out of God, then all creatures proclaimed: Here is God" (DW II, 504f.). How can Eckhart say such a thing? More importantly, how could creatures possibly say such a thing?

For Eckhart, creation is itself a grace. It is an experience of the Creator who is profoundly present in creation. Borrowing from Aquinas and Augustine, he observes that "God is in all things by essence, by virtue and by power. . . . All creatures are like the footprint of God." But he goes even further than Aquinas in emphasizing the presence of God in creation. First, he calls this experience of God in creation "the grace of creation," "the gift of creation," and "gratia gratis data" or grace gratuitously given. (See LW I, p. 235.) This last use of a technical theological term for grace applied to creation is not found in Aquinas.[8]

Isness is God

But Eckhart goes still further in expounding on the grace that creation is when he takes Aquinas' metaphysical declaration that "God is isness" (Deus esse est) and turns it around to say: "Isness is God" (Esse est Deus). Isness is proper to God alone and the fact of the isness of created things is a divine fact, a divine presence. "Each and every being owes to God the fact that it exists, is one, is true, and is good. And every being not only possesses each of these from God himself, but it possesses them from him without any intermediary" (M, 97f). Commenting on Exodus 3:3, God's saying to Moses "I am who am," Eckhart remarks that

"God is his own isness" (M, 113), God's name is isness, an isness that all created things receive. "The one who asks who or what God is, is given the answer: isness." What in fact is the act of creation? It is "the giving of isness from nothing." This giving and sustaining of isness is a constant process and creation never stops. God "always creates." "He does not stop creating, but always creates and begins to create. . . . For creatures are always in the process and beginning of their creation" (M, 95, 86, 90, 92).

Thus we see that for Eckhart, creation, existence or isness are holy in themselves. They come closer to being verbs than nouns. They are of God. And to know and love creation is also to commune with creation's ever-present, ever-active Gift-giver. "Even he who knew nothing but the creatures would never need to think out any sermons, for every creature is full of God and is a book" (CL, 210). He admonishes us to "apprehend God in all things; for God is in all things" (SK, 60). "Every creature is God's word" (LW, p. 183). Thus every creature is a revelation. "All that is good in creatures, all their honey sweetness, is from God" (BL, 144). And this because isness, which is holy, is God's.

> Of this I am certain: if a soul understood the smallest thing that has isness, it would never turn away from it for an instant. The tiniest thing that one knows in God—if one even knew a flower, so far as it has its isness in God—that would be nobler than the whole world. . . . Isness is so noble. No creature is so tiny that it lacks isness. When caterpillars fall off a tree, they climb up a wall, so that they may preserve their isness. So noble is isness. . . . A stone is nobler, insofar as it has isness, than God and his Godhead without isness, if one could deprive him of it (CL, 195f.). (trans. adapted)

All that is is holy for Eckhart—stars and caterpillars, stones and flowers, you and me. Clearly, Eckhart's spirituality is a creation-centered one that makes demands on our everyday awareness of the holy all about us. The Creator is present and actively so.

God's Love and Need for Creation

Eckhart offers still another refreshing insight on the implications of a creation-centered spiritual pathway and that concerns the ecstasy of God at creation. Like Rabbi Heschel who talks of the "pathos" of Yahweh for human history, Eckhart insists that it is not only creatures that get high on creation but God himself does so as well! "God finds joy and rapture in us" (CL, 224). Eckhart compares God's delight and energy to that of a horse let loose in a meadow. Just as the horse would want "to pour forth its whole strength in leaping about in the meadow," so too "it is a joy to God . . . to pour out his nature and his being completely into his likeness, since he is the likeness himself" (CL, 226). "Now I will say what I have never said before: God savors himself. In the sweet savor in which God savors himself, he enjoys all creatures, not as creatures, but as creatures in God. With the savor with which God savors himself, he enjoys all things. . . . God savors himself in all things" (CL, 183).

God's pleasure, in Eckhart's estimation, is clearly due to the fact that, as Genesis insists, creation is good. Being good, it is from God. "From him all things are and are one, true, and good," for God alone is good (M, 94). Like Pseudo-Denys before him, Eckhart considers the goodness of God to be the perfection par exellence of creation. "Goodness is the proper name of God the Creator."[9] So full of ecstasy is all of creation that God the Creator might be therein in busy enjoyment within the tiniest particle of matter or in the vastest reaches of the universe.

Nobility of Human Creation in Particular

While God's panentheistic presence extends to all that exists, God is to be found especially in human beings. "God is in all things, but so far as God is Divine and so far as he is rational, God is nowhere so properly as in the soul—in the innermost of the soul" (SK, 58). Peoples' reason is "the temple of God," God's deepest dwelling place (CL, 207). Eckhart takes quite literally the belief that people are the image and likeness of the Creator. "To create," he says "is an easy thing," but when it came to the creation of people, God did more than create. He made an exact image.

> Then God said: "Let us make one like us." To create is an easy thing; one does it when and how one will. But what I make I make myself and with myself and in myself, and I impress my image into it fully. "Let us make one like us, not the Father, nor the Son, nor the Holy Spirit, but we in the counsel of the Holy Trinity will make one like ourselves."
> When God made man, he wrought an equal work in the soul, his active and eternal work. The work was great and it was nothing other than the soul, and the soul was God's work (CL, 182).

God fell in love with this special creation. "Know then that God loves the soul so deeply that if anyone were to take away from God his love of the soul, he would take away his life and his being and would kill God, if one could put it this way" (CL, 177).

It is not original sin that occupies Eckhart's interest in the creation story but the divine in the very nature of every human being. "How nobly humanity is constituted by nature" he exclaims, for "the seed of God is in us. If it was cultivated by a good, wise, and industrious laborer, it would thrive all the more and would grow up to God, whose seed it is, and the fruit would be like the divine seed. The seed of a pear tree grows into a pear tree, a hazel seed into a hazel tree, a seed of God into God" (SK, 149, 151). The nobility of humans, indeed their divinity, is potential only. It is a seed. It needs work, as Eckhart says, "good, wise and industrious labor" in order to come to fruition. The work is not so much one of being freed from an original sin as it is a return to our divine origins. The fall for Eckhart is a fall into dualisms,[10] a fall into forgetfulness of our divine depths and potential. It is a fall into superficiality or, in his words, a fall into the "outer" rather than the "inner" person. The fall then is *our* fall and not an inherited one only. It is up to us to fall out of the superficial and outer person and into the deep, full, and divine one. The superficial or outer person is vulnerable to "what is wicked, evil, and devilish" while the rooted or inner person is "the field in which God has sowed his image and his likeness . . ., the seed of divine nature" (SK, 150).

We see then that Eckhart's optimism toward human nature is not based on a naive repression of the human potential for the demonic, nor on a denial of sin. Rather it is, in true creation-theology fashion, an emphasis on the goodness of creation as described in the first chapters of Genesis. He refuses to relinquish the creation story to the story of the fall. Here we see why Jesus came primarily to call us back and not to wipe out an original sin. This calling us back is itself redemptive and so here we learn how, within creation spirituality, redemption plays a role. But the role is played within the grace of creation and not prior to it or before it. Jesus comes to call us back to our bigness and our divinity. "When God created all creatures, they were so mean and so small that he could not move in them. But he made the soul so similar to himself and of like nature, so that he could give himself to the soul" (CL, 173). God needs our bigness in which to dwell. It is for God the Creator, not just for human beings, that God the Son became one of us. God needs us. "God's nature, his being and his divinity depend on the fact that he must work in the soul. Praise, praise be to God for this! When God works in the soul, he loves his work there. The work is love and love is God" (CL, 182).

III. THE SECOND PATH:
LETTING GO (ABGESCHIEDENHEIT)
AND LETTING BE (GELASSENHEIT)

In addition to the experience of God in creation, a way of exteriority, Eckhart preaches the way of interiority or the birth of God in the soul of the individual. Before considering the second way (path three below), we ought to ask the question, who needs it? If creation is so full of God, if panentheism is real, why should a way of interiority be necessary at all? Eckhart's answer would be, I think, something like this: "If you think your joy was full from the grace of creation, you haven't seen anything yet! There is much more to come."

The Radical Limits of Creation

The first reason why creation is not the only experience of God is that creation is limited while God and our experience of God is not. Creation is not big enough, one might say, for Eckhart's spiritual expectations. "All the creatures cannot express God, for they are not receptive of that which he is. He . . . the ineffable one, has no name" (CL, 158). God is so much vaster than creatures. "All the creatures that God ever created or could yet create if he chose to do so, are all but small and minute as compared with God" (CL, 176). The point of a needle is larger in relation to the entire sky than is the whole universe in relation to God, he points out.

But there is still another dimension to the limits of creation—a more radical one by far. And that is, that creation is of itself and in relation to the Creator, nothing. How does Eckhart, who as we saw envisioned God omnipresent in creation, come to this startling conclusion? When Eckhart says, as we cite him for saying earlier, above, that "isness is God" he means it. Isness comes, continually, from the Creator. However full of God the creature is, it still depends wholly and absolutely on the Giver of isness. Thus, from the perspective of the Giver of isness, those who receive isness themselves possess none and are therefore nothing. Creatures are—at a root level—nothing because they do not possess isness but must continually receive it. "Everything which is created, in itself is nothing" (LW II, 354). "The whole universe as compared to God is as nothing, every being, is as a middle term between God and nothing" (LW III, 185). Eckhart's following expression was condemned by the Inquisition: "All creatures are a mere nothing. I do not say that they are something very slight or something, but that they are a mere nothing" (CL, 80).

Eckhart is not saying, as gnostic dualisms might, that creatures are bad or morally reprobate or created by an evil spirit. But that, from the point of view of God's isness, they are nothing. That is, that they do not exist by themselves. Another way in which Eckhart describes this situation is by an analogy with color (an accident in scholastic terms) and the thing colored (a substance in scholastic terms). "The color of the wall depends on the wall, and so the existence of creatures depends on the love of God. Separate the color from the wall and it would cease to be. So all creation would cease to exist if separated from the love that God is" (BL, 244).

What is so vital to remember—and the Inquisitors failed to grasp this—is the dialectic that Eckhart is presuming in these surprising statements.[11] The dialectic between creatures as grace and creatures as nothing. Between isness and nonexistence. Between God (who is isness) and creatures (who have no isness that they have not received). Creatures, then, even though full of God are also empty of God. Eckhart is a person who deals in extremes—as any spiritual theologian must. But he is not dualistic; rather he is dialectical in appreciating both ends of a tense, vital, life-process. Ecstasy is both an experience of the infinite and an intimation of the finite. Both experiences occur simultaneously in ecstasy. The one does not falsify the other.

It would constitute a fatal injustice to Eckhart's spirituality and to efforts by persons to live it if one were to ignore the first dimension to this dialectic, namely that of the grace of creation. The latter experience, nothingness, makes spiritual sense only in light of the former experience, which is the fullness (indeed the divine fullness) of isness. Many small-minded and ill-trained spiritualists leap into only the second stage of the dialectic and do great damage to themselves and others by so doing. Here—in failing to love creation well and fully—lies the roots of much sado-masochism in religious circles. For when one fails to love creation well, one loves it badly and that displaced energy reveals itself in masochism (self-hatred) and sadism (control over others).[12] The first path, the grace of creation, is not an option to take or leave in grasping Eckhart's eschatological vision. It lies at the heart of full faith living. The believer who has not tasted the grace and beauty of creation and thus of the first person of the Trinity (God as Creator) is in no position whatsoever to experience the full complement of persons (the Godhead) in the breakthrough that will give birth to God.

A Path Called Letting Go *(Abgeschiedenheit)*

The most radical limit of all to creation is our understanding of creation. It is this above all that has to be transformed so that we pass from knowledge to "divine knowledge." From knowing to unknowing. From learning *about* God to knowing God.

For Eckhart, the nothingness of creatures should not be ignored, forgotten, repressed or covered-up. It should be explored. The adventure of exploring nothingness will itself yield a profound, a truly eschatological, revelation: That there, in the depths of our desert as dependent beings, God not only lives but gives birth constantly to God. That, beyond God who is nameable as Creator lies the Godhead who is unnameable Trinity and who is "a negation of all names" (DW I, 253).

This process of exploring nothingness cannot be accomplished by will power (gritting one's teeth) or by intellect power (the most intense thinking). The process is by definition the surrendering of power, and with it a surrendering of our images and all preconceptions of things as we think they are. It is a *via negationis,* a way of letting go of our thoughts about things. Eckhart describes the process in several ways. "As long as anything of the creature shines within you, you will not see God. . . . The soul that is to find God must jump and leap over all creatures if she is to find God" (CL, 177). "The highest and best of things that are created and made cover and discolor the image of God in us. 'Take away,' says Solomon, 'the dross from the silver, then the purest vessel shall shine forth'" (SK, 154). We have

seen, in discussing the divine origins of the human person, how
Eckhart believed that people were divine in their roots. But
people need to get in touch with that divinity, and they are out of
touch as long as they are out of contact with their deepest self
which includes nothingness as well as isness. The issue is our
slumber, our ignorance. We are as ignorant and asleep about
our nothingness as we are about our isness. When we wake up
about the one we wake up about the other.

How do we so wake up? It is a process, a new attitude, and
Eckhart coined a new word for it, *abgeschiedenheit* or letting
go.[13] To understand this process we need to recall that Eckhart,
as always, was thinking dialectically. Letting go is not so simplistic as separating oneself from creatures. It is more radical than
that; it is separating oneself from the separation itself! It is "the
negation (detachment) of the negation (creature)."[14] The dialectic, we recall, is based on the dialectic of being and nothingness
that constitutes creatures and is therefore a journey of truth or
of coming to the truth of ourselves. Being a journey and a process it is ourselves becoming dialectical, which is ourselves becoming true to ourselves. It is a letting go of all.

> Who are those who honor God? Those who have entirely re-
> nounced themselves, and who do not in the least seek their
> own in anything, whatever it may be, whether great or small,
> who do not look below themselves, or above themselves, or at
> themselves, who love neither goods nor honors, nor comfort
> nor joy, nor advantage, nor devotion, nor holiness, nor re-
> ward, nor heaven, but have renounced all this, and all that is
> theirs (CL, 185).

All goals, then, even heaven itself, need to be suspended in
this particular pathway. The cessation of all discursive thinking
that Eckhart calls for is so total that even the thought of God is to
be abandoned. We need to enter a desert where God is not
defined for us. A God beyond God might then be listened to
whose name is ineffable. "The highest and loftiest thing that
man can renounce is to renounce God for the sake of God" (CL,

225). The unnamed Deity is not subject to our naming. In the depths of us lives the true God, but even our seeking needs to cease for us to find God there. "Truly, 'Thou art a hidden God,' in the ground of the soul where God's ground and the soul's are one ground. The more one seeks Thee, the less one can find Thee. You should seek him in such a way as never to find him. If you do not seek him, you will find him" (CL, 245). We are urged to cease our craving—not because objects are evil but because the very process or dynamics of craving blocks out still greater possibilities. "For as long as the craving for more and more is in you, God can never dwell nor work in you. These things must always go out if God is to enter in" (CL, 219). Cease greed we are told, for greater gifts await you. "This above all, then, be ready at all times for the gifts of God and always for new ones" (BL, 32).

Letting Be (Gelassenheit)

Consequent on letting go, there occurs a deepening experience of reverence for all things—God, self, others, creation. It is a process of letting be (Gelassenheit).

The biggest gift that awaits us is the realization of God. "There where the creature ends, God begins to be. God does not ask anything of you other than that you go out of yourself according to your mode as creature and that you let God be God in you" (DW I, 92). Here lies the crux of this journey: letting God be God (and not just our preconceived ideas of God) in us. It is for this reason that we abandon even the names we have given to God. "I pray God that he may quit me of God" (DP, 308). And we abandon suppositions about Jesus Christ. "It is good that I leave you" Eckhart quotes Jesus as saying to his disciples, and Eckhart comments. "Let images go therefore and unite your-selves to the being without form" (DW V, 430).

One who is truly "poor in spirit" is one who has made this journey of letting go. Such a person has learned that "becoming poor in spirit is letting God be God" (DW V, 432) and possesses an inward poverty wherein one's quests of wanting, knowing, and having are stilled. Eckhart describes this journey of poverty and concludes that "God is identical with the spirit and that is the most intimate poverty a person can find" (DP, 309). The attitude of letting go is clearly the opposite of control, clinging to, grabbing, hoarding. The radical openness that Eckhart advises is a readiness to experience realized eschatology. It is eternal life before death; ecstasy before death; life before death; God now. It is a letting God happen within and among us. It is also an emptying, which is an image that Eckhart employs often. "If a cask is to contain wine, one must necessarily pour out the water; the cask must be bare and empty. Therefore, if you would receive divine joy and God, it is necessary for you to pour out the creatures. . . . everything that is to receive and to be receptive must and should be empty" (SK, 122). Eckhart instructs us in a profoundly antimaterialistic spirituality when he tells us to let go of all objects.

What should never be lost sight of in comprehending Eckhart's nothingness and letting-go-pathway is how it belongs altogether *within* his appreciation of the grace-fullness of creation. One does not let go of objects because objects are bad or inferior but because, as one learns from loving God in creation, our way of knowing requires an emptiness for every fullness, a void for every ecstasy, a desert for every lush meadow.

Methods and Spiritual Tactics

There has been a presumption in the redemption spirituality that has dominated Christianity since the sixteenth century that spirituality is about exercises. And there has been a presumption as well that spiritual theology is "ascetic theology" when in fact that term for spirituality was not employed until the year 1655. Eckhart's wholistic spirituality fortunately antedates all this preoccupation with exercises, methods, and ascetic mortifications that so attract spiritualists. Eckhart is loudly silent on the subject of tactics, exercises, and techniques for the spiritual life. "He does not venture, at least in the texts that we possess, into the domain of techniques of the spiritual life."[15] He possesses "no technique of spiritual prayer, no planned steps in the ascent to spiritual perfection."[16]

Not only is Eckhart unwilling to offer spiritual recipe guides, he is not infrequently overtly critical of such. "You should not restrict yourself to any method, for God is not in any one kind of devotion, neither in this nor that. Those who receive God thus do him wrong. They receive the method and not God. . . . Whether it be weeping or sighing, however much there is of it, it is not God at all" (CL, 235f). One reason Eckhart is so suspicious of methods is that he, true to path one, believes God is quite literally everywhere. "It is a delusion to think that men can obtain more of God by contemplation, or devotion, or sweetness, than by the fire or in the stable. As long as we perform our works for the sake of salvation or of going to heaven, we are on the wrong track" (DW I, 91). He is suspicious here of the confusion of means and ends that occurs in so much tactical mysticism. He is a champion of ends, not means. And the end—God—is quite truly everywhere. "The person who is not conscious of God's presence, but who must always be going out to get him from this and that, who has to seek him by diverse methods, whether by means of some activity, person, or place—such people have not attained God" (DP, 60).

Another objection Eckhart brings to methodical exercises is the externalness of them. They can easily deceive one.

> There are people who in penitential exercises and external practices, of which they make a great deal, cling to their selfish I. May God have pity on these people who know so little of divine truth! These people are called holy because of their external appearances; but on the inside they are asses, for they do not understand at all the correct meaning of divine truth (DP, 304).

Methods weigh us down, make us uptight, interfere with the God of creation and destroy our senses of humor, rendering us more ego-oriented instead of less. We can become their slaves and be rendered more ego-conscious instead of becoming explorers of the id or "the naked being" within us. They render us less than free and spontaneous. "God," Eckhart insists, "did not bind human salvation to any special method . . ." (DP, 78). One *Ave* "uttered sincerely is more potent than a thousand uttered mechanically" since "the heart is not made pure by prayer . . . but rather the prayer is made pure by the pure heart" (BL 238f.).

What exercises conceived of within a redemption spirituality model fail at most of all is that they never allow the letting go experience to happen within the grace of creation itself. In this way they build up a dualistic rather than a dialectical consciousness that one never recovers from. For Eckhart, the letting go applies to spiritual exercises themselves for "no exterior work is so perfect that it may not hinder the inner life" (DP, 444). Eckhart is not forbidding the use of exercises—only counseling that the spiritual life may be a great deal simpler than one might think. For God is everywhere. "Take God and enjoy him in every manner, every thing, and do not deal and hunt all around for your special way: That has been my joy! To this end all kinds of activities may contribute and every work may be a help; but if it does not, let it go!" (BL 250, adapted). "He who seeks God without structure apprehends him as he is in himself" (DW I, 92). "All paths lead to God and he is on them all evenly, to him who knows. . . . Such and such may be the way, but it is not God" (BL 250). His own spiritual development, he has told us, is utterly simple, supported by God's grace and his openness to experience God everywhere. "Nothing is easier for the soul grounded in God's grace than to let go of all things" (DW III, 267).

The path of letting go and letting be, then, is a free and easy path. A path of laughter and freedom—one characterized by the dialectical capacity to laugh at everything—even spiritual exercises. It never puts down creation or things or moralizes about them, for in fact it is a freeing path, an instruction for our overly aggressive and overly rational minds. It is a path within creation and not outside of it or in opposition to it. It is a nonelitist path that anyone with the right intentions might take, for it is in no way restricted to cloistered persons though they are not exempt from it either. It is truly a dialectical, not a dualistic, path. It is a joy-filled path, a freeing path that lets creatures be creatures, self be self, others be others, and God be God.

IV. THE THIRD PATH: BREAKTHROUGH AND BIRTHING OF GOD

The process of letting go reaches a climax at the point of stillness. "Nothing in all creation is so like God as stillness" declares Eckhart (BL 243). "The best and noblest of all that one can come to in this life is to be silent and let God work and let God speak" (DP, 419). Stillness is so holy because it is in stillness that birth is allowed to happen. Silence is active and pregnant for Eckhart. It means nonverbal communion and the entrance of a new word into human history and experience. "It is in a forgetting and in a not-knowing that the word will come. There is no question that the proper way to hear the word is in a stillness and a silence" (DP, 430). Revelation, Eckhart says, takes place in a new word, a new kind of knowledge—one of receptivity and not control. "Then will we know with divine knowledge, and then will our unknowledge be ennobled and adorned with supernatural knowledge. And thus it is that when we allow ourselves to hold back we become fuller than when we work" (BP, 430). In the grace of stillness a new word is born —*the* Word. The birth of the Son of God in us is a major theme of Eckhart's, a major event along the path of our spiritual journeying.

Breakthrough and Deification

When one lets go and thereby overcomes subject/object relationships even between God and people a new and deeper union between God and people occurs. Eckhart coined a word for this occurrence, *Durchbruch,* or breakthrough. The grace of breakthrough is even greater than the grace of creation.

> A great master says that his breaking through is more noble than his flowing out, and that is true. . . . In the breakthrough, where I stand divested of my own will and of the will of God and of all his works and of God himself, there I am beyond all creatures and I am neither "God" nor creature, but rather what I was and what I will remain now and ever more (DW II, 504).

Creation is a flowing out *(Ausfliessen)* and results in only partial God-likeness. But breakthrough is even "more noble" for it results in our "entering spiritually into God." The God we enter into in the breakthrough is not God the Creator but the God-head or Trinity. Notice that in the breakthrough, which is *our* breakthrough or our awakening, Eckhart is not talking of our entering into our inner selves and finding God there but of our "entering into God." In other words, God is already here, there and all over, but we need to awaken to this fact and the awakening is our breakthrough.

Such a breakthrough puts an end to separation, division, and dualism between us and God. "The desert is not productive of anything, even the deity is arid, creates nothing. In the desert everything only begins; but God disappears. The desert is the vast solitude, there is no place for two in the desert. The opposition between Creator and creature is abolished."[17] The I gives way to the we in the desert. The breakthrough "rejoins creation with the creator so radically that there remains neither creature nor creator but only the eternal darkness of the Godhead. All distinction is overcome and there remains only the undivided one."[18]

It is here that deification truly happens. For when a person is united to God, "he or she is more God than creature. . . . Such a person is truly by grace what God is by nature, and even God no longer sees any difference between himself and this person"

(DW V, 22). When God touches the depths of a person, "the soul becomes, by the touch of God, as noble as God himself" (DW I, 171). Our divine origins are revealed once again. "Can we say: 'If man loves God, he then becomes God?' This sounds like heresy.... The prophet says, 'I have said: Ye are gods, and the children of the All Highest.' It sounds strange that man can thus become God in love; yet it is true in the eternal truth. Our Lord Jesus Christ said it" (CL 234). The union is an intimate one and extends to work that people and God do together.

> God and this humble man are entirely one and not two; for what God works, he also works, and what God wills, he also wills, and what God is, he also is: one life and one being... under these circumstances this man is a divine being, a divine being is this man, for here the kiss is exchanged between the unity of God and the humble man (CL 242).

While Eckhart is emphasizing here the very real Christian tradition of deification (much more alive a tradition in Eastern than Western Christianity), he is not suggesting that the identity of God and people is a univocal one. Rather, he sees it as an analogous kind of identity, and at his trial he called it "absurd" to understand this identity as univocal. It is not so much a union of substance as of motion and of journeying. In Schurmann's words, it is *"peregrinale"* or "wandering."[19] In the desert the person who has "let go" becomes the divine space and temple where God works and dwells within the world.

Birthing

The ultimate result of our deification and our letting go to let God happen in us is our giving birth to God's Son in ourselves. Eckhart takes quite literally the words of John (4:4) that we are children of God. This begetting was our creation. "We are the only-begotten Son whom the Father begot eternally." God's love for us is eternal and thus our relation to God as children of God. "When the Father begot all creatures, he begot me also, and I

*Son of God — Logos, reason,
sanity, Torah, illumination, justice,
care, commandment*

flowed out with all creatures and yet remained in the Father" (CL, 212). When we say the words "Your will be done on earth as it is in heaven," says Eckhart, we are saying that "I become he" and that "my will become his will" (SK 59). In the full way in which God dwells in the human person, "The Father begets his Son in the innermost of the soul, and begets you with his only-begotten Son as not less than him." And this, our being born a son of God, is the purpose of Christ's coming into human history. "God became man through and through, in order that he might beget you as his only-begotten Son and not less" (SK, 59).

But for Eckhart we are not only children of God but parents also. "Let yourself give birth to the Son of God." We become, by grace and the breakthrough which is a recognition of grace, generators of God in history, for "the Son of God is always being born" (LW IV, 174). God depends upon us, "he must generate through you" (CL 148). Our giving birth to God marks the echatological era for it is "the fullness of time." "When we have passed beyond the bounds of time and temporal things we are happy and free at all times. This is the fullness of time, when the Son of God is begotten in you" (CL, 219).

Here Eckhart is explaining what becoming Christ-like means to him. It does *not* mean that we are in some static state of perfection but that we are verbs, part of a divine process of giving birth continually to God. "To become like Christ means that the Father is birthing his Son in the soul and the soul as the Son."[20] But who is this God whom we are resembling more and more and introducing to history more and more? God too is a verb, the act of birthing. Birthing is "the divine essence,"[21] for God's highest ideal is "to bear" says Eckhart and only this birthing can exhaust the divine power (DP, 396). Following John's epistles, Eckhart insists that God is quite literally the verb called love.

One wonders whether this central theme of begetting of God by ourselves is not related to Eckhart's long meditation on Mary, the mother of Jesus, with a characteristically Eckhartian imaginative twist. He is saying that we are all mothers, be we male or female, and indeed we are all Theotokos—Mothers (bearers) of God. "Does your heart suffer? You are not yet a mother. You are

Holy Spirit

still on the way to giving birth, you are near to birth" (DP, 321). It is in the very process of giving birth that God and ourselves become one. Birth is truly sacred to Eckhart.

Eckhart sees God as "the process of life giving birth to life, a process which flows into the Trinity itself and then flows over into creatures."[22] He sees people as so God-like and so graced that they are integrally a part of this process of God's grace manifested in the breakthrough. It is no accident that Eckhart is profoundly trinitarian in his spirituality (for all creation spirituality is trinitarian) or that the trinitarian character of his vision climaxes when he elaborates the dialectical process of union of God and persons, fullness and emptiness, isness and nothing. For a living dialectic will always be trinitarian: Two tensions vitally involved create a third. Birth happens from it.

Some persons want to make the breakthrough and consequent birth of God an elitest thing reserved for a few cloistered individuals. Nothing could be further from Eckhart's spirituality. The breakthrough and the birth are potentially everyday events, as near as ecstasy itself. All it requires is our "letting go" so God can happen in us because God wants so badly to happen in us. Ecstasy is letting go.[23] The breakthrough is God's breakthrough, not ours, in the sense that it is a grace. God does it. But it is ours insofar as it is our awakening, and we let it happen by removing obstacles in its way. It is, after all, our slumber that is broken through. We wake up so that we begin to see the truth of the space we live in and begin to see it rightly. We begin to see all reality from within the Godhead and not as a spectator from outside. We begin to see what it means to believe that we are bathed in a sea called God. We begin to see reality as it is.

V. PATH FOUR: COMPASSION: OUR RETURN TO RE-CREATE CREATION

Meister Eckhart's spiritual journey avoids all spiritualisms. It does this, as we have seen, by planting its roots deep within the experience of creation itself and, as we shall see in this section, by returning from its experience within the Godhead to seeing and acting differently in creation. Eckhart avoids entirely the introversion of so much Augustinian and Cartesian spiritualities for he insists on returning *to* creation and to human life of politics and ego-torn worlds as renewed and eschatological persons. Spirituality, he says, "is not to be learned by world-flight, running away from things, turning solitary, and going apart from the world. Rather, one must learn an inner solitude, wherever or with whomsoever he may be. He must learn to penetrate things and find God there" (BL, 9). For Eckhart, spirituality is not a flight from creation but a re-creation of the way we taste creation. Spirituality is our growth in ecstatic consciousness and our sharing of it. As Schurmann points out, even ecstasy for Eckhart is creation-centered or "mundane" and is not neoplatonic for it does not flee from time or the world though it does taste the timeless. "In Eckhart there is no appeal to a privileged experience, no regret of falling back into the body after a repose in the divine, and above all no opposition between a higher world and a lower world into which the soul is resigned to redescend."[24]

Eckhart's spiritual journey is too verb-oriented and therefore too historically conscious to rest on laurels of piety or to wallow in spiritual seances with the divine: It goes to work to transform the world into a recreation worthy of its Creator. His mysticism finds its healthy expression in prophecy. After all, Eckhart himself was not a monk who fled the world or even set up an alternative culture to the world; he was a Dominican friar which means his vocation was to serve the world from within the world. Did he, to take his own life as an example, live quietistically with his personal spiritual experiences? Hardly. "Eckhart was a professor at a great *studium generale,* the administrative head of a vast Dominican province, a famous preacher, the author of voluminous works in two languages, and the spiritual counselor of numerous nuns and friars. There was no time for idleness in such a life."[25] For Eckhart, paths I, II, III treated above are meant for others. In birthing the Son, "by an immense exertion, the dormant spark of the soul is roused to energy and action. Nor does effort cease after mystic union has been attained. The soul rests in God, it is true, but this is not a gospel of inaction. Whatever gifts we have or lack, we must devote them exclusively to the glory of God in all respects."[26] If eternal life has already begun, then the world becomes a stage for re-creation and creation becomes a new name for heaven.

> A person should apprehend God in all things. . . . That person is highly praised by God who perceives all things as divine— more noble than they are of themselves. Now effort and love and a careful attention to the inner person are needed for this and a vigorous, honest, reflective, active knowledge of all one's attitudes toward things and people (DP, 60f).

Eckhart calls for a living in the world with a panentheistic awareness. It demands courage to remain grounded in creation and not flee from it.

> He enunciates a call for a certain type of existence among things. Such is Eckhart's this-worldliness, which is opposed to the other-worldliness of the Neoplatonists. For Eckhart, the first and the last word of his preaching is a deontology of man exposed to risk: . . . Such a deontology of the risk—"you will run the danger of detachment"—proceeds on the level of objects, it teaches an imperative for the use of what falls into our hands.[27]

Because Eckhart's letting go presumes attachment in a prior love of creation, his spirituality has nothing of repression in it. How could anyone who believes "isness is God" repress life? There are divine implications in the decisions we make in this life since in a certain sense God depends on people to carry on the work of re-creation. "Just as little as I can do anything without him, he cannot really accomplish anything apart from me" (CL, 249). Without the hard work of humankind God is not continually reborn and therefore God dies. "We slay God" (CL, 174), and we, human history, die in the process.

Compassion as World-Transformation

For realized eschatology to be authentic it needs to be dialectical. Otherwise, one who believed heaven was on earth would be
blind indeed to the hell that is also on earth. It is this hell, this
not-yet, this chasm between heaven and earth that drives the
mystical believer into prophetic action and consciousness. Eckhart found the not-yet of God's fullness to be most apparent in
the arena of human affairs. He could hardly have been more
blunt about the priority that the suffering of others was to play
in spirituality.

> We should abandon raptures sometimes for the sake of a bet-
> ter love which is to perform a loving ministry of work where it
> is most needed, whether spiritually or physically. As I have
> often said: Were a person in so great a rapture as St. Paul once
> experienced, and he learned of a sick person who needed a
> cup of soup from him, I consider it far better that you leave
> your rapture out of love and serve the needy person with what
> is a bigger love by far (DP, 67).

Notice how Eckhart insists that this is an often repeated doctrine of his and how, matter-oriented that he is, he does not
designate spiritual service as distinct from social or physical needs
of persons. Cheerfulness, he adds, is the essence of such service.
Love of neighbor is a sign of the eschatological person for Eckhart. "We should walk in newness of life by attracting, building
up, enlightening and lighting up our neighbor as John says: 'he
was the light of men.' This ought to be our kind of life also, one
that is the light of men because 'you are the light of the world'"
(LW IV, 154).

Love of neighbor is less a moral imperative for Eckhart (who
hates imperatives and seldom if ever commands) than it is a
logical outcome of the new consciousness that is born of letting
go. A consciousness of the equality of all things and the interconnectedness of all things. A consciousness, one might say, of
compassion.

Whoever wishes to become a son of God, whoever wishes that the Word made flesh dwell in him, must love his neighbor as himself, that is to say, as much as himself.... Whoever has charity in any way does not love his neighbor less than himself, for he loves God who is in all and all things in God; but in the One, there is no longer any distinction, there is neither Jews nor Greeks (LW III, #290).

We have here the political implications of Eckhart's panentheism. "All things are equally my own in him; and if we are to come into our own, so that all things may be our own, we must understand him equally in all things, in one not more than another, for he is equally in all things" (CL, 235). It is this democratic panentheism, the presence of God equally everywhere, that leads us to compassionate service of neighbor. "You should love all people as yourself, esteem and consider them alike. What happens to another, whether it be evil or good, should be the same to you as if it had happened to you" (CL, 234). Compassion includes our rejoicing at the good that befalls others; there is no room for jealousy which implies competition within compassion since to love neighbor is to love self. "The good person praises good people," comments Eckhart—"that is the mark of the good person" (CL, 240). A compassionate person delights at others' delights. "It is just as if he were in heaven and he has more frequent joy than if he only enjoyed his own good" (CL, 172).

Compassion is a way of seeing reality for Eckhart—it is not an additional commandment. It does not require a meditation on how God is in neighbor nor a condescending paternalism toward others. It simply requires a flow of energy from the truth of the unity of things in God and God in things. It is a logical consequence of the consciousness of panentheism and of the new awareness that letting go affords us. There is no dualism in this love of God and neighbor.[28]

Justice and Political Panentheism

The we consciousness that occurs from paths I, II, and III is a political consciousness and Eckhart praises the fact that salvation is public and political (God and us) and not private (God and me). "God has been a common Savior of the entire world, and for this I am indebted to him with much more thanks than if he had saved only myself" (DP, 77). The preference of the "our" over the "my" consciousness is nowhere more evident than in the prayer that Jesus left. Eckhart comments on the "Our" in the *Our Father*. "Note first that it does not say 'my' because prayer which charity elicits pleases many. . . . We should remember that all are our brothers and coheirs and we love them thus, thus we act as brothers, as was said: 'You are all brothers'" (Matt 23:8) (SOD, 4). He comments on the phrase, "Hallowed be thy name, thy kingdom come." "It should be noted that it does not say 'your name be sanctified in me,' but universally, 'let it be sanctified,' 'let it come,' 'let it be,' teaching us to pray for the whole world" (SOD, 8). Eckhart's spirituality is so nonparochial, so universal yet creation-oriented, being as it is for the "whole world."

Commenting on the expression "Give us this day our daily bread," he demonstrates how compassion and unity lead necessarily to acts of justice.

> Bread is given to us not in order that we eat it alone but that others who are indigent might be participants, lest anyone say "my bread given to me for me" but "*our*," as it were given for me and for others through me and to me through others. Still, however, bread and all similar necessities of the present life are for us with others and on account of others and given for others in us. He who does not give to another what belongs to another, does not eat his own bread, but another's at the same time with his own. Thus, when we eat bread acquired justly, we eat our bread; but when bread is acquired by evil means and with sin, we are not eating our own but another's. For everything which we have unjustly is not ours (SOD, 11).

Compassion is not sentimentalized by Eckhart. It is an issue of sharing bread by way of justice and of criticizing the origins of the things we use. For justice, he declares, "is the giving to another what is his due" (DW I, 452). A sign of the true prophet, Eckhart says, will be that such a person will act like a tree which offers shade from the sun and fruit for nourishment. He will offer "shade for the protection of his neighbor and the fruit of his own generosity to his hungry neighbors" (LW IV, 185). Eckhart, when quizzed on whether contemplation or action should take priority, follows the Dominican tradition explained by Aquinas—that love of neighbor takes precedence. "In contemplation you serve only yourself, in good works you serve many people," says Eckhart. But in fact his spirituality wants to cut through such an action/contemplation dualism since compassion is one energy, not two.

> St. Thomas says that the active life is better than the contemplative, for in it one pours out the love he has received in contemplation. Yet it is all one; for what we plant in the soul of contemplation we shall reap in the harvest of action. . . . but it is all a single process with one end in view—that God is. . . . In all he does, man has only his one vision of God (BL, 111).

Eckhart does not ignore the social injustices of his day in which the nonprivileged often lived wretched lives. He raises consciousness about such realities, bringing them into his talks.

> What do the poor people do, who undergo the same or much worse sickness and suffering without anyone to give them even some cold water? They are forced to seek their dry bread in rain, snow and cold, from house to house. Therefore, if you will be comforted, forget those who are better off and think about those who are less fortunate (DP, 107).

He was criticized for confusing the poor people by his sermons whereas in fact he was arousing them to the truth of their conditions. He replied, when he was so accused that "if ignorant people are not taught, they will never learn, nor will they ever know how to live or die . . ." (BL, 73). Mercy is defined by Eckhart as "that which orders man by regulating him to his

neighbor," and he declares that "he who follows mercy finds life
in respect to himself; justice in respect to his neighbor and glory
in respect to God" (LW IV, 124). Eternal life, then, or glory, is
indeed linked up with justice towards neighbor. But the mercy
or compassion that Eckhart speaks of begins with our own attitudes toward ourselves. As he puts it, "we have mercy both
toward our body and our soul" (LW IV, 127). In other words,
compassion reflects the unity that overcomes all dualism, even
that of medieval philosophy between body and soul. Indeed,
Eckhart declares that "the soul loves the body" (DW II, 747).

Eckhart does not cease his spiritual vision with talk of mere
attitudes. He is interested in structural change and liberation as
well as personal, for he knows one feeds on the other. Thus he
distinguishes among what he calls "monastic, political, and
theological virtue" and defines political virtue as that which pre-
pares a person to be a member of a community (*collegio*) of
citizens. It applies to enemies no less than to friends.

> The act of political virtue is this: it produces for friends in God
> and for enemies on account of God; in so far as an enemy
> might be hungry it feeds him; if thirsty, it gives him drink.
> Moreover the fruit that follows from this is not only for citi-
> zens, but is also an appropriate friendship toward enemies. As
> Paul says in Romans 12: "By doing this you will heap coals of
> fire on his head" (LW V, 97).

We see in this commentary as well the politicizing of Jesus' para-
ble of "he who feeds a hungry one feeds me."

Eckhart devotes an entire sermon to an in-depth critique of
the "merchandizing mentality" that the economic capitalist system of his day spawned and another to criticizing the politically
privileged few of his society. In the latter sermon he declares
that "everyone is a nobleman."[29] It is clear that there was nothing privatizing about Eckhart's spirituality. As Schurmann
comments, apropos of Eckhart's institutional criticism: "Meister
Eckhart turns against scholasticism. His preaching is seditious: it

rises up against the project of a culture which reduces the Indeterminate to the disposition of man, which makes it serviceable to spiritual comfort, collective security, academic erudition, and institutions."[30]

CONCLUSION

We have considered the fourfold path of spiritual journeying of Meister Eckhart. All paths intersect and interdepend, one on the other. One cannot separate politics from mysticism in Eckhart's holistic vision. We have seen how a panentheistic awareness of God becomes a democratic and political panentheism as well. All is set in the matrix of realized eschatology, for Eckhart did not believe only *in* Jesus but *that* Jesus inaugurated a new age.[31] A Messianic era that will be characterized by a remembrance and experience of our divine origins and of the divine origins in and through us. Eckhart was one of those rare spirits who believed to the end that the future had already begun.

NOTES

1. Cf. C. F. Kelley, *Meister Eckhart on Divine Knowledge* (Yale University Press, 1977): "It is now admitted by practically all Eckhartian scholars that had the fourteenth-century authorities intelligently and dispassionately investigated all the Meister's writings, he would probably never have suffered a condemnation" (p. 15). As I indicate in the next paragraph, Eckhart follows Aquinas on most of the significant issues in spirituality. It should be remembered in this regard that Aquinas was canonized only three years before Eckhart's trial—which is to say that the cloud of three condemnations of Aquinas lay heavily over Eckhart's entire preaching and writing career.

2. Matthew Fox, *On Becoming a Musical, Mystical Bear: Spirituality American Style* (Paulist, 1976), pp. xviii-xx. See my "Elements

of a Biblical, Creation-Centered Spirituality" in *Spirituality Today* (December 1978), pp. 360–369.

3. DP-111. Most citations from Eckhart himself will be referenced within the text and abbreviated as follows:

LW: *Meister Eckhart. Die lateinischen Werke,* ed. by E. Benz, J. Koch, et al. Kohlhammer ed, vols. I-V. Stuttgart, 1938ff.

DW: *Meister Eckhart. Die deutschen Werke,* ed. by Josef Quint, et al. Kohlhammer ed, vols. I-V except IV., Stuttgart, 1938ff.

DP: Meister Eckhart. *Deutsche Predigten und Tractate,* ed., Josef Quint. Munich, 1963.

M: Armand A. Maurer, trans., *Meister Eckhart: Parisian Questions and Prologues* (Toronto: 1974)

CL: James M. Clark, trans. *Meister Eckhart* (NY: 1957)

SK: James M. Clark and John V. Skinner, *Meister Eckhart* (London: 1958)

BL: Raymond Blakney, *Meister Eckhart: A Modern Translation* (NY: 1941)

4. "Super Oratione Dominica," in Raymundus Klibansky, ed., *Magistri Eckhardi Opera Latina,* I (Lipsiae: S. Sabina, 1934), pp. 8f. Subsequent references will be abbreviated: SOD.

5. Vladimir Lossky, *Théologie Négative et Connaissance de Dieu chez Maître Eckhart* (Paris: Vrin, 1973), p. 188. It is not only theologians who miss Eckhart's realized eschatology. Philosophers try to explain Eckhart without even invoking the concept. Since it is a theological and not a philosophical category, the fact of their lacuna is understandable. However, the results in misinterpreting Eckhart are disastrous.

6. The story is well told by Reiner Schurmann, *Maître Eckhart ou La Joie Errante* (Paris: 1972), p. 202. Especially noteworthy is the fact that Eckhart invoked this passage so critical to his thought at his defense trial. "God, who is undivided and one by essence, is intimate and near to each one of us, 'in him we live, move, and have our being.'" (Cited in Lossky, *Théologie Négative,* p. 361). Aquinas says: "That which is in God is God." (*Sum. theol.,* I, q. 27, a. 3, ad 1).

7. Kelley, *Meister Eckhart,* p. 131.

8. Cf. *Sum. theol.*, I, II, q. 111, a. 1, ad. 2.

9. Schurmann, *Maître Eckhart,* p. 142. See Pseudo-Denys, *In Div. nom.*, IV, 1.

10. For the fall as a fall into dualisms, see Lossky, *Théologie Négative,* p. 58.

11. Cf. Maurice de Gandillac, "La 'dialectque' de Maítre Eckhart," in *La Mystique Rhenane: Colloque de Strasbourg* (Paris: PUF, 1963), pp. 59–94.

12. Ernest Becker, *The Denial of Death* (Macmillan, 1975), p. 139 warns of the "cheap heroism" that sado-masochism can bring about.

13. I translate *Abgeschiedenheit* as "letting go" instead of "detachment" because spiritualist spiritualities in the centuries since Eckhart have appropriated the term "detachment" in the context of ascetic mortifications and with Eckhart no such implications are intended as we shall see below. Schurmann translates it as "detachment" and uses verbs of deliverance as synonyms such as "being freed," "becoming free," "being a virgin," "quitting."

14. Schurmann, *Maître Eckhart,* p. 173.

15. Louis Cognet, *Introduction aux Mystiques Rheno-flamands* (Paris: Desclee, 1968), p. 94.

16. Clarke, *Meister Eckhart,* p. 93. One reason for this that Clarke fails to grasp is that Eckhart does *not* conceive of "spiritual perfection" (a term he never uses) as an "ascent."

17. Schurmann, *Maître Eckhart,* p. 214.

18. John D. Caputo, "Fundamental Themes in Eckhart's Mysticism," *The Thomist* 42, (April, 1978) p. 216.

19. Schurmann, *Maître Eckhart,* p. 98. See p. 204.

20. John Loeschen, "The God Who Becomes: Eckhart on Divine Relativity," *The Thomist* 35 (1971), p. 406.

21. Ibid., p. 412.

22. John D. Caputo, "Meister Eckhart and the Later Heidegger: The Mystical Element in Heidegger's Thought: Part I," *Journal of History of Philosophy* 12 (1974), p. 487.

23. Cf. my naming of ecstasy as the experience of God in Matthew Fox, *Whee! We, wee All the Way Home: A Guide to the New Sensual Spirituality* (Consortium Books, 1976), Part I.

24. Reiner Schurmann, *Meister Eckhart: Mystic and Philosopher*

(Bloomington: Indiana Univ. Press, 1978), p. 15. This is the English translation of *La Joie Errante*. Hereafter all references are to this edition.

25. Clark, *Meister Eckhart*, p. 81.

26. Ibid., p. 96. See p. 170.

27. Schurmann, *Meister Eckhart* p. 97.

28. Because of his profound theology and psychology of compassion, I found myself employing extensive use of Eckhart in my study on that subject, *A Spirituality Named Compassion* (Winston, 1979).

29. See my "Meister Eckhart and Karl Marx: The Mystic as Political Theologian" in *Listening* (Fall, 1978) for a fuller exegesis of Eckhart's talks on the Merchandizing Mentality and on The Aristocrat and for an analysis of the political and economic consciousness he espoused.

30. Schurmann, *Meister Eckhart.*, p. 209. It is not for nothing that Marxist philosopher Ernst Bloch declares that Eckhart was a forerunner of modern socialism. See Ernst Bloch, *Atheism in Christianity* (Herder & Herder, 1972), pp. 63ff. I treat this subject in some detail in my "Meister Eckhart and Karl Marx," *art. cit.*

31. This distinction of Rudolf Bultmann is found wonderfully applied in Jose Miranda, *Being and the Messiah* (Orbis Books, 1977), pp. 84ff.

8

Social and Political Consciousness in the Letters of Catherine of Siena

Carola Parks, OP

English speaking readers, if they know Catherine of Siena at all, tend to know her exclusively through her mystical *Dialogues*. This highly personalized work, usually rendered into flowery language that distracts Anglo-Saxon readers, does not represent by any means the full consciousness of this fourteenth century Doctor of the Church (1333?–1380). Since her letters, which number about four hundred, have been so little available in English, I will present some themes pertinent to the subject of society and spirituality drawing heavily from her letters.

The Dignity of Creation and the Human Person as "Imago Dei"

Catherine's optimism about humanity comes from the human person's dignity and likeness to the Creator. She writes: "We did not have to ask to be created. God himself moved by the ardor of his love created us in his image and likeness in such dignity that the tongue cannot express, nor can the eye see, nor the heart imagine how great is the dignity of a person."[1]

The freedom of the human person appeals especially to Catherine who exclaims:

Know that humanity had hardly been created by God when these words were said to us: "Be it done as you wish." "I make

you free so that you are subject to no other except me." O
Fire of Love, thus you show to us the excellence of your rational creature. All has been created to serve you.[2]

Striking a theme of realized eschatology, Catherine emphasizes
how eternal life is now for those who choose wisely.

Virtue brings sweetness and even now one tastes eternal
life.... Give yourself security and cease confusion. Be constant so that you may have life without death, health without
infirmity since you are a lord and not under the domination of
sin.[3]

Not only is creation itself a divinely blessed happening for
humanity, but for all the goods of the earth. "The things of this
world are good in themselves. It is only the ill will of people who
use them badly which makes them evil."[4] Again, the emphasis is
put on human choosing. It is ourselves and not things in themselves that render things to be "temporal" instead of spiritual for
the temporal is also spiritual. "Every human work can be good
and perfect of whatever nature it may be, whether spiritual or
temporal. It is temporal insofar as the inner motivation makes it
so."[5] In fact, Catherine chastises those who put down the temporal. She makes her point to the Abbess of Santa Maria in
Siena:

If you say to me, "I do not wish to be concerned with temporal
things," I answer you that they are temporal only insofar as we
make them so. It has already been said that everything proceeds from the highest Good. Hence everything is perfect. I
do not wish you to avoid tasks under the plea that they are
temporal, but I would have you be solicitous, with your vision
directed toward God.[6]

She makes a similar point to Joanna the Countess of Naples.

I would not have you think that I have said that riches are
harmful in themselves and death-dealing to humanity. Not so.

It depends upon the disordered affection with which the creature possesses them. If they were harmful, God would not have created them and given them to us. He who is the highest Good cannot will anything but good.[7]

So we learn that the goodness of creation is a gift from the goodness of God. And here lies the starting point for Catherine's spirituality. This is why she can say that "all things serve as an instrument whereby we may practice virtue" and why she considers all kinds of vocations as callings to be "just and faithful servants of one's Creator." For "the truth of God is that God has not placed anything in this life which is an impediment to salvation, unless one wishes it to be."[8] Again, her emphasis is on our choices, our attitudes, and our "wishing."

> In whatever state a person is in, be one a lord of the city or great because of his reputation, his nobility or riches, whether he be consecrated to God by a vow of chastity or live in the married state, whether he has children or not, in every condition he is pleasing to God and is ever in union with him because he loves God wholeheartedly. Whatever actions he performs, even if they appear to be worldly—like maintaining a state of life proper to a grandee or lord, like being with his wife, surrounded by his children, situations which could appear to be worldly actions—everything is directed to God because his soul has set up the principle of regulating and of making all his actions tend to God and the glory of his Name.[9]

Humility as Self-Awareness and Development of Talent

Humility for Catherine is clearly not about self-abasement, put-down of self, or repression of oneself. It is the starting point for all spirituality precisely because it is about self-awareness and will lead to other-awareness, including an awareness of the beauty and grace of God's good creation. But this awareness begins with oneself. Thus she writes to her mother that she desires to see her possess a true knowledge of yourself and of the goodness of God in you. Without this knowledge you are not able to share in the life of grace. You must study with true and holy diligence, acknowledging that you are not, and that you have your being in God and that all gifts and graces which you have received are from him.[10]

The humble person is characterized by the fact that she or he

is thus established in knowledge of self and is able to see better and to discern more sharply the eternal goodness of God. Wherefore, since she knows more, she loves more. The more one loves, so much the more does one acquire perfect humility and patience.[11]

Without the wood of self-knowledge there will be no fire of deep loving. She writes of this to her friend and confessor, Raymond of Capua:

I would have you never to cease increasing the fuel for the fire of holy desire, that is, the wood of self-knowledge. This is the wood that nourishes and feeds the fire of divine love; this love is acquired by the knowledge of self and of the inestimable love of God. . . . The more fuel one gives to the fire so much the more increases the warmth of love of Christ and of neighbor. So remain hidden in the knowledge of self.[12]

One of her favorite images is that of a cell, the cell of self-knowledge. She counsels Alessa Saracini in the following manner:

Make for yourself, dearest daughter, two dwellings, one that of your cell . . . and the other that which you can carry about with you. The latter is the cell of true knowledge of yourself. There you will find awareness of God's love for you. The two cells are as one; while being in one, you ought to remain in the other. Otherwise the soul might suffer confusion or presumption. If you remain fixed in the contemplation of self, you will arrive at a state of confusion. If you persist only in the knowledge of God, you will fall into presumption. . . . In the knowledge of God you will find the flame of divine charity . . . Here consists all our perfection. . . . Here is the principal source from which we derive so much light that we cannot err in our works which proceed from it.[13]

Notice how this knowledge is to lead to action. To Frate Matteo di Francesco Tolomei, a Dominican friar, similar counsel is given:

In that cell one finds another cell, that is the cell of the knowledge of God within oneself. From this come true humility . . . and perfect patience. In the knowledge of God which one finds within oneself there is acquired the most ardent love. Holy and loving desires thus arise.[14]

What comes from this self-knowledge? From this humility? Far from advocating a spiritual masochism or a put-down of self and of one's gifts, Catherine urges a discovery and development of one's talents. She writes: "Everyone ought to be eager to develop his or her own talents. God has given them to us to use and not to bury. . . . We ought to use them at all times, in all places, and toward all creatures."[15] It is our responsibility to know ourselves and come to grips with the image of God in us. "It would be very unbecoming for us rational creatures not to use our reason. To do so would make us like brute animals who are without that gift. Not to use our reason causes us to become impatient and scandalized at the events which God allows. Thus we offend him."[16] What does this responsibility lead to? It leads to love and service of neighbor:

Each one must aid her neighbor according to her own capability—one with learning, another with prayer, another with temporal aid. And if you cannot provide help from your own resources, you should call upon friends to provide it.[17]

Notice how she sees ministry as intellectual for some, prayer for others and temporal aid for still others. There is no sentimentalism, no antiintellectualism and no flight from bodily needs in her spiritual vision.

The Poor

Catherine is continually making her correspondents aware of the plight of the poor. Sometimes she speaks in terms of almsgiving, a favorite medieval and biblical expression. "You who have temporal goods, give to the poor all that you can, disposing of your own riches. Give generously because the poor are the hands which will open the gates of eternal life to you if you give alms with whole-hearted love."[18] At other times she speaks of justice and its perversion by the powerful vis-à-vis the poor. Addressing the magistrates of Bologna, she says bluntly:

> The ruler ought to apply himself above all in cauterizing defects with the flame of love, exercising holy justice by punishing and correcting for example's sake. Instead he sometimes allows himself to be flattered and pretends not to see. He acts in this way toward those who may endanger his position. Toward the poor however who have little and from whom he has nothing to fear, he shows an amazing zeal for justice. Without pity or mercy he imposes upon them the gravest penalties for slight faults.[19]

And she writes to Andreasso Cavalcaboui, a senator in Siena that "we often see some rules adhere to justice strictly in their treatment of the poor—a type of justice that is really injustice—but that in regard to the great and powerful they do not apply such rigidity."[20] Our work of justice is "a part of divine justice" she insists in a letter to the king of France, Charles V:

> Do not close your eyes to the wrongs which your officials commit through bribery or neglect of the poor. Be a father to the impoverished as an almoner of what God has given you. See to it that the crimes committed in your kingdom are punished and that good deeds are exalted and rewarded. All this is a part of divine justice.[21]

She objects to the way the poor are abused by the legal profession who claim to act on behalf of justice. Writing to a lawyer, she says: "Whenever a poor person approaches you who obviously has a just cause but has no one to defend him for lack of money, you would give great honor to God if you would spend yourself on his behalf for charity's sake."[22] Thus the professions *might* be an "honor to God"—if they were undertaken for the sake of the dispossessed. Writing to another lawyer, she observes:

> He despises virtue who has a duty to perform for his neighbor and does not render that service unless he sees some personal advantage for himself. . . . Christ gave his life for us and this fellow does not wish to utter a word on behalf of his neighbor unless he is paid or even overpaid. If his neighbor is poor and is without funds he makes him wait before taking his case and often belittles him. . . . He is cruel toward his own soul because he offends the poor.[23]

What is authentic justice to Catherine? "Holy and true justice seek(s) the common good and not that of an individual."[24]

Institutional Criticism

Catherine was not naive about the rank injustice that infested religious and secular institutions of her time. In fact, she is continually confronting and provoking the very representatives of these institutions, from pope and king to senators and lawyers, to rulers of city-states, businessmen, friars, countesses, queens. To Pope Urban VI she expresses outrage at the schism in the church and at the spiritual and ethical condition of the clergy. They are "stinking" the world with their luxury living, their simony and avarice, their neglect of the poor.

> The world can tolerate no more. Vices so abound, especially among those who were put in the garden of holy church to be fragrant flowers, shedding the fragrance of virtue, and we see instead that they revel in wretched and hateful vices so that the whole world reeks!. . . . Where is the generosity and care of

souls, the distribution of alms to the poor? You know well that men are acting otherwise. With grief I say that your sons nourish themselves on the wealth they are accumulating by their ministry of the blood of Christ, nor are they ashamed of being such money-changers. . . . Where is that deep humility with which to confound the pride of self-seeking? In their great avarice they commit simony, buying benefices with gifts, flattery or vain adornments. . . .[25]

In addition to laying *bare* the corruption of churchmen to the pope, she lends her advice on what makes a good church leader: it is one who puts aside self love as a corrupting "principal motive through which one acts" and "does not suppress the flame of holy desire nor cast from him the pearl of justice." Such a person serves neighbor "wishing to give him that service which it cannot give to God." She admonishes the pope that "it is extremely necessary . . . for you to be rooted in perfect love, wearing the pearl of justice, as I said, in order that you may not be overly concerned with the world." For in doing this you can be "useful to your neighbor." Such a person

does not draw back from pursuing the salvation of their souls and bodies for any ingratitude found in them, nor for the threats or flatteries of man but, in truth clothed in the wedding garment, follows the doctrine of the spotless humble Lamb, that gentle and good Shepherd who, as one enamoured, ran for our salvation to the shameful death of the most holy cross.[26]

She speaks of what a temporal ruler should consider.

We have the example of David and Louis of France who were very saintly people. They actually ruled . . . and the jewel of justice glowed within them with true humility and love. They rendered to each one his due, to the lowly as well as to the great, to the poor as well as to the rich.[27]

To the king of Hungary she urges justice toward the poor. "Exercise justice toward the great as well as toward the powerless, to the poor as to the rich. Do not compromise justice, do not allow yourself to be intimidated by flattery, by threats, by a desire to please."[28]

One of her most persistent themes in dealing with those in power is the theme of "loaning"—all power is as a loan and one will be judged on that stewardship. She tells King Charles V of France to possess "your kingdom as loaned to you and not as your own property. Neither life nor health nor riches nor honor nor royalty are yours by right. If they were truly yours, you could dispose of them at will."[29] Indeed, all of life is a loan!

> A person chooses to be healthy, yet he falls ill; he loves life yet he has to die; he desires riches and is poor; he longs for power and is a slave. Why is this so? Because those things are not his; he enjoys them as long as it pleases God who has loaned those things to him. Well then, how simple and ingenuous is he who considers as his own that which in reality is the property of another. Truly such a one is a robber, worthy of death. Hence I pray that you as a wise man will conduct yourself as a good steward, considering your possessions as loaned to you by God who has appointed you minister and almoner.[30]

To the rulers of Siena she also speaks of the loan they have received. The city itself has been "lent to you" she exclaims:

> One's own city is the city of one's soul; we possess it by means of holy fear founded on fraternal love, on peace and union with God, and on genuine virtue. Now he who lives in hatred, in rancor and in discord, filled with self-love, he who lives so lasciviously that he differs in no way from swine wallowing in filth, such a one does not possess the city of his soul. Poorly will he care for the things loaned him if he does not first tend to directing himself. Loaned domains are those of cities or other temporal governments lent to us and to others. . . . They are lent for a time, as it pleases the divine Will and according to the manners and customs of countries. . . .
>
> I would have you exercise your authority with reverent fear. I assure you that if we wish to preserve spiritual or temporal

authority, there is no other means than by living virtuously. Power and authority are weakened through one's own failings, and in no other way.[31]

Her treatises on what constitutes good government have been called a Christian counterpart to Machiavelli's *Prince*. Her goal is love of neighbor, especially the indigent. Thus she wrote to the newly elected member of Siena's board of rulers, Andrea di Vanni:

> I want to see you a good and just ruler.... I do not understand how we can rule others if we do not first rule ourselves. As the soul governs itself, so does it rule and guide others. Just as perfect charity towards God generates perfect charity towards one's neighbor, so with that perfection with which one rules oneself, thus one rules others.... He who wishes to maintain peace in himself and in his domain ought to act thus, preserving holy justice.... I have said that I would have you be a just and true ruler.[32]

Conclusion

Catherine, like ourselves, was a person of her time and place. I am not suggesting by these excerpts from her letters that she put forth an alternative political-economic structure by which people could live more justly as neighbors. Nor I am suggesting that she transcended altogether the middle class into which she was born. Indeed, her father and brothers held posts in Siena's administration and she no doubt drank deeply of politics as a way of life which is what it was in the Benincasa family. Yet this can certainly be said of Catherine's political-social-spiritual consciousness: She does not encourage the put-down of self-awareness, of love of creation, of this life in favor of another one, of a quest for justice, of professional work as a ministry; of relief of the misery of the poor. Nor did she shrink from taking on the biggest, most powerful, and most corrupt institutions and institutional spokesmen of her time. Faith for Catherine was not in spite of these involvements in social-political affairs: It was with them. It was because of her faith that she was driven to the criticisms that she launched. There is more than one lesson here for us who have our own institutionalized injustices to fight both in society and church six hundred years after Catherine fought her fight in Siena.

NOTES

1. Piero Misciatelli, *ed.*, *Le Lettere di S. Caterina da Siena* (Florence: 1940), I, p. 65, # 21. All excerpts from the letters will be from this edition. Roman numerals indicate volume number; the # sign indicates number of letter. Translations are mine.

2. I, p. 263 # 69.

3. I, p. 80, # 24.

4. II, p. 161, # 112.

5. III, p. 177, # 199.

6. I, p. 114, # 30.

7. V. p. 156, # 345.

8. IV, pp. 104–9, # 259.

9. Ibid.

10. I, p. 3, # 1. The "you are not" is less a psychological than a metaphysical reference common to mystics who are sensitive to the givenness of human existence.

11. III, p. 253, # 216.

12. III, p. 266, # 219.

13. I, pp. 190–2, # 49.

14. II, p. 96, # 94.

15. II, p. 200, # 121.

16. I, p. 42, # 13.

17. IV, p. 81, # 251.

18. IV, p. 276, # 304.

19. IV, p. 149, # 268.

20. V, p. 120, # 338.

21. IV, pp. 11f., # 235.

22. IV, p. 97, # 258.

23. III, p. 151, # 193.

24. IV, p. 149, # 268.
25. IV, pp. 225f., # 291.
26. IV, pp. 221-3, # 291.
27. V, p. 280, # 372.
28. V, p. 220, # 357.
29. IV, pp. 11f., # 235.
30. Ibid.
31. II, p. 210, # 123.
32. V, p. 226, # 358.

9

A Psycho-Spiritual History of Teresa of Avila: A Woman's Perspective

Catherine Romano

William James called her "typical of shrewdom";[1] Walter T. Stace called her "lacking in intellectual power,"[2] Pere Hahn pointed out her physical indication of "hysteria."[3] Kate O'Brien, a sympathetic biographer, comfortably calls her a "saint... alarming... deluded... if you like, mad."[4] Yet the Catholic church canonized Teresa. She is called "the mystical doctor"[5] and honored both within and outside of the church. How can we reconcile a mad shrew who is lacking in intellectual power with this woman called "mystical doctor," "saint," and who, in the last half of her life, not only traveled the length of Spain creating a new religious order, but also wrote a great mystical treatise, *Interior Castle?* Has a patriarchal psychology misunderstood the psycho-spiritual journey of Teresa of Avila? Can today's psychology understand a female at all? Rosemary Ruether reminds us, "There does not exist any truly feminist psychoanalysis or therapy."[6]

This study examines the psychological development of Teresa. It attempts to utilize Freudian insights, but not without critical additions and modifications of orthodox analysis. The reader is reminded that there are many theories of development beyond the orthodox Freudian, and the search for understanding of human behavior follows diverse paths. Up to now no woman has attempted a psychological critique of Teresa. It is time that a woman follows one of these critical paths in undertaking an analysis of the life-journey of this major historical figure of the sixteenth century.

One must look to Teresa's life story and attempt to discover what made her ill, what happened later to make her well, and what this might mean for our own life journeys.

Religious reform in Spain had a sound economic basis. Before Teresa's birth, Isabelle's reign had seen the instituting of the Inquisition (a religious consensus was unifying when politics were unstable). Charles V, as Holy Roman Emperor, followed by Phillip II, instituted a national view on episcopal jurisdiction and prerogatives of the crown. An influx of wealth from colonies and a careful guarding of religious powers left Spain free of bondage to Rome. While Luther's German princes were chafing under the demands of Rome for money to rebuild the Holy City, Spain's main focus of aggression was the identifiable elements of its own population (Jews and Moors). It was as economically sound for Spain to persecute these competitors under the guise of religious reform as for German princes to break loose from an economically draining Rome, again under the guise of religious reform.

No matter what the mundane basis of religious waves may be, always there will be those with some emotional or psychological need that will be fulfilled by what appears to be a sincere personal religious reform.

Her Life

Teresa de Cepeda y Ahumada was born in Avila in 1515. Even in 1515 Avila was a town of cathedrals and hermitages. She grew up surrounded in a home, a community, and a nation characterized by solemn, chivalrous faith and by austere acceptance of the mysteries of the church. Teresa was to grow up in an age of religious fervor, reform, and mysticism.

It is impossible to understand the religious life of Spain or even the history of the Spanish race unless one grasps the importance of Spanish mysticism. . . . The origins of this mysticism go back to an unknown past. . . . Mystical experience and expression developed throughout the Middle Ages and imparted a definite character to a great many theological and devotional works. *The very struggle against the Moors was regarded as a mystical process,* like the conquest of Jerusalem in the age of the Crusades. From these vague adumbrations the great age of mysticism took its starting point with curious suddenness at the beginning of the sixteenth century.[7]

A bright, attractive, extroverted little girl, she was to grow up enduring over twenty years of illness and sufferings, then to recover to reform the Carmelite order, write her own life and illuminating mystical treatise, be regarded as a saint in her own lifetime and, after her death, become canonized and honored as a mystical doctor.

Both of her parents were nobles. Though her father's family was not wealthy, he appears to have been a very proud man, pious and affectionate but lacking in initiative. Her mother, Dona Beatriz, was Don Alonso's second wife and was wealthy, owning properties around Avila. Beatriz was a beautiful woman and a great reader of romantic novels. When she died, Teresa hid all her mother's novels from her father so that she might read and reread them. In her adolescence, Teresa gained much peer esteem for writing one herself.

As a child, Teresa played most often at games of fantasy pretending to be a nun. She had one elder sister and four elder brothers. Five more boys and one more girl were born after Teresa. By her own admission, Teresa was a ringleader at children's games and adventures. When she was six she convinced her older brother that it would be a cunning move on their part to run away and get themselves martyred by the Moors and thus gain everlasting glory with ease. When Teresa and her brother were returned home by a relative who found them upon the road, Teresa defended herself with, "I ran away because I wanted to see God, and one cannot do that without first dying."[8] Such games and ideas are not surprising, considering the severe holiness of her father and the religious atmosphere in which she grew.

Yet, her chosen role in these childhood games of religious life reveals something of Teresa's early personality. Neville Braybrook, an English Teresian scholar writes, "She was a rebellious child by nature and, in many ways, her mind often showed a masculine turn in its readiness to take the lead."[9] It is clear that it was Teresa who would be prioress and her siblings were to respond to her orders and prostrate themselves before her.

She also grew watching her mother age rapidly by continual and debilitating pregnancies. Dona Beatriz died when she was thirty-three, though Teresa records that her mother seemed much older than her years. Teresa was thirteen when her mother died.

It can be assumed that Teresa's father, Don Alonso, was intensely rigid about seeing all of the children well disciplined in religious observances. Teresa mentions that she and her brothers continually reminded one another of "eternity" and the "eternal horrors of hell," a vision that Teresa never seemed to tire of reminding herself. She says, "We often spoke on this subject... often repeating these words 'forever, forever, forever.'"[10]

Still, she seemed to have a childhood normal for her culture. She was a vital, physically healthy child, loved by her parents and siblings. She had her small healthy rebellions (such as secretly reading romances of which her father strongly disapproved) and entered adolescence getting and enjoying her good looks, pretty clothes, and the esteem of her peers. In her later life, she grieves deeply over her adolescent "vanities" and calls them "sins." Don Alonso disapproved of her girl cousins whom he apparently thought encouraged Teresa in her "vanities."

At this time, in the years after her mother's death and when Teresa was blossoming into a healthy young woman attached, as she says later, "to the vanities of the senses," Empress Isabel moved her royal court to Avila. Teresa does not mention in her records this exciting honor of having the country's royal court come to town. She does mention her growing pleasure in social life with friends and makes obscure references that her honor was stained. She was sent to a nearby convent school. "This removal was done with great discretion and caution, for only myself and a relation of mine knew of it" (K, 37). She clearly went somewhat against her own will and at the insistence of her father.

Considering Teresa's own apparent honesty, her position, and her family's religious attitude, it is unlikely that she committed any great indiscretion or any that might be termed a "mortal sin." She appears to have been just a lively, clever girl, with a pious and anxious father.

Up until this time, Teresa appears to be a healthy product of her environment. She enjoyed physical health, she enjoyed adolescent confidences pertaining to marriage (and, no doubt, all that is contained in that exciting subject). Her easy leadership of her brothers implies both intelligence and courage, and her authorship of a romantic novel reveals an ability for expressiveness and organization. She had apparently coped well with her mother's death by expressing her child-like grief intensely and at once and comforted herself with religious ceremonies. She replaced her mother with Mary, Mother of Christ, and felt a security in that idea that was consistent with her culture. She does mention a certain talent she possessed for "pleasing persons wherever I might be" (K, 38). Upon relationships, she seemed to be able to be whatever current significant people admired, and thus was ever successful at making herself "much loved" (K, 38) wherever she was. A friend of hers used the word "tractable" to describe Teresa. She was also very much in love with love, romance, and chivalrous adventure. This latter reflected not only her mother's propensity for romance novels, but also the excitement of the time: the Renaissance hit Europe not long before her time, the Reformation was gathering power, the Middle

Ages had receded, and Spain still felt itself a power in the New World. This was 1531. It was also to be an era of great saints and religious reformers.

Teresa was initially unhappy as a boarding scholar in the Augustinian convent of Our Lady of Grace. She was restless and bored with no novels, no cosmetics, and no more exciting, confidential friendships.

During her eighteen months as a boarder at Our Lady of Grace, Teresa became less restless, made friends, and began to "envy" those about her who appeared confident in their vocations as nuns. She entertained thoughts of being a religious. Her friends encouraged her to seek a religious vocation. She, herself, says "These good thoughts, however, of being a nun, sometimes came into my mind and went away immediately, so that I could not yet persuade myself to be one." She also says, "I was, however, afraid to marry". (K, 39).

At this time, Teresa became so ill that she was obliged to return to her father's house. She also visited her married sister and, following that, she was left with a widowed uncle. This uncle was a very religious man (later, he entered a religious order). He was very much involved with reading religious books and discoursing on God and on the vanity of the world. He also expected Teresa to read the same books. She says " . . . those books he made *me* also read; and though I had no great liking for them, yet I pretended I had; for I always took the greatest care to give pleasure to others, however dear it might cost me . . . " (K, 38–40). Here she learned, she says " . . . that I had just reason to fear if I died (in my present state), I should be sent to hell" (K, 40).

She felt that as a nun she would be more "secure" from punishment and resolved to "force" herself to embrace a religious life.

Her father at first objected to Teresa's choice of vocation, but she adventurously stole off early one morning with her brother (another adventure!) and presented herself at the Carmelite Convent of the Incarnation. Her father yielded and gave his permission to allow her to receive the habit of the mitigated rule of the Order of Mount Carmel in the year 1535. Teresa's first year as a young nun saw an inexplicable loss of health. She admits, in her own record, to no spiritual unhappiness, yet her heart, her nerves, her digestion and her muscular system all began in this year to be racked and reduced by pains and symptoms very difficult to explain. She began having attacks of catalepsy and prolonged periods of near catalepsy. In the first year of her novitiate, Teresa was drawn towards a certain nun who was suffering in the infirmary with a "most grievous infirmity" (K, 46). She envied the sick nun, her holy, much admired patience and expressed a desire to suffer as patiently as the nun she had observed. Her father is once more obliged to carry her away to seek a cure.

In the place where she was taken to be cured, she met a man, a parish priest of good family, intelligent, and of some learning, by her own description. Teresa began to confess to the young man. She expresses her fondness for learned men. She says " . . . he became extremely attached to me. . . . The affection of this man was not bad, though by being excessive, it became evil. He knew well that I was determined not to do anything grievously offensive to God in any account whatever; and he also assured me as much on his part; and thus, our conversations became frequent" (K, 47).

In fact, their conversations became intimate enough that she discovered he had been in liaison with a woman for over seven years, during which time he had continued his priestly functions. Teresa recognized that her attachment to this man was a dangerous one, but she was, in her own words "so frivolous and blind" (K, 47). She longed to save the young man and, in time, charmed him away from his mistress. He returned to a state of grace and he died within the year.

Hope was nearly given up for Teresa's cure. She returned to her father's home and became sicker than before. She wanted often to go to confession. Her father viewed this as a morbid presentment of a coming death and refused to allow her to go to confession. She passed into a catalepsy so absolute and prolonged that she was given the last rites and her grave was prepared. Her father was agonized that he had refused to allow her access to confession. She awoke four days later and eight months later returned to the convent almost totally paralyzed, but able to pray and think. "The effects of this fit were a partial paralysis, that stayed with her until she was forty; and this physical paralysis had its parallel in her spiritual life."[11] In the following years, her health improved somewhat, but was never good.

In 1543, her father died. It is his deathbed statement which Teresa reports in her autobiography, "and in tears he told us about the great sorrow he felt in not having served God, and that he would have liked to be a friar; I mean, he would have chosen one of the *strictest* orders" (K, 62) (emphasis mine).

For twenty years she vomited every morning and every day. Later, she forced herself to vomit before bedtime by tickling her throat. The forced vomiting apparently relieved stomach pain. She was often too sick to eat before noon. In these years, she made attempts to practice a certain method of prayer, similar to meditation. She experimented with prayer, endured difficulties in developing the ability to meditate, studied books, and questioned learned men on the matter. "I voyaged on this tempestuous sea for almost twenty years with these fallings and risings and this evil—since I fell again—and in a life so beneath perfections that I paid almost no attention to venial sins" (K, 66).

Her Conversion

In 1554 at the age of thirty-nine or forty, Teresa experienced a conversion in which she made a final psychological submission to a highly personalized divinity. As she increased her ability to concentrate by different methods, she encountered visions, ecstasies, raptures, that certainly fit the definition given by Arthur Deikmann, for mystic experience in 1) intense realness, 2) unusual sensations, 3) unity, 4) ineffability and transsensate phenomena.[12]

She attempted to define and redefine in her writings the variety of her auditory and visionary experiences, attempting to separate imaginary experiences, devilish visions, and true, God-given revelations. She converses with the Trinity, is covered by white robes by the Blessed Virgin, is given mystical jewels, sees devils frustrated in their attempts to gain certain souls, sees a variety of saints and angels, and endures a tormenting vision of a place reserved for her in hell, should she somehow lose heaven.

Her greatest advances in meditative ability followed her acceptance of meditating on the most sacred humanity of Christ rather than on abstract constructs. Being commanded by spiritual directors to resist these mystic experiences, she says:

> When I began to try to obey the command to reject and resist these favors, there was a much greater increase in them. In seeking to distract myself, I never got free from prayer. It even seemed to me that I was in prayer while sleeping. There was an increase of love and of the loving complaints I was addressing to the Lord; the pain became unbearable, nor was it in my power to stop thinking of Him no matter how much I tried and even though I wanted to (K, 191).

Her relationship with the divinity is always expressed in the same words and terms that one would express a passionate love for another human. But, how else can one express such longings? Christ becomes for Teresa an extraordinary lover with a personality that resembles Teresa's own, an erotic personality.

As Teresa matures, particularly after or about age forty, her exterior life takes on certain changes. Although she tries to remain tractable and obedient to her superiors, she manages to assert her desires to fulfill orders received directly from God. She selects her spiritual advisors and favors "learned men." She begins her reform of the Carmelite order. She travels across Spain founding many chapters of the Primitive Rule. Monasteries for no more than thirteen monks or nuns to live in absolute poverty, enduring *strict austerities,* in *strict* seclusion from the world in contemplative prayer. Along with these changes came an improvement in physical health. Teresa says " . . . afterward, when I wasn't so cared for and pampered, I had much better health" (K, 91).

Her desire to reform the order led her into demanding situations in which she could use the wits and cunning she had obviously possessed as a child. She had once more to deal with worldly concerns, religious and civic authorities, critics and disciples. She was in a leadership position, healthy enough to ride back and forth over country roads on the back of a mule in all kinds of weather. Always, it seems she had a way of finding some pious aristocrat or some wealthy widow who fell under her charm and aided her in building convents. Her reform was not finally released from the jurisdication of the Observance until 1581, so she was often doing her work in "disobedience and contumacy."[13]

Her "saintliness" became known during her lifetime. Yet, she claims she had reached a point where she cared nothing for anyone's opinions. Teresa, in the process of meditation, had reached the point where she truly had only one authority and that authority was the Divinity she met in her own visions.

Little by little, we see the growth of another Teresa, reflecting her earlier childhood personality. Her self-confidence, her problem-oriented nature, her creativity, her air of detachment and need for privacy, and her sense of humor define her as an apparently healthy, actualizing[14] person in her later years. In the end, she seems to have returned to the healthy, intelligent, leadership-oriented personality exhibited in her youth prior to her convent days. She died a peaceful death on October 4, 1582. Sixty-seven years of age was certainly a ripe old age for a sixteenth century woman.

Interpretation of Her Life before Conversion

From the brief review, as has been offered here, one can see that Teresa appears to have gone physically and psychologically through three broad stages. First, an active assertive personality in childhood, with no sign of physical health problems. Second, an adolescent crisis of identity left unresolved which generates twenty years of adult life spent in what appears to have been intense emotional confusion and severe loss of health. Thirdly, from her conversion experience onwards we can trace the growth of a new active Teresa, possessing an assertive confidence, a solid sense of identity and ego strength. This third stage also shows us a Teresa who has given up her symptoms of physical illness.

Teresa would appear to fit into an erotic, libidinal type as described by Freud in *Character and Culture:*

> The erotic type is easily characterized. Erotics are persons whose main interest—the relatively largest amount of their libido—is focused on love. Loving, but above all, being loved, is for them the most important thing in life. They are governed by the dread of loss of love, and this makes them peculiarly dependent on those who may withhold love from them. It seems easy to infer that, when persons of the erotic type fall ill, they will develop hysteria. . . . [15]

Teresa appears to fit the erotic type. She goes out of her way to please others so that they will love her. As a child with her mother, she surely gained love and affection by showing her mother's passion for romantic novels. Later, she wants the esteem of her peers. She seeks and gains her father's and uncle's approval by religious behavior. She freely admits that she has a talent for winning the love of whoever she is with by seeking to please them even by doing things she has no desire to do (K, 39). In more mature visions of Christ, he is always her tender lover. She projects onto her vision of Christ her own erotic personality and he, too, longs for love.

Let us look first at her childhood. Keep in mind that Teresa grew up in a patriarchal culture, where the male (and activities viewed as masculine) was considered superior. Women's roles were limited and narrow leaving most females with the choices of either marriage or convent, the latter offering females greater opportunities to leadership and managerial roles. As a child, Teresa exhibited what Braybrook termed her "masculine turn" of mind. She was a leader even of her older brothers. She longed for adventure and fed her mind on the romantic adventure novels supplied by her mother. Her world was full of soldiering and new worlds to conquer. The action was male. The values were male. Any gross favoritism was likely to have been of a brother, not a sister. The boys would expect to grow up into an active life, to bring to the family name new honor or new wealth. For the females of the family, their objective was a passive one, that is, to do nothing that would bring dishonor. For a girl of Teresa's energies and talents, it would have been very difficult not to envy the possession of a penis. Not because in lacking one she felt defective, but because the privileges and opportunities for activity and adventure were denied to the half of the species that did not possess one.

Let us not call this penis envy in the Freudian sense, which signifies some innate biological basis for its development. A more reasonable analysis suggests Teresa's developing what Karen Horney termed the masculinity complex of woman. That is " . . . the entire complex of feelings and fantasies that have for their content the woman's feeling of being discriminated against, her envy of the male, her wish to be a man and to discard the female role . . . "[16] Teresa envied male power. "The penis does not give men biological superiority over women, but is the symbol of their social domination over women."[17]

Teresa's early observation of her mother's sexual role most likely contributed profoundly to this masculinity complex. What did she see as the result of her mother's continual and debilitating pregnancies? Only her mother's premature aging and young death, a traumatic loss to Teresa in those early years when she herself was entering adolescence and the ambiguity that accompanies adolescence for girls in a patriarchal culture. We are here already within the realm of the unconscious.

In cases of favorable female development in male-valuing cultures, the woman submerges narcissistic penis envy in the object-libidinal desire to have a child (preferably a *male* child). In Teresa's case, she would have found it difficult to choose what appeared, in her family, as a not very preferable alternative.

Even as a child, Teresa was beginning to struggle against unconscious impulses. Her practice of constantly reminding herself of eternity and the eternal horrors of hell and her compulsive-like repetitions of "forever, forever, forever" may have been a reaction-formation defense against some unacceptable impulses. Some wish threatened to surface to a conscious level, and Teresa fought to push it back with her "forever, forever, forever." Braybrook reminds us that Teresa was always subject to nightmares. Her unconscious wishes surfaced too near to consciousness when she slept. Even disguised in dreams, her impulses were too threatening and caused anxiety.

Her first attempts at blossoming into adolescent love interests are quickly blunted by her hasty incarceration at Our Lady of Grace. She is forced to suppress her natural sexuality in order to keep her father's love and to win the love of her new religious authority figures. Before her father's death, she succeeds at drawing her father to her through her illness. Later he visits her at the convent to discuss her progress in the practice of prayer, but she admits to having deceived her father when she was practicing at prayer so as to avoid any loss of love or esteem in his eyes.

Wanting love and having a sensitivity to rejection are not in themselves abnormal. Teresa, though, shows symptoms of a *neurotic* need for love. The neurotic need for love is compulsive and indiscriminate. She will behave situationally in order to win the love of everyone. She cannot bear the possibility of not being loved by anyone. This extreme sensitivity to rejection occurs frequently among people with hysterical characteristics.

But, what generates this neurotic need? In Teresa, it may have been the inevitable rivalry for her father's affection in a society that valued sons above daughters. Her mother's premature death (abandonment) occurred before Teresa had resolved feelings of competition with a "perfect" mother and may have been a contributing factor to her neurosis. Her sensitivity to rejection was aggravated, no doubt, by her father's sending her away from him to the convent school. This sensitivity to rejection and the intense hate following rejection must be repressed, because to express any hostile impulses would threaten the security of the erotic personality. The guilt that follows repressed anger increases anxiety and leaves the erotic personality with a feeling of helplessness in a hostile world. For the most part, the individual is not aware of the source of anxiety, but develops other fears (e.g., fear of pregnancy) or physical illnesses that restrain their anger by crippling them in some way. The physical suffering (punishment), which they may endure, alleviates some of the guilt.

Teresa also reacted with submission, another method the neurotic uses to protect herself. If she sought always to be pleasing and never demanded anything, no one would hurt her. There are other methods of dealing with this anxiety and neurotic need for love which Teresa discovered later in life.

Teresa's first symptoms appear after being sent away from her father, apparently for some adolescent indiscretion that her father felt was a threat to her virtue. She seeks to be pleasing and loved in her new surroundings. She considers becoming a nun, but does not feel a strong calling. She also expresses a fear of marriage. This latter fear, no doubt, stems from having watched her beautiful mother die after a married life of several pregnancies. Teresa seemed a vital, healthy adolescent, interested in her new sensuality. She is sensuous, but fears marriage. She probably fears pregnancy. Had she been allowed to develop in the midst of her peers, she might have overcome this fear and matured into an exciting sensual woman. Her sudden confinement within convent walls led her to repress her own sensuous healthy desire. Her anxiety over choosing a vocation forced her to find some mechanism to cope with the choice situation. Teresa wished not to make a choice. Her illness, whether it was hysterical or not, forced her father to remove her to his home again. "The hysterical symptom is, like other mental products, the expression of a wish fulfillment."[18] She flees into illness, thus escaping the need to make a choice.

This first illness may have been a real illness which led to a rescue by her father. It was to be the first use of physical illness to gain attention or escape threat. Writing about conversion hysteria, Freud says:

> In persons who are disposed to be neurotic without having yet developed a neurosis on the grand scale, some morbid organic condition—perhaps an inflammation or injury—very commonly sets the work of symptom formation in motion; so that the later process swiftly seizes upon the symptom supplied by reality, and uses it to represent those unconscious phantasies that have only been lying in wait for some means of expression.[19]

Teresa, after having experienced her first real illness, is then thrust into an environment with her fanatically pious uncle, where her old childish fears of eternal damnation are reawakened. She sees a religious vocation as her only security and flees to another convent to begin her novitiate.

Teresa wants to be loved, to be esteemed by her peers and, no doubt, longs for her father's approval and recognition. She mentions the admiration given to a sick nun and longs for similar suffering and similar patience to endure it. She almost immediately becomes ill. So ill that her father must come for her again. Her illness has won her quick attention and "love" from her significant male.

While away to be cured, she has a romantic relationship. She is obviously loved by the young priest. Her vocation demands that she love the man "for God." She does win him over away from a life of sin with another woman and realizes her charm is in her virtue. Her culture and her character demand that she repress her natural desires. She must forcefully eject from consciousness shameful experiences or impulses which are incompatible with her evaluation of herself. The problem becomes moot due to the young man's death. Teresa returns to her father's home and becomes sicker. She cannot bear being touched, she has heart pain, she cannot eat. All might be a reaction to repression of the certain traumatic impressions and experiences with the young man who loved her. "The hysterical symptom is the memory symbol of the operation of certain (traumatic) impressions and experiences."[20] She becomes, in her illness, insensible. Her senses all leave her. She thus totally represses any memory sensations, an option that may serve the purpose of some sexual gratification. "The hysterical fit is an equivalent of coitus... Even the ancients called coitus a 'minor epilepsy.'"[21]

Teresa's sickness here is climaxed by a total loss of consciousness. She passes into a catalepsy. Freud observes more than one purpose that such hysterical conversions serve, whether these losses of consciousness are fleeting or of duration.

> A loss of consciousness, the "absence" of the hysterical attack, is derived from the fleeting, but unmistakable, loss of consciousness which can be observed at the climax of very intensive (also auto-erotic) sexual gratification... This gap in consciousness, which may be called a physiological one, is then extended in the service of repression until it takes up everything which the repressing faculty rejects.[22]

This specific fit was also effective in punishing her father for a manipulative gesture.

It can be assumed that Teresa remained abstinent, despite her natural longings, but at this stage in her young life, she was not as successful at deflecting her sexual excitement into higher channels. There is no need to assume that Teresa's libidinal desires were even at a conscious level, although it would not be irreverent to assume that, at times, her desire did become conscious.

> Unconscious phantasies have either always been unconscious and formed in the unconscious or, more often, they were once conscious phantasies, daydreams, and have been purposely forgotten and driven into the unconscious by "repression."[23]

Teresa returned to the convent eight months after her four-day catelepsy. She was paralyzed and not able to function in her religious obligations. Her young man had functioned as a priest for seven years while living in sin with a woman. Teresa's paralysis, which disappeared without explanation, may have been either a compensation for his failure or a guard she set upon herself to protect her from acting out in any overt way.

A symptom often has more than one meaning and serves to represent several unconscious mental processes simultaneously. Initially, Teresa's flight into illness may have involved a saving of psychical effort. It was a convenient solution to mental conflict. Her years of suffering and being unable to function may have served to somehow undo the seven-year liaison her dead young priest enjoyed. Her confinement may have had later advantages including long hours of opportunity to deal in fantasies. A second advantage would be that her patient suffering gained her love and esteem from other significant persons in the convent and in her father's eyes. Also, it may reflect a fear of having earlier made a "false step" in her relationship with the young priest.

> The motive for being ill is, of course, invariably the gaining of some advantages. . . . But, in every neurotic illness, a paranosic gain is also to be discerned. In the first place, falling ill involves a saving of psychical effort; it emerges as being economically the most convenient solution when there is mental conflict, even though in most cases the ineffectiveness of such an escape becomes manifest at a later stage. This element in the paranosic gain may be described as the *internal* or psychological one, and it is, so to say, a constant one. But beyond this, external factors may contribute motives for falling ill; and these will constitute the *external* element in paranosic gain.[24]

An epinosic gain, to Teresa, may have been the love and attention she gained for her suffering. Teresa, herself, records some of her rewards gained through her hysterical illness.

Right away I was in such a hurry to return to the convent that I made them bring me back as I was.... I suffered all those years and—if not in the early sufferings—with great gladness. For it was all a trifle to me.... I spoke much about God in such a way that I was edifying to everyone, and they were amazed at the patience the Lord gave me. For, if this patience had not come from the hand of His Majesty, it seemed it would have been impossible to suffer so much with so great contentment (K, 51f.).

This "belle indifference" toward her paralyzed condition is another signal that her later illness and all of her paralysis were hysterical in nature. Interesting, too, is the revelation that her dysfunctions did not conform to the symptoms of her disorder. Her paralysis lasted over three years, but failed to produce the atrophy of muscle that would be expected to occur in any case of a physically based paralysis. It must be remembered that following Teresa's conversion experience when she was to give up her old neurosis and create a more functional one, her health improves dramatically. She writes, " . . . afterward, when I wasn't so cared for and pampered, I had much better health." (K, 91)

It is difficult to place the years in which another interesting symptom appears in Teresa. She records that she endured twenty years of vomiting every morning and was only rarely able to eat before noon each day. Her mother had been married for nineteen years. This symptom might reflect an identification with her mother, who was pregnant for so much of her married life. It may be a sign of her unresolved Oedipal desire for her father's love.

Interpretation of Her Life After Conversion

While Teresa had been making attempts to lead a life of prayer, she had been far too distracted by her needs to be loved by those in the world, by her feelings of guilt, and by an inability to concentrate. A general life of anxiety filled by a preoccupation with her unusual illnesses and her desire to show herself as a good, lovable, tractable person prevented her spiritual progress.

At the age of thirty-nine or forty, Teresa experienced a spiritual conversion. William James describes a conversion experience:

> To be converted, to be regenerated, to receive grace, to experience religion, to gain an assurance, are so many phrases which denote the process, gradual or sudden, by which a self hitherto divided, and consciously wrong inferior and unhappy, becomes unified and consciously right superior and happy, in consequence of its firmer hold upon religious realities. This, at least, is what conversion signifies in general terms, whether or not we believe that a direct divine operation is needed to bring such a normal change about.[25]

Freud would explain the internal resynthesis that leads us out of neurotic dysfunction in another way: "Probably the most prevalent way of resolving conflicts is that of fusion or integration. The person finds a way to satisfy both the opposing forces in a single activity."[26]

When Teresa left childhood behind and had to choose a woman's role in her society, she became a self divided. A strong, talented leader, romantic and adventurous, she could choose either to imitate her mother and sister and become a quiet and submissive wife and mother or to live a life of passive obedience as a nun. Whichever the choice, hell (the fire which burns "forever, forever, forever") had to be avoided. And, in this life of the flesh, love must be won. Impulses had to be denied or controlled and Teresa had found that one way of winning attention (love) and avoiding choice and controlling dangerous impulses was to cripple herself. She had fled into illness. This held the reins of her passionate personality but left little satisfactory outlet. Something was bound to occur which would release the years and years of building tension within her. An acceptable alternative to her hysterical symptoms had to be found.

Teresa had been her own love object. Her neurotic need to be loved and admired by others had made her appear tractable. Her "brave" endurance of physical pain and suffering had won admiration and attention, but at great expense. Her attempts to be an example of prayer had proven more successful at gaining paternal approval, but her anxiety and poor health caused her to be rather mediocre in that practice. She was being pulled between heaven and earth, experiencing some shame about presenting herself to others as a prayerful religious and, at the same time, being unable to pull herself away from her enjoyment of this pastime. Her semi-awareness of this building ambiguity implies activity in her unconscious mind in its attempts to find suitable outlets for increasingly strong wishes or impulses. She says:

> On the one hand, God was calling me; on the other hand, I was following the world. All the things of God made me happy; those of the world held me bound. It seems I desired to harmonize these two contraries—so inimical to one another—such as are the spiritual life and sensory joys, pleasures, and pastimes. (K, 62f)

Teresa's unconscious wanted everything. She wanted love and admiration of others (particularly from her father and later from "learned" men); she wanted the adventure and excitement which she had dreamed of in her youth; she wanted to win heaven and avoid the pains of hell; she wanted to do wonderful things and be her own boss (she had always played the hand-clapping prioress in childhood games); and she wanted the perfect lover with whom she could find outlets for her sensuality. She wanted what she had wanted as a small child, she wanted "to see God."[27] Her superego demanded that she restrict her behavior and express her needs and attain her pleasure in morally and socially acceptable ways. Her ego had dealt with such conflicts very inadequately up to Teresa's fortieth year of life. Now there was to be a change.

Teresa spent twenty years of nausea (metaphorically, disgust), identifying with and atoning for her mother's life of child-bearing and debillitation. She had crippled herself physically for years atoning for the sinful priest she had saved, or possibly punishing herself for her own guilt and anger. Now she was forty. She would never have a child, a male child, of her own through which she could live vicariously and achieve all that was denied her as a female in a male world. She needed no longer to fear pregnancy or marriage or sinful lusts of her own or of males. Her body had attained that neutered state. No reminder came monthly of her own female flesh role. While so many guilts were being resolved and so many fears lessening, new roads, too, were being presented.

In chapter nine of her autobiography in which she presents her conversion, she says:

> I was very devoted to the glorious Magdalene and frequently thought about her conversion. . . . At this time, they gave me *The Confessions of St. Augustine.* It seems the Lord ordained this because I had not tried to procure a copy, nor had I ever seen one. . . . It seemed I could find help in them and that, since the Lord had pardoned them, he could also pardon me. As I began to read the *Confessions,* it seemed to me I saw myself in them (K, 71f.).

Teresa was hard at work building a new superior identity for herself. Any sins she had committed were certainly not comparable in reality to sexual prostitution or a life of lusty fornications, yet she identified herself as far worse than this. She was to write page after page of self-condemnation, for God had courted her and she had been slow in responding to his courtship. Thus, when she at last surrenders to the wooing of God, she becomes in her own eyes, a singularly fault-filled creature (but one who must publicly endure constant manifestations of the Lord's hot desire for her soul and her services on earth).

The moment of submission to her own unconscious desires

comes when Teresa, tired in soul, enters the oratory of the convent and sees before her a new statue borrowed for a celebration. The statue represented the "much wounded Christ" (K, 70). Teresa becomes utterly distressed in seeing him that way. "My heart broke," (K, 71) she says. She is suddenly struck by the moment's meta-awareness that she is so very much loved that a man, a divine man, would suffer so for her sake.

Can we rephrase this experience? Did Teresa see this wounded person and subliminally react against a tyrannical superego and say within her unconscious "*I* will not suffer like this anymore!" "I love myself." "I am punished enough!" "No more! Return me to myself!"? She threw herself to the floor before him and attained at last the gift of tears. Compunction, that pricking of the sympathic conscience, is the needle which opens the doors of psychic process for Teresa. The dam has burst and the wishes and impulses of the id, the restrictions and commands of the superego, and the reality or changing face of need of the ego are released and readied for a resynthesis, a new order of dominance within Teresa's psyche which will allow her to function more egotistically and creatively.

Teresa prayed with a new ego. "I think I then said that I would not rise from there until he granted what I was begging him for. . . . from that time I went on improving" (K, 71).

What happened, did not happen in an isolated moment. Teresa's history had predicted the need for such a moment to occur. Hysterical, erotic personalities demand such drama. Teresa was well prepared by her reading, first of romances, and later, of Augustine, to create a moment like this and like the many manifestations which were to occur later. William James discusses studies of personalities prone to sudden "striking" conversions and the subliminal (unconscious?) preparation for them: "Voices are often heard, lights seen, or visions witnessed; automatic motor phenomena occur; and it always seems, after the surrender of the personal will, as if an extraneous higher power had flooded in and taken possession."[28] James attributes this sudden change largely to some unconscious incubation of thought and maturing motives deposited by the experiences of life. Teresa was ripe. Humans who have had such experience tend to be unusually suggestible hypnotic subjects or hysterical patients. James continues:

> In the wonderful explorations by Binet, Janet, Bruer, Freud, Mason, Prince, and others, of the subliminal consciousness of patients with hysteria, we have revealed to us whole systems of underground life, in the shape of memories of a painful sort which lead a parasitic existence, buried outside of the primary fields of consciousness, and making irruptions thereinto with hallucinations, pains, convulsions, paralysis of feeling and of motion, and the whole procession of symptoms of hysteric disease of body and mind.[29]

Teresa was to go with her newly structured psyche having received, in the ideation content dictated by her culture and experience, a divine permission to express her long bound impulses. She sought and received confirmation of her new reality by seeking out confessors to strengthen her new perceptions either by agreeing with these perceptions or by testing them.

Teresa's old structure was one of total repression. All of her energies were being used to keep unacceptable impulses from surfacing. There was no energy left for fueling the productive creativity of which she was capable. The impulses surfaced in limited and distorted fashion (hysterical illness). Her new structure allowed a sublimation rather than a repression. Rather than denying and fighting impulses, Teresa found acceptable outlets for her own personal wishes. She was to creatively examine herself, accept herself and find a less distorting personality adjustment to mediate the conflicting demands of id and superego.

> For if we break the false wishes created in us by society and get in touch with, and follow, the deeper wishes that reveal the orientation of the infancy libidinal energies, we may be led to a cultural creativity, art or religion that prolongs the libidinal

bent in us and enables us to sublimate our instinctual energies in the creation of a humane society.[30]

She finds new ways of making her wishes acceptable—her primary method being to project her wishes onto her Divine Lord and having him command her to do what she has long yearned to do.

In chapter thirty-two of her life, she writes of someone mentioning to her how desirable it would be to possibly found a strict enclosed monastery like the discalced. "Since I was having these desires," she writes, "I began to discuss the matter with that lady companion of mine, the widow I mentioned who had the same desires" (K, 216f.). Teresa goes on to say that she was really perfectly content where she was though and that attempting to found a new house was not likely to succeed. She prays over the matter. Quickly she receives an earnest command from "His Majesty," her Lord, to strive for this new monastery with all her power.

The rest of her life, her Foundation and her letters clearly reflect a Teresa who is forever receiving special commands straight from the top to get out there and be herself. In 1561, at the age of forty-six or forty-seven, she receives divine permission to refuse obedience to her superiors: "As for what the Queen of Angels said concerning obedience, it pertained to the fact that it distressed me not to give obedience to the order, but the Lord had told me it wasn't suitable to give it to my superiors. He gave me reasons why it would in no way be fitting that I do so" (K, 226). Instead, he told her she should petition Rome. Clearly her ego, dressed in divine clouds, had regained control in her life.

This founding of strict and enclosed monasteries satisfied Teresa's longing to be a leader in an active life and also reflects her desire to fulfill in some way her father's death-bed wish to have joined the strictest of orders. Her foundations service both her active wishes for her own life and her desire to be loved by her father by doing for him what he expressed a desire to have done for himself. How significant to Teresa was her father's last wish for what might have been his dying expression of existential guilt?

One must consider that Teresa began writing her life twenty-two years after her father's death. He is mentioned far more often than any other family member, first by a description of his piety and exceptional goodness, then by three separate references to his caution about her actions and effect on the family's reputation, including Teresa's account of being sent unhappily off to a convent school (again for the good of reputation). She records his denial of permission to allow her to take vows and a vision of him in heaven following his death. But the longest narrative section concerning him pertains to her deception of her father about her prayer habits and culminates in his dying. After Teresa's account of her father's last days of life, she writes, "I don't know why I have told this . . . " (K, 62). A very spontaneous remark indicating input from her unconscious that the conscious mind must then rationalize. We can hypothesize that she told us of this wish of her father's because it was such an important moment in her life. Although one can perceive that Teresa wanted to be the religious leader even in childhood games, her father's wish added to her own unconscious wish came as added fuel to an internal fire that her earlier hysterical defense mechanisms would fail to contain. The strict order she was to found could atone for many guilts.

So we see the conversion experience as a product of a variety of Teresa's experiences, foremost of which being a resynthesis of ego, a new resolution of old conflicts. The old neurosis, so dependent on passivity and hysterical illnesses, was not only less and less adequate in resolving inner conflict, but also we see some impulses growing stronger, some fears (due to physical and environmental changes) growing stronger, some fears (due to physical and environmental changes) growing weaker, and some identifications and expiations being concluded. Fueling this resynthesis was a budding identification with Mary Magdalene and St. Augustine. This identification gave opportunity for pressing sexual ideation to surface into consciousness without being totally owned or identified by Teresa as her own sexual impulse.

The catalyst of this resynthesis of Teresa's impulses, repressions, and realities was compunction. This compunction or remorse followed a period of incubation of ideas, some unconscious, some not. For nearly twenty years Teresa had been sporadically searching for a new spiritual psychic life for herself. Her attempts and failures at prayer, her efforts to rechannel impulses toward acceptable alternatives had been sabotaged primarily by her old neurotic pattern: excessive dependence on others; a neurotic need for love; unexpressed anger turned in upon herself; and her need to punish herself due to guilt over that anger. She was a self divided (a fact which facilitated her identification with Augustine).

Erik Erikson might describe her condition as that of one who has never successfully resolved her adolescent crises of identity or as one who had assumed a sick identity that was not capable of integrating her body, her role and her individuality. What our present day psychology still insists on calling a "masculine mind," we can call Teresa's early adolescent feelings of competence, goal-directedness, capacity for leadership and love of challenge and adventure. In later adolescence, her attempts to integrate her past, competent self with present and future female roles failed miserably.

Teresa's will to change, to evolve into a spiritual and psychological maturity, was being hampered by her neurotic pattern of dealing with her identity conflict.

Exhaustion of old defenses and self-surrender to another force was Teresa's way out of her old pattern. Her conscious will had not been able to bring her into a unified wholeness. When she surrendered that conscious will, she also momentarily ceased resisting and repressing unconscious impulses such as her anger, her sexual drives and her need to lead and dominate. That gift of tears was a weeping for herself, a new conscious recognition of impulses once repressed, now released. She saw her anger and wept, she recognized unconsciously and consciously her own humanity through recognizing consciously and unconsciously the humanity of Christ. In accepting his forgiveness at both levels of consciousness, in accepting salvation at both levels of consciousness, Teresa forgave herself and saved herself and her weeping signifies this moment of release from the bonds of her old neurotic pattern. William James describes this surrender: " . . . the crises described is the throwing of our conscious selves upon the mercy of powers which, whatever they may be, are more ideal than we are actually, and make for our redemption, you see why self-surrender has been and always must be regarded as the vital turning-point of the religious life. . . . "[31] A humanistic scientist may infer that force to be the unconscious mind. A Christian may infer that force to be one external from the person, that is, an external supernatural force, or a combination of internal and external forces or God working through such a force.

Teresa's Crisis of Generativity

Erik Erikson goes beyond Freud's early psychosexual developmental theories and includes stages in adulthood and social influence.[32] Psychosocial development or development of the personality does not freeze into an unbreakable pattern following puberty, but continues to evolve, meeting various crisis points through life. In Erikson's stages, Teresa's fortieth year would have ushered in the psychosocial crisis of generativity, a new stage in life where ego identity will reintegrate. This crisis occurs in young or middle adulthood and the issue of such a crisis will determine whether the personality will become exceedingly self-absorbed, rejecting concern with society and opportunities to be productive or, if the crisis is positively resolved, whether the adult personality will be productive and concerned with the common good. A person who has resolved the crisis positively will care for self and for others and will choose to act.

Teresa's conversion was a part of her crisis of generativity. Since the second half of Teresa's life was active and productive far beyond the first half of her life, we can assume that she reintegrated into the positive generating personality. Erikson explains the "crisis of generativity" thus:

> The crisis of generativity occurs when a man looks at what he has generated, or helped to generate, and finds it good or wanting, when his life work as part of the productivity of his time gives him some sense of being on the side of a few angels or makes him feel stagnant. All this, in turn, offers him either promise of an old age that can be faced with a sense of integrity, and in which he can say, "All in all, I would do this over again," or confronts him with a sense of waste, of despair.[33]

Following her conversion experience she was to re-enter the world and produce a new Teresa and create for herself an environment of activity in which she was to play the leading role. Her initial work at this period of her life was to develop a new pattern to replace her discarded old neurotic pattern. The new neurosis was simply a new, more economical, more functional, and more rewarding way of resolving conflicts. It was a creative way to satisfy all of her opposing internal forces in a single activity. Why say a *new* neurosis rather than a healthy adjustment? (Of course, I am speaking here according to modern standards.) Because she continues to project her wishes and impulses onto Christ rather than coming completely to accept their existence within her own self. The eroticism, the anger, and the desire to act as a leader continue to be accepted only as acts of obedience to Christ and never as acts generated by her own wish.

Teresa's method of prayer included intense self-examination, along with a willingness to completely surrender her critical adult mind and allow her thoughts to flow freely, censoring no thought. This exercise in nondiscursive thinking which she adapted for her own needs is similar to the methods used in psychoanalysis where the patient contracts with the therapist to surrender her intellect to the therapist, in an atmosphere of safety and acceptance. The patient agrees to allow the therapist to be the interpreting adult while the patient, often through free-association of thought, allows an exit for the unconscious.

Teresa, in her surrender to a divinity, now had a safe, accepting father/lover figure upon which to transfer. This figure was a product of her own ego's projection, unconsciously, but at a conscious level, was a reality. This figure, this divinity, gave permission to Teresa to examine herself closely. The probability that this figure was in actuality Teresa's own ego kept the situation safe, but Teresa appears to have made a true effort, a brave effort to examine herself, her "fault," her soul as closely as possible and to become an attentive and dispassionate self-oberver. She calls herself "so filthy and malodorous a dung heap" (K, 78) following a self-examination. She insisted that it was important to know one's own nature.

She appeared to reach what in analysis with a therapist is the halfway point of therapy. She could not, of course, by herself get beyond this transference. Her libido had been forced away from her old symptoms, and loosened from its previous attachments. In place of her original illness, we see now an artificially acquired transference. In place of a variety of unreal objects of her libido, there was finally only one object, in the person of Christ. Through prayer, meditation, and a method of a free-flowing self-examination, unconscious conflicts had been allowed to surface partially to a higher mental level and be worked out partially as a normal mental conflict. Opposition between Teresa's ego and libido was lessened and energies once used to maintain repressions were now free to be used otherwise in a creative life.

Anger, which in the early neurotic pattern had been turned inward, could now be aimed safely at others. I say safely because in Teresa's new neurotic pattern, she resolved conflict over anger by consciously attributing the source of the anger not to herself but to Christ. When her superiors forbade her to practice prayer (her intimate relationship with her spouse, Christ), Teresa reports the order to Christ (to her ego) and finds anger.

"When they forbade me to practice prayer, it seemed to me he was annoyed. He told me to tell them that now what they were doing was tyranny" (K, 191).

Teresa found acceptable paths by which her unconscious erotic fantasies could surface. She had, in the visions of Christ, an acceptable object with which to satisfy sexual aims. Rather than retreating into cataleptic seizures, hysterical absence, or crippling illness to deny or repress her erotic fantasies, she could see such raptures as favors the Lord granted her. Any shame connected with these events could be rationalized at a conscious level. The shame could be consciously acknowledged and less expenditure of libido was needed to aid in a total repression of the event. She writes: "So when these experiences of recollection or rapture began, which I couldn't resist even in public, I was left so ashamed afterward that I didn't want to be where anyone would see me" (K, 207).

Attempts to avoid such occasions led to increased erotic dreaming. The unconscious would find a way to surface at all costs, but now that the experiences were put into an acceptable form, they could appear less disguised. She writes:

> When I began to try to obey the command to reject and resist these favors, there was a much greater increase in them. In seeking to distract myself, I never got free from prayer. It even seemed to me that I was in prayer while sleeping. There was an increase of love and of the loving complaints I was addressing to the Lord; the pain became unbearable, nor was it in my power to stop thinking of Him no matter how much I tried and even though I wanted to (K, 191).

Her new neurosis then served the purpose of better consolidating many dysfunctioning symptoms into fewer more functional ones of which her environment (mystical Spain) had to be supportive. Her new neurosis, too, was to open up for Teresa opportunities to rationalize her future activities as a worldly business administrator, traveler, writer as a service she would just as well have let someone else provide, but which she was *ordered* by God to do herself. Her new neurosis was highly functional for her unconscious motive.

> Hysterics are undoubtedly imaginative artists... making attempts at solving their conflicts and appeasing their pressing needs which, when they are carried out in a fashion that has binding force for the majority, go by the names of poetry, religion, and philosophy.[34]

Sister Grace Anthony Gaircy, in an article entitled "St. Teresa–Psychologist," highlights Teresa's ability to spot potential sources of mental problems among the nuns, her useful instructions in caring for them and, in general, her common sense insight into psychic life and its expression in behavior.[35] In some cases, we can see Teresa projecting her own neurosis onto others, but in many it is possibly a recognition of her neurosis in others and the sources of it. Freud found it a very common thing for patients to recognize, in other people, connections which they were incapable of perceiving in themselves.[36]

Keep in mind Teresa's age at the time of her conversion experience. At that time she may have already entered or was about to enter her menopausal stage. The most common symptoms of this stage in a woman's life consist of characteristic flushes involving the head, neck, and upper parts of the thorax and the so called "flashes," typified by hot or tingling sensations over the entire body. Some women experience sensations of even more bizarre natures, and many fear some decompensation of their personalities. I am suggesting a possibility that should not be ignored, that is that many or some of Teresa's later experiences may have been a consequence of attributing some bizarre physical symptoms to the most available cue[37] ... a divine effect of her passionate involvement with her vision of Christ.

In her visions of Christ, he more than once gave to her gifts of valuable jewels. Once these jewels were in the form of a cross.

Symbolically, these jewels may be said to represent an offering of male genitals. Teresa senses a piercing within her. She may have been "deflowered" in this particular ecstasy. Her "morning sickness" may have aided her unconscious to realize a fantasy of pregnancy. This is a subject she must have had some knowledge of, having watched her sickly mother grow old being almost always pregnant during Teresa's life. It may also reflect Teresa's real fear of marriage which she expressed in her first year at Our Lady of Grace. She was now a bride of Christ and, in her own visionary experiences, she sees Christ in bodily form, including "his most lovely and divine mouth ... our Lord always appeared in his glorified flesh" (K, 189f.).

As Teresa grew more practiced at meditation, more skillful at willfully entering states of ecstasy, she also became more confident. Her own ego became stronger. She later recognized only one true authority in her life and that authority was the Christ of her visions. She was free to transfer all her love onto her Christ (in service to her own ego).

She found confessors that served as reference authorities to validate her revelations. Within her culture, her experiences were acceptable. She lost the need to totally repress her sexuality. She was able to sublimate and rechannel her libido into an acceptable area of life. She succeeded in deflecting her sexual excitation into higher channels. The Christ of her visions reflected a healthy combination of her own ego and the portion of her superego that was consistent with the demands of her cultural environment. In an acceptable way, she found a suitable love object and established a rewarding and lasting relationship with this perfect lover. Little by little, she relinquished the hysterical symptoms that interfered the most with her physical functioning. Her hysterical attacks became confined to moments of ecstatic union with her lover.

This style contrasts sharply with the patriarchal male's approach to God the Father as in the example of Luther, who canceled notions of debt to the Father figure and strove to become his own father. In Luther's case, the Oedipus complex is enlarged. In Teresa, the oedipal desire is fulfilled with passion and grace. She manages by psychic manipulation to achieve erotic unity with the Father as both a father and a lover and dies happily a "daughter of the Church."

Conclusion

In assessing Teresa's life as a model for our own, we must remember that the ideation content of Teresa's experiences was dictated by her culture. Had she displayed an ideation content differing from her culture, she would have appeared insane or possessed to the people of her time and place in history.

To a reader who may somewhat share Teresa's belief systems, her life appears to be a series of miracles. Approaching her writings from another belief system, she remains a remarkable and creative woman. If one is not inclined to say that Teresa found God is it not also wondrous to say that Teresa found herself? That she approached the center of her own being and permitted the expression of a more "whole" Teresa? That she came as close as was humanly possible to healing herself? Neurotic patterns, once established, are difficult to change and, yet, through intense work, she changed her own. She managed to combine in her later lifestyle and self-image both the active and passive Teresa. She developed both the "masculine" and "feminine" of herself to express a unified exciting person. She found her own way of allowing her unconscious to surface and serve her needs. Whether we attribute her final successes to divine grace or to courageous struggle, or to both, it still was a process which produced a person remarkably healthy in the two basic areas that Freud used to measure healthy integration: love and work. Within her culture, Teresa succeeded in her work and in her love. It was not an easy task. The courage it took to transcend the boundaries of her very patriarchal time and place brings to mind the response of Adrienne Rich when she was asked what it is she most wishes for her three sons: "That they might grow up to be as courageous as women."

NOTES

1. William James, *The Varieties of Religious Experience* (Mentor, 1958), p. 269.

2. Walter T. Stace, *The Teachings of the Mystics* (Mentor, 1960), p. 175.

3. G. Hahn, "Les Phenomenes hysteriques et les revelations de sainte Therese," *Revue des Questions Scientifiques 13* (1883), pp. 568–569.

4. Kate O'Brien, *Teresa of Avila* (Sheed & Ward, 1951), p. 93.

5. Titus Cranny, "Teresa: Daughter of the Church," *Spiritual Life* (Spring, 1965), p. 66.

6. Rosemary Ruether, *New Woman New Earth* (Seabury Press, 1975), p. 158.

7. Trevor Davis, *The Golden Century of Spain 1561–1621* (London: Macmillan & Co., 1961), p. 290.

8. Lady Alice Lovat, *The Life of Saint Teresa* (London: Herbert & Daniel, 1912), p. 11.

9. Neville Braybrook, "Celestial Castles," *Spiritual Life* (March, 1957), pp. 45ff.

10. Kieran Kavanaugh and Otilio Rodriquez, *St. Teresa of Avila* (ICS Publications, 1976), p. 34. Subsequent citations from Teresa's work are from this edition unless otherwise noted and are abbreviated in the text as K.

11. Neville Braybrook, "St. Teresa of Avila", *Spiritual Life* (Fall, 1961), pp. 253ff.

12. Arthur Deikmann, "Deautomatization and the Mystic Experience," in *Altered States of Consciousness,* ed. Charles T. Tate (Doubleday, 1972), pp. 37ff.

13. O'Brien, *Teresa,* p. 85.

14. See A. H. Maslow, *Toward a Psychology of Being* (Van Nostrand, 1968).

15. Sigmund Freud, *Character and Culture,* ed. Philip Rieff (Collier Books, 1963), pp. 211–213.

16. Karen Horney, *Feminine Psychology* (W. W. Norton, 1967), p. 74.

17. Ruether, *New Woman,* p. 142.

18. Sigmund Freud, *Dora; an analysis of a case of hysteria,* ed. Philip Rieff (Collier Books, 1963), p. 149.

19. Sigmund Freud, *A General Introduction to Psychoanalysis,* trans. Joan Riviere (Pocket Books, 1953), p. 399.

20. Freud, *Dora, ed. cit,* p. 149.

21. Ibid., p. 157.

22. Ibid., p. 156.

23. Ibid., pp. 146f.

24. Ibid., pp. 59f.

25. James, *Religious Experience,* p. 157.

26. Cited in Calvin Hall, *A Primer of Freudian Psychology* (Mentor, 1954), p. 122.

27. Lovat, *Life,* p. 11.

28. James, *Religious Experience,* p. 185.

29. Ibid., p. 189.

30. Gregory Baum, *Religion and Alienation* (Paulist Press, 1975), p. 233.

31. James, *Religious Experience,* p. 172.

32. See Erik Erikson, *Young Man Luther: A Study in Psychoanalysis and History* (Norton Library, 1962).

33. Ibid., p. 243.

34. Sigmund Freud, *Character and Culture, ed. cit.,* p. 225.

35. See Sister Grace Anthony Gaircy, "St. Teresa-Psychologist," *Cross and Crown,* (March, 1954), pp. 35ff.

36. Freud, *Dora, ed. cit.,* p. 97.

37. S. Shacter and J. E. Singer, "Cognitive, Social and Physiological Determinants of Emotional State," *Psychological Review 69,* (1962), pp. 379–399.

10

Spirituality and Politics: Seventeenth Century France

Daniel G. DiDomizio

Until very recently the word "spirituality" has rarely evoked political images. The pursuit of spirituality led one to consider matters of "spirit," not of "flesh," certainly not the sordid affairs of politics. If this principle was firmly adhered to theoretically, in practice, as the history of Christian life illustrates, people of flesh and blood never in fact maintained this clear-cut isolation of the two realms. The incarnational principle, rooted in the very dynamic of human life, has always been operative. The Spirit lives and breathes in real people, in concrete cultures and political situations. The contrary belief expressed a common, highly treasured approach to spirituality, namely the neo-platonic, in which somehow the human spirit could rise above real life and surge towards its heavenly counterpart. That this spiritual worldview befitted certain eras of Christianity and pro-duced spiritual giants cannot be denied. Ironically, the era under consideration here witnessed a noble but tragic rebirth of the neoplatonic as well as its definitive demise in the creation of the scientific age.

Worldview and Social Class

Every age develops its own worldview, or, more accurately, its own set of worldviews. These worldviews serve not only as the

296

context for events, but also as the very expression of the period of time in question as well as the generative source of the era's major cultural and political happenings. Understood thus, the concept of worldview functions as an indispensable interpretive instrument for studying the theological phenomena and spirituality of a given period. Faith, far from being seen as an isolated act or state, becomes a stance which shapes and is shaped by the particular structures and events which characterize the age. The spirituality of a people must of necessity flow from their worldview.

A worldview, observes Lucien Goldmann, represents "the whole complex of ideas, aspirations and feelings which link together the members of a social group and which opposes them to members of other social groups."[1] Key to the notion of worldview is the socio-political reality of social classes. A social class is simply a group of people bound together by common economic, social, political, and intellectual background and experience. By the same incarnational principle, the spirituality of such a group, honed by similar advantages and stresses, will evidence characteristic elements. Few would deny, for instance, the divergence in spirituality or Christian lifestyles and vision of an affluent, U.S. suburbanite and a disenfranchised Chilean peasant. The gospel is never read with neutral, apolitical eyes.

These observations provide a context for the study of the Jansenist movement in the seventeenth century and its characteristic worldview and spirituality. In this context, too, the personage and work of Blaise Pascal appear as the most authentic and consistent interpretation of the Jansenist worldview as well as a uniquely significant expression of Christian faith. To view an author and his/her work apart from the worldview of his/her social class runs the risk of overlooking some of the deeper social implications of the work and, in this sense, of misinterpreting the meaning of the work in its particular setting. In other words, to understand and interpret a cultural work, including a religious and theological phenomenon, one must be mindful of the reciprocal movement or flow between the individual and the group, between individual expression and worldview. The discovery of the group's worldview provides the key to understanding the interaction.

Jansenism: The Tragic Worldview

The movement towards absolute monarchy in France took place over a long period of time. The feudal monarchy gradually gave way to a more centralized one. This evolution was interrupted by the religious wars which devastated much of France at the close of the sixteenth century. During the transition the strengthening of the monarchy's position came at the expense of the old feudal nobility, whose prestige steadily declined, despite the nobility's sporadic rebellion against the relentless royal absolutism. Allied with the king, a new *noblesse de robe* emerged who were bound to the monarchy by a loyalty born of economic interdependence. Though not of royal blood, these officers, or office holders, played a key role as the king's tax collectors and local administrators. To wage war and build up and maintain the trappings of a central bureaucracy, the French monarchy experienced an increasing need for financial resources. Positions as revenue collectors were sold to lawyers and other public figures in various parts of France; such offices, moreover, could generally be passed on to one's descendants, often with the payment of an annual fee. Indeed the buying and selling of such offices furnished the king with a substantial revenue. The office holders, though bound to the king, nevertheless maintained a certain independence due to the relatively permanent nature of the positions in the families. Thus they formed a definite, noble class. Yet even they were not deeply imbued with the new nationalism which strove to put the king and the nation above group interests.

With the rise to power of Cardinal Richelieu, the evolution towards absolute, centralized power moved with even greater speed. In Armand-Jean de Richelieu the French monarchy found a unique public servant. Richelieu was born to a family of high standing whose financial status, however, dwindled during his childhood. Perhaps it was this tension which helped form the temperament which drove him to restore the fortunes and dignity of his family and later of France herself.[2] Giving up a military career, Richelieu assumed the bishopric of Luçon as a family benefice. As bishop he displayed an authentic concern for his people and the duties of his post. Though not austere in his style of life, the bishop of Luçon maintained a simple profile and a certain modesty in his wealth. He supported the reform efforts in the French church at that time, notably those of the Capuchins and of Cardinal Bérulle; the latter founded the second oratory for young priests in Luçon during Richelieu's episcopacy.[3] Around 1616 Richelieu began to involve himself in the political affairs of the realm. His early political career was checkered. Yet his ability to analyze situations, weigh and choose political options, and to make useful alliances eventually brought him success and prominence. Most of all, his loyalty to France and the king knew no limits. He lived, in his own eyes, as the faithful servant of his two kings.

Richelieu faced a number of grave situations in his efforts to solidify the power of the monarchy. He needed to control the nobles, whose lingering feudal mentality made them natural enemies of an absolute national monarchy. In addition, the Huguenots, though defeated in the religious wars, remained a constant political force in certain sections of France. Add to these political tensions the delicate foreign maneuvers of Richelieu to establish a balance to the powerful Catholic block of Spain and the Hapsburgs.

Under Richelieu the possession of the various offices was increasingly subjected to the whim of the central power. Here too the chancellor displayed his usual singlemindedness. Any opposition to official positions met with stern reprisals. Gradually a system of "commissars," more closely tied to the central bureaucracy, began to replace the more autonomous *noblesse de robe*. The Parliament, whose influence also was declining, found its natural allies in this group of officers. The conflict reached a critical point towards the end of the 1630s. In March, 1638, for example, a number of investors, members of the *noblesse de robe,* protested the failure of the government to pay interest on loans. Richelieu responded by arresting and imprisoning several members of the group. Etienne Pascal, father of Blaise, escaped the Bastille only by fleeing Paris and living in relative secrecy for one year. Through the good graces of friends who had Richelieu's ear and the charm and wit of his daughter Jacqueline, later a nun at Port Royal, the elder Pascal was pardoned and given a position in Rouen, an office which was subsequently embroiled in the political turmoil which marked that province.[4]

Pascal's situation was typical of other members of the *noblesse de robe.* What is significant here is the fact that many of the key personages in the Jansenist movement of the mid-seventeenth century, the Arnaulds, the Pascals, the Abbé of Saint-Cyran, Antoine Lemaître and others came from this social class, a group of people whose position in the world of the French aristocracy and whose financial stability were rapidly deteriorating due to the ruthless political machinations of Cardinal Richelieu. Burdened with the trappings of aristocracy, these families began to experience the threat of poverty and diminished prestige. Life in the "world" gradually lost its appeal. The political setting was established for a distinct spirituality, viz., "flight from the world."

During the same period under discussion, the intellectual life in France was in a similar state of transition. Among intellectuals the work of Descartes was widely discussed and debated. Cartesian philosophy coexisted with the Aristotelianism of scholastic philosophy, though the thrust of the former would ultimately undermine the structured world of the latter. Indeed, the logic of Cartesian philosophy even went beyond the personal life stances of its author. Descartes, for instance, saw himself as a faithful member of the Catholic community; yet the methodical doubt which anchored the perception of reality in the "I" of self implied the demise of this very sense of believing community. Philosophical individualism was the logical outcome. Though he was a sincere believer, Descartes implicitly set aside any outside source of order and values—God in the traditional view of the time. This philosophical autonomy contrasted sharply with the sense of transcendence inherited from the medieval past. In sum, the very structure of society no longer had a theological basis. It was for the Enlightenment of a century later to draw out these conclusions. In the seventeenth century, the two philosophical views existed side by side. Empiricism had its foundation, though it did not immediately abolish the structured universe of Greek philosophy. Blaise Pascal, for example, a brilliant mathematician and scientist, both appreciated and integrated positive elements of empiricism into his own thought. Yet he also saw the limits and insufficiency of this position. Indeed, for Pascal in his *Pensees* the mathematical method represented the best of human rational possibilities, but beyond it lay the infinite realm of grace; this alone was supreme. Hence Pascal frequently found himself at odds with the rationalist vein of Cartesian philosophy during several personal meetings with Descartes.[5] The seeds of rationalism and even skepticism, however, were already sown. Here, too, the members of the *noblesse de robe* in general found themselves in an alien world.

Significantly, renewal in the church in the early seventeenth century took a totally different direction, that is, away from major institutional changes and new philosophical trends. The devastation of the religious wars had taken a heavy toll in the church. The numbers and morale of the clergy declined drastically. The intellectual formation of both clergy and laity in general was of a poor quality. Many church buildings were leveled and the clergy dispersed. The renewal in seventeenth century France pursued the direction of the postreformation church elsewhere, namely the renewal of the inner life of the Spirit. Even Cardinal Richelieu, as was mentioned above, was a early supporter of the work of Vincent de Paul with the poor and of Cardinal Bérulle in deepening the spiritual life of the clergy.

Under the influence of the Teresian reform in the sixteenth century Spain, a circle of "spirituals" came together in Paris to form a network of persons committed to a deeper life of prayer and religious commitment as a means to reform the church. But their influence in fact set the direction of French spirituality in general during the seventeenth century and beyond. Persons such as Madame Acarie, Benedict of Canfeld, Francis de Sales, Oratorian Charles Condren, Cardinal Bérulle, Sulpician Jean-Jacques Olier, Vincent de Paul, Abbé of Saint-Cyran, Mère Angelique Arnauld of Port Royal, Blaise Pascal himself, and Francis Fénélon form a chain which spanned most of the century. Though significantly different as individuals, they represent a definite spiritual heritage: the priority of the spiritual over the affairs of politics; the quest of God over worldly success; the reform of individual faith life as a prelude to institutional reform. These men and women were, however, by the nature of the times, political figues as well. Hence the dramatic events which shaped their lives.

The early members of this spiritual movement, Canfeld and Bérulle in particular, were especially drawn to mysticism as the culmination of prayer and the Christian life. They borrowed heavily from the Rheno-Flemish school of mysticism of the thirteenth and fourteenth centuries and studied the writings of Meister Eckhart, John Ruusbroec, and John Tauler, writers not unknown for their influence on movements in their time and culture. The theological works of Cardinal Bérulle reveal a clear neoplatonic thrust.[6] His hierarchical structure of the universe eminating from the Godhead closely resembled the theological anthropology of Pseudo-Dionysius. Such an overall spiritual, even mystical, emphasis could not but be on a collision course with the spirit of the age represented by the politics of Cardinal Richelieu and the philosophical tenets of both Descartes and the new declining scholasticism.

These various cultural movements of the seventeenth century, however, were anything but isolated from each other. Indeed Jansenism, with the monastery of Port Royal as a symbol, represented the convergence of the economic, political, philosophical, and religious currents of the century. During the 1620s and later, Cardinal Bérulle, in addition to his role as spiritual leader, was also at the head of the "Catholic" party in opposition to Richelieu's alliance with the German Protestant princes against Catholic Spain. Though a former collaborator with Bérulle,[7] Richelieu's vengeance in victory was complete. Discredited, Bérulle died in 1629.[8] The Abbé of Saint-Cyran, a disciple and collaborator of Bérulle, was also to win the disfavor of Richelieu. In 1634 Saint-Cyran became spiritual director of the convent of Port Royal. In addition to his association with Bérulle, he had ventured theological opinions which were suspect in court circles: his defense of his friend Cornelius Jansen in the controversy over the work *Augustinus;* his position in the debate on contrition; and his growing pessimism regarding the possibility of leading an authentic Christian life in the politico-social milieu of that time. Further, he was an outspoken critic of the politics of the realm. The climax of this conflict came in 1637 when August Antoine Lemaître, a promising young lawyer, abruptly left public life and became the first solitary at Port Royal under the direction of Saint-Cyran. Using the pretext that Saint-Cyran was depriving the state of its most gifted citizens as well as leveling vague accusations of "illuminism" at the Abbé, Richelieu had Saint-Cyran arrested and imprisoned,[9] where the Abbé remained almost until his death in 1643. Others, however, both clerics and laymen soon joined the ranks of the solitaries at Port Royal. Thus the nucleus of the Jansenist movement was formed, a nucleus which received support from a wide section of French aristocratic society, particularly from the *noblesse de robe,* the office holders and some members of Parliament. Subsequent theological issues which were to have political ramifications include the controversy over frequent communion and the condemnation of five propositions of Jansen by Pope Innocent X in 1653. In each case Port Royal became the symbol of conflict.

This sketch of historical events and cultural movements traces the patterns of the emerging worldview of this segment of French society, namely the *noblesse de robe.* Opposed to the absolutism of the monarchy for both practical and theoretical reasons, these aristocrats with a certain lingering feudal mentality were at the same time too dependent on the monarchy economically to desire the demise or even radical change in the structure. Blended into this political turmoil were several theological polemics involving members of the same social class. The ordered world of neoplatonism clashed harshly with the skepticism generated by Cartesian philosophy and political nationalism. Thus the paradox arose of a social class politically disenfranchized, threatened on every side by cultural and intellectual trends, feeling the alienation which suggested a flight from the world, and yet at the same time keenly aware that by the nature of life itself they were compelled to be in and of the world. The worldview thus described merits the term used by Lucien Goldmann—"tragic."

> The nature of the tragic mind in seventeenth-century France can be characterized by two factors: the complete and exact understanding of the new world created by rationalistic individualism, together with all the invaluable and scientifically valid acquisitions which this offered to the human intellect; and, at the same time, the complete refusal to accept this world as the only one in which man could live, move and have his being.[10]

Blaise Pascal: The Tragic Vision and the God of Paradox

By reason of temperament, profession, and social class: Blaise Pascal embodied the tragic worldview. Born in 1623 the son of an officer, his mother died when he was three years old. Etienne Pascal, mathematician and amateur scientist, undertook the education of his own children. Blaise's interest and genius in regard to mathematics appeared very early. In 1631 the family moved to Paris where the personality of Richelieu dominated the political scene. The disruptive events of 1638 leading to his father's exile gave Blaise a first-hand experience of life in the "world."

In 1646 on the occasion of Etienne's convalescence after a fall, family friends introduced the Pascal family into the religious views and fervor of Port Royal and of Saint-Cyran's writings in particular. The response was profound and lasting. Some have called this occasion Blaise Pascal's first conversion. Meanwhile he continued his scientific work, completing major experiments with atmospheric pressure. Upon the death of Etienne Pascal in 1651, his daughter Jacqueline entered the convent of Port Royal, an occasion which precipitated a painful rift between Blaise and his younger sister regarding the inheritance. Between 1652 and 1654 Blaise pursued his interest in science. He was sought after as a speaker on scientific questions and tried to market his invention of 1642, a calculating machine. His companions were among the more liberal thinking men of the era in Paris. He pursued the "good life."

Thus Pascal arrived at a critical point of his life in the fall of 1654, a leading proponent of the new scientific era, man of business and of the world, who maintained nevertheless a certain religious fervor through his contact with the Jansenism of Port Royal. In September of that year Blaise went to see his sister Jacqueline at Port Royal, aware of a growing dissatisfaction with his present life.[11] On the night of November 23 Pascal underwent a profound religious experience during which he felt with great intensity the truth of the "God of Abraham, God of Isaac, God of Jacob, not of the philosophers and scientists," as he wrote in his famous *Memorial;* "forgetting the world and all things, except only God."[12] "Fire" was the image which dominated his description of the experience.

In January, 1655 Pascal retired temporarily to live among the solitaries at Port Royal. He began to take a more critical stance towards much of the liberal thinking of his time. When the theologians of the Sorbonne condemned Port Royal's defense of Jansen and Port Royal's existence itself was threatened, Pascal and several others launched the *Provincial Letters,* a sustained attack against certain contemporary theological opinions and the casuistry of the moralists in particular. The prime target was the

Jesuits.[13] The *Letters* were characterized by a keen, incisive wit which held up to ridicule not only the opinions but also the theologians and clerics responsible for them. The public followed the exchange closely, taking delight in the clever attack upon those close to the realm. Though published anonymously, the *Provincial Letters* further divided Port Royal from the court of Louis XIV where the Jesuits served as confessors. In September of 1657, the *Letters* were placed on the Index.

Meanwhile the arrival of the Bull of Pope Alexander VII condemning Jansen in March of 1657 precipitated another personal crisis for Pascal. He was torn between "obeying God or obeying the pope," as he put it.[14] Pascal experienced a growing sense of distress at the prolonged debate and began to move away from the logic and close reasoning of the *Provincial Letters* towards the paradoxical, almost skeptical approach found in the *Pensées.*[15] How live faithful to God who remains absent from the world? How pursue the temporal when only eternal values are worthy of human endeavor? Yet, in the apparent absence of the eternal, where else must one struggle but in the world of affairs? The *Pensées* represent Pascal's personal apologia, his attempt to build a reasonable argument for faith in Jesus Christ amid the contradiction and even absurdity of human life.

If the *Pensées* express the paradox of the tragic worldview, they accurately reflect the last four years of Pascal's own life. Though close to the life of Port Royal, he never retired there permanently. Though critical of the scientific viewpoint, he pursued his scientific experiments, and only months before his death he organized the first bus service in Paris. In a letter to a fellow scientist Pierre Fermat in 1661, Pascal wrote, " ... I consider geometry to be the highest exercise of the mind, but at the same time hold it so useless that I would make little distinction between the man who is a geometer and nothing more and one who is a skillful artisan ... for my part, I would not as much as walk down the street for geometry's sake."[16]

As his health worsened, his life became more austere. During his final years much of his time and meager financial resources were devoted to caring for the poor and infirm. While fellow Jansenists could say yes to God in the certainty of his existence and thus reject the world in as absolute a fashion as possible, Pascal maintained both the yes and the no which best expressed the tragic vision. When a person sincerely searches his heart, God's existence is sensed as an absolute necessity; the world of human events fades in comparison. Yet the same person who must see the world as the context and reality of his very existence searches in vain for God's presence in the world of politics, or philosophy and science, the world of human exchange. Reason obscures what the heart reveals. "The eternal silence of these infinite spaces terrifies me," wrote Pascal.[17] For Pascal God is a totality and hence the unifier of polarities. To affirm one pole and reject the other is to falsify the situation. But the tragedy lies in the fact that reason seems to say yes to one pole, the world, and in an absolute fashion, while the thrust of the human heart affirms only God, and then too in an absolute way. In the practical living out of one's life, one must choose, wager, and yet be willing to live out the tragedy. In the long run, for Pascal, one has more to gain by opting for faith in God.

> The conditions in which it is easiest to live according to the world are the most difficult in which to live according to God; and the reverse: nothing is more difficult in the eyes of the world than the religious life; nothing is easier in the sight of God. Nothing, according to the world, is easier than to hold a great office and to enjoy a great fortune; nothing, according to God, is more difficult than to live like that, without participating in it and developing a taste for it.[18]

If Jansenism stood for the tragic worldview in mid-seventh century France, Pascal ironically was more Jansenist than the very inhabitants of Port Royal. When the Formulary asserting the condemnation of Jansen was presented to the nuns of Port Royal, some, including Jacqueline Pascal, refused to sign it under any conditions and were later removed from Port Royal.

Their yes to God was absolute and was confirmed by their no to the world. Blaise Pascal himself refused to sign the Formulary and indeed stated in a letter of 1661 that no one ought to sign a condemnation of Jansen. Yet in his final deathbed confession of July, 1662, he stated that he had completely accepted the pope's authority since August of 1661.[19] The tragic vision implies not yes *or* no, but yes *and* no to both God and the world. The refusal of the world is only valid when carried out within the world itself. Faith in God is only authentic when it entertains the possibility of his total absence. History was to prove this stance to be a genuine insight in the evolution of modern faith and spirituality.

Pascal in Religious History

Blaise Pascal holds an honored position among the "spirituals" of the seventeenth century. Yet when one scans this list of persons of exceptional spiritual stature, it is clear that what binds them together was not similarities of personality, nor doctrinal foundations, nor position in the church. Indeed, only the sense of belonging to a particular social class appears as the common cultural link among these men and women. Again the impact of social groups is profound. Countless elements of daily life in fact shape the vantage point from which a significant number of this group views the larger world and interacts with its current thought-patterns and formative events. A worldview finds its most authentic expression, furthermore, in the literary and intellectual works of its gifted members, namely those men and women who reflect the maximum possible awareness of the situation of the group to which they belong. In turn, a grasp of the worldview of a social group enables the reader to reach a more objective interpretation of the work of one of the group's important artists or thinkers. Even the detailed analysis of such a work and an understanding of the author's personality can still fail to pinpoint the underlying intent of the work in question. The principle is an old one: to fully understand a part, one must situate it in the totality. Individuals, whether intentionally or not,

can separate their thoughts from their daily lives; a social class
cannot do so consistently over a long period of time.

The social class in question here was a pivotal one in seventeenth century France. The *noblesse de robe* as a class bore the
greatest impact of the profound political and cultural changes of
the seventeenth century. Hence these gifted persons represent
not so much the emergence of a new doctrinal development, nor
an artistic or literary trend; rather, as representatives of a social
class, they formed a movement, a movement whose inevitable
destination would be tragic. In touch both with the newer cultural and political tendencies and with the eternal foundation of
the older order, the *noblesse de robe* could only perish in the
unavoidable conflict of the two worldviews. The real conflict,
however, took place not so much between this class and the
monarchy or the liberal theologians, or any other outside group;
the true confrontation was enacted between these divergent positions within the hearts and minds and lifestyles of the *noblesse
de robe* itself. In this sense, the experience of the *noblesse de robe* in
France at that time stands as a paradigm of the modern confrontation between a traditional faith in a caring, ever-present God
and a far-reaching empiricism whose structures seem to uproot
the very foundations of faith. As a fitting symbol of this class,
Blaise Pascal can be aptly called, in Lucien Goldmann's words,
"the first modern man . . . the first of a long line of thinkers who
go beyond—and integrate—both the Christian tradition and the
achievements of rationalism and empiricism and create a moral
attitude which is still valid today."[20]

The devastating critiques of Jansenist theology and moral attitudes, expressed with vehemence and some skill by Abbé H.
Bremond[21] as well as by Ronald Knox,[22] have been accepted
virtually without question by religious historians of the past century. Saint-Cyran is said to have been a vain, stubborn man. The
nuns of Port Royal and some of the solitaries come down to us as
proud, better-than-thou religious fanatics. Pascal himself is
often presented as exemplifying the moral and spiritual rigidity
of Jansenism, a man who at times displayed the harshness to-

wards others born of such religious intensity. The existence of certain of these individual and group traits seems in fact verified by history. Yet the issue of deepest concern transcends this moral critique. Our age allows its heroes mistakes, even glaring faults. Instead we tend to cherish that which they hand on to us which has the insight and power to speak to our own most pressing human questions. We treasure most of all their solidarity with us in our human condition.

In this light the events of seventeenth century France and the life of Blaise Pascal in particular emerge as sketching a unique style of faith. Gone was a faith buttressed by stable philosophical and theological systems rooted in the Greek sense of order; gone too was a faith which found adequate, or at least meaningful expression in culture and art. Instead Pascal in the *Pensées* suggests a faith in a God who is no longer mediated by life in the world, be it cultural, political, or philosophical life. God from now on is a hidden God. The universal skepticism of the seventeenth century and afterwards created a vacuum; faith must live in this vacuum. For Pascal and other modern people faith lives in a void by making choices, choices about the meaning of life and about the resultant deeds and style of life. Faith becomes not the once-and-for-all option, nor a familial heritage, but a continual process of probing, of discerning, deciding, and acting.

Moreover, the fragment, the basic literary element in the composition of the *Pensées,* becomes the characteristic expression of the modern person's spiritual testimony. The fragment suggests a momentary insight, not a total system, or a summa. The fragment attempts to order an experience; its very form implies the lack of any overall, timeless order. We will never know what final form the *Pensées* might have taken in Pascal's hands. Yet the fragment as an expression of faith bespeaks a movement or process, a search for order and continuity— indeed a search for God. In the words Nikos Kazantzakis puts on the lips of his St. Francis, " ... perhaps God is simply the search for God. ... If so, woe unto us."[23] Such a search is tragic, for it foresees no final achievement this side of death.

The Contemporary Crisis of Faith

One might point to a number of contemporary figures as symbols of today's crisis of faith. I would like to propose three persons whose lives and faith stances, though widely divergent, appear both paradoxical and fragmentary—indeed tragic. The major impact of Dietrich Bonhoeffer has not come from his more traditional works but from his *Letters and Papers from Prison,* a tentative, haunting set of fragments, full of both doubt and confidence. The God who cannot tolerate genocide and murder, can he save the person who murders the tyrant? Need one risk the unforgivable to respond to the gospel? The contrast Bonhoeffer suggests between traditional Christian faith and the faith tempered by the horror of war continues to challenge our contemporary reflection on faith. Not enough time has passed yet for history to cast its perceptive eye on the faith of the post-Vietnam, American Christian. But Bonhoeffer's religious categories are not likely to pass into time unused.

The Holocaust brought forth numerous expressions of faith, among them the tales of Elie Wiesel, the Jewish story teller, whose faith in the God of the Covenant perished with the remains of the six million. He is obsessed by the memory. Can the remembering find a reason and somehow heal the wounds? Can there ever be a reason or a healing for the death of six million? Yet Wiesel's tales are a search for a Presence, for a chance to believe again in life, in the future, in God.

Finally, the literary pilgrim, Nikos Kazantzakis, comes to mind, whose characters from Zorba to Jesus Christ are as much enigmas as their author. During his lifetime Kazantzakis was fittingly described as fervent Christian and heretic, mystic and rationalist, sensual lover and celibate, the traditionalist who proclaims the new age of the proletariat. Each of his novels is a fragment—a tentative insight into the meaning of life, of love, of God.

For Pascal, faith, though it be an affair of the heart, needs expression in everyday life, in politics and economic life, in cul-

ture and philosophy, in moral values and patterns of life.
Spirituality must encompass all of these. But what really
mediates God's presence in this world of paradoxical human
events? This is the underlying question that emerges from the
conflicts of seventeenth century France. This question remains
with us today, in a new context, and with a new set of terms. Our
response today can echo Pascal's: everything and nothing
mediates God's presence to us! How resolve the paradox?
Perhaps Professor John Dunne's remark regarding Pascal and
Kierkegaard gives us a hint: "Only the man who stands on the
leading edge of modern experience . . . can taste the victory (of
faith)"[24] People who live in paradox, not flawlessly but nonetheless creatively, can best speak to the issue of faith.

NOTES

1. Lucien Goldmann, *The Hidden God,* trans. Philip Thody
(Humanities Press, 1964), p. 17.

2. D. P. O'Connell, *Richelieu* (World Publishing Company,
1968) p. 23.

3. Ibid., p. 19.

4. Jean Steinmann, *Pascal,* trans. Martin Turnell (Harcourt
Brace and World, 1966), pp. 20–23.

5. Ibid., pp. 43–44.

6. Cf. *la Vie de Jésus* and *les Grandeurs de Jésus.* The hierarchical structure of the universe and the threefold division of the
human soul both reflect the ordered universe of Pseudo-
Dionysius. Louis Cognet, *La Spiritualité Moderne: 1500–1650* (Au-
bier, 1966), chapter IX, pp. 310 ff.

7. O'Connell, *Richelieu,* p. 23.

8. Cognet, *Spiritualité,* p. 324.

9. Ibid., p. 494.

10. Goldmann, *Hidden God,* p. 33.

11. Steinmann, *Pascal.,* p. 76.

12. Robert W. Gleason, ed., *The Essential Pascal* (Mentor-
Omega, 1966), p. 205.

13. The relatively new Society of Jesus had already made a profound impact on European cultural life. In France in the seventeenth century the influence of the Jesuits was felt both in theology and politics. Theologically they represented a more humanistic approach to the relationship between the human being and God. Their teachings often met opposition in more traditional circles. The debate concerning grace was a prime example. However, it was in the realm of moral theology that Pascal saw Jesuits teaching and practice as dangerous to Christian life. Pascal accused the Jesuits of laxity and hair-splitting in morality, a tendency, according to him, which negated the gospel itself. As confessors for the king and many of the nobility, the Jesuits exercised considerable political power as well.

14. The expression is taken from notes of what would have been the nineteenth Letter. Goldmann, *Hidden God,* p. 84.

15. Ibid., pp. 170–71.

16. Cited by Goldmann, pp. 50–51.

17. Martin Turnell, trans., *Pascal's Pensées,* (Harper, 1962) fr. 392.

18. Ibid., fr. 705.

19. Goldmann, *Hidden God,* pp. 188–89.

20. Ibid., p. 171.

21. Cf. Henri Bremond, *Histoire du sentiment religieux.* IV.

22. Ronald A. Knox, *Enthusiasm* (Oxford University Press, 1961), chapters IX and X.

23. Nikos Kazantzakis, *St. Francis.* (Simon and Schuster, 1962), p. 37.

24. John Dunne, *A Search for God in Time and Memory* (Macmillan, 1969), p. 69.

PART II:
ECUMENICAL ROUTES

11

Seeking a Moist Heart: Native American Ways for Helping the Spirit

Mary José Hobday, OSF

The Papago Indians of the Southwest tell the story of the Elder Brother, who was killed, and, after a few days, struggled to come back to full strength and renewed life. To gain this, he went in search of a moist heart, a heart with new blood. He had to make several stops, for there were enemies determined to prevent his finding new life. But with each victory, he grew stronger, the blood flowed more powerfully, and his heart became more and more moist. Finally, he stood in full vigor, with a very moist heart.

Maybe it is time for America to seek a moist heart. Maybe it is time for spiritual battles that will bring new blood to the heart of America, blood that can truly moisten the heart for deep feeling, great generosity, spiritual living. Nearly a century ago an old Dakota wiseman said:

> Everything as it moves, now and then, here and there, makes stops. The bird as it flies stops in one place to make its nest, and in another to rest in its flight. A man when he goes forth stops when he wills. So the God has stopped. The sun . . . moon . . . trees . . . animals are all places where he stopped. The Indian thinks of these places and sends his prayers there to reach the place where the God has stopped. He hopes to win help . . . and a blessing.[1]

Maybe America is stopping to wonder about itself. Maybe it is looking for help and a blessing. Maybe it is time to listen to those who have stopped here on this land for thousands of generations, who have loved this land, who have been broken by fights over it, but who will surely heal into a stronger people. Maybe there is, in the Native American tradition, a way for the people of this country to make a stopover. There might be something to learn. There might be a deeper way of breathing. There might be a beat that could include a new heart, a better earth, and a more joyful Spirit dance. There might be a way to unity. Maybe the hoop can be mended. Maybe the people can form a circle that is holy, that is strong, that would be a blessing for the greater circle of the world. Maybe.

Let us sit down together and speak of some Indian ways that help the Spirit, that help the heart keep moist and strong. There is the way of silence, the way of remembering the dead, the way of loving the land, the way of seeking a vision, the way of telling stories. There are other ways, too, but we will not be greedy.

Silence Helps the Heart

About three hundred years ago, an Indian chief said to the governor of Pennsylvania:

We love quiet; we suffer the mouse to play; when the woods are rustled by the wind, we fear not.[2]

The American people need to learn from the Native Americans the love of silence. For many non-Indians in this country, it is tolerated, held in awe, suspected, perhaps desired, occasionally cherished, but rarely cultivated. Silence is part of the traditional way of living for the native American. It is an easy way, for it gives the soft distance between spoken words, body signals, and action choices. To live with Indian people is to discover a beautiful enhancement of the spirit through silence. Unless they have succumbed to the rush and noise of the main-stream style of life in this country, Indians still reveal this gift of silence.

They walk with a lighter step—easy on the grasses as they pass through, easy on the dispositions of others. They judge with a held breath, easy on the frailties of fellow human beings. They wait with a long and strong patience, easy on the strains of change and upheaval. They smile with a quiet peace, easy on the contradictions of daily living. You might say, "All Indians do this?" Perhaps not all. But many. Most.

The Indian way of eating is one of the best ways to understand their companionship with silence. Eating is slow, deliberately so, and is given enough space to happen. The bread is dipped with attention into the sauce, observed with appreciation, taken to the mouth with a kind of lingering anticipation. I enjoy watching those around me separate the food with care, relish the individual flavors, consider the time it took to prepare each, wonder from whose kitchen or pot it came. It is not that Indians do not speak during a meal, but conversation is not primary. Eating is. It gets full and unembarrassed attention. Usually when the people gather for a celebration or a memorial meal, there is an impressive gathering of foods. The lowly pinto bean receives its share of interest and appreciation. Soups provide ample occasion for reflection. I have found the *act* of eating with Indian peoples is usually a quiet, pleasant meditation of gifts. Feelings of gratitude come easy. Much communication goes on during the meal, but talk is not steady. Because eating is so daily, there is a beauty in that kind of quiet, thoughtful sharing.

A friend of mine once visited me on a reservation. We had given a young man a ride for a short distance. After he left the car, my friend remarked, "What a quiet manner he has. And the way he got out of the car and walked away—it was like a poem spoken without sound." Most Indian people are very comfortable with silence. They can sit in one another's presence without words for long periods of time. This does not mean that nothing is happening—Indians are highly attuned to nonverbal communication. They pick up movements without seeming to notice; they know impatience or nervousness without a glance up. Practiced silence is a great strength. The Indian children who seem most at peace and least fretful are usually controlled by silence rather than by harsh or loud reminders. A steady look, a quiet smile, calm presence to fussy demands seem to work best. Often, a child is simply gathered up and held, with no direct notice of its crying.

Part of the understanding of silence as a spiritual value has to do with waiting, with not being impatient. Impatient pacing, persistent watch-checking, aggravated comments—all these are usually lacking at Indian gatherings and meetings. Somehow, the Indian tradition allows more space for individuals at common assemblies. They wait, giving everyone time to get settled. And they wait in silence. In worship services, in ceremonials, there are often long silences. But the waiting is part of the action, not divorced from it.

Love the quiet? It can become friend. Suffer the mouse to play? It is an extraordinary creature of adaptation. Fear the wind? It teases the imagination into courage if given a chance.

It Is Good To Walk With The Dead

In his speech delivered to the governor of the Washington Territory in 1854, the Swamish chief, Seattle, reveals the feel of the Native American for their dead.

> To us our ancestors are sacred and their resting place is hallowed ground. You wander far from the graves of your ancestors and seemingly without regret. . . . Your dead cease to love you, and the land of their nativity, as soon as they pass the portals of the tomb and wander way beyond the stars. They are soon forgotten and never return. Our dead can never forget the beautiful world that gave them being. . . .
>
> Every part of this soil is sacred in the estimation of my people. The very dust upon which you now stand responds

more lovingly to their footsteps than to yours, because it is rich with the blood of our ancestors, and our bare feet are conscious of the sympathetic touch.

And when your children's children think themselves alone in the field, the store, the shop, upon the highway, or in the silence of the pathless woods, they will not be alone. At night when the streets of your cities and villages are silent and you think them deserted, they will throng with the returning hosts that once filled and still love this beautiful land. The white man will never be alone.

Let him be just and deal kindly with my people, for the dead are not powerless. Dead, did I say? There is no death, only a change of worlds.[3]

For the Native American, part of life is living with death and the dead, keeping alive the memory of those who have gone ahead. To allow the memory of the dead to die is in itself a kind of death. It is not only an action of selfishness and ingratitude, it is a betrayal of the history of the family and of the tribe.

Whatever the particular ceremonies at the death and burial, whatever the specific understanding of life after death, Indian people keep alive to the dead and keep the dead alive to themselves. A significant way of remembering is the yearly memorial feast, which commemorates the death of the person. The first memorial is held one year after the death. Memorial feasts are marked by personal prayer, prayer vigils with other family members and friends, by feasts open even to passersby, and often by gift-giving, known as giveaways. In some tribes the giveaway includes a dance by family members. Gifts are given to anyone who may have been especially kind to the deceased or the family; gifts are given, also, to those who have shared the sorrow of the death.

Where Indians still have use of their reservation land, they often commemorate the *place* of death with a marker, a shrine, or a flower arrangement. Those who are not acquainted with their customs may think these are graves, but they are not. They are markers to show just where the spirit left the body to journey to the other world. Once a boy drowned in an open tank in the school yard, and the family set up a marker right on the school property. In villages that are alive to tradition, the cemeteries are lovingly cared for and show many touches of respect and sentiment. How a village cares for its cemetery is usually a sign of the spiritual vigor of the people living there.

What does this hold for non-Indians? The Indian attitude toward the dead links the memory of those who have died with those who still live. The dead and the land are intertwined in memory, but also with many signs of public and private reminder. Continuity with the past gives strength to the present and offers hope for the future. Perhaps a great sense of the rootlessness of the Western world is its separation from the dead. Familiarity with the dead, communion with the dead, can lessen the fear of death. The Indians expect a friendly greeting in the other world. But leaving this world through death does not mean a loss of land that has shared tears and laughter, sorrow and joy. A Navajo song sings that the dead are lonely for the living, and tug at them gently, trying to draw them away from this life. But Indians do not believe that time and space can separate; rather, time and space create a new way of being.

The Beloved Land

The tradition of the tribe is that each person, and the entire tribe, have a moral, an ethical, relationship with the land. The land is the Mother. The grass is her hair. She is fertile and generous with her gifts, yielding life and beauty in abundance. She provides nourishment for the living and a welcoming embrace for the dead. She is not prejudiced, for she treasures the so-called weeds as readily as the more resplendent flowers. Not only do Indians love the land because it mingles with the dust of the dead, but because it is vital and alive, and is part of the life of each person. Indians are close to the sources—to earth and water, fire and air, climate and seasons. Many of their spiritual ceremonials move around the seasons. Many take place out-of-doors. Often the high places, the faraway places, the places anointed with austerity, beauty, or memory are most holy. The Indians have never apologized for being intoxicated with the beauty, the power, the mystery of the land. They cultivate the ways that the land can transport them, can teach them the secrets and mysteries of nature. The land is not only the soil. It is the four-leggeds, the winged creatures, the growing plants and trees. It is the directions which teach courage, birth, warmth, and death, as well as what in life is up, what is down, and what is inside. The land can be touched and heard, smelled and brushed against. It can be inhaled and rubbed into the skin. It can be caressed and admired. But it can also be violated, raped, wounded, scarred, and grieved. The lessons can be learned or discarded, but the land will not be ignored.

Native Americans include nature's raw gifts in their ceremonials. They prefer to pick a branch from a nearby tree, rather than use an instrument of precious metal. They like to burn what comes from their own land. They choose the scent of pine and cedar, of sage and sweetgrass, over the fragrance of an imported incense. They enjoy "holy" smoke, whether it curls from a cooking fire, a ritual fire, or a cigarette smoked meditatively. All are part of the land, the whole world, and are reverenced.

Those who do not understand may think the Indian way of speaking of holy stones, sacred mountains, mystery caves, and blessed trees as mere superstition. More often, such respect is an identification with the past, with a story of valor or goodness, with the hidden ways the Great Spirit speaks to us through what is plain and lowly. Indians are sometimes criticized as passive or lacking in ambition because they do not relate to nature with the white attitude. Indians do not consider nature to be only the servant of humans, and often they will be inconvenienced rather than disturb a beautiful mountain. They feel it is more gracious to yield at times, to take the long way around, rather than tunnel through or slice the top off a mountain. They do not consider a swift passage necessarily superior to a beautiful one. Indians have always had a more accommodating spirit toward the land, because they believe the land shares the Great Spirit. The white mentality has been to conquer, to dominate: *Make* the land fit! *Force* the land to yield! Indians feel white people do not know how to obey what is holy and reasonable in nature, and this is partly why white culture has such little patience and reverence for the land. The land has its own needs, apart from humans. These days there is much wailing and crying about waste and neglect and scarcity. But these evils come when the earth itself is sore from the touch of plundering and greedy people.

Thomas Merton has suggested that the people in America, other than the Indians, will never develop a truly American spirituality until they pay more attention to the wisdom of the native people. White people are recent immigrants, even those who can trace back a few hundred years. Often they came selfishly, rushing to take for themselves, to fence off as much as possible and keep everyone else away. They did not believe that no one owns the land; the earth is the Creator's gift to all, from the Indian view. Now the land is giving back the treatment it has received. Greed and waste and heavy steps have left the land breathless, littered, and worn to poverty.

Native Americans have had about twenty thousand years longer than anyone else to understand the spirit of the land called America. They have come to know the ways and whims of this part of the earth, not through dominance, but through friendship. The land, like all life, is strong, but it is also fragile. These past decades it has become almost delicate in its needs for refreshment. It requires love and care and sacrifice to bring it healing and a steady beat. If the American people do not want to be treated as strangers, even as enemies, by the land, they must grow in wisdom and respect for the balance of nature. Community sharing, rather than personal greed, must find a stronger path.

Do Not Be Afraid To Seek The Vision

Though many Native American tribes have moved away from the actual tradition of the vision quest, of vision seeking, others

have retained at least portions of this adventure of the spirit. It is
helpful to think about some of the characteristics of vision seeking, because wisdom and understanding can come from the
quest. All spiritual traditions consider what is noble, what leads
to peace and good living with others, what teaches the most
generous way to give oneself away to life, in order to come to live
with meaning and direction.

Going apart is important in vision seeking. Once there is an
inner stirring—which may be fostered by the leader, a friend, a
holy person—one is coming to the sense of wanting to seek a
vision. A readiness, an eagerness of spirit, is like an eagle inside,
trying to take wing. So one begins to look for the right place. It
may be a high place, or a very isolated place, maybe a place with
a holy memory. But it must be where daily routine cannot inter-
rupt, where waiting in stillness is possible. In the peyote ceremony, the seekers may sit together in a circle within a tipi, letting
the long night lead the group into prophetic dreams or visions.
Those who have taken the peyote in ceremony tell that the
visions can be strange and wonderful. But if one seeks the vision
alone, it is good to give several days and nights so that there is
time for unfolding.

When one is seeking a vision, the person must be ready to fast
and pray. Fasting is the space that is needed. If any food is taken,
it is in the tradition of ceremonial replenishment or symbolic
eating, rather than to satisfy hunger or pleasure. It is necessary
to dry out, to be spent through the body, to make room for
understanding and purified breath. Looking to the Greatest
Spirit, the Source of life, sharpens the seeing power. Crying out
for help, humbling the heart to remember its littleness and
weakness, offering everything, waiting for power: this is what
helps the vision seeker know desire.

Facing the unknown is part of the quest. It is important to look
into the fears, possibly even hidden terrors, that may be lurking
in the shadows of one's life. Solitude in a wild place makes the
spirit reach out to understand the power of the plants and animals. It teaches the seeker to become a warrior against darkness,

against what might be born in the imagination. It is a call to learn to walk in the wilderness of beauty. Facing the unknown, the fears that linger, keeps the seeker awake and alert. For long years, many Indian tribes have been asleep, overcome by white people, by disease, by alcohol, by ways of living that are not true to hospitable living. Questing for a vision wakes up all the senses.

The vision may be a private one which the seeker needs to live out quietly. But it may also be for the good of all the people and have to become public. Visions often hold warnings and promises, as did Black Elk's.[4] But visions are about how to live. How can healing be learned? What makes the strength for overcoming evil? What are the highest desires? How can the pieces of the puzzle of life be put together? In everyday life we climb and hunt. We search, and sometimes we find. But always we are gathering the strength for the climb to the top of a great mountain. We must always be fasting, praying, waiting for light from the One who gives all visions. Vision questing is spiritual adventure, and it may have many names. Vision questing wants to find what makes the person free, what gives the spirit space to roam.

There is the story of the Spear Woman who was singing to some buffalo behind a fence. While she was singing her song to them, she reminded them that they would not know what she meant when she sang of the old days. She told them it would not be possible for them to know, for they were just calves. "You cannot remember," she said, "because you are like my own grandchildren. Like you, they have been born inside the fence." The vision quest seeks to take the fences down, to make space for the spirit to travel far.

Life Has Many Stories

All the religious traditions have their stories, their legends, their tales of the journeying of the spirit. Stories are central to the Native American way of understanding and passing on spiritual values. The written language has not been part of the Indian history. It is the oral tradition that has kept the stories alive.

Therefore, storytellers have always been important in communicating Indian values. When there is no written language, the memory is sharpened to a remarkable accuracy. Stories are ways of helping memory, of seeking out hidden meanings, of separating the literal from the implied. They come with the voice of the teller, with tone and inflection and a special setting. They ask for close listening, because the memory must hold them for consideration and for sharing with others. Stories come with a history, but they make a place for the imagination to play. They can make us afraid or happy; they can amuse or puzzle us. But the good story has a way of finding a path into the heart as well as the mind. A good story will come out in song or dance. It may come alive in dreams or when the gaze is on a distant mesa. Stories ask for listening, for believing. They say, "Put aside your doubting for awhile." Storytellers will pass on, listeners will come and go, but the story takes on a life of its own. It is like a wisdom river flowing through the generations, offering refreshment to this one, direction to that one, amusement to another, and an ideal to yet another.

Often in the Native American traditions the stories are of "animal people," closing the distance between people and animals, savoring the mystery of what is alike, and yet pointing up the differences. It is the differences that usually amuse us, for people think themselves wiser. Jaime de Angulo's *Indian Tales* is a charming collection.[5] In these stories, it is sometimes hard to tell whether an animal or human is talking. The animals make so much sense, and sometimes the people sound so silly! There is wisdom and laughter in these tales, and many surprises. One tale is about how the person's shadow lives a life of its own. Each night, when one lies down to sleep, the shadow departs, going out to explore the world it is not free to explore during the day. The shadow may become quite intrigued by the large and strange world, and be reluctant to return home at daybreak. So it is necessary for the person, early in the morning, to hum the shadow home. Each person has a song that only its shadow will recognize, and the shadow must obey the hum. If one is too busy, or too thoughtless, to hum the shadow home, the whole day will be difficult. Until the shadow comes home, the person is not whole, is not all together. It is like the person who got up on the wrong side of the bed—part of him is still missing. Humming the shadow home is necessary for harmony, for inner unity. Not too many people seem to know their morning hum when you ask them about it.

Many of the stories are spiritual reading, and are meant to be that. The story is valuable, but it always points to more than is told. Such books as Morton Kelsey's *Tales to Tell* (Seneca Legends)[6] and the Iroquoian epic, *The Secret of No Face*,[7] might help take a few fences down that are keeping your spirit from adventure and wisdom.

In quite a few tribes, certain rules for telling and listening to stories are observed. The storyteller begins when the children are quiet (though the grownups can usually be found on the outer circle). The children must learn to stay awake, to keep very still, and not spoil the story for anyone. Should a child drop off to sleep, the story ends. Then everyone is deprived of the story for that evening. There is the quiet, but strong, language of peer pressure to keep all the children awake. The storytellers are not boring, and a good evening can be ruined by the lack of discipline or selfishness of only one. Is it expecting too much for children to stay awake? The Indians feel it is not. Children have the choice to listen or not to be part of the circle. But if they join the circle, they also enter into an obligation to all the listeners. The storyteller can lose his position if the stories become dull or colorless. Too many children falling asleep or not joining the circle can mean a change of tellers. But this seldom happens, because storytelling is an art, a gift for the others.

Conclusion

These are some of the ways that the heart can be moistened, that the blood of healthy and spiritual living can flow. It is not only the Elder Brother who must struggle to keep coming back to life. Each person meets death in many ways, and it takes courage and a new, moist heart to keep journeying on. It takes a moist heart to walk with our brothers and sisters, a moist heart to be at peace with ourselves, a moist heart to serve the people well. The created world, those who have gone before us, silence, seeking, and stories can help massage the heart, can keep it from drying up and shriveling away.

The stories are friend to us. The silence is friend. The land is friend to us. The dead are friend. The quest is friend to us. It is simple to be a friend, but it is not easy. It must be learned.[8] Take care, Friend, and may your heart stay moist.

NOTES

1. Eastman (Ohiyesa), *The Soul of the Indian*, p. 45.

2. Cited in Paul Jacobs and Saul Landau, *To Serve the Devil*, vol 1, "Natives and Slaves," (Vintage, 1971), p. xxvii.

3. Archie Binns, *Northwest Gateway* (Binford: 1949), pp. 100ff.

4. See John G. Neihardt, *Black Elk Speaks* (University of Nebraska Press, n.d.).

5. See Jaime de Angulo, *Indian Tales* (Ballantine Books, 1953).

6. See Morton T. Kelsey, *Tales to Tell* (Dove Publications, 1978).

7. See Chief Everett Parker & Oledoska, *The Secret of No Face* (Native American Publishers, 1972).

8. To assist in the learning and befriending of this rich spiritual tradition, in addition to the works cited, I can recommend the following studies: William Willoya and Vinson Brown, *Warriors of the Rainbow* (Native American Publishers, 1962); N. Scott Momaday, *The Gourd Dancer* (Harper & Row, 1934); Virginia Armstrong, ed., *I Have Spoken* (Swallow Press, 1971); T.C. McLuhan, *Touch the Earth* (E.P. Dutton & Co., 1971); A. Grove Day, *The Sky Clears* (University of Nebraska Press, 1951); Ruth M. Underhill, *Papago Indian Religion* (Ams Pres, 1946). The works by Momaday and Day treat Native American poetry.

12

Gifts and Insights from the Hasidim

Monika K. Hellwig

At the turn of the century the philosopher Martin Buber began to open up for the Western world the treasury of folk tales of the eastern European peasant tradition of spirituality known as Hasidism. Gradually the power of the stories attracted wider and wider attention, not wholly for their spiritual import but largely for their literary merit as folk tales. Buber himself relates[1] how in his case what began as academic research aimed at recording and interpreting from the point of view of an outsider, penetrated his consciousness so deeply and so thoroughly that it became a profound personal conversion not only of his thinking but of his being. He further testifies that he pursued the matter so far in his writings and publications because he came to have an overwhelming sense of mission to do so.[2] Indeed his studies not only of the legends but of the whole way of life of the Hasidim, have stimulated many further studies and translations, opening up a wealth of resources even for those who do not read either Hebrew or Yiddish.[3] As this has happened, the pervasive influence of this traditional piety of poor and excluded and often persecuted Jews, has become interior and transforming not only for sophisticated Jews long alienated from their own traditions of piety, but also for increasing numbers of Christians alienated for various reasons from Christian traditions of piety, folklore, symbolism, and ritual. An ever increasing number of readers is rediscovering or first discovering with a certain sense of homesickness, the healing power of this tradition and its whole way of life.

The term "hasidim," the pious, had been used to describe other groups earlier in Jewish history, but the tradition to which the burgeoning present literature refers arose in the eighteenth century in eastern Europe, was strong still in the nineteenth and is experiencing something of a revival in the United States and elsewhere at this time. Though one cannot actually point to one moment in time at which the tradition of the Hasidim began, they themselves customarily point to the person and teachings of the "Besht" as the source of their way of life and piety. The title, "BeShT," an abbreviation of Baal Shem Tov, or master of the good name, refers to Rabbi Israel, son of Rabbi Eliezer, of a small town in Wallachia. Of his life, c.1700–1760, little is known. Extant accounts are highly stylized, not altogether unlike the canonical gospels of Jesus the Christ. In these accounts[4] his future birth is announced to his pious father in a vision by the prophet Elijah, when both parents are already far advanced in years.[5] His mission to the community was preceded by years of prayer and seclusion in the forest,[6] and by a hidden life to the age of thirty-six.[7] His public life is characterized by great simplicity, supernatural wisdom, miracles, prophetic vision into hidden thoughts and future events, passionate prophetic denunciations of hypocrisy, pomposity, self-righteousness, and elitism on the part of the learned. Most important of all, however, are the testimonies of a constant, deeply transforming, often ecstatic and usually intensely joyful, mystical union with God, lived in conditions of great poverty and deprivation under constant danger of active and vicious persecution.[8]

The community that clustered around him and continued after his death, was marked by a great warmth, by enthusiastic and joyful styles of worship, and by the commitment to share the most sublime mystical prayer with the most ordinary people. Indeed, there are charming stories of the efforts of *zaddikim*, that is, holy leaders or spiritual fathers, to share their light and their contemplation with people who could not understand their words. Thus the story is told of one such spiritual leader, "the Ladier," that he noticed as he spoke to his followers that a certain old man was listening intently but understanding not at all, so he took him aside and sang him a song without words until his heart was filled with an overwhelming desire to be united with God. Further, the story ends with the observation that after that the Ladier always included that song without words in his discourses, evidently in his concern not to exclude those who had difficulty following the meaning of the words.[9]

The mysticism of the Hasidim was deeply and firmly rooted in the classic Jewish traditions of mysticism, and was in fact consciously and deliberately cultivated according to the principles of the traditional teachings, especially the tradition of the Kabbalah. What was new, however, was the attempt to open this tradition to popular participation.[10] This was done through the mediation of the person of the *zaddik,* by encouraging discipleship of living saints whose task it was to draw their disciples into their own devotion, their understanding, their prayer, their enthusiasm. Gershom Scholem, a very careful scholar, does not hesitate to refer to Hasidism as a revivalist movement and to point a cautioning finger towards the dangers of personality cult in such a movement.[11] In fact, the leadership of a *rebbe* or *zaddik* is constitutive of each hasidic community.

The objective of hasidic spirituality is to become aware of God and united to God everywhere and in all things with sustained, passionate and joyful self-abandonment. For the Hasidim, the presence of God everywhere and in all things was understood literally. Therefore intimate union with God was to be sought not only in seclusion but in the everyday life of the community. For the Hasidim as elsewhere in Judaism, the quest for mystical union with God was not understood to demand a renunciation of family life or of the marital relationship, nor yet of craft, trade, or business ventures. It is not a matter of redeeming souls (consciousness, or reflexive self-awareness) out of the world of human affairs and human intercourse and social structures, but rather a matter of redeeming that world, of uniting to God not individuals in their isolation, but the community in all the complexity of its activities, structures and relationships. Underlying this is the traditional kabbalistic understanding that the *shekhina,* that is the divine indwelling, radiance, or glory in creation is in exile until the hour of redemption. Therefore the task and privilege of the mystic is to seek out the *shekhina* in its exile, and to offer it companionship.[12] For the Hasidim this seems to have become a community task, and must surely be seen as a way of hastening the redemption.

Martin Buber discerns as the central thrust of Hasidism "the powerful tendency, preserved in personal as well as in communal existence, to overcome the fundamental separation between the sacred and the profane."[13] This is surely a basic Jewish thrust, and equally a basic Christian thrust, but it would seem that in both traditions we have been facing severe problems based on the modern trend towards secularization. The notion of a realm of the sacred and an outer region of the profane is more or less universal in thought and experience. Characteristic of monotheism is the growing conviction that the division is based on our inadequate perception; that the whole world is the place of God; that all aspects of life are to be hallowed and brought into the sphere of the sacred; that the division of sacred and profane is best seen as provisional and strategic, providing a focus, marking off that which perceptibly has already been hallowed and therefore perceptibly mediates our union with God. However, a contrary trend has also been working in our experience. To the extent that we are and have been victims of magical misconceptions of the realm of the sacred, every advance in power, knowledge, and control by human persons with the help of science and technology, seems to demand not an extension of the realm of the sacred but a reduction of it in favor of expanding autonomy of the profane. Hence the thrust of secularization in which religion or faith, prayer, and fidelity, must exercise less and less influence on social structures, values, and the whole way of life. There is here an overcoming of the separation by progressive elimination of the sacred rather than by progressive elimination of the profane. Perhaps the key to the sense of homesickness with which both Jews and Christians are discovering the hasidic tradition, is precisely that it offers a viable solution to the contemporary problem of the vanishing sphere of communion with God in the context of modern technological and social sophistication—and this in spite of its peasant origins, or possibly even because of them.

Abraham Joshua Heschel wrote of the east European Jews including the Hasidim, "They did not make the mistake of thinking that the good is attained unwittingly and that hours have merely to be lived in order to arrive at the goals of living."[14] Even among Jews the Hasidim stand out as those who order all things to promote conscious union with God. Heschel sees their particular contribution as this, that they "brought heaven down to earth" by banishing melancholy and rediscovering joy.[15] As asceticism of arbitrary renunciations and self-deprivations was seen as contrary to their objective of union with God always, everywhere, and in all things. Far-reaching renunciations are certainly part of this way of life, but they are never arbitrary; they follow from the ordering of all aspects of life to mediate the merciful power, presence, and exigence of God. In such a context the capacity of wonder is preserved and therefore miracles, the wonderful works of God, are not impossible.

According to Buber,[16] the characteristics or "virtues" cultivated in hasidic communities in order to overcome the separation of the sacred and the profane are four. The first of these is *hitlahavut,* the fire of ecstasy. It is this that all observers of the hasidic communities seem to notice first. There is a sense of having tasted the goodness of God, of having anticipated in some way the joy of heaven. There is even the assertion that, no matter how virtuous they may be, those who have not learned to yield themselves to the fire of ecstasy in their lives are not really capable of the true joy of paradise (heaven) when they pass beyond death.[17] To a Christian, the testimony of the Hasidim on this may strike the familiar notes sounded by the apostolic community of the early days of Christianity when the sharing of the community's experience of the resurrection of Jesus was recognized and proclaimed as the ecstatic foretaste of the coming reign of God. For Christians today it is not so much the quality of the ecstasy of the Hasidim that is noteworthy, but rather its extraordinary diffusion through whole communities. The Hasidim diligently fostered the experience and were confident that they could draw ordinary people into it—not only the rare and exceptionally gifted person. In our present Christian experience one might draw a comparison in this respect with the best of the charismatic groups. What the Hasidim had, however, and turned to such evident advantage, was the cultural condition of an isolated and oppressed people clinging desperately to a rich cultural as well as religious heritage in which the identity, dignity, and hope of the people is concretely expressed. What the Hasidim did with that heritage was to keep it open as the channel of their constant communion with the living God.

Balancing *hitlahavut,* the fire of ecstasy, is a second cultivated characteristic or virtue, *avoda,* work or service.[18] This includes worship and teaching and observance. It is constant human effort to let creatures "ascend" to God, to live a life that is properly in focus. It is a communal as well as an individual effort and it manifests itself concretely in ways that support and guide others. Such service is realized in sublime but also in everyday and simple matters and activities. It is realized by great saints and sages but also by quite ordinary people, as is underscored in the story of the Baal Shem Tov's approving response to the retarded boy who insisted on blowing his whistle in the house of prayer on Yom Kippur.[19] Community, love, and service of the neighbor and even prayer for one's enemies are acknowledged as elements of *avoda.*[20]

The coupling of *avoda* with *hitlahavut* as seen by the Hasidim speaks urgently to the Christian dilemma of increasing tension and even partisan rivalries between the upholders of the mystical and the political dimensions of the Christian faith. There is complementarity rather than intrinsic opposition between these two ways to God, these two ways of salvation. Perhaps it is in the nonelitist understanding of mysticism that the hasidic tradition seems to find its way so easily to a dynamic balance between the two elements. It is after all a way of salvation and a way to mystical union with God that is not for monks but for artisans and laborers, people with family responsibilities under political and social conditions of maximal stress and anxiety. It is for such as these that the way of the hasidim is open.

Yet this nonelitist character makes it none the less demanding. This is quite evident in the third characteristic cultivated and fostered, that is *kavana*, inner devotion, intention, or singlemindedness that sees only one goal in life rather than many goals that divide. By such inner devotion or singlemindedness not only people but things (material objects as well as social structures and human activities) are as it were liberated and brought back to their true goal in God.[21] This seems to be an inner dimension of the overcoming of the separation of sacred and profane. Both Buber and Scholem seem to have difficulty in describing *kavana* in a way that would be meaningful to those outside the tradition. It is really only in the continuities and repetitions within the various collections of the tales of the Hasidim that the meaning emerges. Eli Wiesel, more boldly, ventures to define the term as "spiritual concentration on prayer or the religious act to prepare for *devekut*—compliance with the Divine Will."[22]

The final characteristic of the four that Buber selects as central is that of *shiflut*, humility, which means among other things that one must be content to be uniquely oneself and not ape the ways that are appointed for others.[23] It means that one knows oneself as part of a community, in complementarity with others, part of a whole so very much greater than oneself. This humility has nothing to do with thinking oneself worthless. Humility is only possible when one does not compare oneself with others, when one does not reflect on the comparative or "market" value of one's thoughts and actions. This is possible, of course, not as the outcome of efforts directly bent upon acquiring such humility, but only as the outcome of an all-absorbing living in and with the others. This understanding reconciles the heights of mystical union with God with the fullness of a multidimensional commitment to community with others in their struggles, their needs and their own growth in union with God.

Intention and humility thus understood are also, of course, complementary to each other, as ecstasy and service are. Singlemindedness in turning to God, "spiritual concentration," is bound to be liberating from unproductive habits of mirror-gazing, while freedom from the latter in turn certainly means freedom for the genuine singleness of intention. The role that community plays in that liberating process gives the spirituality of the Hasidim a character of immersion in the world rather than withdrawal from it. Louis Newman, following S. Dubnow, sees strong parallels between the hasidic and the Franciscan spiritualities, especially with reference to Moshe Leib of Sassov,[24] but it may be said that in terms of this mysticism of world-immersion and in terms of the complementarity of ecstasy and service, of intention and humility, there are very strong parallels with the spirituality taught by Ignatius of Loyola.

The account here offered has been abstract rather than preserving the concrete story form that is the proper medium of most hasidic instruction and tradition. Moreover, this account has ignored problems and contradictions due to certain gnostic elements in the older traditions taken over by the Hasidim. It has also by-passed the tendency to magic which all knowledge-able authors discern in the history and structure of Hasidism. Newman sees this, sympathetically, as a parallel with Christian experiences.[25] The foregoing account has concentrated on aspects of Hasidism that seem to hold some gifts and insights for Christians in the context of our contemporary questions and problems concerning the shaping of our own tradition for the future in a progressively more pluralistic, more secularized and more critically conscious society.

The first and particularly valuable gift that seems to come to Catholics from an encounter with the Hasidim is a resounding confirmation of the sacramental principle. By sacramental principle is here meant not only the understanding that the encounter with God is mediated through concrete things, events and persons in cosmos and history, but also the conviction that the community of faith by its worship and its ways of life and organization constructs the world so as to provide such mediation of the encounter with God. In other words, it is the task of the community so to interpret space and time and relationships in the world as to make God palpably present to the members of that community. Within Christianity, it has been especially the Catholic tradition that has been committed to this understanding. Hence the double calendar of mysteries of redemption in Jesus the Christ and of festivals of saints. Hence also the elaboration of ritual and, at some times, of observances. Hence the complex organizational structure, the iconography, the lore of saints' lives, the music and hymnody, the multiplicity of colorful devotions, of pilgrimages, shrines, processions, and so forth.

The Catholic community in our times, however, appears to be in danger of losing its nerve and thinking it safer to ape Protestant ways than to explore and enjoy its own particular charisms. There seem to be several reasons. First of all there is a pervasive Hegelian assumption that religion moves to maturity by dropping the particular, the concrete, the poetic, the mysterious and becoming more philosophical and abstract, or more universal, in its formulations and more exclusively ethical in its preoccupations. The sacramental principle asserts exactly the opposite; that there can be no reduction from the concrete, the particular, the poetically mysterious and picturesque that is not at the same time a tragic loss of essential elements, because there is always much that eludes our understanding. Perhaps the enthusiasm for the encounter by Christians with wisdom, folklore, and piety of the Hasidim is due at least in part to the fact that we see the importance of the sacramental principle reasserting itself with such evident vigor and justification in another tradition where our own anxieties do not impede our vision as they do in matters closer to home.

Another reason for Catholic anxiety over the many manifestations of the sacramental principle in the Catholic tradition appears to be the realization that sacrament and magic are at all times very apt to be confused. Indeed the line between authentic religion and magic has been very tenuous in all traditions of the human race, but it is certainly more acutely troublesome in a community marked by fervor, antielitist attitudes, and highly concrete, imaginative modes of expression. Perusal of the tales of the Hasidim shows that magical attitudes and expectations have seldom been completely absent from hasidic communities. It also shows, however, that the great saints of the tradition, though looking far beyond magical interpretations, were for the most part not greatly troubled by the instrusions of magic in the popular understanding. Magic is, after all, based on the understanding that wonderful things may happen because the creation is far more mysterious and wonderful than our everyday vision of it reveals. When we, as Christians, look at the testimony of the Hasidim, we are likely to discover that our own extreme anxiety to avoid all that might carry the faintest suspicion of magic, is based less on concern to practice authentic religious faith than on certain strong cultural biases of our society which tends to exclude the transcendent and the supernatural.

A second gift and insight that comes to us as Christians from the acquaintance with the piety of the Hasidim is the reassertion of a joyful and enthusiastic spirituality, immersed in the world of God's creating and in the community of human persons and families. Peasant traditions of Catholicism have been marked with the spirit and talent for celebration. They have let imagination run riot in iconography, hymnody, festivals, pilgrimages and shrines, processions, and devotions. To worship was to enjoy. To go to church was to make holiday. The self-conscious cosmopolitan and homogenized Catholicism of our postcritical, pluralistic societies is in danger not only of forgetting how to celebrate but also of forgetting that it is important to do so. Out of the encounter with the spirituality of the Hasidim comes the unmistakable testimony of the authenticity and health of this

kind of piety. It is healthy, among other reasons, because it is
inclusive, nonelitist, because it draws in people of all stages of
awareness and maturity, of all levels of sophistication or lack of
it, of all degrees of family, social, and business responsibilities, of
all stages of personal faith or lack of it. It is a style of spirituality
for natural, inclusive communities. The encounter with the
Hasidim points us back to the wealth that we have in our own
tradition and frequently fail to recognize for what it is.

A third gift is the demonstration that mystical union with God
is not reserved by divine ordinance to rare souls under conditions of strict seclusion of life from ordinary mortals, but is compatible with an active life in a needy community making many
and urgent demands in justice and charity. The Hasidim assure
us that one need not be placed in a privileged and protected
position in society to be called to a life of exalted contemplation,
but that this might more properly be considered the vocation of
the human person as such, and indeed the vocation of the
human community.

A final gift, not to be despised, is surely the convincing message that the truths of faith, true spiritual teaching, true wisdom
about the divine, are better and more fully conveyed in the
persons of living witnesses and in the stories, images, and symbols of the tradition than in the language of philosophical
abstraction and universal formulations. The ordinary channels
for their teaching were short, concrete stories, sometimes needing considerable reflection before they could be understood.
The teaching of Jesus was not different from this. Again, the
attraction to modern secularized Christians of the literature of
the Hasidim is certainly partly due to this. Alienated as we tend
to be from our own roots in cosmos and history, many of us still
recognize the ring of what is authentic. The Hasidim seem to
testify that God can speak to us more clearly in the concrete
givenness of particular situations and events, before they are
buried under human interpretations and generalizations that
are apt to be self-serving, short sighted, and culturally biased. It
is small wonder that the Hasidim should exercise much magnetic

attraction for Christians of our times, for they offer gifts and insights that seem to have the ring of the authentically human and of the authentically Christian.

NOTES

1. Martin Buber, *Hasidism and Modern Man* (Harper & Row, 1966), pp. 47–69.

2. Ibid. His publications in the field are many. Gershom Scholem, *Major Trends in Jewish Mysticism* (Schocken, 1961), p. 443, cites ten different works of Buber on Hasidism, and this list is not complete.

3. Many English language titles are included in the six page bibliography by Dan Ben-Amos and Jerome R. Mintz, *In Praise of the Baal Shem Tov* (Indiana University Press, 1970), pp. 273–279. A critical assessment of the available English language literature is given by Fritz Rothschild and Seymour Siegel in *The Study of Judaism: Bibliographical Essays*, ed. Jacob Neusner (Ktav, 1972), pp. 128–132. A good introduction to the tradition might include: A. J. Heschel, *The Earth Is the Lord's* (Harper and Row, 1966); Martin Buber, *Ten Rungs* (Schocken, 1947); Martin Buber, *Hasidism and Modern Man* (Harper & Row, 1966).

4. See, e.g., Ben-Amos and Mintz, *Baal Shem Tov*, and Louis Newman, *The Hasidic Anthology* (Block, 1944).

5. Ben-Amos and Mintz, *Baal Shem Tov*, p. 11.

6. Ibid., p. 11 ff.

7. Ibid., p. 13 ff.

8. Ibid., passim.

9. Newman, *Anthology*, p. 283.

10. Gershom Scholem, *Jewish Mysticism*, chapter 9, especially pp. 338 ff. Cf. also Newman, *Anthology*, pp. lxxviii ff., and Heschel, *Earth is the Lord's*, passim.

11. Scholem, *Jewish Mysticism*. See, e.g., p. 343ff.

12. Cf. Buber, *Hasidism*, Book III, especially section on "ecstasy."

13. Ibid., p. 28.

14. Heschel, *Earth is the Lord's*, p. 18.

15. Ibid., p. 75.

16. Buber, *Hasidism*, Book III, passim. Scholem, while in general agreement with Buber's observations, lists the cultivated characteristics rather differently (*Jewish Mysticism*, ch. 9). The outsider to the tradition, reading the two accounts, is left with the impression that Buber is considerably more in sympathy with the way of the Hasidim.

17. Buber, *Hasidism*, p. 74. Cf. also the reiteration of this idea in the tales, e.g., *In Praise of the Baal Shem Tov* (where it is diffuse) and *The Hasidic Anthology*, especially section 1, pp. 1-6.

18. Buber, *Hasidism*, p. 84 ff. But cf. Scholem on revolutionary and conservative elements of Hasidism (*Jewish Mysticism*, pp. 337-344).

19. Buber, *Hasidism*, pp. 93-94.

20. Ibid., pp. 243-256.

21. Ibid., pp. 98-108.

22. Elie Wiesel, *Souls on Fire* (Random House, 1972), p. 263.

23. Buber, *Hasidism*, pp. 110-122.

24. Newman, *Anthology*, p. lxxiii.

25. See, e.g., the section on Jesus and the Besht, ibid., pp. lxx-lxxiv.

13

Fullness in Emptiness: The Development of a Russian Spiritual Vision

James Kenney

> In a recent interview with a young Soviet dissident
> we read that he sounds more like a traditional Russian
> fatalist, willing to endure suffering and deprivation
> rather than submit to what he views as tyranny....
> "Being sent to a camp will be my reward. A big re-
> ward. It comforts me to know that millions of our peo-
> ple—and the best people in Russia—have gone to
> camps. So I will be sharing the fate of our best peo-
> ple. That is a great reward."

It is often the case that a genuine insight into the particular
religious intuition which undergirds a given culture emerges as
the single most illuminating factor in the effort to come to some
real understanding of that culture. Few would deny that the
fascination which Russian culture has held for the West derives
in some measure from the deep, brooding religiosity of the Russian spirit. The compelling and complex characters who dwell in
the pages of the tortured novels of the golden age of Russian
literature, the humble yet sternly righteous figures evoked by
the recital of the names of the monks who gave medieval Russian
monasticism its particular flavor, the revolutionary, the nihilist,
the anarchist—all these breathe deeply of the Russian religious
atmosphere.

Clearly, even the atheist who militantly denounces the hypocrisy and emptiness of religion, its values and institutions, cannot efface the imprint on his or her own personality and intellection of the complex symbolic network that constitutes his or her religious cultural heritage. Precisely because it must employ symbols to aid in the approach to ineffable ultimate reality, religion exerts an influence—often so subtle as to be nearly imperceptible—over literature, music, art, philosophy, and human experience itself, an influence which we ought not to ignore. This study will attempt to probe a critical aspect of the Russian religious phenomenon as it has manifested itself throughout the thousand-year history of Russian Christianity and in the myriad artistic expressions of the Russian soul.

The characteristic identification of the Russian experience with seemingly endless suffering and of Russian literature with the anguished cry of the soul, while clearly a deceptive over-simplification, nonetheless serves to point up the central importance of suffering to the Russian mystique. We are reminded of the perplexing question—lying at the heart of the problem before us—posed by Fyodor Dostoevsky in his *Notes From the Underground:*

> And why are you so firmly, so triumphantly, convinced that only the normal and the positive—in other words, only what is conducive to welfare—is for the advantage of man? Is not reason in error as regards advantage? Does not man, perhaps, love something besides well-being? Perhaps he is just as fond of suffering? Perhaps suffering is just as great a benefit to him as well-being? Man is sometimes extraordinarily, passionately in love with suffering, and that is a fact.[1]

I. THE FORMATIVE PERIOD: THE HOLY MARTYRS BORIS AND GLEB

We will begin our exploration of suffering and Russian religion with a look at the seminal epoch of Slavic Orthodoxy, the period of the Christianization of the principality of Kiev, in the tenth and eleventh centuries. The conversion of the people known as the Kievan Rus', in or around 988, had vital significance for the development of Russian culture, primarily because it meant the dramatic impact of Byzantium on the embryonic nucleus of the great Russian empire-to-be. As Nicholas Riasanovsky has pointed out:

> It must be kept in mind that Christianity came to Russia from Byzantium, not from Rome. . . . It meant that Russia remained outside the Roman Catholic Church, and this in turn not only deprived Russia of what that church itself had to offer, but also contributed in a major way to the relative isolation of Russia from the rest of Europe and its Latin civilization . . . and it brought religion, in the form of a readily understandable Slavic rite, close to the people and gave a powerful impetus to the development of a national culture.[2]

Vladimir, the Great Prince of Kiev, whose decision it was to cast Russia's spiritual and cultural lot in with the Greeks, was canonized by the young church and is still celebrated as "the baptizer of the Russias."

The Germination of the Russian Ideal of Kenotic Sainthood

While one can easily understand that the fledgling spiritual community would rush to the official sanctification of its patron, Vladimir was not the first canonized saint of the Russian church. Rather, two of his sons, the young princes Boris and Gleb—murdered by their elder brother in his seizure of the throne made vacant by the death of Vladimir—were the first to be venerated as Russia's own spiritual heroes. In his penetrating study of the development of Russian Christianity, Georgi Fedotov poses a vital question with regard to the canonization of the two princes. Noting that the Greek metropolitan presiding at the time over the new Russian flock, "nourished some doubt of the holiness of the new thaumaturges,"[3] who certainly do not seem to have conformed to the prevailing Greek notions of sanctity, Fedotov asks: "In what did the Russian church and all the nation perceive the holiness of the princes and the meaning of their Christian achievement?"[4] The question has tremendously important implications for any attempt to unravel the mysterious tangle of Russian spirituality.

Of the three extant hagiographic works dealing with the passion and death of Boris and Gleb, two stand out as most influential: the *Lection (Chteniye)* attributed to the monk Nestor, and the anonymously-penned *Legend (Skazaniye)*. The two works differ from normative "lives of the saints," as that genre was developed in Greek hagiography, in that they contain (in the case of Nestor's account) only scanty details of the lives of the princes before the hour of their deaths, or (as is the case with the *Legend*) no mention whatsoever of any such details. Clearly, the piety (or, for that matter, impiety) of the princes before their arrival at that fateful moment is of importance neither to Nestor nor to the author of the *Legend*. Only the moment of voluntary acceptance of suffering and death has any ultimate bearing on the sanctity of the brothers. Indeed, as regards the younger brother, Gleb, it can be pointed out that only in the final moments of his ordeal do his terror and pleading give way to a quiescent and forgiving acceptance of his fate: "If you wish to satiate yourselves with my blood, I am in your hands and in those of my brother, your prince."[5]

A distinction can nevertheless be drawn between the two accounts of the "martyrdom," which underscores the importance of the far greater popularity enjoyed by the *Legend* among the peasants who comprised the rapidly-formed cult to the memory of Boris and Gleb. Nestor's version (the *Lection*) stresses the duty of the younger brothers to defer in all things to the will of the elder: "Do you see brethren, how great is the obedience which thy saints had to their senior brother . . . ? If they had resisted him they would hardly have been granted such miraculous gifts."[6] Needless to say, Nestor's hymn of praise to sibling fealty and clan loyalty reflects a moral-political code no longer truly relevant to Russian spirituality. The *Legend,* on the other hand, lays its emphasis squarely upon the fact of voluntarily-accepted suffering. As we read the author's long and highly dramatic account of the death of Boris, who dismisses his retinue and waits in anguish for the murderers to fall upon him, we dwell with the young prince on his impending martyrdom, refracted for him by the passion of Christ, transfigured and made fully meaningful by the paradigmatic suffering of the incarnate Logos: "Lord Jesus Christ, who appeared in this form on earth, who allowed himself to be nailed on a cross and who accepted suffering for the sake of our sins! Make me also able to accept suffering."[7]

For Boris, the paramount fact of human existence emerges in the agonizing confrontation with certain death: suffering purifies, ennobles and saves the one who accepts it willingly and in full consciousness of the model afforded by the suffering, death, and resurrection of Jesus Christ. Yet even so, Boris' final minutes hardly seem tranquil or in any way mystically-beatified. His terror is palpable. He laments his untimely exit from the "charm of this deceitful life,"[8] and clearly wishes that the cup would pass. Yet when death finally comes, Boris blesses his killers and the brother Sviatopolk, who sent them. Fedotov suggests that the essential feature of the religious spirit manifested by the popular demand for the canonization of Boris and Gleb is its celebration of suffering, acceptance, and forgiveness—in emulation of the life and death of Jesus. The question posed above— "in what did the nation perceive the holiness of the princes?"— yields a simple and yet powerful answer: The sainthood of the two brothers hinges upon their voluntary offering of self, a Christ-like self-emptying, which Fedotov terms, "kenosis" (from the Greek *kenós,* "empty"). Timothy Ware sounds the same theme in the following characterization of Russian Orthodoxy's remembrance of its first saints:

> If any blood were to be shed, Boris and Gleb preferred that it should be their own. Although they were not martyrs for the faith, but victims in a political quarrel, they were canonized,

being given the special title of "Passion Bearers": it was felt
that by their innocent and voluntary suffering they had
shared in the Passion of Christ. Russians have always laid great
emphasis on the place of suffering in the Christian life.[9]

In the Orthodox view, we are called by the example of Boris
and Gleb to passive acquiescence in the face of suffering, to the
practice of the virtue of humility and to *hope* in the redemptive
and resurrective power of the act of suffering as it is transfigured by God's love for humankind. This theme, enunciated
countless times in Russian hagiographic literature, finds what
may be its most beautiful expression in the idealized accounts of
the eternal martyrdom of the Russian peasant.

After exploring and documenting his contention that the
models of Boris and Gleb are preeminent in Russian Orthodox
liturgy and cultic practice, Fedotov observes that the memory of
the princes was regularly invoked in the subsequent canonization of numerous victims of political assassination. Here we
come face to face with one of the most difficult and perplexing
features of Russian kenoticism, for the proliferation of "passion-bearers" would seem to suggest a serious adulteration of the
religious ideal:

> Certainly one is entitled to see in this development the degen-
> eration of the idea of kenotic holiness.... But we are here in
> the very core of the Russian religious world. Many a Russian
> saint was canonized for the only obvious reason: his violent
> death.... Children are particularly numerous in this group,
> their natural innocence adding to the purification by blood.
> The underlying idea, evidently, is that of the redeeming and
> purifying merit of suffering and death. In a correct, orthodox
> form, willing, self-offering nonresistance is needed to bring
> the victim into conformity with the suffering kenotic Christ.
> In many cases, however, the condition is simply hypo-
> thetical.[10]

Nevertheless, we can discern in "the order of 'sufferers,' the
most paradoxical order of the Russian saints,"[11] the undiluted

essence of the dominant element in the Russian exaltation of self-emptying: the belief in the transforming power of suffering itself. The canonizations of Andrew Bogoliubsky, assassinated Prince of Vladimir, Iuliania of Viazma, the victim of her lover's wrath, and the infant prince Demetrius, last of the ancient dynasty of Riurik and murdered for political expedience, may be understood as expressions of a deeply-rooted faith in the promise implicit in Christ as suffering exemplar. Similarly, the emergence of the cult which posthumously venerated the Tsar Paul—a capricious and tyrannical autocrat killed in a palace revolt in 1801—ought not necessarily be regarded simply as a distortion of the "pure" kenotic ideal. On the contrary, although the operative religious intuition—in the canonization or veneration of political victims—may not be identical with that which brought about the elevation of Boris and Gleb, it is nevertheless directly corollary to the development of the Russian religious focus on suffering as the key to the emulation of Christ, and it constitutes a particularly Russian expression of faith in the miraculous transfiguring power of the redemption.

To be sure, when Boris met his death, the *Legend* recounts, his experience of pain and terror was imbued with significance by the heroic and Christ-like manner of his encounter with it. Obviously, the voluntary acceptance embodied in his hagiographic image is absent in the majority of cases of political murder. Still in all, whatever one might wish to argue with respect to the social consequences of the religious adulation of an assassinated tyrant or mere political pawn, the inclusion of "the sufferers" in the canon of the Russian saints represents an important and genuine movement of faith. It symbolically proclaims that suffering—the very bane of human existence is at the same time the key to transcendence, the philosopher's stone which alone can effect the ultimate transmutation.

In the strictest sense, true kenosis depends upon an act of the will, and is necessarily voluntary in character. It involves the conscious opting for suffering, whether or not escape might have been possible. However, will alone cannot produce the salvific effect inherent in the experience of Boris and Gleb. Will only forms that experience; its substance is the primal purifying element of suffering itself. One cannot simply dismiss the far-reaching religious import of the symbol of the saint whose holiness consists for the believer in his or her violent death alone. The murdered leader emerges in the Russian milieu as the natural analogue to the suffering peasant. (The abiding loyalty of the common people to the Prince and the Tsar—a characteristic feature of life in pre-Revolutionary Russia—clearly bears on the development of this mode of kenotic imagery.) In the idealized life of the *prince struck-down,* the daily agonies of the common person are writ large. Sainthood is brought symbolically within the reach of all, prince and commoner alike, and life's suffering takes on new meaning. The voluntarily-accepted suffering of Boris and the anguish of the unwilling victim of assassination equally reflect the chronic pain of existence—now accepted, now resisted. Moreover (and herein lies the significance of the Christian concept of sainthood), they offer to the believer a variety of models for personal holiness and a source of continued religious inspiration.

Theological Dimensions of the Concept of Kenosis

The word "kenosis" ("emptying") is drawn from Paul's Epistle to the Philippians, the second chapter, in which the Apostle recounts how Christ "emptied himself, humbled himself and became obedient unto death, even death on a cross" (Phil 2: 7–8). Interestingly enough, this typically Pauline theme was very little developed in Western Christianity. The attention directed to this particular passage—by the Fathers and by later Western Christian theologians—resulted largely from the concern with the implications of Christ's "emptying" for Christology. In other words, they sought to determine whether the unincarnated Logos emptied into the Incarnate Christ, or whether it was the human Christ who underwent kenosis in the form of the submergence of the human self in the redemptive agony of the crucifixion. This was the kenosis which concerned the religious thinkers of the Christian West.

In the Orthodox Church of Byzantine Greece, the idea of kenosis as the willful acceptance of suffering—as a means of imitating of following Christ—was also curiously rare. Indeed, the notion of Christ cherished by the Byzantine Church (and Empire) was that of Christ Pantocrator, triumphant Lord of the Universe, Christ as Creator of All, as Godhead. Understandably, the Greeks were less familiar with the image of a helpless, pitiful, or even despairing Christ. But in the Russian church, this identification with Christ Suffering has been a dominant theme of the quest for the spiritual life.

In the phenomenon of the acceptance of suffering as a means of cultivating Christ-like existence, Fedotov sees "the great discovery of the first Christian generation in Russia: the kenotic Christ of the Russian saints."[12] Kenosis, in this view, constitutes the fundamental Russian religious insight or intuition. Clearly, this does not imply any Russian monopoly on the kenotic mode of spirituality. Rather, it simply emphasizes the centrality of that mode in the Russian Orthodox heritage and suggests that an understanding of the kenotic phenomenon must accompany any attempt to penetrate the enigmatic Russian character.

The emergence of the kenotic motif in Russian Orthodoxy represents a variation on a familiar Christian theme: that the suffering and death of Jesus Christ somehow redeems fallen humankind and restores the possibility—and therefore the hope—of meaningful existence. Individual suffering (which proceeds from the existential encounter with human limitation) finds its meaning and ultimate vindication in the tears of the man Jesus and the transcendent mystery of the incarnation, crucifixion, and resurrection of Christ: this is the animating promise of Christianity. Needless to say, this rich symbolic complex gives rise to a symphonic variety of interpretation and accentuation. The kenotic approach to understanding and praxis—the focus on suffering as a channel of divine grace and a means to self-transcendence—flows easily from the symbol of Christ's voluntary self-emptying to the belief that suffering, in and of itself, may be transforming and salvific, precisely because it can be a mode of our own self-emptying and sanctification.

For Russian spirituality, no element of the Christian message is more central than that of the kenosis of Jesus Christ, and perhaps no words from scripture are more powerful than the testimony that, "Jesus wept."

II. THE PARADIGM: THE EXPERIENCE OF THE RUSSIAN PEASANT

If, indeed, suffering and its passive acceptance are pivotal to the Russian Christian spiritual life, to what extent can the passion of the Holy Martyrs Boris and Gleb be said to be the point of origination, the source of this tendency? After entertaining for some time the notion that the two passion-bearers represent the introduction of a new theme to the Russian religious mind, I now feel that the events surrounding their martyrdom and canonization comprise a *node,* a point of concentration or crystallization in the evolution of the Russian Orthodox consciousness.

The dominant theme of the story of Boris and Gleb, as it is recounted in the *Legend,* embodies a primal Russian motif: the fruit of the unrelenting struggle with the elements which occupies the time, energy, and resolve of those who would try to make a home and build a life in the forbidding Russian forest. It is a theme which finds nourishment in the unenviable history of the peasants, those whose experience is woven into the fabric of the Russian soul. Never in the thousand years of Russian Christian history has the peasant known much more than a hint of self-determination or real freedom. Indeed, he or she may insist with all seriousness that no such thing as freedom can possibly exist. Long-enslaved and usually beset by a variety of existential travails, the Russian peasant of the nineteenth century, as portrayed in the works of that golden age of Russian literature, seems nevertheless content. Simple, yet frequently blessed with a telling wit, the *muzhik* displays the roughest of manners and yet is remarkably strong in faith. The peasant farmer may well be an inveterate sinner, and he almost certainly drinks to excess, but he is likely to be securely grounded in the knowledge that all human beings are sinners, that sin is the necessary product of our unnatural separation from God and, finally, that the incarnation, passion, and death of Christ have infused the human experience of suffering with the redeeming power of divine mercy.

The suffering motif which predominates in the *Legend* could not be a purely novel or coincidental development; nor can it be fully explained in terms of the influence of the gospels or of Pauline Christology. The *Legend* is important because it captures a unique moment of the Russian people's response to the stimulus of a religious model totally new to them. The message might well have been that of a different religious tradition, the response might have been a different one; but those whose answer to the Christian call finds expression in the *Legend* and the popular reaction to it tell us a great deal about their milieu, their perception of reality, and their experience of the human condition. Obviously, more is involved than the individual decisions made by Boris and Gleb; for if the account of the martyrdom did not strike some nerve in the common people, if it did not resonate with the developing religious spirit of the Russian peasant, then it simply would not have become the major religious landmark that it has.

Thus, the events surrounding the martyrdom of the princes, their subsequent elevation by the Russian faithful to the status of heavenly patrons of the new church and the further elaboration of kenosis as a mode of Christian life are all particularly Russian spiritual phenomena. In the kenotic flavor of Russian Orthodox devotion, the life experience of the peasant finds its religious reflection.

James Billington, the eminent cultural historian, offers a fascinating insight into the complex symbolic ambience which we are attempting to probe. He writes:

> Even stronger . . . in the forest was the fear of, and fascination with, fire. . . . Russians often mention Christ's statement that, "I have come to send fire on the earth," and the fact that the Holy Spirit first came down to man through "tongues of

fire."... A basic metaphor for explaining the perfect combination of God and man in Christ had long been that of fire infusing itself into iron.... Heat not light, warmth rather than enlightenment, was the way to God.... Small wonder that fire was the dominant symbol of the Last Judgment in Russian iconography... After the fundamentalists had been anathematized in 1667, many of the Old Believers sought self-immolation—often with all their family and friends in an oil-soaked wooden church—as a means of anticipating the purgative fires of the imminent Last Judgment.[13]

This apocalyptical preoccupation with the purifying power of fire, which Billington attributes to modern-day Russians as well as to the Kievans, seems a particularly potent symbol for the Russian focus on suffering. The pain of human experience serves the spiritual person just as fire serves the farmer who burns off his fields to render them more fertile. Fire as symbol evokes, in different contexts, fear, thoughts of destruction, the remembered pain of a long-forgotten burn, or—conversely—feelings of security, warmth, renewal, consecration, etc. As a consequence, it rather aptly embodies or symbolizes the Russian view of suffering. This is not to imply that there is a conscious association of fire with suffering in the Russian mind (although there well might be); rather, it is simply to suggest a very appropriate metaphor, one very Russian in form, which can serve as a powerful poetic image to illustrate the ambivalence of the spirit of the Russian peasant with respect to the fact of human suffering.

III. THE FLOWERING OF THE IDEAL: THE CELEBRATION OF HUMILITY

Evocative expressions of the Russian experience of kenosis have emerged in the formation and the refinement of Russian Christianity. This is so especially in terms of the development of those modes of *emptying* which do not involve physical suffering as such: poverty, humility, obedience, and—perhaps most important, since it underlies and gives meaning to all of the various kenotic virtues embraced by Russian Orthodoxy—*hope*.

The conversion of Kievan Russia in the tenth century meant the wholesale adoption of a highly developed and quite venerable religious tradition by a people who lacked most of the cultural background and context which gave life to that tradition. It was inevitable, from the earliest of the Byzantine transfusions of Greek culture into the relatively undeveloped Russian spiritual and intellectual milieu, that Orthodoxy would begin on Russian soil to take on a Russian character. We can perhaps capture something of the flavor of the russification of Orthodoxy by considering a few of the religious figures who came to the fore in the centuries of transformation and who continue to occupy special places in the Russian religious consciousness. We will, in the course of the discussion, pay considerable attention to the lives of a handful of the most important of the later Russian saints. We shall do so not out of any sense that their spiritual careers *shaped* the Russian religious intuition, giving it a character which it might not otherwise have possessed, but rather because—as canonized saints and legendary religious heroes— they embody the gradual refinement of a particular spiritual ideal. The hagiographic genre, in every religious culture, emerges as a sort of archival repository of religious idealism. The saints of the Christian traditions, the legendary rabbis, teachers, judges, caliphs, and kings of Judaism and Islam, the rishis and bodhisattvas of the East: all stand as culturally-determined symbols of persistent human faith in the tremendous possibilities inherent in existence. Russian Christianity speaks to itself and to us through its prayers, its music and iconography, its ritual life and its heroes. Those who are remembered and what is remembered about them can tell us a great deal.

The Monk Theodosius

Theodosius of the Kievo-Pecherskaya Monastery, one of the co-architects (along with St. Antony) of the Russian monastic movement, stands alongside Boris and Gleb as a classic embodiment of the kenotic follower of Christ. A very concerned social critic, he evolved a radical response to the challenge which is implicit in the encounter of a religion with social implications as broad as those of the gospels with the fact of hunger and poverty as widespread forms of human suffering. Theodosius, like Francis of Assisi in the West, embraced poverty and practiced strict self-effacing humility. His clothes were rags, his portion always the smallest. Though he was the highly respected abbot of the greatest of the early Russian monasteries, he worked at humble tasks, and he was often overlooked by those who had come to the monastery hoping to catch a glimpse of the famed abbot—whom they certainly did not expect to find busy at weeding the monks' garden or washing plates in the refectory. Yet this same Theodosius was the sought-after adviser and confidante of princes and nobles, never reluctant to challenge the members of the aristocracy in the matter of their moral responsibility as Christian rulers and their personal participation in the communal life of Orthodoxy.

Theodosius "turned his back on wealth and indeed on asceticism to lead the monastery of the caves into a life of active counsel and charity in the city of Kiev."[14] The kenosis which he displayed consisted quite simply in the cultivation of a profound and transfiguring humility. His biographer repeatedly stresses this single concept, the self-emptying simplicity of the humble follower of the Suffering Christ. The abbot became, after Boris and Gleb, the third canonized saint of the Russian church, and Fedotov compares his spirituality with that of the murdered princes:

> The brothers followed Christ in their sacrificial deaths—the climax of his kenosis—as Theodosius did in his poverty and humiliation. Humility and love, if not poverty, are present also in the suffering of the princes. We have seen their eloquent expression.[15]

Theodosius' discovery of the kenotic potential of poverty and humility is paralleled in Western Christianity by the development of theological understanding of the monastic vows of poverty, chastity, and obedience. Interestingly, the Pauline text which yields the term *kenosis* (Phil 2:7–8) is perhaps the most frequently cited passage in the Western discussions of the role of the vow in the Christ-like life. As can easily be seen, the essence of the vow as a mode of Christian experience is kenotic. The vow of poverty embodies a willful denial of the acquisitive, grasping, clinging self. At the same time, it opens the way for the emergence of genuine humility (as a positive rather than a negative quality). Similarly, the other two vows deny a fundamental mental ego-related aspect of the personality and substitute the kenotic abandonment of the ego-self, "for the sake of Christ."

Sergei of Radonezh, the Peasant Saint

Another important manifestation of the Russian understanding of sanctity—as flowing in to fill up the vessel emptied by the kenotic emulation of Christ—emerges in the life of St. Sergei of Radonezh, founder of the famed Holy Trinity Monastery and one of the most remarkable exponents of Russian Christianity. He is the man most often acclaimed as the national saint of the Russian people. Nicholas Zernov describes Sergei as "the peasant saint . . . the man who continued to the end of his life, in spite of all his spiritual achievements, to pursue the usual work of a Russian peasant."[16] In light of the importance of the role of the peasant in the evolution of the Russian spiritual model, the story of Sergei has considerable significance for the present study. Although the majority of its most influential or powerful figures were individuals with aristocratic backgrounds, the Russian Orthodox Church is primarily rooted in the deep piety of the peasants. In characterizing Sergei as he does, Zernov underscores those attributes which mark the saintly monk as the paradigmatic pious *muzhik:*

St. Sergius knew all the joys and sorrows of the peasant's lot, he was a master of all peasant crafts, he was scorched by the

sun during long and exhausting summer toil, he suffered
from frost during severe Russian winters. . . . His strong, indefatigable body, his skillful hands, his practical mind, his endurance, were those of a typical peasant. There was nothing
extravagant or exotic about this humble, hard-working man.[17]

Zernov here touches indirectly on that quality of the peasant
which we have already noted and which emerges as the most
religiously significant of all his or her earthy characteristics: the
abiding acquaintance with suffering and the consequent humble
acknowledgement of human impotence in the face of nature,
the state, and the divine. Powerless to alter the course of events,
the Russian peasant "realizes that sometimes one can achieve
better results by an outward submission than by an open rebellion. He feels himself to be part of the universe, to partake of the
same stream of life which is shared by all living creatures."[18] St.
Sergei of Radonezh became, in the pages of his inspirational
biography (one of the most widely-read books in pre-Revolutionary Russia), a compelling symbol of the spiritual potential
of the fundamentally kenotic experience and outlook of the
Christian *muzhik*.

In his capacity as abbot of Holy Trinity Monastery, Sergei was
the instrument of a far-reaching spiritual revival which spread
out from the monasteries and whose source of inspiration was
Holy Trinity and Sergei himself. In the latter part of the period
of Byzantine decline (the late thirteenth and early fourteenth
centuries), the emergence of the mystical movement known as
Hesychasm proved to have a strong influence on the development of the Russian religious attitude and on the spiritual renewal preached by Sergei. The Hesychasts insisted that there
exists "a direct personal way to God available to man through the
'inner calm' (*hēsychia*) which came from ascetic discipline of the
flesh and silent prayers of the spirit."[19] The Russian monks, cut
off as they were from classical systematic theology as it was practiced in Latin Christendom, were "ripe for a doctrine emphasizing direct contact with God."[20] The closeness of monks like

Sergei to the wonders of nature combined with the new mystical currents to produce what Billington has termed, "an almost Franciscan manner (of contemplation) on the theme of God's involvement with all creation."[21] The most intriguing result of the interplay of these various forces was in the emergence of the expectation that the *eschaton,* the culmination of the history of salvation, would bring not only a resurrection of the body but a transformation or transfiguration of the entire cosmos.

The growth of the Hesychast movement within the context of Russian spirituality was unquestionably facilitated by the kenotic predisposition displayed by the best-remembered saints of the Orthodox tradition. The path of self-emptying through the willful acceptance of life's chronic suffering and the cultivation of profound humility seems ideally suited for the development of the mystical *hēsychia.* The "inner calm" sought by the mystics consists in the quieting of the self and the diminishment of the demands of the ego so that the life of the spirit can begin to take root. One can discern in the spiritual testament of a Sergei the reiteration of the promise implicit in Paul's affirmation that, "It is now no longer I that live but Christ that lives in me."

The next crystallization of the diverse currents flowing through Russian religion formed about a dispute between two of the most gifted of the disciples of Sergei, Joseph of Volotsk and Nil Sorskii. Zernov refers to the controversy in the following passage, in which he attributes Sergei's unique place in history to the fact that,

> ... he achieved a synthesis of the opposite tendencies of Russian spirituality. The real importance of St. Sergei for the Russian nation can be best seen in the light of the conflict between the "Possessors" and the "Nonpossessors" which, like a storm, descended upon the Russian church one hundred years after his death.[22]

The central issue over which the church was divided in the early years of the sixteenth century was the matter of the legitimacy of church land holdings. (This became, at any rate, the most visible of the many points of controversy which separated the two groups.) It seems apparent that the Nonpossessors, led by Nil Sorskii, constituted another manifestation of the phenomenon of Russian kenoticism.

In essence, the Nonpossessors insisted that ecclesiastical wealth, especially in the form of monastic land-holdings, were a serious violation of the vow of poverty, one of the cornerstones of the monastic edifice. Nil's career reflects the advancement during the fifteenth century of the principles of the development of the "inner spiritual life" and the Hesychast movement. It is not therefore surprising that he demonstrated a very strong opposition, not only to church ownership of property (and, of course, of serfs), but also to church involvement in matters of state, the coercion of heretics by physical force and the substitution of detailed and disciplined external ritual for a rich and vital inner spirituality. The "Testament" left by Nil upon his death in 1508 suggests, moreover, that Nil's personal religious style was of the familiar kenotic type:

> Cast off my body in the desert to be eaten by beasts and birds; for it has sinned much before God and is not worthy of a funeral. My striving always was, as much as was in my power, not to take part in the honor and glory of this world; and just as it was in this life so be it also after my death. I beseech all to pray for my sinful soul, to pardon me and accept my pardon. May God pardon all of us.[23]

In this soberingly grim farewell, Nil offers an insight into his lifelong effort to follow the gospel's injunction to be *in* the world but not *of* it. The impulse is clearly kenotic: the self is the agent of attachment to the pleasures of the world; to empty the self is to eliminate attachment to the world. By the same token, the deep sense of sinfulness is a typical product of kenotic self-effacement. At the heart of the matter, we can detect the fundamental Orthodox intuition that, as long as he or she remains separated from God, the human person cannot live naturally and cannot find complete contentment. The deep kenotic sense of unworthiness, however, must never cross over into despair, for the hope of God's forgiveness is always at hand.

IV. KENOTIC HOPE: THE DIALECTIC OF TRANSFORMATION

In the expectation of final transformation which reverberates through Russian religiosity, we can discover an animating principle which—as the corollary to profound humility and passive suffering—seems ever-present in the Russian articulation of the fundamental nature of the relationship of the human being to God. Once again, the principle at work is unabashed *hope* in the saving power of the incarnation. The bleakness and drudgery which typify the experience of the peasant are recast by the cultivation of humility into the very real hope of complete transformation of all things in Christ. Hope can be described as the corollary to humility precisely because the emptying of self, the kenosis implicit in following Christ, eliminates the aggressive reliance on one's own ego and makes possible the openness and trust which give rise to the transfiguring experience of hope. (And, regardless of the particular religious or philosophical context in which it is found, hope is a revitalizing and transforming experience.) This then is the most spiritually profound manifestation of the life of the Russian church: the remarkable persistence of hope in the face of the continued adversity encountered by the common people.

As has become increasingly apparent, the kenotic approach to Christ is a mystical approach. The very image of *emptying,* so illustrative of the Russian understanding of holiness, is a classic mystical image. It would seem that the saints elevated by the Russian church were individuals with a profound awareness of suffering and a corresponding sense of humility, rooted in personal experience. Their religious genius inheres in that quality which separates them from those others whose suffering is not offset by the prospect of deliverance, and whose search for the hidden significance of the pain of life has been futile: the suicides. Indeed, perhaps only the thinnest of lines divides the two psychological realms; and that line, one can argue, is simply the threshold of religious hope.

There may be more to the notion of hope than might at first be assumed. To speak of transforming hope in any meaningful sense is at best difficult. Obviously, the varieties in personal religious experience complicate the matter enormously. Yet, whatever one's personal religious point of view, it seems scarcely possible to deny that the transforming power of a religious way far outreaches the familiar social influence of a religious institution. (By religious "way," I mean the path, the spirituality, or the profound sense of direction which seems to be opened up to the believer at the deeper levels of religious involvement in any of the major religious traditions.) It is an incontrovertible fact that religious experience exists and that it transforms. Religious genius consists in the intuitive discovery of the religious way which is most appropriate to the life-situation of an individual or a people, the *way* which can most deeply transfigure the life of the believer.

Commitment to a religious way or path, when viewed from a slightly different perspective, seems equivalent to the experience of faith or hope, or both. Only the religious person can know the meaning and the depth of his or her own faith; the internal transformation remains hidden. But the external reshaping of human affairs by individual experiences of religious faith is not so difficult to examine. Similarly, while we may not be able even to imagine a genuine moment of religious hope, we can nevertheless contemplate at our leisure the extraordinary creations which have been wrought at every period of human history by the astonishing daring of true visionaries.

I have introduced the notion of religious experience as a meaningful category in the study of culture development because of the unique intensity of the kenotic approach to Christianity and the powerful imagery which it generates. Just as the vision of Mother Russia evoked by some of her greatest literary masters, painters, and sculptors seems at once both forbidding and enticing, so too, the kenotic mode of spirituality, constantly refracted in the literature and art of the Russians, attracts and repels one at practically the same moment. On the one hand, we cannot fail to notice and admire the Russian saints who display a remarkable fortitude and capacity for loving service. The athletic holiness manifested by Sergei or the tranquil poverty of Nil, both seem to be expressions of the noblest side of human nature. On the other hand, however, the gnawing, negative distrust of the world, a distrust which seems at times too close to despair, is the obverse of the kenotic nobility of the Russian saints.

The question which must therefore be raised at this point is this: given that the central motif of the Russian Orthodox pursuit of holiness is kenosis and that this fascination with emptying is somehow a reflection of the rigors of Russian life during the formative period of the church and the suffering which has always been the lot of the peasant, how is it that the Russian religious life has managed to maintain the balance that it has? What prevents a life of preoccupation with sinfulness, the vanity of the world, suffering as the inescapable lot of the human person, and the need for the most ruthless attack on the self—the emptying of the ego—from producing simply a deepening of despair? What is the source of the nobility and strength of the Russian Orthodox tradition? It seems likely that the answer must be sought in terms of the Orthodox persistence in hope.

The Russian religious life involves (as spirituality so often does) a tremendous gamble. To the extent that it flows from an understanding of suffering, it requires that the religious person engage in profound contemplation of that suffering which is everywhere visible. In the dark visions of the saints—which are strongly reflected in the literature of nineteenth-century Russia—are the same seeds which develop into the suicidal emptiness reflected, as Billington notes, in the nineteenth century's absorption in "the Hamlet question . . . the question of whether or not to take one's life."[24] We see here, once again, the "thin line" of hope which separates kenotic religious intuition from pure despair. It would appear that the strength of kenotic imagery and the reality of suffering in the life of the Russian can only be forged into the remarkable hope of salvation in the face of the seemingly overwhelming nature of sinfulness.

The Russian saints were believed to have discovered an experience of fullness through their pursuit of emptiness. The testimony of the Hesychasts, the examples afforded by Theodosius, Sergei, Nil, and, of course, by Boris and Gleb, and the scriptural promise voiced by St. Paul, all strongly suggest to the believer the existence of a level of consciousness and a mode of living which can be reached through self-emptying, the passive acquiescence in the face of suffering and the nurturing of a hopeful humility. In short, Russian Orthodoxy proclaims the possibility of a radically different perspective on life for the person who responds to its symbolic content and its promise of fullness in emptiness. Clearly, it is one thing to identify suffering and redemption on the symbolic level, and quite another to experience somehow that same identity. Nevertheless, the continued vigor of Russian spirituality—in spite of the diminishment of the numbers of the faithful and the compromise of Orthodox institutions under the Soviet regime—testifies to the richness of the Russian way.

The kenotic element manifests itself again and again in the actions and the conscious testimony of those individuals whose personal experience of religious hope animates the spiritual dimension of the Russian people. It is more than a literary theme. It is the reflection of some common religious experience, shared in to varying degrees by all who have found solace in Russian Christianity. Moreover, the kenotic mode of expression by way of symbols and images has come to be employed by the religiously experienced to convey to others or to evoke in them that same transforming moment of kenosis, or faith, or hope. Kenotic themes have become characteristic of much of Russian literature and art and as a result, they have won secure places in the

Russian consciousness. The young Russian atheist partakes of the same heritage as the seminarian, although her value structure and attitudes may differ radically; and at some critical points in her experience, her response to stimuli must have a great deal in common with that of her religious counterpart.

V. THE PROMISE OF RUSSIAN SPIRITUALITY

While Russian kenoticism will certainly seem imbalanced or even psychologically unhealthy to many in the modern West, others will see in it a particularly moving and beautiful example of the transformative power of religious vision. While one's own spiritual mode may seem to diverge dramatically from the passive self-emptying celebrated in Russian Orthodoxy, one may nevertheless come to respect and to understand and perhaps even to feel the power of the kenotic experience.

Beyond doubt, the considerable difficulty which one usually encounters in the study of any religious tradition derives in large measure from the dialectical nature of so many of the basic formulations of the religious mind. Dialectic—the contrapuntal opposition of diametrical concepts—lies at the heart of all religious experience. Ever confronted by the contradictory character of human experience, religious intuition strives for a synthesis which often transcends the limits of conceptualization. Clearly, the kenosis embraced by Russian Christianity is thoroughly dialectical, for it consists in the paradoxical promise of fullness in emptiness, the realization of self through self-denial, the attainment of joy through the experience of suffering.

Fyodor Dostoevsky, whose writings give expression to some of the most profound achievements of Russian theological inquiry,

... discovered the paradox of the coexistence in men's hearts of intense fear of suffering and of readiness for it. Man, according to him, was prepared at first to sell his freedom in the hope of escaping suffering, but once he became a slave he revolted against his captivity and was ready to plunge back into the ocean of struggle and affliction in order to regain his freedom.[25]

In this paradox lies an important clue to the power of the kenotic motif to inspire the Russian religious mind. The dialectic of self-emptying achieves the synthesis of the fear of suffering and the readiness to endure it, yet no simple conceptual formula can express that synthesis. The gamble remains, and only one's own religious experience can offer the certainty which we call faith. Hope, the willingness to engage life's contradictions, is by nature a dialectical phenomenon. It energizes the pursuit of meaningful synthesis. The task of religion consists, in this regard, in the nurturing of the dialectical hope, in the proclamation of the possibility of transcendent synthesis and in the gradual refinement of the religious ideal which guides and sustains the seeker.

Frithjof Schuon, in his *The Transcendent Unity of Religions*, writes: "The truth is, however, that every religious form is superior to the others in a particular respect, and it is this characteristic that in fact indicates the sufficient reason for the existence of that form."[26] This statement gives succinct expression to the attitude which makes real interreligious encounter possible. True ecumenism demands of the religious individual a secure grounding in his or her own system of belief and practice *and,* at the same time, a real openness to the religious genius which gives life to other religious paths. Whatever else may be said of it, religion is a human phenomenon. It consists in the human response to the experience of existence. Whether it proceeds from revelation, discovery, instinct or need—or, indeed, from all of these—it takes on many forms within the dynamics of human life and interaction. For the Russian Christians, to take up religion means to take up the cross. Indeed, the Russian word meaning "to christen, to baptize" (*krestit'*), comes from the word for "cross" (*krest*), as does "*krestyánin,*" a particularly beautiful word in spoken Russian, "the peasant."

NOTES

1. Fyodor Dostoevsky, *Notes From the Underground,* cited in Walter Kaufmann, *Existentialism: From Dostoevsky to Sartre* (World Publishing Co., 1970), p. 78.

2. Nicholas Riasanovsky, *A History of Russia* (London: Oxford University Press, 1969), p. 39. See also Francis Dvornik's *Byzantine Missions Among the Slavs* (Rutgers Univ. Press, 1970) for a detailed account of the Christianization of the Slavic peoples. The outlines of Byzantine religious thought are well presented by John Meyendorff in his *Byzantine Theology* (Fordham University Press, 1974). For the pre- Christian period, see Samuel H. Cross, trans., *The Russian Primary Chronicle* (Cambridge: Medieval Academy of America, 1953) and Serge A. Zenkovsky, *Medieval Russia's Epics, Chronicles and Tales* (E. P. Dutton, 1963).

3. G. P. Fedotov, *The Russian Religious Mind* (Harvard University Press, 1966), p. 95.

4. Ibid., p. 95.

5. Ibid., p. 101.

6. Ibid., p. 97.

7. "Gospodi Iisus' Xriste, ižhesim' obras'm' iavisia no zemli, iavolivy voleju prigvozditisia na kr'stě i priim' strast' grěx' radi nashix'! S'podobi i mia priiati strast'." In D. I. Abramovič, ed., *Žitija svjatyx mučenikov Borisa i Gleba i služby im* (Pamjatniki drevnerusskoj literatury, 2; p., 1916), p. 34. (This remains the best edition of texts on Sts. Boris and Gleb. The *Skazanie (Legend)* is written in Old Church Slavonic. The translation is mine.)

8. "...ot' prel'cti žhitija sevo l'ct'naago." Ibid., pp. 35–36.

9. Timothy Ware, *The Orthodox Church* (Middlesex: Penguin, 1963), p. 88. (Ware is himself an ordained Orthodox monk, Father Kallistos.) See Nadejada Gorodetzky, *The Humiliated Christ in Modern Russian Thought.* (Macmillan Co., 1938) for a dated but compelling treatment of the kenotic theme in post-revolutionary Russian thought.

10. Fedotov, *Russian Religious Mind,* pp. 109–110.

11. Ibid., p. 104.

12. Ibid., p. 131.

13. James Billington, *The Icon and the Axe* (Knopf, 1966), pp. 24–25. This work is an excellent cultural history of the Russians. Billington has a remarkable flair and is a thorough scholar as well.

14. Ibid., p. 8.

15. Fedotov, *Russian Religious Mind,* p. 130.

16. Nicholas Zernov, *St. Sergius—Builder of Russia* (Ann Arbor Reprints, 1975—reprint of the original Macmillan edition), p. 66.

17. Ibid., p. 66.

18. Ibid., p. 67.

19. Billington, *Icon,* p. 51.

20. Ibid., p. 52.

21. Ibid., p. 51.

22. Zernov, *Sergius,* p. 73.

23. Nil Sorskii, "Testament," cited in Fedotov, *Russian Religious Mind,* vol ii, p. 267.

24. Billington, *Icon,* p. 354.

25. Nicholas Zernov, *Three Russian Prophets: Khomiakov, Dostoevsky, Soloviev* (London: S.C.M. Press, Ltd., 1944), p. 92. It is Zernov's contention that one must look to Russian literature to find the sort of religious expression usually found in the musings of theologians. In his assessment, Dostoevsky and Tolstoi, for example, are among the most important theological writers in the Russian language. In this connection, see Tolstoi, Lev, *My Confession, My Religion* and *The Gospel in Brief* in The Works of Lyof N. Tolstoi (sic) Vol. XVII (Charles Scribner's Sons, 1904).

26. Frithjof Schuon, *The Transcendent Unity of Religions* (Harper and Row, 1976, Revised ed.), p. 33.

14

Yoga and the Western Consciousness

Justin O'Brien

Before classical yoga can dialogue fruitfully with Western science and spirituality, some preliminary points need to be appreciated.

Although it belongs to an ancient source of perennial wisdom, classical yoga is not an Oriental import.[1] It is a definite, experimental science, but hardly recognized as such in Europe and North America. People are more familiar with the postures and some breathing aspects, Hatha yoga as it is called, than with the more advanced stages of the science.

To probe classical yoga, one has to examine the premier texts—Patanjali's *Yoga Sutras* and the *Samkhya Karika*. These scriptures are the basis for the theory and practice of scientific yoga.

Yoga's traditional ground for thousands of years has been the Himalayan Mountain regions. Yet it remains unassociated with ethnic, religious, or political persuasions. Does one speak of the cardio-vascular system or the law of gravity as being Eastern or Western? Much less should any discussion on yoga assume that it is indigenous to the Eastern world.

To speak of yoga as a wisdom means that it transcends cultural labels. As a noncultural contribution to human development, it is applicable to any citizen of any country. It shares with other wise traditions a timeless quality that makes it a continual resource for human enrichment. Yoga's contribution lies in its study of human nature and its intrinsic unfoldment from the primary existence of consciousness. It attempts to interpret the person, not for a particular period of history, however beneficial, but on a perennial basis. It outlines its remarks from a universal perspective that regards the person holistically—body, mind, and spirit.

Yoga postulates that people carry within themselves a dynamic impulse or appetite towards self-perfection. People strive to actualize their total nature, to experience life as richly, as enjoyably, as maturely as possible; the world of culture and science are a partial manifestation of this living drive for perfection. In order to achieve this integral goal, a person must consciously activate these inherent laws of his or her multileveled nature. To embark on the practice of yoga, one enters not an intellectual adventure, but a transformative process that systematically awakens, coordinates and realizes the latent resources in human nature for peaceful living in full self-awareness.

With these few clarifications, the question may be asked, what can yoga offer to the human problems in Western consciousness?

I. THE RANGE OF CONSCIOUSNESS IN CONTEMPORARY SOCIETY

Western society is in continual pursuit of cultural patterns to eliminate strife and guarantee a modest program of the "good life." Its undaunted reliance upon its reasoning faculty—*ratio*—has nourished a confident tradition that makes its vision of life synonymous with the efforts of its discursive mind. It has engaged its environment rationally in order to resolve the intricacies of meaningful survival. The history of these engagements has accumulated into the human enterprise called culture, which itself becomes an index of the search for the true *humanum*—those humanitarian values of society for disclosing to man and woman their dignity.

The Reduction of Consciousness to Discursive Reason

The important questions revolving about the social, economical, and political issues are argued and dispatched, however tenuously, within the arena of discursive thinking. At the same time, stimulated by the success of the scientific, industrial, and technological revolutions, the gratification of the mass of human desires has proliferated into the complexity of modern living. In order to satisfy the expanding ingredients of these contemporary life styles, the promotion of institutions and policies is ever increasing—a work of discursive reason.

To sustain its dignity while justifying the treatment of natural resources and the expenditure of human energies, Western society has opted for a rational usefulness in producing the modern degree of cultural prosperity. Its vision for it has transpired from the medieval insistence of a rigidly defined social and static worldview to the dynamic optimism and experimental modes of contemporary living. By its discursive ingenuity, modern society has been exceeding the cultural limitations of the past generations. By enlarging the abundance of cultural advantages to overcome the universal problem of human privation and nonfulfillment, the successful termination of this dreadful recurrence would soon seem to be looming upon the modern horizon. It is only a matter of time and priority.

Throughout this historic evolution of discovery and self-expression, concentration upon strictly discursive methods have yielded the achievements and benefits.[2] The use of human consciousness in this discursive manner has been the inspiration furnishing the prevalent understanding of human nature. The resulting cultural accomplishments in turn have determined people's self-image, as well as confined them equally to its consequences.

Forced by history to inherit the practical consequences of discursive thought, people find themselves in a strange predicament. The concrete betterment of passing decades has not always been an edifying episode for everyone concerned. The echo of recorded history narrates that howsoever modern society has enjoyed its newly civilized status, the improved standard of living eventually suffered a painful obsolescence. As society continued to objectify its cultural desires, each generation repeatedly found the lingering benefits from the past improvements too restrictive for their taste. However well instigated were the latest programs for emancipation, history demonstrates that as each cultural advance stabilized, it soon spawned its own oppressiveness.

Ironically, men and women find themselves cramped and manipulated by the very tools of liberation. The discursive enlightenment has brought them from the dark ages to our present level of civilization and succeeded in replacing medieval restrictions with modern ones. Our recent ecological sensitivity exposes the fact that the industrial-technological worldview enforces a way of living that supports its own disintegration. Amid the expansion of today's prosperity, unsuspected forms of obsolescence and insecurity have emerged. If one were to place men and women totally within cultural history, an argument could be readily fashioned for supposing inner strife and social alienation as irreplaceable portions of human nature. In view of its diminishing returns, discursive consciousness cannot but stand ambivalent toward the meaningfulness of its future.

The Discursive Illusion

Replacing the standard of culture with concrete improvement gives hope to human progress. Nature and the universe are yielding their secrets to research. A more hopeful future does seem credible. In so doing, modernity has banked on the faculty of reason for the displacement and raising of culture. Contemporary people, as a result, remain perpetually struggling to unburden themselves from its results. The latent tensions, the restive feelings of antagonism that eventuate from discursive consciousness' newest forms of cultural progress recur with every succeeding advance. Pollution, the attrition of natural resources, the escalating arms race are but a few signals for people's concern. To replace one form with another newer model does not answer the underlying problem. If modern society cannot resolve the inherent obsolescence accompanying discursive consciousness then it resigns itself to a destiny of futile optimism.

Modern culture is not only the product of discursiveness but encourages an habituated way of experiencing life. Discursive thinking and its projects define the legitimate field for human reflection and stimulate the motivational center of people. Since a culture tends to see only what can be incorporated into its established frame of reference, the discursive plane and its products are taken as the whole or predominate way of life. A society thus insures its future stability.

The cultural rationale or established beliefs influence the mind's perceptions of reality, providing a logic of self-approval for the mind's desires. In this way, discursive thinking does not mirror life so much as it screens the horizon of human experience to find correlations with its striving impulses. Even the most critical, scientific, or detached looking becomes a verification search. One sifts through the possibilities of life for a confirmation—one that will strengthen the hypotheses or rationale that generates the cultural search. The overall social fabric is sustained by the discursive agreement on which phenomena are currently acceptable to society. Thus, the mind represents the world to itself and responds to its own representation.

But, as history recalls, the structures and policies founded on discursive reflection are inherently susceptible to erosion. For the rising cultural epoch protests against the current limitations of the inherited status quo. The culture of the previous generation is felt now as an unfair boundary, impinging on the self-expression rights of its successor. The expected introduction of new cultural programs to overcome the "old conditions" have arrived; the latest arrival has yet to sow its own unsuspected ills. And so on.

These great cultural failures in human liberation are not the fault of the human spirit's apparently indomitable quest for fulfillment; rather the flaw resides in the nature of the discursive mind. When the conditions for human fulfillment under the present cultural expectations begin showing their aging limits, society suffers until it recalls the discursive mind to introduce newer models of rescue. Even though these cultural remedies may statistically reduce the incidence of certain afflictions, their insertion into the dynamic complexities of society produces strains and pressures in another segment of society. Each epoch lives from one cultural reprieve to the next. Here the perpetual disclosure of ever new regimes of plans and systems supplies the grand illusion: total human fulfillment and the elimination of human misery in all its forms—everything within patient discursive reach.

In constructing the next future from the dissatisfactions with the current epoch, the plan occurs entirely on the same cognitive plane. The expansion or renovation of cultural boundaries does not require a radical alteration of consciousness. The advance by the mind is only lateral; the change of plans remains within the dimensions of reason—the same field of consciousness as before. Hope still throbs. And in keeping with this hope, the human spirit continues to subject itself to the pressure for the total unburdening of pains, a quest which in its concrete implementations, consistently seems to drain the future of its promise.

The Restive Quest of the Ego

Let us return to the question of why after all is the discursive manifestation of mind an illusion in its hopes?

A study of Yoga philosophy points out that the thrust of self-consciousness to objectify itself into the world promotes a sense of ego. "I" need to know the world; knowing gives me a sense of personal identity. The objectifying brings into play the discursive level of mind, with which the ego identifies. Because the ego desires enrichment, self-consciousness presumes it cannot survive without the external world; it uses the discursive faculty through the bodily senses to secure the presumption. Thinking that thinking and the sensory environments are demanded for essential existence, the confused self becomes harried with ego-sustaining desires. At any given moment, the emergence of desire tends to function in a selective process for locating those aspects of the phenomenal world which correspond to the exigencies of the ego's mood. Ignorant of its real nature, the already free self-conscious life force is now being entangled by the ego's ambitions for it.

Buoyed as well as compelled by the quest to experience life, the ego's embodiment into the phenomenal world necessitates relentless waves of desire to satisfy its presence there. Thus it is in the ego's best interest to prolong concern with worldly fashion and experiment with the latest trend. How else to satisfy the quest?

On the other hand, human experience in the world demonstrates again and again that concrete desires have saturation levels. It is only a matter of time before they produce ennui in the experiencer. The irony for the ego is that the quest is characterized by infinitude, while desire is specified by finitude. Consequently, the ego's ceaseless efforts with the discursive mind cannot ever match the quest. In association with the ego, one remains on a treadmill of desire to satisfy it.

Transposed to the realm of culture—the amplitude of culture being only the grosser manifestation of consciousness—our analysis finds society with all its sincere hopes and model systems to alleviate the complex ills producing only temporary success. The finite quality of the remedies uncover or influence, however unintentionally, newer forms of human limitation.[3] Unavoidably, the self encounters estrangement from its own quest!

The question of cultural failure may be asked differently: why should man encounter estrangement?

Presuming the mind's ego-discursive arrangement the norm of waking consciousness, one would expect accumulative fulfillment to resolve the quest. But the more I experience, the more I search. Estrangement persists. The quest beckons. Immediately, the ego impels the mind to try to close the gap between fulfilled desires and the unrelieved quest. In complying with desires, the ego is realizing its nature. Everything seems to be in proper order. But consciousness cannot evade sensing the distance between the ego's completed goals and the uncompleted quest. No matter how often the ego completes desire, one is always running competition with the painful void of nonfulfillment.

The awareness of the uncompleted void is available only if the structure of consciousness were not entirely coincident with ego. The event of this insight in consciousness does not result from discursive scrutiny but is given unsuspectedly in spontaneous awareness. The new awareness leaves room for the mind to reconsider its self-understanding beyond the boundaries of ego-consciousness: the self is more than ego. With this broader basis for identity, the ego cannot be held solely responsible for the unyielding quest. Rather the insight of self-awareness recognizes the discrepancy between the relentless demand for all-inclusive fulfillment and the partial limited responses by the ego. The quest arises from self-consciousness, not ego-consciousness. The ego attempts to mimic self-consciousness. The ego's searching is the opposite of what is already present in self-consciousness. The quest is constituted by nothing other than abiding self-awareness unfulfilled in the ego.

In support of this inquiry into the nature of consciousness, yoga offers another approach in understanding the limits of the discursive mind.

Four States of Consciousness[4]

Given the prevailing state of mind in society, the display of ego dependency upon the world sums up what most persons accept for self-consciousness. If this relationship between the self and the world at large is essentially unalterable, and if the existence of personal consciousness requires the relationship, then the following experiment could not be performed. In the very act of thinking, one can be aware of mental activity as it develops. One can step back, as it were, and simply observe the busy functioning of the discursive machinery at work in one's own mind. Whether it is puzzling out problems, listening to conversations or composing ideas, anyone of these illustrate some of the ways the thinking mind may occupy its own attention. No matter how the thinking mind may be occupied at the moment, one can simultaneously be aware of the occupation. Being able to be witness to one's own mental processes provides the experimental evidence for not defining human consciousness entirely with discursive activity.

In addition, if the existence of self-consciousness were entirely equated with discursive activity, then one could neither experience sleep nor dream. For in acknowledging sleep, in recalling a dream, who does the sleeping and acknowledging, the dreaming and recalling? In none of these experiences does the person cease to exist. The same self has perdured, manifested in differentiated states. Throughout these experiences, the surviving substrate, the self, underlies these three modes of consciousness and forms the continuity between them. Since one can proceed through these modes in experiential sequence, self-consciousness cannot be identified with any one of them. This arrangement of consciousness infers the presence of a fourth state, wherein the self recognizes that it can abide in itself and yet through any of the other three states without being permanently fixed therein.[5]

In our inquiry into the range of consciousness, we have tried to examine aspects of consciousness that may be underestimated in our pursuit of cultural fulfillment. Prone as modern society is to suspect whatever is offered in freedom, even more does it oppose what lessens its appreciation of discursive accomplishments. The suggestion of using nondiscursive awareness for self-discovery can easily threaten the very ego-esteem built into the relative security of the current culture. Our purpose in this essay is not to evoke anxiety but wonder.

Suffering from a melancholia of abundance, modern society

fails to connect its restlessness with a serious absence of a human experience other than discursive thinking. Overwhelmed by the potentials of technology, it resists the possibility that another form of genuine knowing may be humanly satisfying and necessary to contend with life. Yet the hustling pace at which hard, practical thinking can drive itself is still surprised with another more subtle form of knowing. The strain of thinking is often accompanied with sudden, unanticipated insight. The "eureka" feeling, the creative breakthrough, the sense of awe that swells one with wonder, all are disclosures of a consciousness that may not be reduced to the labor of *ratio*.[6] Western antiquity understood this form of knowing as *simplex intuitus* or *contemplatio*, what we today call intuition. The intuitive way of knowing distinguishes itself from the exertion of *ratio* by its effortless disclosure of reality, akin to the way the truth of a landscape simply offers itself to the eye of the beholder. Almost through no fault of one's own, awareness takes hold. Plato referred to these happenings as a kind of divine mania, wherein the experience surpasses the person's straining efforts, coming as a gift, an insight, reminding him or her of their divine origin. If the mind was purely discursive, there would be no room for these surprises.

Western history further indicates that the holy writers of the Bible, along with the wise of antiquity, have always venerated the intuitional promptings of the spirit. They have transpired this awareness into their aphorisms, poems, allegories, and stories, using these vehicles for describing the truths of their experience. Their preference for this way of knowing and expressing reality did not eliminate the genuine role of discursive thought, but assumed it into a higher synthesis of truth. Although careful to preserve the ordinary means of conceptual communication, they were not willing to abandon people to it. In reading their writings one senses that the inspiration for their communication exceeds the use of rational concepts at hand; they live from a range of consciousness transcending the field of reason.

Although the aesthetic sense has not pioneered Western culture, nevertheless the priceless awe that one feels before the presence of the beautiful in reality serves as another instance exceeding purely rational communication. The great artists, like the biblical narrators, operate from a different center of awareness than the functional relations of concepts to the production schedule at work. The beholder and the artist participate in an act of heightened astonishment whereby the gifts of intuition disclose enriching levels of reality whose existence reason could not begin to suspect. The recognition and practice of these cognitive experiences in a discursive oriented society may not replace people's interests, but they are a challenge to the exclusive obligation of *ratio*.

The unannounced illumination in problem solving and art, the feeling of estrangement with desire, the witnessing to the mind's discursive activity and the sequence of three conditional modes of consciousness—all these experiences extend the perimeter of human knowing beyond the boundary of *ratio*. These discoverable instances expose ego-consciousness for not being the measure of self-consciousness and provide the internal evidence for redefining human nature: people's identity now infers the presence of nonconceptual awareness. For charting this new vista, we may turn to an ancient map.

II. AN ANCIENT REMEDY FOR MODERN ILLS

There is an ancient story about a man who was pierced by a poisoned arrow. His companions immediately wanted to fetch a physician from a nearby village. The victim would not hear of it. Instead, before permitting medical aid or the removal of the arrow, he obliged his concerned friends to inquire about the name of the archer, his town and family circumstances. Next, the victim instructed them to find out the type of construction for the bow and the materials used in the arrows. Furthermore ... and then he died. The same plight, according to yoga, afflicts modern society.

Modern society knows that it is alive, but not alive with optimum life. The wound in it is the presumption of reason. It resorts wholly to *ratio* for solutions to life's dilemmas. Like the storied victim, it prolongs its injury by pursuing unprofitable questions. Unknowingly reason's concoctions only endanger his recovery. Rational man and woman "merely see the diversity of things, with their divisions and limitations . . . they have impure knowledge."[7] Humankind only fools itself into arguing that it is reason's destiny to find the universal unity in life.

For thousands of years yoga has supplied a program for complementing reason, not for the sake of leisure, but precisely to reconcile humankind with the world. A paper solution, involving coherent ideas to satisfy the intellect? No. Yoga feels that people's unpredicatable anxieties will hardly be resolved through careful rationalizing alone.

For society's sake, yoga poses a critique of culture. Whenever people become complacent or discouraged with their current level of civilization, yoga quietly insists upon a special feature of human nature. No matter how bogged down or overwhelmed a person may become with his or her involvement with society, he or she possesses a transcendental nature. In spite of their endless worries and tribulations, yoga reminds people that they are more than their body, their mind, their career, their momentary success or failure with life. For they possess a center of life, wisdom, and strength within that makes their nature wider than history and its vicissitudes.

> There is a bridge between time and eternity;
> and this bridge is Atman, the spirit of man.
> Neither day nor night cross that bridge, nor
> old age, nor death, nor sorrow.[8]

Yoga sees people embroiled in a world of ineluctable change and suffering. Starting from this inescapable condition of humankind yoga refuses to be abstract about suffering. Five year renovation plans are not proffered. Instead, a different tack: an applied philosophy of life, one that only reveals its intelligibility in the act of performance. More, an investigation of human consciousness whereby consciousness uses as its chief tool living awareness itself; self probing self, an inner alchemy of spirit.

> It is this spirit that we must find and know:
> man must find his own soul. He who has found
> and knows his soul has found all the worlds,
> has achieved all his desires.[9]

Yoga views people's aggravation with life as stemming from a profound ignorance, a metaphysical veil, if you will, so thick with confusion and error that a person innocently feels he or she has entered a nightmare existence. Humankind's sense of wonder may have occasioned hellenic thought, but its feeling of bondage inspired yoga. Yoga traces the root problem of life to people's painful ignorance about the truth of their spirit. Yet pain can spur emancipation. Life's afflictions can have an ironic impact: suffering goads a desperate search for salvation. Addressing a person as a patient too long in the hospital who finally gets sick of being sick, yoga nourishes that fundamental appetite in us for liberation, *moksa*. Humankind's sense of bondage beckons the ancient visitor to make his rounds and dispense his remedies.

Highly optimistic, with centuries of practitioners to embody its claim, yoga insists that a person's normal state is healthful, free, serene, and beyond all suffering. The key to his or her recovery, as well as the lessening of society's turmoil, lies in his or her ability to restore through experience the eternal vision of his or her spirit. One cannot think pious thoughts or quote perennial remarks of sages to get oneself there. One must do it to oneself; a spiritual praxis of integrating one's inner world of consciousness on all its levels as one goes about making one's mark in the world. Familiarity with the world alone profits a person surface knowledge and success; combined with a systematic self-exploration, he or she can develop tranquil confidence that leaves one undisturbed amid the flux of culture. Time and eternity, like every antithesis in life find their crossroads in a person. The meaning for their conjunction, and their enjoyment, dawns past the boundaries of rational inquiry.

To understand the mystery of history and the cosmos, one must perceive from within—without reason's aid. For a person is a complete microcosm, who is reflected in the creativity of nature. All the principles of matter and energy, the archetypes of creation, are contained with his or her own spiritual evolution. These truths one must experience not by the route of intellectuality, but as a comprehensor, *evamvit,* one who verifies in one's person. This discovery of oneself as the inner center of the universe is through the methodology of nondiscursive meditation, *dhyana.* Meditation leads to abiding intuition. Like a concentrated spaceship plunging above earth's gravitational pull, consciousness moves past the attractions of mind and body, entering into the silent inner space of his microcosm to sight hidden galaxies of knowledge.

> When the vision of reason is clear,
> and in steadiness the soul is in harmony;
> when the world of sound and other senses is gone,
> and the spirit has risen above passion and hate ... [10]

An unlearning process expands within. Leaving aside conventual thoughts, images, and fancies, one allows inner awareness to go its natural way. Gradually, a strange paradox takes shape: the more one recedes inward, the more one encompasses the world at large—without opposition. Through meditation, the epigenic unfolding of matter and form, body and soul, the individual and society, the past as well as the future, even life and death—every apparent contradiction and dichotomy resolves into a glorious unifying experience. The person of *samadhi* knows the oneness in the diversity by absorbing it. One knows oneself in a superconscious comprehension state.

> When a man dwells in the solitude of silence,
> and meditation and contemplation are ever with him;

when too much food does not disturb his health,
and his thoughts and words and body are in peace;
when freedom from passion is his constant will . . .
and his selfishness and violence and pride are gone;
when lust and anger and greediness are no more,
and he is free from the thought "this is mine";
then this man has risen on the mountain of the highest:
he is worthy to be one with God.[11]

Fully conscious at last, one lives in unalloyed bliss and peace, peace that the world neither gives or understands. No longer baffled by any event of existence, the realized person now strives to fulfill his or her compassionate goal of bringing freedom to all living beings by annihilating the mental causes of their agonies. Only then does one seek final transcendence.

Rational man and woman, attempt world peace without first preparing themselves to experience the truth of peace within themselves. Modern psychology can attest to the observation that people reflect in their outer lives the interior world of their self-understanding. A world without peace is a people living out of interior distress. The rational mind is only a small function of self-consciousness.[12] Important and useful for dealing with reality in the space-time-continuum, it becomes obsolete itself as a means to discovering the significance of human nature and its destiny. Cultural consciousness will not begin to resolve its almost universal dilemmas until people recognize that their problems, from disease to loneliness, start and end with their consciousness of themselves.

In summary, then, as long as humankind believes its ultimate realization resides in the phenomenal world, its spirit invites ennui and antagonism. And as long as the future of human culture waters the tree of its life only from its discursive font, people will remain unquenched. Our inquiry into Western consciousness suggests a complementary route. The exact nature of its horizon before embarking can only be hinted at by reason. For Christian citizens yoga offers a complementary invitation to foster the peaceful perfecting of themselves as God's image, while renewing society.

NOTES

1. Classical yoga is often known as raja or "royal" yoga. The emphasis and methodology of this praxis is upon experiential verification. Each aspirant explores his or her own consciousness on the various levels and dimensions, being guided by a competent teacher. There are other forms of yoga—Bhakti, Karma, Jnana, and so on. These major approaches are already included in classical yoga, which utilizes these traditions to bring the practitioner to his or her goal. cf. Rama, Swami, *Lectures on Yoga* (Himalayan International Institute, Honesdale, Pa., 1973).

2. For some interesting literature of varying evaluations upon the role of discursive reason, see: J. Ellul, *The Technological Society* (A. A. Knopf, 1964). A. Toffler, *Future Shock* (Random House). B. Fuller, *Operating Manual for Spaceship Earth* (Massachusetts Institution of Technology Press, 1969). L. Ferrer, *The Scientific Intellectual* (Basic Books, 1963). M. Polanyi, *Personal Knowledge* (University of Chicago Press, 1959). F. Matson, *The Broken Image* (Bragiller, 1964).

3. As an example, medical advances in the last few decades have produced a drug-remedy approach to curing ailments. The immediate startling recoveries have heralded a demand for instant cures. Only later, when the incidence of unexpected pathological reactions set in does society become more cautious with these chemical panaceas. In the meantime, society tends to look to external items for relief from what is essentially an internal problem and thus needing internal or intangible remedies. Cf. Ivan Illich, *Medical Nemesis: The Expropriation of Health* (Pantheon, 1976).

4. The philosophical analysis of the four major states of consciousness is the leading concern of the *Mandukya Upanishad*. This treatise is considered by yogis as the most terse of all the hundreds of Upanishads. The entire compilation of Upanishads are the philosophical distillations of the Vedas. They are not the product of discursive reasoning but are universal truths received in the highest state of consciousness—*samadhi*.

5. The full awareness of the fourth state of consciousness is referred to *turiya*, synonymous with samadhi. Cf. Swami Rama, R. Ballentine, and Swami Ajaya, *Yoga and Psychotherapy* (The Himalayan Institute, Glenview, 1976).

6. Descartes received his breakthrough in analytical geometry in a series of three dream-visions; he never investigated this mode of knowing as a new possibility for consciousness. Cf. T. Roszak *Where the Wasteland Ends* (Doubleday, 1973). William James commented how rational consciousness is but one type, and that many other forms of consciousness are available to one's self-pursuit. William James, *The Varieties of Religious Experience* (New American Library, 1958).

7. *Bhagavad Gita*, 18.21, The "Song of the Lord" is a series of eighteen chapters taken from the longest epic extant, the "Mahabharata." These chapters reveal a dialogue between two characters, Arjuna—the aspiring one, and Krishna—the lord of the universe. The ensuing story has an everyman quality and may be interpreted on many levels. Arjuna is the struggle of the human soul perplexed with incongruous problems and unexpected reverses.

8. *Chandogya Upanishad*, 8.4.1.

9. Ibid., 8.7.

10. *Bhagavad Gita*, 18.51.

11. Ibid., 18.52–53. In *samadhi*, man's total nature becomes self-evident.

12. In some unusual experiments at the Menninger research laboratories, Swami Rama demonstrated under scientifically controlled conditions that one's consciousness was other than one's brain or nervous system. By allowing his material body to remain asleep, he nevertheless stayed aware of his environment without the normal means of sensory and brain stimulation. When asked the explanation, he replied, "All the body is in the mind but not all of the mind is in the body." E. E. & A. Green, "The Ins and Outs of Mind-Body Energy," *The World Book Science Annual, 1974.*

15

Spiritual Insights of the American Transcendentalists

Jon Alexander, OP

One of the first students of the effects of the democratic revolution on the personality was that astute observer of the manners and customs of the American republic, Jean de Crèvecoeur. Writing in 1782, Crèvecoeur found that the citizens of the new republic were fabricating a new civic identity: "He is an American, who leaving behind him all his ancient prejudices and manners, receives new ones from the new mode of life he has embraced, the new government he obeys, and the new rank he holds."[1] A generation after Crèvecoeur's examination another observer of American life, Alexis de Tocqueville, found that democratic life had affected the personal identity of Americans. "Thus not only does democracy make every man forget his ancestors, but it hides his descendents and separates his contemporaries from him; it throws him back forever upon himself alone and threatens in the end to confine him entirely within the solitude of his own heart."[2]

The features of the American personality described by Crèvecoeur and Tocqueville were signs of the process called modernization by social scientists. Modernization is characterized by the replacment of the traditional moorings of custom, family, church, and position by a rationalized, uniform social system and a capitalistic economy which allow for a higher degree of individual autonomy, mobility, and diversity than existed in traditional society. It was this increase of individual autonomy which invited the Jacksonian American to seek a station commensurate with his (and to some extent her) ambitions, or a denomination compatible with his/her personal faith experience that seemed to Tocqueville to isolate the American "in the solitude of his heart."[3]

Jacksonian America was an epitome of the spiritual and intellectual contradictions of a society well into the modernization process. In the North the forces of democracy were moving apace to level such remaining distinctions of the past as state supported churches at the same time that nativists and Know Nothings were pressing for new ethnocentric distinctions. Individuals were experiencing a new degree of autonomy in realizing their potentials, yet the popularity of phrenology, which promised a quick, scientific determination of one's personality and potential, indicates a widespread wish to escape from the uncertainties and anxieties of freedom. Democratic boosters celebrated the advance of American civilization, but the urbanization and industrialization underlying these advances had dramatically raised the mortality rate. Churchmen proclaimed the fatherhood of God, the brotherhood of man, and the accessability of grace at the very time that large numbers of Americans were confronting evil in America's labor systems or in the premature death of a loved one.[4]

DEMOCRATIZING THE DIVINE

The contributions of the Transcendentalists to spirituality arose from their effort to address the contradictions experienced by the democratic persons, emerging in Jacksonian America. Despite their diversity as a group, the Transcendentalists were united in the hope that the increased autonomy of democratic society afforded the context for the development of a more creative and harmonious person. Yet they were keenly aware that freedom held a dark potential. The Transcendentalists knew from their own experiences the anxiety and despair faced by the democratic persons of their generation.

Characteristic of the group was Emerson who struggled with waves of doubt and despair throughout his life. An entry in an early journal recounting the conflict between his youthful aspiration and misfortune is typical. "The spring," Emerson wrote, "is wearing into summer and life is wearing into death; our friends are forsaking us, our hopes are declining; our riches are wasting; our mortifications are increasing, and is the question settled in our minds, what objects we pursue with undivided aim? Have we fixed ourself by principles? Have we planted our stakes?"[5] Later the death of his first wife Ellen and his son Waldo compelled him to face again the question of the meaning of human existence.

Although the specifics were different, the experiences of the other Transcendentalists were cut from the same crepe as Emerson's. Margaret Fuller battled the intense loneliness faced by an intelligent woman seeking to realize her potential in American society. Bronson Alcott saw the collapse of his communal and educational experiments; Theodore Parker suffered the enmity of many of his Unitarian colleagues. Thoreau was frustrated in his effort to launch himself as an activist reformer of society; while the efforts of Hawthorne, Melville, and Emily Dickinson to transcend the melancholy of their lives remain one of the prominent themes of nineteenth century American literature.[6]

The spiritual problem of the Transcendentalists was in a significant respect a vocational crisis. The positions available in Jacksonian America held little appeal for them. The traditional form of the ministry was too constricting for Emerson and George Ripley. Emerson confessed, "It is the best part of the man, I sometimes think, that revolts most against his being the minister." Margaret Fuller found little precedent for her goal of becoming an active and cogent intellectual. Assessing herself, she confided to her journal in the early 1830s, "I look not fairly to myself, at the present moment." Thoreau, the iconoclast, ventured a symbolic departure from society to discern his essential needs and goals.[7]

The vocational crisis of the Transcendentalists was intensified by feelings of isolation, impotence, and uselessness. As Jacksonian society sped along on its railways the Transcendentalists experienced a Sisyphean impotence. Emerson lamented, "Health, action, happiness. How they ebb from me!" Fuller complained, "I have indeed been forced to take up old burdens, from which I thought I had learned what they could teach. . . ."[8]

During the 1830s the Transcendentalists groped their way toward an understanding of the self in American democratic society which Emerson would later articulate in his essay "Self-Reliance." To the Transcendentalists, self-reliance was a far cry from the rugged individualism later preached by American captains of industry. Rather it was a view of the self as a creative, morally responsible agent in an essentially benevolent and purposive universe. It meant being true to one's conscience and intuition of things, and avoiding the "prison uniform" of parties and social pressures to conform to roles one felt to be dead. In his old age Theodore Parker saw his youthful break with the custom of his playmates as a turning point in his life. About to strike a tortoise with a stick, ". . . something checked my little arm, and a voice within me said, clear and loud, 'It is wrong!' "[9]

For the Transcendentalists embracing self-reliance was akin to a religious conversion. The break through their despair over the constraints of custom yielded a whole range of insights which gradually led them to reconceptualize some of the main themes of Western philosophy and theology. Pushed back on their own resources, the Transcendentalists discovered in self-reliance a true form of reliance on God. Rebelling against Lockean and Scottish rationalism and sensationalism, the Transcendentalists held up intuition as the primary means of knowing. Intuition was the way God spoke to the individual; it was the primary channel of revelation; the principal source of religion. In touch with God through intuition, the democratic person could safely rely on the self rather than religious institutions, customs, or scriptures. As a vehicle of revelation self-reliance and intuition fulfilled the criteria of the Transcendentalists. As Margaret Fuller explained, "What I want, the word I crave, I do not expect to hear from the lips of man. I do not wish to be, I do not wish to have, a *mediator* .... "[10]

The intuitional epistemology of the Transcendentalists put the whole subject of human relation and perception in a new light. Because God was present in the intuition of every individual, isolation was transcended. Bronson Alcott explained: " ... Nature is not separable from me, she is mine alike with my body; and in moments of true life, I feel my identity with her: I breathe, pulsate, feel, think, will through her members, and know no duality of being." Walt Whitman's epiphany through identification with all creation, "The simple, compact, well-joined scheme, myself disintegrated, every one disintegrated yet part of the scheme" expressed poetically the insight couched in Emerson's image of the transparent eyeball. Emerson explained: "Standing on the bare ground, my head bathed by the blithe air, and uplifted into infinite space—all mean egotism vanishes. I become a transparent eyeball. I am nothing. I see all. The currents of the Universal Being circulate through me; I am part or particle of God." God was present in the self and with God's presence so was all of creation.[11]

The experiences of the Transcendentalists which eventuated in their epistemological reinterpretation provided a rationale for their critique of traditional religious doctrine and practice. From their view the critical self had little need for the mediation of religion since the divine was directly available through intuition. For the Transcendentalists, Christianity required a radical house cleaning, a sifting of the permanent from the transient on the basis of a reason guided by intuition. Since the religious experience was universally available to all persons, it could not be confined to a particular tradition. In their enthusiasm the Transcendentalists saw the permanent religious insights behind the transient myths of all religions. In Emerson's view, "Whenever a mind is simple, and receives a divine wisdom, old things pass away—means, teachers, texts, temples fall—it lives now, and absorbs past and future into the present hour." The great clash between the Transcendentalists and the Unitarians concerning miracles was based on the Transcendentalists' abhorrence of the historical particularism of the Unitarian position. For the Transcendentalists the real miracle was the presence of the divine in the self and nature—not the particular recollections of past events handed down in particular traditions. As Emerson explained, " ... in the Universal miracle, petty and particular miracles disappear."[12]

Democratizing the divine by making it available to all persons, and reinterpreting the religious tradition by sifting the permanent from the transient, the Transcendentalists adapted religion to the person whose experience of the whirligig of modernization had called into question much of tradition and emphasized the importance of one's individual resources. Reinterpreting the supernatural in secular terms the Transcendentalists redefined providence as progress, prayer as a state of perception or consciousness, salvation by election as freely chosen self-reliance. The heart of this reinterpretation involved trust. Here the Transcendentalists endeavored to move the object of trust from institutions and traditions to God alone who spoke through the critical self. Although the Transcendentalist reinterpretation of trust was not a novelty, in the historical context of Jacksonian America, where so much religious writing was preoccupied with apologetics and proofs, its shift of the locus of authority to the self through intuition, reason, and feeling represented something of a Cartesian revolution. The impetus behind the revolution was the personal experience of the Transcendentalists and the pastoral experience of those who served in the ministry. Theodore Parker was a little surprised to discover that his reinterpretation of religious authority spoke to the needs of his congregation. After he finally preached two sermons he had hesitated to share for a year he reported that his parishioners "thanked me for the attempt to apply common sense to religion and the Bible. ... I could not learn that any one felt less reverence for God, or less love for piety and morality. It was plain I had removed a stone of stumbling from the public path." Emerson's preaching had a profound effect on Margaret Fuller. " . . . From him," she explained, "I first learned what is meant by an inward life. Many other springs have since fed the stream of living waters, but he first opened the fountain. . . . Several of his sermons stand apart in memory, like landmarks of my spiritual history."[13]

EVIL AND THE THEORY OF COMPENSATION

The greatest challenge faced by the Transcendentalists in their translation of religion into democratized and credible terms was accounting for evil. To this challenge Emerson proposed the theory of compensation which provided a naturalistic interpretation of good and evil. As he explained, "Every act rewards itself, or, in other words, integrates itself. . . . " Evil flows from evil acts, and good from good acts in proportion to their nature. This was not to deny the reality of good or of evil acts, but to make their consequences universal and democratic. No special grace could nullify nor any particular mediator meliorate the consequences of evil acts. On the other hand, the experience of good and evil were also compensatory. Each benefit imposed its particular limitation, each reverse held its own opportunity for growth in self-reliance. As Emerson explained: "In the view of compensation nothing is given. There is always a price. Purity is the price at which impurity may be sold. If I sell my cruelty I shall become merciful of necessity. No man ever had pride but he suffered from it or parted with it for meekness without feeling the advantage of the blessed change."[14]

The theory of compensation was grounded in the moral order of the universe which the Transcendentalists maintained could be seen by the critical self. By entailing the consequences of actions in the actions themselves, by finding a compensation in the experience of advantage and reverse Emerson stoicized traditional Christian theodicy by placing reward and punishment in this world, and by making their effects equal and uniform on all persons. Compensation provided a hoist by which an individual might transcend any situation: finding benefit in personal reverse, sobering limitations in success, and an antidote for the envy or pity of others.

Embedded in the theory of compensation was a dialectical perception of existence which Emerson called polarity. He described it as the " . . . action and reaction we meet in every part of nature: in darkness and light; in heat and cold; in the ebb and flow of waters; in male and female. . . . " More profoundly Emerson saw that "An inevitable dualism bisects nature, so that each thing is a half and suggests another thing to make it whole. . . . " Because of compensation the critical self could transcend the polarities of physical and moral, universal and particular by achieving a broader scope in which to understand things. From this compensatory perspective things which had seemed contradictory or evil when viewed in terms of themselves could now be viewed correctly as moments in the harmonious concerto of the hospitable universe.[15]

Yet, somehow, compensation seems tainted with the flavor of sour grapes. Emerson worked out the theory of compensation during a period of intense affliction which culminated in the death of his first wife and his resignation from the ministry. During this period of trouble Emerson filled his journals with numerous observations on the burdens of success which are juxtaposed to lamentations on his frustrated ambitions in a pattern that suggests his efforts to cope with his personal reverses. Emerson's articulation of the theory of compensation at this point implies that the theory was to some extent, itself, a compensation. However, if compensation was indeed the universalization of a personal rationalization, it was a rationalization which had a wide appeal in Jacksonian America.[16]

Taken as a public theory compensation provided a support for those who had lost a traditional faith but wished a reasonable explanation for the moral order of the universe. But it was not a satisfactory answer to the question of how evil could exist in a benevolent universe. The descriptions of the suffering of innocents in the writings of Hawthorne and Melville were a direct critique of compensation.[17] In practice compensation could easily degenerate to indifference, as in Emerson's facile rationalization of the slave trade: "A tender American girl doubts of Divine Providence whilst she reads the horrors of the 'middle passage' and they are bad enough at the mildest; but to such as she these crucifixions do not come: they come to the obtuse and barbarous, to whom they are not horrid, but only a little worse than the old sufferings. They exchange a cannibal war for the stench of the hold."[18]

Indeed, at bottom compensation was more rationalization than rational; a faith for faith's sake or a faith in faith itself. As Emerson confessed in his journal, compensation is simply better " . . . in the view of the mind than any other way. Whatever is better must be the truer way." Like Emily Dickinson's poetical critique of compensation which begins with a recognition of the self as nobody, proposes a community of nobodies, and concludes by comparing the identity of a somebody to a frog croaking its name "to an admiring bog" the theory of compensation leaves the suspicion that everyone is inevitably a nobody (in modern society). In this light, compensation is surely as dismal as anything that ever came out of Calvin's Geneva.[19]

EVALUATION OF TRANSCENDENTALISM AS A SPIRITUALITY

The inadequacies of compensation suggest some of the basic problems of Transcendantalism as a spirituality. Although it provided a context for a significant literary flowering, a platform for the budding intellectual life of Jacksonian America, and a witness to the importance of aesthetic appreciation and feeling in religion, it failed to provide a spirituality or an ideology capable of transforming large numbers of democratic persons into intuitive activists. Those Transcendentalists who became involved in reform followed the customary patterns of

American politics or dissent. While Transcendentalism spawned numerous experiments in community life, such as Brook Farm and Fruitlands, these experiments failed to survive. Hawthorne found the roots of these communal failures in Transcendentalism's inability to inspire self-sacrifice and cooperation. He saw an inherent aversion to society in Transcendentalism because society inevitably makes claims on its members which limit them to distinctive roles. By placing the source of ultimate authority in the individual's intuition Transcendentalism set the individual against the claims of tradition and society. Implying that the individual was to be his/her own redeemer Transcendentalism tended to justify an infantile imperial identity in which the world is seen as revolving around the subject. At its extreme this tendency suggested that the reliant self was possessed of the power to dispose of the whole felt and imagined world with its own consciousness. Such views are inherently incompatible with society or effective reform.[20]

Other contradictions limited Transcendentalism's appeal as a spirituality. It was unable to bridge the active and contemplative polarities of life. Margaret Fuller who as both a participant and a commentator on the Italian Revolution of 1848 came closest to the Transcendental ideal of critical activist achieved her synthesis in Europe, not in America. Emerson seemed more at home in contemplating action than in acting. Indeed, much of Transcendentalist activity possessed the character of a media event; the character of an activity soon to be turned into a lecture or essay. In the hands of the Transcendentalists the experience, consciousness, and action which they praised so highly seemed to function as raw material for a literary form where the variables of experience could be brought under the control of the mind. Again, the Transcendentalist's criticism of the particularity of traditional religions can be turned against them. Emerson's confession that compensation was true because it was better raises the question better for whom? Since it appears that most people throughout history, as well as most of Emerson's contemporaries (who flocked to revivals to "get religion"), preferred to believe in a personal God, in miracles, and merciful mediators, one wonders if the Transcendentalists were not guilty of seeking to present their preference and the insights of their experience as universal truths. Indeed, in this light Transcendentalism appears to be a particular form of enthusiasm— "the evangelism of the highbrows," as Richard Hofstadter once put it.[21]

In spite of these inadequacies and contradictions Transcendentalism was more than a tempest in a Boston teapot. Its greatest legacy lies in the questions it raised and the experiments it fostered rather than in any specific answer it proposed. As a movement of questioning and experiment it cogently addressed the spiritual problems of the self in modern democratic society. In grappling with religious traditions it proposed many of the directions which would be taken by the historic churches in their efforts to translate and renew their traditions. In addressing the question of the transient and permanent in religion Transcendentalists suggested approaches to the study and appreciation of the world religions which provided an impetus for their study. Its understanding that the nature of modern society demands a redefinition of the self which draws on a greater articulation of subjective feelings and intuition is now taken as commonplace truth. In proclaiming the presence of the divine in the self and in the universe the Transcendentalists encouraged some of their contemporaries to brave the path of introspection and reflection. In this respect they can be seen as the precursors of the psychological movement which would later sweep Western culture in a more sophisticated clinical form.

The Transcendentalists' message that faith in the self and the universe was justified by the presence of a moral divinity in both, places them in a long line of Western spiritual teachers. Although the Transcendentalists would have been scandalized to think that their insights were highly colored by the fads and fancies of Jacksonian America, the mind of the twentieth century, sensitive to that historical dimension which the Transcendentalists often tried to transcend, may regard their particularism as a sign of authenticity, and their spiritual insights as a valuable, though particular, contribution to the quest for viable spiritualities for the modern world.[22]

NOTES

1. Jean de Crèvecoeur, *Letters from an American Farmer*, in *The American Tradition in Literature*, ed. Sculley Bradley, Richmond Beatty, and E. Hudson Long, 4th ed., 2 vols. (Grosset and Dunlap, 1974), 1:184.

2. Alexis de Tocqueville, *Democracy in America*, trans. Henry Reeve, rev. Francis Bowen and Phillips Bradley, 2 vols. (Vintage Books, 1960), 2:106.

3. Richard D. Brown, *Modernization the Transformation of American Life 1600–1865* (Hill and Wang, 1976), pp. 9–18, 100–108; Michael Zuckerman, "The Fabrication of Identity in Early America," *William and Mary Quarterly*, ser 3, 34 (1977), 213–214.

4. The histories of Jacksonian America from which these impressions are drawn are: Lee Benson, *The Concept of Jacksonian Democracy: New York as a Test Case* (Atheneum, 1965); Marvin Myers, *The Jacksonian Persuasion: Politics and Belief* (Vintage Books, 1957); Arthur M. Schlessinger, Jr., *The Age of Jackson* (Little and Brown, 1945); Fred Somkin, *The Unquiet Eagle: Memory and Desire in the Idea of American Freedom 1815–1860* (Cornell University Press, 1967); Alice Felt Tyler, *Freedom's Ferment: Phases of American Social History from the Colonial Period to the Outbreak of the Civil War* (Harper Torchbooks, 1962); Glyndon G. Van Deusen, *The Jacksonian Era 1828–1848* (Harper and Brothers, 1959). For phrenology and mortality statistics respectively see Russel Blaine Nye, *Society and Culture in America 1830–1860* (Harper Torchbooks, 1974), pp. 334–336; 339–340. For a consideration of the relationship between American nativism and the anxieties resulting from cultural pluralism see John Higham, *Strangers in the Land: Patterns of American Nativism 1860–1925*, 2nd ed. (Atheneum, 1968), pp. 3–11.

5. *The Journals and Miscellaneous Notebooks of Ralph Waldo Emerson*, ed. William Gilman et al., 13 vols. (Cambridge: Har-

vard University Press, 1960 —-), 3:238. (In quoting Emerson's Journals I have omitted his cancelations and included his insertions. For the Transcendentalist's perception of the dark potential of freedom see Joel Porte, "Emerson, Thoreau and the Double Consciousness," *New England Quarterly* 41 (1968), 40–41, and Donald N. Koster, *Transcendentalism in America* (Twayne, 1975), p. 15.

6. For Emerson's struggle with despair see: Jonathan Bishop, *Emerson on the Soul* (Harvard University Press, 1964), pp. 165–176, 181, 187–202; Stephen Whicher, "Emerson's Tragic Sense," in *Emerson, A Collection of Critical Essays,* ed. Milton Konvitz and Stephen Whicher (Prentice-Hall, 1962), pp. 39–45. For Fuller see Ann Douglass, *The Feminization of American Culture* (Knopf, 1977), pp. 259–288. For Alcott see Paul Boller, Jr., *American Transcendentalism 1830–1860: An Intellectual Inquiry* (G. P. Putnam's Sons, 1974) p. 122. For Parker see Henry Steele Commager, *Theodore Parker Yankee Crusader* (Beacon Press, 1960), pp. 86–90. For Thoreau see Lawrence Buell, *Literary Transcendentalism: Style and Vision in the American Renaissance* (Cornell University Press, 1973), pp. 299–302. For Hawthorne and Melville see Charles Feidelson, Jr., *Symbolism and American Literature* (Phoenix, 1959), pp. 9–15, 211–212. For Dickinson see Glauco Cambon, "Emily Dickinson and the Crisis of Self-Reliance," in *Transcendentalism and Its Legacy,* ed. Myron Simon and Thornton H. Parsons (University of Michigan Press, 1966), p. 125.

7. Emerson, *Journals,* 3:318; *Memoirs of Margaret Fuller Ossoli,* ed., William H. Channing, J. F. Clarke, and Ralph W. Emerson, 2 vols. (Philips Sampson Co, 1852), 2:98; Henry Nash Smith, "Emerson's Problem of Vocation," in *Emerson,* p. 71.

8. Emerson, *Journals,* 3: 45; *Memoirs of Margaret Fuller Ossoli,* 1:310; Leo Marx, *The Machine in the Garden Technology and the Pastoral Ideal in America* (Oxford Press, 1964), pp. 178–179.

9. Theodore Parker, "Recollections of Boyhood," in *Theodore Parker: An Anthology,* ed. Henry Steele Commager (Boston: Beacon Press, 1960), p. 21; Emerson, "Self-Reliance," in *The American Tradition in Literature,* 1:1107–1128; William Clebsch, *American Religious Thought: A History* (University of Chicago Press, 1973), pp. 106–111.

10. *Memoirs of Margaret Fuller Ossoli,* 1:311.

11. Alcott [Orphic Saying] "xxxv, Nature," in *The Transcendentalists: An Anthology,* ed. Perry Miller (Cambridge: Harvard University Press, 1960), p. 311; Whitman, "Crossing Brooklyn Ferry," in *The American Tradition in Literature,* 1:1778; Emerson, "Nature," in ibid., 1:1043.

12. Emerson, "Self-Reliance," in ibid, 1:1117. For an example of Emerson's demythologization see "Compensation," in *The Works of Ralph Waldo Emerson* (Charles C. Bigelow and Co. [192?]), 1:70–72; for Theodore Parker see "The Transient and Permanent in Christianity," in *Theodore Parker: An Anthology,* pp. 38–62. I have borrowed the expression "critical self" from Professor Glebsch's masterful examination of Emerson in his *American Religious Thought.*

13. Parker, "Experience as a Minister," in *Theodore Parker: An Anthology,* p. 341; Fuller, *Memoirs,* 1:194.

14. Emerson, "Compensation," in *Works,* 1:68; Emerson, *Journals,* 3:79.

15. Emerson, "Compensation," in *Works,* 1:64 Robert Lee Francis, "The Architectionics of Emerson's Nature," *The American Quarterly* 19 (1967), 50; Kenneth Burke, "I, Eye, Ay— Emerson's Early Essay 'Nature:' Thoughts on the Machinery of Transcendence," in *Transcendentalism and Its Legacy,* p. 5.

16. See, for example, Emerson, *Journals,* 3:26, 45, 60, 68, 74, 77–79, 83.

17. For a summary of the criticism of the Transcendentalists see Koster, *Transcendentalism in America,* pp. 80–83; for Hawthorne's direct criticism see *The Blithedale Romance.*

18. "The Tragic," in *The Portable Emerson,* ed. Mark Van Doren (The Viking Press, 1946), p. 223.

19. Emerson, *Journal,* 3:317; Dickinson, J[ohnson number] 288, "I'm Nobody! Who are You?" in *The American Tradition in Literature,* 2:95. On the nature of faith see Wilfred Cantwell Smith, *The Meaning and End of Religion: A New Approach to the Religious Traditions of Mankind* (Mentor Books, 1964), pp. 154–173.

20. Bishop, *Emerson on the Soul,* p. 23; Quentin Anderson, *The Imperial Self: An Essay in American Literature and Cultural History* (Knopf, 1971), pp. 5, 56.

21. Ann Douglass, *The Feminization of American Culture,* pp.

283–288. For the activist-contemplative tension see Daniel B. Shea, "Emerson and the American Metamorphosis," in *English Institute Essays for 1975,* ed. David Levin (Columbia University Press, 1975), p. 49; Bishop, *Emerson on the Soul,* pp. 184–185. Richard Hofstadter, *Anti-intellectualism in American Life* (Vintage Books, 1962), p. 48.

22. Although most of the Transcendentalists were more humanistic than mystic as Patrick F. Quinn has demonstrated ("Emerson and Mysticism," *American Literature* 21 [1950], 397–414) there are similarities between the message of the Transcendentalists and such mystics and spiritual teachers as Hugh of St. Victor, St. Bonaventura, Meister Eckhart, Giordano Bruno, and Baruch Spinoza. The Platonic tradition is very evident in Transcendentalism. Indeed, Emerson's image of the naked eyeball was borrowed from Plotinus (Boller, *American Transcendentalism,* p. 85).

16

The Spirituality of Franz Rosenzweig

Ronald H. Miller

The picture is not easy to forget. A man in his early forties, propped up in his bed, paralyzed, a neck support fastened to the bedstead to keep his head from falling forward, the moustache and shock of dark hair, his piercing eyes looking out through rimless glasses at a world soon to be plunged into the blood-bath of World War I. Few philosophies are more intimately bound to flesh and bone than Franz Rosenzweig's. Few spiritual theologies flow more immediately from personal stories than his.

His Life and Times

Less austere pictures than the final one emerge from the album of his life. Cassell, Germany, and his family home—an imposing building perched on the edge of town. Above the town, the spacious and lovely Park Wilhelmshöhe; from there the young Rosenzweig could see the impressive castle, the Hercules monument and the expanse of his thousand-year old home city. He was the only child of an affluent and assimilated Jewish family, and the world stretching out before him seemed beautiful indeed.

After graduating from the Friedrichs-Gymnasium in 1905, he began his university career, studying at Germany's best academic centers in those halcyon days before World War I. Manifesting all of a nineteen-year-old's eagerness for the years to pass and a golden maturity to emerge, Rosenzweig wrote to his parents from college, "I wish I were a symphony of Beethoven, or something else that has been completely written. What hurts is the process of *being* written."[1] His youth spared him the realization that the process ends only when life does.

Göttingen, Freiburg, Munich, Leipzig, Berlin, medicine, history, music, literature, philosophy—a survivor of many universities and many examinations, Rosenzweig finished an impressive doctoral study of Hegel's political philosophy in 1912. But fiercer examinations were taking place in his soul and after a heart-wrenching conversation with a young teacher and friend, Rosenzweig abandoned the skepticism of his youth and opted for conversion to Christianity. He believed, however, that he should enter the Christian community as a Jew and not as a pagan, thus deciding to attend the autumn high holiday services before his baptism. And so it is that Yom Kippur of 1913 found him at a small orthodox synagogue in Berlin.

A turning point was reached—whether through a sudden illumination or a long churning of experience and self-knowledge.[2] He was twenty-seven when he wrote the friend he had chosen to be his godfather, " ... I have reversed my decision. It no longer seems necessary to me, and therefore, being what I am, no longer possible. I will remain a Jew."[3] He had earlier decided that Jesus was the way to the Father and this had been the basis of his choosing to convert to Christianity. But now he writes, "We are wholly agreed as to what Christ and his Church mean to the world: no one can reach the Father save through him. No one can reach the Father! But the situation is quite different for one who does not have to reach the Father because he is already with him. And this is true of the people of Israel (though not of individual Jews)."[4] Rosenzweig's decision, then, was not against Christianity. To the end of his life he maintained the conviction that Christianity is a true religion, an authentic spiritual path. But it was not to be his path. He would remain a Jew.

Other pictures follow in quick succession: an Unteroffizier in the Kaiser's army on the Balkan front where he began to write his monumental *Star of Redemption* on army stationery. After the war, we see him as the newly-wed husband of Edith Hahn and as a teacher of Judaism, eschewing university appointments to be the director of Frankfurt's Free House of Jewish Study. And shortly thereafter he appears as the proud father at the circumcision of his eight-day-old son, Raphael.

Raphael means "God heals" and it was a custom to give that name to a boy whose parent was seriously ill when the child was born. Rosenzweig had recently received the death-sentence diagnosis of a terminal paralysis. But life did not stop. There emerged the saint and sage of Frankfurt, transforming his sickbed into study and synagogue as he continued for six years as an indefatigable scholar. To the end, he was Rosenzweig the Jew, choosing life, even in the embrace of death. Martin Buber read a psalm when his forty-three-year-old friend and colleague was laid to rest and someone recalled a rainbow shimmering in the distance beyond the Jewish cemetery and the silently flowing Main river.

This was the man. His thought is intimately connected with his life, his spirituality with his story. It is the spiritual path which led him from agnosticism to observance and faith, from Hegelianism to his own philosophy of dialogue, from almost total assimilation in a Christian culture to an unshakeable realization of Jewishness. His way led him from the battlefields of World War I to a much more intense combat with disease and death. In this protracted struggle, his confidence grew that all his ways were in the hands of God. Carved large on his tombstone are the words of Psalm 73, words he chose, words addressed by the believer to his God: *ani tamid imcha,* "I am always with Thee."

His Spirituality

Where do we touch the spirituality of this man? The Hebrew word *halacha* comes from the root *holech,* meaning "to walk." *Halacha,* the 613 commandments of orthodox Judaism, is the

Jew's response to God's covenantal love. It is traditional Jewish spirituality. If God revealed a spiritual path to Israel in giving Torah, then what other spirituality could there be than walking that path through the observance of the prescribed commandments?

Immediately apparent here is the intimate connection between one's understanding of revelation and one's perspective on spirituality. The spiritual path one follows relates quite naturally to what one believes has been revealed. People who believe laws are the content of divine revelation find their spirituality in obedience to laws. Those who consider dogmas the prime constituents of revelation judge the authenticity of a spiritual path by its adherence to certain doctrinal formulations. But what if revelation has no content other than revelation? What if revelation is presence?

In a letter dated June 5, 1925, Rosenzweig wrote to his friend Buber, "Revelation is certainly not lawgiving. It is only this: revelation. The primary content of revelation is revelation itself. 'He came down' (on Sinai)—this already concludes the revelation; 'He spoke' is the beginning of interpretation."[5] This represents a radical stance on revelation. No human articulation—neither Torah nor *halacha*—can be identified with revelation. They are interpretations, legitimate interpretations, but interpretations nonetheless.

This step catapults Rosenzweig from the secure world of objective religiosity to the careening and challenging currents of subjective religious reality, an experienced and existential spiritual dynamic. Copernicus pulled the solid earth from under our feet by hypothesizing the movement of our planet. Kant alluded to this paradigmatic shift of perspective in his own epistemological reversal based on his conviction that our concepts do not conform to reality but what we call reality has already conformed to our conceptualization.[6] It is this same kind of change of viewpoint which is introduced to religion when it is recognized that there is no knowledge in theology which is not somehow grounded in human experience. In other words, what comes first is not *halacha* or even *Torah* (in Judaism) or creed (in Christianity) but the encounters of men and women with the revealing presence we call God.

This changed perspective—whether in science, philosophy, or religion—often proves initially disconcerting and unsettling. Comfort of a sort lies in the triple illusion of *terra firma,* a known reality not affected by our knowing it and a knowledge of God untouched by the human channels communicating it. But all is not lost when this security is relinquished. On the contrary, an immensely richer universe emerges with the realization that our planet participates in the ongoing mystery of the physical universe, that our knowing processes shape our experienced reality, that our religious language is inadequate to the mystery it so falteringly interprets. It is liberating to acknowledge with Tillich that God is after all the symbol of God.[7]

Rosenzweig is criticized for his unabashedly subjective perspective on religion, though he never loses his historical rootedness in the Jewish experience stretching from the Exodus/Sinai events forward. Gershom Scholem argues that this view of revelation "necessarily destroys its authoritative character." He also expresses the fear that there is "no great distance from such a subjective conception, which transfers revelation into the human heart, to a secular-humanist conception." And he accuses both Buber and Rosenzweig of fundamentally acknowledging only one kind of revelation—the mystical one.[8]

Rosenzweig might well plead guilty to all three charges. Religious authority deserves to be destroyed whenever it becomes idolatrous, i.e., whenever it identifies itself with the ultimate mystery of God. Secondly, revealed religion and the secular-humanist conception are more connected than most people are willing to admit. In 1921, Rosenzweig wrote to a friend, "The Bible is different from all other books. You can know what is in other books only by reading them. But there are two ways of knowing what is in the Bible: first, by listening to what the Bible says; second, by listening to the beating of the human heart. . . . *The Bible and the heart say the same thing.*"[9] And, finally, although they both would have been loathe to use the term, Buber and Rosenzweig do have a mystical theology of revelation. For the mystical phenomenon is their paradigm of primary, subjective, revelatory experience. And the universality of mysticism is but another indication that the mystery of divine presence in the world is deeper than the diversities of religious interpretation. diversities of religious interpretation.

The subject should not be forgotten, whether in science, philosophy, or theology—and most certainly not in spirituality. The central focus of spiritual theology is precisely the path the subject walks in response to the revealing mystery of God. Personal religious experience is not an addendum for a theological appendix or footnote. It is the beginning, the source of what we call religion. A human being experiences ultimate reality. Let us call this experience *a*. She assures us that *b, c,* and *d* are facilitative of this divine encounter. Her disciples observe that *e, f,* and *g* are helpful aids in preparing for *b, c,* and *d*. And then some four hundred years later, adherents of the movement are asking why they are supposed to be doing *u, v,* and *w*—and no one remembers.[10] Reestablishing the links, building the bridge back to *a*, this is the nature of all religious reform, all renewal of religious traditions, and of Rosenzweig's thought in particular.

This radicalization of religion revolves for Rosenzweig around three key terms: *Gesetz, Gebot,* and *Heutigkeit*. "Law (*Gesetz*) must again become commandment (*Gebot*) which seeks to be transformed into deed at the very moment it is heard. It must regain that living reality (*Heutigkeit*) in which all great Jewish periods have sensed the guarantee for its eternity. Like teaching, it must consciously start where its content stops being content and becomes inner power, our own inner power."[11] Authentic spirituality must be a reality *today* (*heute,* the root of *Heutigkeit*). Laws are general prescriptions applying to strangers as well as children of the house. But commandments are in the second person singular—"thou shalt" or "thou shalt not." And this is the pronoun of intimacy, the German *du*. In comandments, heart speaks to heart.

This, then, becomes the essential project of spirituality for the Jew. Not the choice of total fulfillment of the 613 commandments or total avoidance of them. The "love it or leave it" policy shows itself to be as simplistic in spirituality as it is in politics. Religious reality must be the experiencing today of the inner power of the divine. And, therefore, it is not a matter of doing everything but of doing something where that something can be real. "Therefore, whether much is done, or little, or maybe nothing at all, is immaterial in the face of the one and unavoidable demand, that whatever is being done, shall come from that inner power. As the knowledge of everything knowable is not yet wisdom, so the doing of everything do-able is not yet deed. The deed is created at the boundary of the merely do-able, where the voice of commandment causes the spark to leap from 'I must' to 'I can.' The Law is built on such commandments, but only on them."[12] Rosenzweig's analogy is telling. The gap between mere knowledge and wisdom is not less than that between mere religious observance and spirituality.

And yet, just as knowing something can open the door to wisdom, so the storehouse of Jewish observance can be the beginning of spirituality. The Jew seeking spiritual growth must choose something she can do, something flowing from her reality—lighting Sabbath candles, studying Torah, praying the psalms. It is not the quantity of do-able things which is significant but the quality of expectation and readiness. Readiness for what? In a letter to his mother, Rosenzweig wrote, "It does not at all depend on whether one 'believes' in the 'dear Lord' but only on whether or not one opens his five senses and sees the facts— but alert to the dangerous possibility that the dear Lord might appear right there."[13] The beginning of spirituality lies in doing whatever is at hand to do but with a readiness for meeting God.

Every moment contains the possibility of encountering the divine. Isn't that the meaning of what Buber writes about his own sense of religion? "I have given up the 'religious' which is nothing but the exception, extraction, exaltation, ecstasy; or it has given me up. I possess nothing but the everyday out of which

I am never taken. The mystery is no longer disclosed, it has escaped or it has made its dwelling here where everything happens as it happens. . . . I do not know much more. If that is religion then it is just *everything*, simply all that is lived in its possibility of dialogue."[14] Reality's ultimate presence may break through in any moment of any day. The beginning of spirituality is attentiveness. As Rosenzweig himself wrote, "The highest things cannot be planned; for them, readiness is everything."[15]

Barred from this perspective is every form of cramped and crabbed religious absolutism. Yes, this is a Jewish spirituality, with its own identity and authenticity. But it breathes the humility and openness of the deepest spiritual teachings in all the great world traditions. In a striking passage, Rosenzweig sees far beyond the two traditions of Judaism and Christianity which he knew best: "Did God wait for Mount Sinai or, perhaps, Golgotha? No paths that lead from Sinai and Golgotha are guaranteed to lead to him, but neither can he possibly have failed to come to one who sought him on the trails skirting Olympus. There is no temple built so close to him as to give man reassurance in its closeness, and none is so far from him as to make it too difficult for man's hand to reach. There is no direction from which it would not be possible for him to come, and none from which he must come; no block of wood in which he may not once take up his dwelling, and no psalm of David that will always reach his ear."[16] On his own path Rosenzweig walks with confidence, never needing the false security of feeling that his way is the only one.

Attentiveness, readiness, expectancy—these are no less important for the privileged channels of religious tradition than for the everyday moment with all its possibilities. Rosenzweig's mature life was spent close to the text of the Bible. He was collaborating with Buber on the monumental task of translating the Hebrew Bible into German at the time of his death. But he never makes an idol of the Bible; he approaches it with the same sense of expectancy so central to his spirituality: "As a searchlight detaches from darkness now one section of the landscape and now another, and then leaves these again dimmed, so for such a man the days of his own life illumine the Scriptures, and in their quality of humanness permit him to recognize what is more than human, today at one point and tomorrow at another. . . . This humanness may anywhere become so translucid under the beam of a day of one's life, that it stands suddenly written in his innermost heart; and the divine in human inscription becomes as clear and actual to him for that one pulse beat as if—at that instant—he heard a voice calling to his heart. Not everything in the Scripture belongs to him—neither today nor ever. But he knows that he belongs to everything in them, and it is only this readiness of his which, when directed towards the Scriptures, constitutes belief."[17] With the Bible as with life, readiness is everything.

A Dialogue of Love

What, then, results from this spirituality? The kind of person whom Rosenzweig calls "the beloved soul." Like many mystics before him, Rosenzweig finds the paradigm of the beloved soul in the *Song of Songs*. For many scripture scholars it is a matter of some embarrassment that the *Song of Songs* was ever included in the Bible. So it is not without some surprise that one reads in Rosenzweig, "We have recognized the *Song of Songs* as the focal book of revelation."[18] For revelation is a dialogue of love, not a content. And spiritual growth means learning to be a lover.

In the opening chapters of the *Song of Songs* we find a progression paralleling Rosenzweig's understanding of revelation and spiritual maturation. This can be traced in the opening cry of the beloved for her lover and the response of the lover to her pleading: "O that you would kiss me with the kisses of your mouth! For your love is better than wine, your anointing oils are fragrant, your name is oil poured out. . . . "[19] Our attention here is directed to the kiss, the mouth, and the word.

Two triangles, placed on top of each other and pointing in opposite directions, make up the six-pointed Star of David.

Rosenzweig speaks of the human face as an analogous config-uration.[20] The first triangle is formed by the forehead (to which belongs the nose) and the cheeks (to which belong the ears). This upward pointing triangle is the structure of the receptive or-gans: the nose inhaling the fragrance and the ears receiving the sound. A second triangle, superimposed on this first one, is formed by the two eyes and the mouth. This downward pointing triangle constitutes the active organs of the face: the eyes shining with the communicative power which is then given a twofold expression in the spoken words of love and the kiss. The star, the face—both are models of Rosenzweig's spirituality. For the first triangle is readiness; the second, response.

Returning now to the lines of the text, we note that the beloved knows the name of her lover and she is asking now for the kiss of his mouth. He who has already heard her voice (the passive triangle of his countenance) is asked now to see her and kiss her (the active triangle). And yet, he is already her lover, and there-fore, we can presume that he has been active towards her before. To understand this is to comprehend the basic rhythm of spirituality, how it is a matter of relationship and not simple existence or knowledge, how it is both a word and a kiss, how it is both a plea and an acceptance, how it rediscovers in the present the love which was already there in the past, but how there really is a new love in the present, in this "today."

The words of the lover in the second chapter constitute a song of love and springtime. Springtime is the season of revelation, because the prophecy contained in the winter existence of na-ture is fulfilled in the second creation or revelation of spring: "Arise, my love, my fair one, and come away; for lo, the winter is past, the rain is over and gone. The flowers appear on the earth, the time of singing has come, and the voice of the turtledove is heard in our land. The fig tree puts forth its figs, and the vines are in blossom; they give forth fragrance. Arise, my love, my fair one, and come away. O my dove, in the clefts of the rock, in the covert of the cliff, let me see your face, let me hear your voice."[21] The soul is called to spiritual maturity; she now becomes the beloved soul.

The lover speaks in imperatives. The command is a calling forth of the beloved. The winter of enclosedness is past; now is the time for the brightness of sunshine, the budding of flowers, and the song of birds. The lover wants to see the face of his beloved and hear her voice. He compares her to a dove hidden in the clefts of the rock, an image which calls to mind Rosenzweig's statement that, "It is only, after all, in the love of God that the flower of the soul begins to grow out of the rock of the self."[22] This is the condition of spiritual growth—the beloved's enclosedness must open so that she can see and speak and become a living soul.

In the context of this dialogue of love, we are at the heart of Rosenzweig's spirituality. He sees the analogy of love as central; in fact, it is more the substance itself than an analogy. "Thus it is not enough that God's relationship to man is explained by the simile of the lover and the beloved. God's word must contain the relationship of love to beloved directly. . . . And so we find it in the *Song of Songs*. Here it is no longer possible to see in that simile 'only a simile.' Here the reader seems to be confronted by the choice either to accept the 'purely human,' purely sensual sense and then, admittedly, to ask himself what strange error allowed these pages to slip into God's word, or to acknowledge that the deeper meaning lodges here, precisely in the purely sensual sense, directly and not 'merely' in simile."[23] Spirituality is not spoken *about* in the *Song of Songs;* it is spoken.

God's presence re-creates the human partner in dialogue. Warmed by God's love, the mute self comes of age as eloquent soul.[24] It is only now that she finds the strength to exist in the face of death. It is only the beloved soul, called from muteness to eloquence, who can sing: "Set me as a seal upon your heart, as a seal upon your arm; for love is strong as death, jealousy is cruel as the grave. Its flashes are flashes of fire, a most vehement flame. Many waters cannot quench love, neither can floods drown it."[25] God's loving initiative wakens something in creation as strong as death. This new creation is the beloved soul—what Rosenzweig calls "the unearthly in earthly life."[26]

In Rosenzweig's spiritual dynamic, not only does the human

person come alive in a new way—no longer merely the recepta-
cle for a "deposit of faith" or a statistic of halachic observance—
but God too emerges from dusty objectivity. Rosenzweig avers
that "Divine love does not, like light, radiate in all directions as
an essential attitude. Rather it transfixes individuals—men, nations, epochs, things—in an enigmatic transfixion."[27] God's love
has an infinity of time in which to meet his creation and re-create
it through the disclosure of himself as lover. God is much more
the lover in pursuit of the beloved than a static essence of First
Cause. That is why prayer, not knowledge, is the final
touchstone of spirituality: "Prayer is the last thing achieved by
revelation . . . to be able to pray: that is the greatest gift presented to the soul in revelation."[28]

It is only after the calling into being of the beloved soul that we
can really speak of the doing of God's will. As Rosenzweig writes:
"God's first word to the soul that unlocks itself to him is 'Love
me!' and everything which he may yet reveal to the soul in the
form of law, therefore, without more ado turns into words which
he commands *today*."[29] Readiness allows the soul to respond.
Response brings her to spiritual and personal maturity. Maturity
enables the beloved soul to live and to love profoundly, to find
the "dearest freshness deep down things" today and to love others towards that tomorrow which is God's future and promise.

NOTES

1. Nahum N. Glatzer, *Franz Rosenzweig: His Life and Thought*
(Schocken, 1953), p. 3. This is the best introduction to
Rosenzweig. Henceforth referred to as FR.

2. There are two viewpoints on this. Glatzer (p. xviii in the
introduction to FR), basing his view on communications with
Rosenzweig's mother, understands the Yom Kippur event as a
sudden illumination. Rosenzweig's wife, whom I spoke with in
Berlin in March of 1976, sees the whole process as a gradual one.
Given the interplay of conscious and unconscious movements in
any major decision, both views may be correct from differing
perspectives.

3. FR, p. 28.

4. FR, p. 341.

5. Franz Rosenzweig, *On Jewish Learning*, ed. N. N. Glatzer (Schocken, 1965), p. 118. Henceforth referred to as JL.

6. Immanuel Kant, *Critique of Pure Reason*, trans. Norman Kemp Smith (London: Macmillan, 1964), p. 22.

7. Paul Tillich, *Dynamics of Faith* (Harper & Row, 1958), p. 46.

8. Gershom Scholem, "Jewish Theology Today," *The Center Magazine*, March/April 1974, pp. 62f., 63.

9. Franz Rosenzweig, *Briefe* (Berlin: Schocken, 1935), p. 402. Translation my own. Henceforth referred to as BR.

10. I heard this alphabet analogy in an impressive lecture delivered by Quentin Quesnell in St. Marys, Kansas sometime in 1966.

11. JL, p. 85.

12. Ibid., p. 86.

13. BR, p. 406. Translation my own. "Dear Lord" seemed to be the only idiomatic equivalent of "lieber Gott."

14. Martin Buber, *Between Man and Man*, trans. Ronald Gregor Smith (Macmillan, 1966), p. 14.

15. JL, p. 65.

16. FR, p. 202.

17. Ibid., p. 258.

18. Franz Rosenzweig, *Star of Redemption*, trans. W. W. Hallo (Beacon Press, 1964), p. 202. Henceforth referred to as *Star*.

19. *Song of Songs* 1:2-3a.

20. *Star*, pp. 422-3.

21. *Song of Songs* 2:10-14.

22. *Star*, p. 169.

23. Ibid., p. 199.

24. Ibid., p. 198.

25. *Song of Songs* 8:6-7.

26. *Star*, p. 326.

27. Ibid., p. 164.

28. Ibid., p. 184.

29. Ibid., p. 177.

17

Mysticism, Protestantism, and Ecumenism: The Spiritual Theology of William Ernest Hocking

Richard Woods, OP

Few Americans have written so extensively or so profoundly of spirituality and its ecumenical implications as William Ernest Hocking. Born in Cleveland in 1873 and reared in Illinois and Iowa, Hocking was above all American in his themes and approach. But he was also keenly aware from his studies abroad of the importance of continental thought. In his mid-years, he also traveled extensively in the Orient. His career as a professor of philosophy took him from Berkeley to Yale and then to Harvard where he held the Alford Chair from 1920 to 1943. He retired at that time to Madison, New Hampshire, where he died in 1966, just prior to his ninety-third birthday.

A Methodist in his youth, Hocking attended the Congregational church throughout most of his active life. But he also considered himself a member of "the Catholic church of the future."[1] His importance today with regard to ecumenical spirituality lies, I believe, in his highly original yet deeply traditional sensitivity to the mystical element in all religions. Here he found the basis for a coming "world faith." But as he began his career as a religious thinker, the value of mysticism was by no means an indisputable question. Many of his views earned him the heated opposition of the dominant theologians of the day.

The Recovery of Mysticism

Following the controversies and condemnations concerning Quietism at the end of the seventeenth century, Catholic spiritual writers began to distinguish sharply between the "ordinary" life of the Christian and the "extraordinary" stages of mystical experience with its special graces, odd phenomena, etc.[2] Similarly, under Calvinist and later Lutheran influence, Protestant theologians had already all but stifled the mystical element of religion in England, Germany, and the Low Countries.[3] Despite the protests of many great mystics and theologians, the tendency to reduce mysticism to the quaint, odd, or pathological and thereby to the irrelevant periphery of ordinary Christian life continued both to sunder Catholic "ascetical" and "mystical" theology and also to pit Protestants against each other regarding mysticism versus prophecy well into the twentieth century. At that time, the work of Catholic and Protestant mystics (and scholars) began to reverse the trend.

The Historical Context: Prophecy and Mysticism

Hocking's attempt to formulate a theory of mysticism consonant with the American philosophical tradition involved him in an effort to undercut a prevalent view in America and Europe which held mysticism to be opposed in principle to the socially-active, prophetic character of Christianity. Hocking's thesis, and the occasion of his clashes with neo-orthodox theologians, affirmed the dynamic identity of mysticism and prophecy, which represented the theological equivalent of asserting that the meaning and structure of mystical experience were radically social. For in the late nineteenth century, the idea of prophecy was closely identified in Protestant thought with social activism and reform. This understanding was characteristic, for instance, of the "Social Gospel" as set forth by Walter Rauschenbusch, a disciple of Ritschl and Troeltsch, and refined by Reinhold and H. Richard Neibuhr.[4] It was no less associated with the neo-orthodox movement inaugurated by Karl Barth and continued by Emil Brünner and Hendrick Kraemer, the latter's *Christian Faith in a Non-Christian World* (1938) being directed squarely against Hocking.[5]

The fundamental opposition between the prophetic character of Christianity and mysticism, according to the neo-orthodox point of view, entails an essential conflict between the historical, contingent, this-worldly but ultimately transcultural nature of the Christian mission and the timeless, absolute, other-worldly, and hellenistic nature attributed to mystical religion.[6] With regard to social reform, this opposition is expressed as a tension between involvement and escape. With regard to faith and salvation, however, prophetic action was held to rely chiefly on grace, whereas mystical quietism represented a subtle dependence on a form of "works," being a merely human endeavor to reach God.

Hocking's contention that mysticism and prophetic action can be reconciled, being in effect complementary stages of a unified process, thus involved him in a head-on collision with some of the most influential theologians of his time.

Against the "Protestant" view that mysticism is radically anti-social, a privatized form of pseudo-religion based on a flight from the real world to the untroubled recesses of "inner experience," Hocking contended that all authentic human experience, including mystical experience, is not only radically intersubjective but also inevitably social in expression. Against the recent "Catholic" position that mystical experience is essentially extraordinary, differing from ordinary experience in kind rather than degree, being characteristic of a few elite souls called to a life of religious perfection denied the majority of mankind, Hocking claimed that God was a direct and immediate factor in all human experience and, as a consequence, that all human persons were at least latent mystics.

Hocking answered the first objection by incorporating it into his dialectic of experience, showing that social withdrawal was but a preliminary, negative phase of the mystic's fuller involvement in society. He met the second by acknowledging that while religious genius was rare, the accomplishments of the saints presupposed a foundation common to all men. If not everyone in fact reached the heights of mystical development, all were nevertheless capable of reaching as much fullness as they desired and sincerely strove for. In effect, Hocking not only enlarged the scope of mysticism temporally, he extended it socially. In thus democratizing mysticism, Hocking not only reclaimed the venerable tradition of classical Christianity, but in some respects anticipated the contributions of later exponents of mysticism.

Hocking's writings on mysticism thus did not appear in a neutral setting, but one charged with deeply felt issues and lively debate. How Hocking responded to this situation, coming to it already convinced of the fundamental "rightness" of the mystic's vision, can best be seen in terms of his own development as a philosopher of religion and, in fact, a mystic.

Hocking's Dialectical Development

From the relatively scant information available concerning Hocking's childhood, it seems clear enough that his religious experience began at a very early age.[7] His parents were devout Methodists, and young Ernest grew up in a household permeated by a strong sense of faith and duty. Rouner recounts a crucial "conversion experience" at a prayer meeting when Hocking was twelve, quoting Hocking's remembrance of the event seventy-three years later:

> Hocking did not long remember what the evangelist said in his sermon, nor was he very much aware at the time. But there was, he said, "a presence felt, a reality perceived" which was beyond the details of the service and including them. When the call came to "come down and be saved," this boy of twelve—tears streaming down his face—suddenly saw things "in a new light." He saw "the real" in a way which "combined a new resolve with a new insight." He saw himself as part of a "great procession of humanity in which each man had an im-

mortal soul." He had a vision, as he puts it, of "men like souls walking."[8]

Hocking was possessed thereafter of what he later identified as the "mystic's sense of the universe." This view was severely shaken, however, when Hocking came into contact with the writings of Herbert Spencer a year later.[9] Several years of disillusionment followed, during which, however, he experienced another "mystical" insight. Hocking's powerful description of this episode not only illustrates his own experience but also represents the almost prosaic *kind* of ordinary life-events that are the stuff of mysticism:

> The time is 1892, more or less. The scene is the right-of-way of a single track railroad, between Aurora, Illinois, and Waukegan.... It is a summer day. A lone figure carrying a pot of white paint and a brush, stoops every 100 feet to cover a chalk mark on the inside of a rail with a vertical line of paint, and every 500 feet to paint a number. The crew of the civil engineering department are measuring the track of the railway for inventory purposes. The chalk markers, with the steel tape, have moved ahead of the painter, who doesn't mind being alone. He has become interested in the numbers.
> ... The painter is painting the number 1800. He is amused to note the possibility of putting this number series into one-to-one correspondence with the years of the century. He begins to supply the numbers with events, at first bits of history—Civil War and family background. This imaginary living-through-past-time becomes as real an experience as the rail-painting, and far more exciting! 1865, 1870—suddenly 1873, my birth year.... Every mark, from now on, numbered or not, is entangled with personal history. But very soon, 1892, *the present:* the painter's story and the actual story coincide: I paint the Now! From this point, memory is dismissed; it gives place to anticipation, dream, conjecture—there is something relentless in the onmoving of these numbers, to be filled with something—but with what? 1893.... 1900.... 1950, fairly old, very likely gone. 1973, a hundred years from

birth—surely gone. . . . I see myself as dead, the nothingness of nonbeing sweeps over me. . . . For the first time I realize, beyond the mere clack of words, the blankness of annihilation. And no doubt, just because of this swift sense of no-sense, the shock was intense as I realized, with the same swiftness, that *it was I, as surviving,* who looked upon myself as dead, that it had to be so, and that because of this, annihilation can be spoken of, but *never truly imagined.* This was not enough to free me from the spell of Spencer, but it cracked that spell: the rest of the day was spent in a new lightness of heart, as I had come upon a truth that was not to leave me.[10]

This crack in Spencer's spell was subsequently widened and Hocking's youthful confidence in the mystical vision of the world was restored by his reading William James' *Principles of Psychology* while an engineering student at Iowa State College in 1894, when he was twenty-one. Hocking later related that from that moment.

I began to regain confidence that the mystic's sense of the universe is in substance a true sense, quite apart from his theological symbols. I was sure that the real world is more like the world of James' imagination than like that of Spencer's, and from that time it became my first business to define the difference and to capture some rational account of it (SSP, 388).

Hocking was so impressed by James that he resolved to go to Harvard. Once there, however, he found not James, who was in Scotland for his Gifford Lectures, but rather Josiah Royce, whose critical-skeptical interest in mysticism stimulated the young Hocking's imagination further. But James' return to Harvard in 1903, the manuscript of *The Varieties of Religious Experience* in hand, provided the occasion for Hocking to pass beyond the critique of theoretical mysticism inspired by Royce. Having begun to realize that the active non-ego of our experience must also be a self, he recognized in it "the Absolute of

Royce's teaching. But I also recognized it as the object of that mystic experience whose significance James had begun to do justice to" (SSP, 392).

It was thus in reconceiving mysticism that Hocking began to reconcile the elements of James' and Royce's antipodal philosophies, creating in the process an original interpretation, indeed a mystical philosophy of human experience.

The most influential event of Hocking's early career was his marriage to Agnes Boyle O'Reilly in 1905. Not only did Hocking dedicate his magnum opus, *The Meaning of God in Human Experience*, to her, "an unfailing source of insight," she was in no small way responsible for much of its content and eventual "shape." Even more fundamentally, in their love Hocking realized the truth of his most important insight—that the isolation of individual from individual is an illusion. All experience is, rather, intersubjective from the beginning, or "social" as Hocking described it in 1912:

> I have sometimes sat looking at a comrade, speculating on this mysterious isolation of self from self. Why are we so made that I gaze and see of thee only thy Wall, and never Thee? This Wall of thee is but a movable part of the Wall of my world; and I also am a Wall to thee: we look out at one another from behind masks. How would it seem if my mind could but once be *within* thine; and we could meet and without barrier be with each other? And then it has fallen upon me like a shock—as when one thinking himself alone has felt a presence—but I am in thy soul. These things around me are in thy experience. They are thy own; when I touch them and move them I change *thee*. When I look on them I see what thou seest; when I listen, I hear what thou hearest. I am in the great Room of thy soul; and I experience thy very experience. For *where art thou?* Not there, behind those eyes, within that head, in darkness, fraternizing with chemical processes. Of these, in my own case, I know nothing, and will know nothing; for my existence is spent not behind my Wall, but in front of it. I am there, where I have treasures. And there art thou, also. This world in which

I live, is the world of thy soul: and being within that, I am within thee. I can image no contact more real and thrilling than this: that we should meet and share identity, not through ineffable inner depths (alone), but here through the foregrounds of common experience; and that thou shouldst be—not behind that mask—but *here,* pressing with all thy consciousness upon me, *containing* me, and these things of mine. This is reality: and having seen it thus, I can never again be frightened into monadism by reflections which have strayed from their guiding insight.[11]

As Rouner relates, the "comrade" whom Hocking was addressing was Agnes herself (WHE 44). In regard to his love for her and its impact on his philosophy, we find here perhaps the finest illustration of Hocking's reliance on his own experience with its assumed resonances in the common experience of "everyman." Such love is preeminently a paradigm as well as a source of ordinary mystical experience.

When his magnum opus was published, Hocking was an assistant professor at Yale, having moved there in 1908 from the University of California at Berkeley where he had taken a position two years earlier. In 1914 he was called back to Harvard. During the First World War, he saw active duty as a military engineer. On his return, he was appointed Alford Professor of Natural Religion, Moral Philosophy, and Civil Polity in 1920. Between then and 1940, he produced eight major books and over sixty articles and reviews. In 1930, he and Agnes were appointed to the Laymen's Foreign Mission Inquiry, an investigating committee representing seven Protestant denominations concerned about the state of their foreign missions.

As chairman of the group, Hocking was enabled thereby to travel widely in the Orient, broadening his understanding of Eastern religions and the possibilities of ecumenical relations. The report which resulted from this investigation, *Re-thinking Missions,* involved Hocking and other members of the group in long and bitter controversies with neo-orthodox theologians. Not the least factor in the conflict was Hocking's manifest influence on the final report.[12] One of the less controversial if far-sighted recommendations entailed "a serious inquiry into the religious value of meditation, and a study of the ways in which a further place for his function can be brought into the Christian church. . . . "[13]

At this time, Hocking's attention began to widen from a preoccupation with religion to include social, legal, and political issues.[14] But his involvement with the missions controversy awakened him further to the promise of ecumenism among Christian denominations as well as among different faiths. This in turn enabled him to reconceive the role of the mystic as a harbinger of religious unity on a world scale, a theme that would become dominant in the writings of his later years.

In 1936, Hocking was honored with appointments to several lectureships which, in effect, crowned his academic career. The first of these was the Hibbert Lectures at Oxford and Cambridge, later published as *Living Religions and a World Faith,* his ecumenical ground-plan. In the same year, he also delivered the Ingersoll Lectures at Harvard and the Thomas Lectures at the University of Chicago, published together in 1937 as *Thoughts on Life and Death* (revised and augmented in 1957 as *The Meaning of Immortality in Human Experience*). In 1938, Hocking was invited to present the prestigious Gifford Lectures at the University of Glasgow, perhaps his greatest honor in the field of religious studies. While never published in book form, these lectures, *Fact and Destiny,* provided material for reflection which occupied Hocking until his death—including his first insight into the self as a "field of fields," the central concern of his mature metaphysics.

When Hocking returned from Scotland, he was then sixty-five and due to retire from Harvard. He was, however, invited by President Conant to continue teaching for an additional five years. After his actual retirement in 1943, Hocking enjoyed several guest professorships and an occasional lecture. His writing continued unabated.

The Second World War created a critical period in Hocking's life. Not only did the outbreak of war in 1939 disrupt his plans to publish *Fact and Destiny*. It significantly altered his outlook on world problems, deepening his understanding of the creative potential of suffering in the emergence of any future world community united in its shared experience of God's silent presence. The war also provided the occasion for his third major mystical experience, which he related years later in the preface to *The Meaning of Immortality in Human Experience*.

He had been lecturing on metaphysics at Harvard during the autumn of 1941. The war was much on his mind. One evening as he walked along the Charles River, "It was though for a moment Nature were holding still—caught in a spell of quiet and tense glory, unwilling to fade" (MIHE, xivf.). In the following passage, he described his sudden insight into a "truth about the world, as well as about the self,"[15] again providing a paradigm of a mystical experience mediated by space as before it had been occasioned by a perception of time:

> Here was quiescence—no seminar, no discussion, no labor of categories, also no war. Time had stopped, and the world was now drenched in unmoving space. Space was endless; it was *my* space, running out far beyond the solitary evening star; running also through the earth, and out the other side. There were armies at night, minds full of battle-plans for tomorrow's action. Was it truly the same space? Could that space, crowded with fighters' strategies, be the same as my space, spellbound in peace?
>
> Yes, it must be the identical space; it is the same world for all of us. Yet it cannot be the same. For no one else saw the world I saw; if I had not happened along, that marvel of a sky-moment might have passed unknown. It was certainly not known to itself, was it? Those colors, lights, shadows, shapes, could exist only for a creature with eyes, stationed at or near where I was standing (MIHE, xv).

Falling back on the idea of plural spaces about which he had theorized as early as 1912, Hocking was able to organize the elements of an actual experience of plural spaces into a new insight. He continued,

> Our various spaces, all infinite, must be and cannot be identical. The answer? *Space is not single, but plural.* There is a world-space, identical for all included persons. But for each one, there is also a private space, perhaps spaces, holding private responses to qualities, holding also futurities, not yet existent—plans, battle-plans perhaps, plans that can be detained, modified, canceled, as events in the identical world-space cannot be.
>
> Space must have a plural—this we were saying in the seminar. And more than this, each person envisages plural spaces. Then, *the position of the person,* the self, toward this his plurality, how shall we describe it? Each space can be called a "field," a continuum on which infinite positions, potentials, etc., can be distinguished and held-together. Could the self, as envisaging plural fields, be a *field of fields?* (MIHE, xv).

Out of that experience came a new assurance in the reality of human freedom, immortality, and God—an assurance not the result of an inference, but a conviction based on immediate experience. But commenting on the significance of this and similar episodes, insofar as they are in some sense extraordinary, Hocking noted, years later, that

> The function of unusual experiences is, as a rule, not so much to answer questions as to open them. They stir us out of our habitual assumptions. They may illuminate; but the final answers must be in the common experiences of mankind—this has become my firm conviction. If there is any truth in "mystic experience," it is what every man subconsciously knows, and what thought can eventually validate (MIHE, 216).

In these events in Hocking's life, from which we may safely infer his own mystical sensitivities, it is possible to detect concrete elements which provided the basis for his more analytical articulation of mystical experience.

Hocking's Concept of Mystical Experience

As developed over a lifetime of reflective analysis, mystical experience consisted for Hocking in a direct and immediate apprehension of the presence of God mediated by one's own psychic objects, nature, and society. In other words, it was an explicit awareness of God as the Field grounding the elements of what Hocking called "nuclear experience"—the structural interrelatedness of "I, It, and Thou." As the cultivation of mystical experience, mysticism—the "practice of union with God, together with the theory of that practice"[16]—constituted for him a practical development of this awareness of this Field of all experience in terms of the realities of everyday life.

Hocking held that mystical experience itself had two phases—first, a primordial, constant but subliminal experience of God's presence underlying our nuclear experience of self, nature, and society and, second, the explicitation of that presence in moments of feeling-charged insight, whether as spontaneous occurrences or in the form of deliberate shifts of attention from the objects of daily experience to their ground in the world as a whole, conceived of as a medium of the divine presence. These moments range in explicitness from a simple awareness of the underlying unity of the world to a more or less continual and intense consciousness of union with God.

Hocking also held that developed mysticism as the cultivated practice of such explicit consciousness always tends to find expression in social action. Hence, mysticism was structually also a temporally dynamic process alternating between the inward pole of God-consciousness and the outward pole of prophetic activity. For Hocking, mysticism was thus essentially dialectical, manifesting itself processively in action and reflection according to the fundamental principle he called the "law of alternation." The prophet is the mystic in action; the mystic is the prophet in reflection and worship.[17]

In terms of spirituality and ecumenism, Hocking's teaching on mysticism and prophecy from two of his later works are of particular importance—"The Mystical Spirit"[18] (1944) and *The Coming World Civilization*[19] (1956).

"The Mystical Spirit"

This article, the most direct treatment Hocking accorded mysticism at this period, appeared, significantly, in a symposium entitled *Protestantism* in which he took the occasion to parry some of the chief objections to his position. He did this chiefly by identifying mysticism not merely as the ground of prophecy, but as the equivalent in many respects of the Protestant Spirit itself.

Even more than in his previous writings, Hocking now acknowledged the validity of both theoretical and practical mysticism, pursuing the theoretical aspect farther into the regions of logic, where he claimed that the mystic had made a distinct contribution.[20] But again, he subordinated mystical theory to practice: "*the theoretical mystic ought to turn into the practical mystic,* who has a way of gaining union with God other than by concepts" (MS, 188). For mysticism is, first, largely common in practice rather than content; it is, moreover, neither extraordinary nor elite:

> The position of mankind toward the whole wonderful history of mysticism would be vastly improved if attention were given to the extent to which the reports of the great mystics corroborate one another and indicate a common nature in the paths proposed; and it were further shown how deeply the more extraordinary varieties of mystical experience are akin to very normal and, indeed, inescapable experiences of men everywhere (MS, 189).

All human persons are at bottom mystics. Moreover, all true mysticism is fundamentally religious insofar as it is a direct (even if unrecognized) encounter with God:

> The characteristic assertion of mysticism in all its forms is that there is a vitally important and nonconceptual experience of

God available to men who meet its conditions. The simplest and most usual expression of this thesis is that all men at all times are directly dealing with God, whether they know it or not (MS, 189).

Such encounter is made possible by the power of nature, self, and society to reveal the presence of God to those open to that possibility:

The principle of the mystical consciousness is the *transparency of intermediaries*. Vital awareness deals with what intermediaries *represent*. And if the Real is God, it is with God that we have to do from moment to moment of daily living. For each action the world concentrates itself into a point of resistance and support; and that point is a Thou, not an It (MS, 190).

This is but one of the three assertions, both fundamental and apparently incompatible, which Hocking claimed were the central doctrinal points on which the great mystics agree and which provide the connection with the spirit of Protestantism:

Man is always aware of God. Man must struggle to become aware of God. Man is neither aware of God by nature, nor can he win this awareness by his own efforts; but God must, by his own act, make himself known to man—the essential act of grace (MS, 190).

Concerning the first point, the awareness of God is, as Hocking saw it, continuous. It is also so radical in man that it is largely taken for granted:

... It is remarkably easy to overlook what is always present, just because it is an invariable element of experience: there is no absurdity—on the contrary, it is one of the commonest events—that we discover what it is that we have been presupposing or unconsciously relying on; [further] ... if the God found were different from the power that always surrounds and sustains our being (and in this sense is always "there") it would not be God that was found (MS, 191).

Secondly, the condition for the possibility of consciously experiencing God through the mediation of nature, society, and one's own psychic structure is primarily *moral*: the willingness to see.

But, finally,

> The mystic has not infrequently asserted, on the basis of his own experience, that there comes a stage of effort in which effort must be set aside in favor of a purely receptive attitude. His effort has been chiefly (as the "negative path" suggests) to put aside the obstacles in his own nature to receiving that vision. He recognizes the danger that his "trying" may be a trying toward some preconceived goal and therefore impede his perception of the true goal, whose character is such that it cannot have been preconceived. He must render himself passive and wait in hope that God will vouch-safe to reveal himself (MS, 190).

This openness to grace provides the basis for the identification of the mystical and Protestant spirit.

Hocking was not insensitive to the social emphasis in Protestant thought when he reiterated his basic position on the social dimension of mysticism. He likewise acknowledged the importance of individual experience, a key element of the "Protestant Principle." But he also insisted, "It has its own need of steadying, corroboration, interpretation, development. This [the mystic] must find in the equally original experiences of other minds and in whatever has become for them the guide of the community" (MS, 191).

The main thrust of his argument was demonstrating not only the compatibility of mysticism and Protestantism, but their virtual identity. This he did by an analysis of three fundamental and common values: "the actuality of certitude, the possibility of new religious insight, the importance of a stable corpus of faith" (MS, 192). These are the three fundamental characteristics of religion itself, made more explicit in mysticism.

Overall, in this not over-subtle reply to his opponents, Hocking was not compromising but rather developing his own original insights, and yet provided a basis for Protestant acceptance. He also discerned in the mystical spirit a basis for closer rapprochement between Protestants and other Christian and non-Christian groups, a theme that he would develop further in his last major work on religion, *The Coming World Civilization*.

The Coming World Civilization

In this important book, Hocking continued the line of development begun in *Living Religions and a World Faith*—a possible world community must have a common foundation in shared experience which can provide men with sufficient assurance and incentive even to attempt bridging the enormous gaps dividing person from person and nation from nation. This common factor is the presence of God in individual, corporate, and historical experience. Thus, the mystic represents the future citizen of the coming world civilization as an embodied "anticipation of attainment." He is the prophet of a world brotherhood united not along political lines, but in spirit.

Insofar as the mystic represents all men, then all must be mystics at least in principle. Further, as Hocking had proposed before, mystical experience is thus a *commom* element in human experience and history as a whole:

> The "mystic" here is simply that "any man" in any religion who opens the door of his self-built enclosure, and sees the world, perhaps for the first time, in his own experience, as not his alone but God's world, and therewith every man's world, as held in God's care, the ego's personal entity included (WC, 100v.).

Hence, mystical experience cannot be isolated, extraordinary or bizarre:

> Such seeing is not a rare and privileged event; it is not unnatural; it is a passing from the unnatural to the natural and true. It is present in some degree in every wakening of the mind to love, and every opening of the eyes to beauty. . . ."[21]

Thus, Hocking singled out as the basis of a world faith which could alone ground a humane world civilization, the mutual values and practices of the mystics rather than any shared doctrinal tenets (CWC, 140f.). Moreover, he recognized a yet deeper foundation, one underpinning the unanimity of the mystics despite real divergences in practice as well as theory: "Whatever their departures from one another in practice and theory, there is a tendency for the mystics in various traditions—selectively—to understand one another."[22]

Working from this basis, Hocking postulated three elements regulating the encounter among the great religions as they edge toward a world-wide ecumenism:

(a) The true mystic will recognize the true mystic across all boundaries, and will learn from him;

(b) Every man's religion must be "a" religion, having its own simplicity of essence, its organic integrity, and its historic identity;

(c) To every man belongs the full truth of religion—the unlosable essences in whatever context they appear, and also their interpretation through history (CWC, 141f.)

Thus, the world-faith will be *catholic*—united on the basis of the deepest character of all human persons, their intersubjective experience of God and, in that, of other persons, especially those whose eyes have also been opened. It will also be *pluralistic*—historically and culturally particular. Finally, it will be *protestant*—individualized in the experience of each person, albeit in the content of a concrete tradition.

Even so, the long history of mysticism indicates that "the several universal religions *are already fused together, so to speak,* at the top." And hence, "the primary identity involved in recognition of mystic by mystic is the essence of the religious world view, the perception of Being as beatitude—God is, and God is One." Such a vision is, moreover, not specialized or reserved to the few: "With this final and universal truth, whatever is implied in it, and that is much, is already implicitly the possession of every believer within his own faith" (CWC, 149).

With direct experience of the richness and aptness of various religions to meet the individual needs of persons themselves particularized by the historical contingencies of existence and destiny, Hocking did not envision some vast conglomerate religion which would replace particular religions. He rather anticipated a faith which would find expression in cultural and historical "peculiarities." The common faith of mankind would be neither a vacuous generality nor a totalitarian dictatorship of the spirit. He envisioned it, mystically, as a "concrete universal," the Whole, the One, realized in the parts, the Many, each adapted to the exigencies of its place and time.[23]

The common faith of the future, as anticipated in the religion of the mystic, would find its natural expression in action, the work of love and justice, governed by the principle of alternation. But the mystic-prophet is not simply regulated by the alternation of action and contemplation; he is driven by an incentive to manifest his vision of the unity of all persons by concrete deeds. That motive is love:

To "love one's neighbor" would be to deal with him, not blindly but with responsible provocation, on the basis of his favorable possibilities *as creatively discerned by you,* including therein that not actual but potential divinity which your deed may elicit. Then one understands that startling statement,

"Inasmuch as ye have done it unto one of the least of these my brethren, ye have done it unto me."[24]

Conclusion

In Western experience, perhaps the most crucial development since the Cartesian "revolution" was the shift in thought from a monarchical, absolutist perspective to one characterized by the democratic outlook, which recognizes the value of the common experience of everyman. Royce and especially James attempted to secure the success of the transition in American thought, and with Dewey the achievement can be said to have been consummated. Hocking's accomplishment in this regard can be fairly described as the execution of the crossing with respect to what until his time had largely been taken as a bastion of esoteric elitism, the last refuge of absolutism: mysticism. By democratizing mystical experience, and with it the Absolute, i.e., locating them within the capacities of everyone, Hocking established the tie between the classical Western tradition and the spirit of the New World in the area of religion and religious experience.

In synthesizing realism and idealism in mysticism, Hocking's insistence on the necessity of mediation was a key element. By it, he reconceived the absolutist model of mystical union, often conceived of as an ontological merger of subject and object. This is true, for example, of John E. Smith's characterization (and subsequent rejection) of mystical union as "the individual's merging with an ultimate reality or . . . his becoming absorbed in the object of his quest."[25]

Hocking's triadic model of experience precludes the simple absorption of subject by object insofar as *all* experience of an object by a subject is mediated by "thirds," that is, some other entity. In the integrity of mystical oneness. God remains God, the creature remains creature.[26] On a social plane, this insight has specific ecumenical implications. For Hocking the prophet of the coming world faith was the mystic, but the intermediary agencies in the converging religious experience of individuals and societies are particular religious traditions, especially those with a universalizing tendency—Buddhism, Christianity, Judaism, Islam, and, to a lesser extent, Hinduism.

Regarding Hocking's own mysticism, he was clearly not an ordinary mystic. Like Plato, Plotinus, Eckhart, and Schelling, he was a philosopher-mystic (or a mystic-philosopher; it makes little difference). He was not a religious figure in exactly the sense that Eckhart was, much less John of the Cross or George Fox. Yet he was a religious leader in his time and, as a man of action, both reformer and critic. As such, he was no less a prophet.

No one who reads with an open mind Hocking's "Confessio Fidei"—the epilogue to *Types of Philosophy*[27] can miss the fact that the mystical element of religion extensively permeated his thought and life. But Hocking proposed a "realistic mysticism" (or a "mystical realism"—which, again, amounts to the same thing). His was a reconceived mysticism in which the residual absolutism perhaps inevitable in any mysticism was strongly tempered by the pluralistic realism of everyday experience. Such a mysticism not only accords better with the "Gospel Christianity" Hocking professed, but by its openness also admits of comparison and exchange with the temperate absolutism he found at the heart of all great religions.

NOTES

1. Cf. Leroy S. Rouner, "The Making of a Philosopher," *Philosophy, Religion and the Coming World Civilization,* ed. Leroy Rouner (The Hague: Martinus Nijhoff, 1966), p. 22; hereafter referred to as PRCWC.

2. Cf. Reginald Garrigou-Lagrange, O.P., *Christian Perfection and Contemplation,* trans Sr. Timothea Doyle (B. Herder Book Co., 1937), pp. 12–47.

3. Cf. F. C. Happold, *Mysticism* (Penguin Books, 1970), pp. 294, 306; cf. also *The Protestant Mystics,* ed. Anne Fremantle, intro. by W. H. Auden (New American Library, 1964), p. xi.

4. Cf. Herbert Schneider, *Religion in the Twentieth Century* (Atheneum, 1964), pp. 98ff.

5. For a discussion of the Hocking-Kraemer dispute, cf. Rouner, *Within Human Experience: The Philosophy of William Er-*

nest Hocking (Harvard University Press, 1969), pp. 235–38, 280–82. Hereafter WHE. Cf. also Hendrik Kraemer, "The Role and Responsibility of the Christian Mission," PRCWC 235–49.

6. Cf. A. Leonard, "Studies in the Phenomena of Mystical Experience," *Mystery and Mysticism* (London: Blackfriars Publications, 1956), p. 72.

7. On Hocking's early life, cf. "Some Second Principles," *Contemporary American Philosophy,* ed. George Adams and William P. Montague (Russell and Russell, 1930), pp. 385–93; hereafter referred to as "SSP." Cf. also Rouner, WHE 1–12 and PRCWC 5–22.

8. Rouner, WHE 2. Cf. also PRCWC 10–11.

9. "SSP" 387. CF. also "A Philosopher of a Single Civilization," *This is My Philosophy,* ed. Whit Burnett, (London: Allen and Unwin, Ltd., 1958), p. 287.

10. *The Meaning of Immortality in Human Experience* (Greenwood Press, 1973), pp. 213–14; hereafter referred to as MIHE.

11. *The Meaning of God in Human Experience* (Yale University Press, 1963 ed.), pp. 265–66. Hereafter referred to as MGHE.

12. Cf. Stephen Neill, *A History of Christian Missions* (Wm. B. Eerdmans Pub. Co., 1965), pp. 455–56.

13. *Re-thinking Missions: A Laymen's Inquiry after One Hundred Years* (New York: Harper and Brothers, 1932), p. 45–6.

14. Cf. Rouner, WHE 188.

15. Cf. MGHE 362, 450.

16. MGHE xxviii. The connection of Hocking's earlier mystical doctrine and his later articulation of nuclear experience is found explicitly in the 1962 introduction to MGHE.

17. Cf. MGHE 511ff.

18. In *Protestantism: A Symposium,* ed. William K. Anderson (Books for Libraries Press, 1969), pp. 185–95; hereafter referred to as "MS."

19. *The Coming World Civilization* (Harper and Bros., 1956.) Hereafter referred to as CWC.

20. Cf. "MS" 187–192.

21. CWC 101. He further amplified this idea: "what I mean by 'the true mystic' is simply the person who in the course of his own experience has in some moment become aware of the nature of things as supreme good." He continued, "Such vision

may come wholly outside the lines of formal religion.... Or it may come in the way of meditative discipline.... Or still more simply and widely, in the waking of the mind to love and the opening of the eyes to beauty, when these experiences are as they may be, entrance gates to the nature of Being" (CWC 138–39).

22. C..C 141. Cf. Evelyn Underhill quoting Claude de St. Martin, "All mystics ... speak the same language and come from the same country." (*Mysticism* [World Publishing Co., 1955], p. xiii.)

23. Cf. CWC 180, MGHE 407.

24. CWC 184. Cf. MIHE 232.

25. John E. Smith, "In What Sense Can We Speak of Experiencing God?" Journal of Religion 50 (1970), p. 231.

26. Cf. especially MGHE 390.

27. *Types of Philosophy* (Charles Scribner's Sons, 1939. Revised ed., with the collaboration of Richard Hocking, 1959.)

Index to Spirituality Themes